T0373300

Mercedes-Benz
C-Class Diesel
Owners Workshop Manual

Martynn Randall

(6389 - 304)

Models covered

C-Class (W204 Series) C200 CDI, C220 CDI & C250 CDI
Saloon (from June 2007) & Estate (from March 2008) with 2.1 litre (2143cc/2148cc) turbo-diesel engines

Does NOT cover petrol models, C320/C350 CDI with 3.0 litre diesel engine, four-wheel-drive ('4Matic' transmission) or Coupe
Does NOT cover new C-Class range (W205 Series) introduced February 2014

© Haynes Group Limited 2017

A book in the **Haynes Owners Workshop Manual Series**

ABCDE
FGHIJ
KLMNO
PQR

ISBN **978 1 78521 389 2**

British Library Cataloguing in Publication Data
A catalogue record for this book is available from the British Library.

Printed in India

Haynes Group Limited
Sparkford, Yeovil, Somerset BA22 7JJ, England

Haynes North America, Inc
2801 Townsgate Road, Suite 340, Thousand Oaks, CA 91361

Disclaimer

Contents

LIVING WITH YOUR MERCEDES-BENZ C-CLASS DIESEL

Introduction	Page	0•4
Safety first!	Page	0•5

Roadside repairs

If your car won't start	Page	0•6
Jump starting	Page	0•7
Wheel changing	Page	0•8
Identifying leaks	Page	0•9
Towing	Page	0•9

Weekly checks

Introduction	Page	0•10
Underbonnet check points	Page	0•10
Engine oil level	Page	0•11
Brake/clutch fluid level	Page	0•11
Coolant level	Page	0•12
Electrical systems	Page	0•12
Battery	Page	0•13
Wiper blades	Page	0•14
Screen washer fluid level	Page	0•14
Tyre condition and pressure	Page	0•15
Power steering fluid level	Page	0•16

Lubricants and fluids

	Page	0•16

Tyre pressures

	Page	0•16

MAINTENANCE

Routine maintenance and servicing

Servicing specifications	Page	1•2
Maintenance schedule	Page	1•3
Maintenance procedures	Page	1•6

Contents

REPAIRS AND OVERHAUL

Engine and Associated Systems
2148 cc engine in-car repair procedures   Page **2A•1**

2143 cc engine in-car repair procedures   Page **2B•1**

General engine removal and overhaul procedures   Page **2C•1**

Cooling, heating and ventilation systems   Page   **3•1**

Fuel and exhaust systems   Page **4A•1**

Emission control systems   Page **4B•1**

Starting and charging systems   Page **5A•1**

Preheating system   Page **5B•1**

Transmission
Clutch   Page   **6•1**

Manual gearbox   Page **7A•1**

Automatic gearbox   Page **7B•1**

Driveshafts, propeller shaft and final drive   Page   **8•1**

Brakes and suspension
Braking system   Page   **9•1**

Suspension and steering   Page **10•1**

Body equipment
Bodywork and fittings   Page **11•1**

Body electrical system   Page **12•1**

Wiring diagrams   Page **12•28**

REFERENCE
Dimensions and weights   Page **REF•1**

Fuel economy   Page **REF•2**

Conversion factors   Page **REF•6**

Buying spare parts   Page **REF•7**

Vehicle identification numbers   Page **REF•7**

General repair procedures   Page **REF•8**

Jacking and vehicle support   Page **REF•9**

Tools and working facilities   Page **REF•10**

MOT test checks   Page **REF•12**

Fault finding   Page **REF•16**

Glossary of technical terms   Page **REF•24**

Index
                                                           Page **REF•29**

The W204 Series Mercedes-Benz C-Class replaced the previous Series in June 2007. Available initially as a 4-door Saloon, it was launched with a range of in-line turbocharged diesel engines. Theses engines are developments of well-proven engines used in many Mercedes-Benz vehicles. In March 2008 an Estate model was launched. In February 2009, revised versions of these engines were introduced, to bring them up to Euro 5 emission standards. All of these engines are fitted, longitudinally with the transmission mounted behind the engine. Both manual and automatic transmissions are available.

Fully independent suspension is fitted front and rear, with MacPherson type front suspension, and multi-link rear suspension with separate coil springs and dampers.

All models feature anti-lock brakes, traction control, ESP, along with a multitude of equipment to enhance the safety, convenience and efficiency of the vehicle.

Provided that regular servicing is carried out in accordance with the manufacturers recommendations, the C-Class should prove very reliable and durable. The engine compartment is well designed, and most of the items requiring frequent attention are easily accessible.

This manual covers the following models:
- 4-cylinder in-line 2143 cc and 2148 cc diesel engines
- Two wheel drive Saloon and Estate models
- Manual and automatic transmissions
- Does not cover petrol engines, V6 diesel engines, Coupe, AMG or 4 wheel drive models

Your Mercedes C-Class manual

The aim of this Manual is to help you get the best value from your vehicle. It can do so in several ways. It can help you decide what work must be done (even should you choose to get it done by a garage). It will also provide information on routine maintenance and servicing, and give a logical course of action and diagnosis when random faults occur. However, it is hoped that you will use the manual by tackling the work yourself. On simpler jobs it may even be quicker than booking the car into a garage and going there twice, to leave and collect it. Perhaps most important, a lot of money can be saved by avoiding the costs a garage must charge to cover its labour and overheads.

The manual has drawings and descriptions to show the function of the various components so that their layout can be understood. Tasks are described and photographed in a clear step-by-step sequence. The illustrations are numbered by the Section number and paragraph number to which they relate – if there is more than one illustration per paragraph, the sequence is denoted alphabetically.

References to the "left" or "right" of the vehicle are in the sense of a person in the driver's seat, facing forwards.

Acknowledgements

Thanks are due to Draper Tools, who provided some of the workshop tools, and to all those people at Sparkford who helped in the production of this manual.

This manual is not a direct reproduction of the vehicle manufacturer's data, and its publication should not be taken as implying any technical approval by the vehicle manufacturers or importers.

We take great pride in the accuracy of information given in this manual, but vehicle manufacturers make alterations and design changes during the production run of a particular vehicle of which they do not inform us. No liability can be accepted by the authors or publishers for loss, damage or injury caused by any errors in, or omissions from, the information given.

Project vehicles

The main vehicle used in the preparation of this manual, and which appears in many of the photographic sequences, had a 2143 cc Type 651 engine.

Mercedes-Benz C-Class W204 Saloon

Working on your car can be dangerous. This page shows just some of the potential risks and hazards, with the aim of creating a safety-conscious attitude.

General hazards

Scalding

• Don't remove the radiator or expansion tank cap while the engine is hot.
• Engine oil, transmission fluid or power steering fluid may also be dangerously hot if the engine has recently been running.

Burning

• Beware of burns from the exhaust system and from any part of the engine. Brake discs and drums can also be extremely hot immediately after use.

Crushing

• When working under or near a raised vehicle, always supplement the jack with axle stands, or use drive-on ramps.
Never venture under a car which is only supported by a jack.

• Take care if loosening or tightening high-torque nuts when the vehicle is on stands. Initial loosening and final tightening should be done with the wheels on the ground.

Fire

• Fuel is highly flammable; fuel vapour is explosive.
• Don't let fuel spill onto a hot engine.
• Do not smoke or allow naked lights (including pilot lights) anywhere near a vehicle being worked on. Also beware of creating sparks (electrically or by use of tools).
• Fuel vapour is heavier than air, so don't work on the fuel system with the vehicle over an inspection pit.
• Another cause of fire is an electrical overload or short-circuit. Take care when repairing or modifying the vehicle wiring.
• Keep a fire extinguisher handy, of a type suitable for use on fuel and electrical fires.

Electric shock

• Ignition HT and Xenon headlight voltages can be dangerous, especially to people with heart problems or a pacemaker. Don't work on or near these systems with the engine running or the ignition switched on.

• Mains voltage is also dangerous. Make sure that any mains-operated equipment is correctly earthed. Mains power points should be protected by a residual current device (RCD) circuit breaker.

Fume or gas intoxication

• Exhaust fumes are poisonous; they can contain carbon monoxide, which is rapidly fatal if inhaled. Never run the engine in a confined space such as a garage with the doors shut.

• Fuel vapour is also poisonous, as are the vapours from some cleaning solvents and paint thinners.

Poisonous or irritant substances

• Avoid skin contact with battery acid and with any fuel, fluid or lubricant, especially antifreeze, brake hydraulic fluid and Diesel fuel. Don't syphon them by mouth. If such a substance is swallowed or gets into the eyes, seek medical advice.
• Prolonged contact with used engine oil can cause skin cancer. Wear gloves or use a barrier cream if necessary. Change out of oil-soaked clothes and do not keep oily rags in your pocket.
• Air conditioning refrigerant forms a poisonous gas if exposed to a naked flame (including a cigarette). It can also cause skin burns on contact.

Asbestos

• Asbestos dust can cause cancer if inhaled or swallowed. Asbestos may be found in gaskets and in brake and clutch linings. When dealing with such components it is safest to assume that they contain asbestos.

Special hazards

Hydrofluoric acid

• This extremely corrosive acid is formed when certain types of synthetic rubber, found in some O-rings, oil seals, fuel hoses etc, are exposed to temperatures above 4000C. The rubber changes into a charred or sticky substance containing the acid. *Once formed, the acid remains dangerous for years. If it gets onto the skin, it may be necessary to amputate the limb concerned.*
• When dealing with a vehicle which has suffered a fire, or with components salvaged from such a vehicle, wear protective gloves and discard them after use.

The battery

• Batteries contain sulphuric acid, which attacks clothing, eyes and skin. Take care when topping-up or carrying the battery.
• The hydrogen gas given off by the battery is highly explosive. Never cause a spark or allow a naked light nearby. Be careful when connecting and disconnecting battery chargers or jump leads.

Air bags

• Air bags can cause injury if they go off accidentally. Take care when removing the steering wheel and trim panels. Special storage instructions may apply.

Diesel injection equipment

• Diesel injection pumps supply fuel at very high pressure. Take care when working on the fuel injectors and fuel pipes.

⚠️ *Warning: Never expose the hands, face or any other part of the body to injector spray; the fuel can penetrate the skin with potentially fatal results.*

Remember...

DO

• Do use eye protection when using power tools, and when working under the vehicle.

• Do wear gloves or use barrier cream to protect your hands when necessary.

• Do get someone to check periodically that all is well when working alone on the vehicle.

• Do keep loose clothing and long hair well out of the way of moving mechanical parts.

• Do remove rings, wristwatch etc, before working on the vehicle – especially the electrical system.

• Do ensure that any lifting or jacking equipment has a safe working load rating adequate for the job.

DON'T

• Don't attempt to lift a heavy component which may be beyond your capability – get assistance.

• Don't rush to finish a job, or take unverified short cuts.

• Don't use ill-fitting tools which may slip and cause injury.

• Don't leave tools or parts lying around where someone can trip over them. Mop up oil and fuel spills at once.

• Don't allow children or pets to play in or near a vehicle being worked on.

The following pages are intended to help in dealing with common roadside emergencies and breakdowns. You will find more detailed fault finding information at the back of the manual, and repair information in the main chapters.

If your car won't start and the starter motor doesn't turn

- ☐ If it's a model with automatic transmission, make sure the selector is in 'P' or 'N'.
- ☐ Open the boot lid or tailgate, lift up the floor panel, and unclip the battery cover. On Estate models, unclip the cover from the battery on the right-hand side of the spare wheel well.
- ☐ Check the condition and security of the battery connections.
- ☐ Switch on the headlights and try to start the engine. If the headlights go very dim when you're trying to start, the battery is probable flat. Get out of trouble by jump starting using a friends car.

If your car won't start even though the starter motor turns as normal

- ☐ Is there fuel in the tank?
- ☐ Is there moisture on electrical connections under the bonnet? Switch off the ignition, then wipe off any obvious dampness with a dry cloth. Spray a water-dispersant aerosol product (WD-40 or equivalent) on ignition and fuel system electrical connectors like those shown in the photos.

A Check the security of the pre-heating system components wiring plugs

B Check the mass air flow sensor wiring plug

C Check the engine compartment fuses

D Check the security and condition of the battery terminal clamps

Check that electrical connections are secure (with the ignition switched off) and spray them with a water-dispersant spray like WD-40 if you suspect a problem due to damp

Jump starting

HAYNES HiNT *Jump starting will get you out of trouble, but you must correct whatever made the battery go flat in the first place. There are three possibilities:*

1 The battery has been drained by repeated attempts to start, or by leaving the lights on.

2 The charging system is not working properly (alternator drivebelt slack or broken, alternator wiring fault or alternator itself faulty).

3 The battery itself is at fault (electrolyte low, or battery worn out).

When jump-starting a car, observe the following precautions:

Caution: Remove the key in case the central locking engages when the jump leads are connected.

✓ Before connecting the booster battery, make sure that the ignition is switched off.
✓ Ensure that all electrical equipment (lights, heater, wipers, etc) is switched off.
✓ Take note of any special precautions printed on the battery case.
✓ Make sure that the booster battery is the same voltage as the discharged one in the vehicle.

✓ If the battery is being jump-started from the battery in another vehicle, the two vehicles MUST NOT TOUCH each other.
✓ Make sure that the transmission is in neutral (or PARK, in the case of automatic transmission)

HAYNES HiNT *Budget jump leads can be a false economy, as they often do not pass enough current to start large capacity or diesel engines. They can also get hot.*

1 Slide open the cover and connect one end of the red jump lead to the positive (+) terminal at the engine compartment bulkhead.

2 Connect the other end of the red jump lead to the positive (+) terminal of the booster battery.

3 Connect one end of the black jump lead to the negative (-) terminal of the booster battery.

4 Connect the other end of the black jump lead to the body earth point in the engine compartment.

5 Make sure that the jump leads will not come into contact with the fan, drive-belts or other moving parts of the engine.

6 Start the engine using the booster battery and run it at idle speed. Switch on the lights, rear window demister and heater blower motor, then disconnect the jump leads in the reverse order of connection. Turn off the lights etc.

Wheel changing

Warning: Do not change a wheel in a situation where you risk being hit by another vehicle. On busy roads, try to stop in a lay-by or a gateway. Be wary of passing traffic while changing the wheel – it is easy to become distracted by the job in hand.

Preparation

☐ When a puncture occurs, stop as soon as it is safe to do so.
☐ Park on firm level ground, if possible, and well out of the way of other traffic. If jacking on a slope is unavoidable, chock the wheel diagonally opposite the one to be removed on the downhill side, using the chock provided in the toolkit.
☐ Use hazard warning lights if necessary.
☐ If the ground is soft, use a flat piece of wood to spread the load under the jack.

1 Rotate the toolkit carrier anti-clockwise and remove it

2 Chock the wheel diagonally opposite the one being removed

3 Use the special adapter to slacken the locking wheel nut

4 Position the head of the jack under the sill jacking point

5 Undo the bolts and remove the wheel

6 Fit the spare wheel and tighten the retaining bolts

Caution: If a temporary 'space-saver' spare wheel is fitted, do not exceed 50 mph (80 kmh), and take particular care when cornering.

Finally

☐ Remove the wheel chocks.
☐ Stow the punctured wheel and tools back in the luggage compartment, and secure them in position.
☐ Check the tyre pressure on the tyre just fitted. If it is low, or if you don't have a pressure gauge with you, drive slowly to the next garage and inflate the tyre to the correct pressure. In the case of the narrow 'space-saver' spare wheel this pressure is much higher than for a normal tyre.
☐ Have the punctured wheel repaired as soon as possible, or another puncture will leave you stranded.

Identifying leaks

Puddles on the garage floor or drive, or obvious wetness under the bonnet or underneath the car, suggest a leak that needs investigating. It can sometimes be difficult to decide where the leak is coming from, especially if the engine bay is very dirty already. Leaking oil of fluid can also be blown rearwards by the passage of air under the car, giving a false impression of where the problem lies.

 Warning: Most automotive oils and fluids are poisonous, Wash them off skin, and change out of contaminated clothing without delay.

 The smell of a fluid leaking from the car may provide a clue to what's leaking. Some fluids are distinctly coloured. It may help to clean the car carefully and to park it over some clean paper overnight as an aid to locating the source of the leak. Remember that some leaks may only occur while the engine is running.

Sump oil

Engine oil may leak from the drain plug...

Oil from filter

...or from the base of the oil filter.

Antifreeze

Leaking antifreeze often leaves a crystalline deposit like this.

Brake fluid

A leak occurring at a wheel is almost certainly brake fluid.

Power steering fluid

Power steering fluid may leak from the pipe connectors on the steering rack.

Towing

Press-in the mark on the front towing eye cover

☐ When all else fails, you may find yourself having to get a tow home – or of course you may be helping somebody else. Long-distance recovery should only be done by a garage or breakdown service. For shorter distances, DIY towing using another car is easy enough, but observe the following points:

☐ Use a proper tow-rope – they are not expensive. The vehicle being towed must display an ON TOW sign in its rear window.

☐ Always turn the ignition to the 'on' position when the vehicle is being towed, so that the steering lock is released, and that the direction indicator and brake lights will work.

☐ The front towing eye socket is located in the front bumper. Press-in the lower section of the cover **(see illustration)**.

☐ The rear towing eye socket cover is located in the rear bumper. Press-in the mark on the cover.

☐ Before being towed, release the handbrake and make sure the transmission is in neutral.

☐ Note that greater-than-usual pedal pressure will be required to operate the brakes, since the vacuum servo unit is only operational with the engine running, and no power assistance will be available for the steering.

☐ The driver of the car being towed must keep the tow-rope taut at all times to avoid snatching.

☐ Only drive at moderate speeds, and keep the distance towed to a minimum. Drive smoothly, and allow plenty of time for slowing down at junctions.

☐ Mercedes state that the vehicle should be towed at a speed of no more than 50 mph (80 kmh) for a distance of no more than 50 miles (80 km). If being towed a longer distance, the propeller shaft must be removed as described in Chapter 8 Section 7.

Introduction

There are some very simple checks which need only take a few minutes to carry out, but which could save you a lot of inconvenience and expense.

☐ These Weekly checks require no great skill or special tools, and the small amount of time they take to perform could prove to be very well spent, for example:

☐ Keeping an eye on tyre condition and pressures, will not only help to stop them wearing out prematurely, but could also save your life.

☐ Many breakdowns are caused by electrical problems. Battery-related faults are particularly common, and a quick check on a regular basis will often prevent the majority of these.

☐ If your car develops a brake fluid leak, the first time you might know about it is when your brakes don't work properly. Checking the level regularly will give advance warning of this kind of problem.

☐ If the oil or coolant levels run low, the cost of repairing any engine damage will be far greater than fixing the leak, for example.

Underbonnet check points

◀2148 cc (Type 646) engine

A *Engine oil level dipstick*

B *Engine oil filler cap*

C *Coolant expansion tank*

D *Brake/clutch fluid reservoir*

E *Screen/headlight washer fluid reservoir*

F *Power steering fluid reservoir (under cover)*

◀2143 cc (Type 651) engine

A *Engine oil level dipstick*

B *Engine oil filler cap*

C *Coolant expansion tank*

D *Brake/clutch fluid reservoir*

E *Screen/headlight washer fluid reservoir*

Engine oil level

Before you start
✔ Make sure that your car is on level ground
✔ Check the oil level before the car is driven, or at least 5 minutes after the engine has been switched off.

The correct oil
Modern engines place great demands on their oil. It is very important that the correct oil for your car is used (see *Lubricants and fluids*).

HAYNES HiNT *If the oil is checked immediately after driving the vehicle, some of the oil will remain in the upper engine components, resulting in an inaccurate reading on the dipstick!*

Car care
● If you have to add oil frequently, you should check whether you have any oil leaks. Place some clean paper under the car overnight, and check for stains in the morning. If there are no leaks, the engine may be burning oil (see *Fault finding*).
● Always maintain the level between the upper and lower dipstick marks. If the level is too low severe engine damage may occur. Oil seal failure may result if the engine is overfilled by adding too much oil.
● On all diesel models it is located on the left-hand rear side of the engine. See *Underbonnet Check Points* for the exact location of the dipstick.

1 Withdraw the dipstick. Using a clean rag or paper towel, wipe all the oil from the dipstick. Insert the clean dipstick into the tube as far as it will go, then withdraw it again.

2 Note the oil level on the end of the dipstick, which should be between the upper mark and the lower mark.

3 Oil is added through the filler cap on top of the engine. Rotate the cap through a quarter-turn anti-clockwise and withdraw it. Top-up the level. A funnel may help to reduce spillage. Add the oil slowly, checking the level on the dipstick often. Do not overfill.

Brake (and clutch) fluid level

⚠ *Warning: Brake fluid can harm your eyes and damage painted surfaces, so use extreme caution when handling and pouring it.*
⚠ *Warning: Do not use fluid that has been standing open for some time, as it absorbs moisture from the air, which can cause a dangerous loss of braking effectiveness.*

Note: *The fluid level in the reservoir will drop slightly as the brake pads wear down, but the fluid level must never be allowed to drop below the "MIN" mark.*

Safety first!
● If the reservoir requires repeated topping-up this is an indication of a fluid leak somewhere in the system, which should be investigated immediately.
● If a leak is suspected, the car should not be driven until the braking system has been checked. Never take any risks where brakes are concerned.

1 The brake master cylinder and fluid reservoir are mounted in the engine compartment on the right-hand side of the bulkhead. The MAX and MIN level marks are indicated on the side of the reservoir and the fluid level should be maintained between these marks at all times. The MAX level is also indicated within the filler neck.

2 On manual transmission models, the clutch master cylinder is supplied with fluid from the brake master cylinder reservoir. If topping-up is necessary, wipe the area around the filler cap with a clean rag before removing the cap. It's a good idea to inspect the reservoir. The fluid should be changed if dirt is visible.

3 Carefully add fluid, avoiding spilling it on surrounding paintwork. Use only the specified hydraulic fluid; mixing different types of fluid can cause damage to the system and/or a loss of braking effectiveness. After filling to the correct level, refit the cap securely. Wipe off any spilt fluid.

Coolant level

Warning: DO NOT attempt to remove the expansion tank pressure cap when the engine is hot, as there is a very great risk of scalding. Do not leave open containers of coolant about, as it is poisonous.

Car care

● With a sealed-type cooling system, adding coolant should not be necessary on a regular basis. If frequent topping-up is required, it is likely there is a leak. Check the radiator, all hoses and joint faces for signs of staining or wetness, and rectify as necessary.

● It is important that antifreeze is used in the cooling system all year round, not just during the winter months. Don't top-up with water alone, as the antifreeze will become too diluted.

● The coolant level varies with the temperature of the engine. When the engine is cold, the coolant level should be level with the marker bar withing the filler neck. When the engine is hot, the level will rise approximately 15 mm.

1 If topping-up is necessary, wait until the engine is cold, then slowly unscrew the expansion tank filler cap anti-clockwise, to release any pressure in the system, and remove it.

2 Add a mixture of water and antifreeze through the expansion tank filler neck ...

3 ... until the coolant is level with the marker bar in the filler neck. Refit the cap, turning it clockwise as far as it will go until it is secure.

Electrical systems

✔ Check all external lights and the horn. Refer to the appropriate Sections of Chapter 12 for details if any of the circuits are found to be inoperative.

✔ Visually check all accessible wiring connectors, harnesses and retaining clips for security, and for signs of chafing or damage.

HAYNES HiNT *If you need to check your brake lights and indicators unaided, back up to a wall or garage door and operate the lights. The reflected light should show if they are working properly.*

1 If a single indicator light, brake light or headlight has failed, it is likely that a bulb has blown and will need to be replaced. Refer to Chapter 12 Section 6 for details. If both brake lights have failed, it is possible that the stop-light switch operated by the brake pedal has failed. Refer to Chapter 9 Section 17 for details.

2 If more than one indicator light or headlight has failed, it is likely that either a fuse has blown or that there is a fault in the circuit (see Chapter 12). The main fusebox is located in the right-hand side of the engine compartment, with a further fusebox beneath the luggage compartment floor. To access the main fusebox, release the clips and remove the cover.

3 Prise open the cover to access the fusebox on the right-hand side of the luggage compartment

4 To replace a blown fuse, pull it out directly from the fusebox. Fit a new fuse of the same rating, available from car accessory shops. It is important that you find the reason that the fuse blew (see "Electrical fault finding" in Chapter 12).

Battery

Caution: Before carrying out any work on the vehicle battery, read the precautions given in "Safety first" at the start of this manual.

✔ Make sure that the battery tray is in good condition, and that the clamp is tight. Corrosion on the tray, retaining clamp and the battery itself can be removed with a solution of water and baking soda. Thoroughly rinse all cleaned areas with water. Any metal parts damaged by corrosion should be covered with a zinc-based primer, then painted.

✔ Periodically (approximately every three months), check the charge condition of the battery as described in "Chapter 5A Section 3 ".

✔ If the battery is flat, and you need to jump start your vehicle, see 4.

✔ The battery is located in the left-hand corner of the engine compartment, or under the luggage compartment floor panel. Release the clips and remove the cover over the battery, or lift out the luggage compartment floor panel as applicable. The exterior of the battery should be inspected periodically for damage such as a cracked case or cover.

HAYNES HiNT *Battery corrosion can be kept to a minimum by applying a layer of petroleum jelly to the clamps and terminals after they are reconnected.*

1 Release the clips…

2 …and remove the engine compartment battery cover

3 Check the tightness of the battery cable clamps to ensure good electrical connections. You should not be able to move them. Also check each cable for cracks and frayed conductors

4 On models equipped with 'Stop-Start', an additional battery is located under the luggage compartment floor panel

5 If corrosion (white, fluffy deposits) is evident, remove the cables from the battery terminals, clean them with a small wire brush, then refit them. Automotive stores sell a tool for cleaning the battery post …

6 … as well as the battery cable clamps

Wiper blades

Check the condition of the wiper blades. If they are cracked or show any signs of deterioration, or if the glass swept area is smeared, renew them. For maximum clarity of vision, wiper blades should be renewed annually, as a matter of course.

Rear wiper blade

1 Pull the blade away from the screen, and press it from the arm.

Front wiper blades

Set the wipers in the 'Service position' by switching on the ignition, setting the wiper switch to continuous slow wipe, then when the arms are in the vertical position, turn off the ignition.

Fold the wiper arms away from the windscreen.

Caution: Do not attempt to fold the arms away from the windscreen when they at not at the vertical position, otherwise damage to the bonnet may result.

2 Depress the release button...

3 ... and slide the blade from the arm.

Screen washer fluid level

● Screenwash additives not only keep the windscreen clean during foul weather, they also prevent the washer system freezing in cold weather – which is when you are likely to need it most. Don't top up using plain water as the screenwash will become too diluted, and will freeze during cold weather.

 Warning: On no account use coolant antifreeze in the washer system – this could discolour or damage paintwork.

1 The reservoir for the windscreen and rear window, and healight (where applicable) washer systems is located in the front right-hand corner of the engine compartment. If topping up is necessary, open the cap.

2 When topping-up the reservoir a screenwash additive should be added in the quantities recommended on the container.

Tyre condition and pressure

It is very important that tyres are in good condition, and at the correct pressure – having a tyre failure at any speed is highly dangerous. Tyre wear is influenced by driving style – harsh braking and acceleration, or fast cornering, will all produce more rapid tyre wear. As a general rule, the front tyres wear out faster the the rears. Interchanging the tyres from front to rear ("rotating" the tyres) may result in more even wear. However, if this is completely effective, you may have the expense of replacing all four tyres at once!

Remove any nails or stones embedded in the tread before they penetrate the tyre to cause deflation. If removal of a nail does reveal that the tyre has been punctured, refit the nail so that its point of penetration is marked. Then immediately change the wheel, and have the tyre repaired by a tyre dealer.

Regularly check the tyres for damage in the form of cuts or bulges, especially in the side walls. Periodically remove the wheels, and clean any dirt or mud from the inside and outside surfaces. Examine the wheel rims for signs of rusting, corrosion or other damage. Light alloy wheels are easily damaged by "kerbing" whilst parking; steel wheels may also become dented or buckled. A new wheel is very often the only way to overcome severe damage.

New tyres should be balanced when they are fitted, but it may become necessary to re-balance them as they ear, or if the balance weights fitted to the wheel rim should fall off. Unbalanced tyres will wear more quickly, as will the steering and suspension components. Wheel imbalance is normally signified by vibration, particularly at t certain speed (typically around 50 mph). If this vibration is felt only through the steering wheel, then it is likely that just the front wheels need balancing. If, however, the vibration is felt through the whole car, the rear wheels could be out of balance. Wheel balancing should be carried out by a tyre dealer or garage.

1 Tread Depth - visual check
The original tyres have tread wear safety bands (B), which will appear when the tread depth reaches approximately 1.6 mm. The band positions are indicated by a triangular mark on the tyre sidewall (A).

2 Tread Depth - manual check
Alternatively, tread wear can be monitored with a simple, inexpensive device known as a tread depth indicator gauge.

3 Tyre Pressure Check
Check the tyre pressures regularly with the tyres cold. Do not adjust the tyre pressures immediately after the vehicle has been used, or an inaccurate setting will result.

Tyre tread wear patterns

Shoulder Wear

Underinflation (wear on both sides)
Under-inflation will cause overheating of the tyre, because the tyre will flex too much, and the tread will not sit correctly on the road surface. This will cause a loss of grip and excessive wear, not to mention the danger of sudden tyre failure due to heat build-up.
Check and adjust pressures
Incorrect wheel camber (wear on one side)
Repair or renew suspension parts
Hard cornering
Reduce speed!

Centre Wear

Overinflation
Over-inflation will cause rapid wear of the centre part of the tyre tread, coupled with reduced grip, harsher ride, and the danger of shock damage occurring in the tyre casing.
Check and adjust pressures

If you sometimes have to inflate your car's tyres to the higher pressures specified for maximum load or sustained high speed, don't forget to reduce the pressures to normal afterwards.

Uneven Wear

Front tyres may wear unevenly as a result of wheel misalignment. Most tyre dealers and garages can check and adjust the wheel alignment (or "tracking") for a modest charge.
Incorrect camber or castor
Repair or renew suspension parts
Malfunctioning suspension
Repair or renew suspension parts
Unbalanced wheel
Balance tyres
Incorrect toe setting
Adjust front wheel alignment
Note: *The feathered edge of the tread which typifies toe wear is best checked by feel.*

Power steering fluid level

Before you start

Note: *This procedure is only necessary on 2148 cc models. 2143 cc models are equipped with electrically powered steering.*

Before you start

✔ Park the vehicle on level ground
✔ Set the steering wheel straight-ahead
✔ The engine should be cold and turned off

Note: *For the check to be accurate, the steering must not be turned once the engine has been stopped.*

1 Remove the plastic cover from the top of the engine.

2 The reservoir is mounted at the left-hand side of the engine compartment.

3 Wipe clean the area around the filler cap, then unscrew it from the reservoir. The level should be at the MAX mark on the dipstick, depending on the temperature of the fluid. MAX and MIN marks on the dipstick are given for 80°C and 20°C

4 If topping-up is necessary, use the specified type of fluid – do not overfill the reservoir. Take care not to introduce dirt into the system when topping-up. When the level is correct, securely refit the cap.

Lubricants and fluids

Engine oil:
Models without diesel particulate filter . . . . 5W/30 meeting Mercedes specification 228.3/228.5/228.51/229.3/229.31/229.5/229.51. Eg. Castrol Edge 5W30

Models with diesel particulate filter . . . . 5W/30 meeting Mercedes specification 228.51/229.31/229.51. Eg. Castrol Edge 5W30

Coolant . . . . Mercedes Benz Long life coolant to specification M325.6*

Manual gearbox . . . . Mercedes Benz specification MB345.0 part No. A 001 989 24 03*. Eg. Pentosin CHF 11 S

Automatic transmission:
Five speed: . . . . Mercedes Benz ATF specification MB 236.14 part No. A 001 898 68 03. Eg. Shell ATF 134

Seven speed . . . . Mercedes Benz ATF specification MB 236.15 part No. A 001 898 78 03. Eg. Shell ATF 134FE

Final drive . . . . Mercedes Benz 75W-85 specification MB 235.7/237.74 Hypoid gear oil part No. A 001 898 33 03*. Mobilube FE 75W-85

Brake/clutch fluid . . . . Hydraulic fluid DOT 4 Plus

Power steering fluid . . . . Mercedes Benz ATF specification 345.0 part No. A 001 989 24 03. Eg, Pentosin CHF 11 S*

Check with dealer for latest specifications.

Tyre pressures

The pressures for the standard fitment tyres are given on a sticker attached to the inside of the fuel filler flap.

Chapter 1
Routine maintenance and servicing

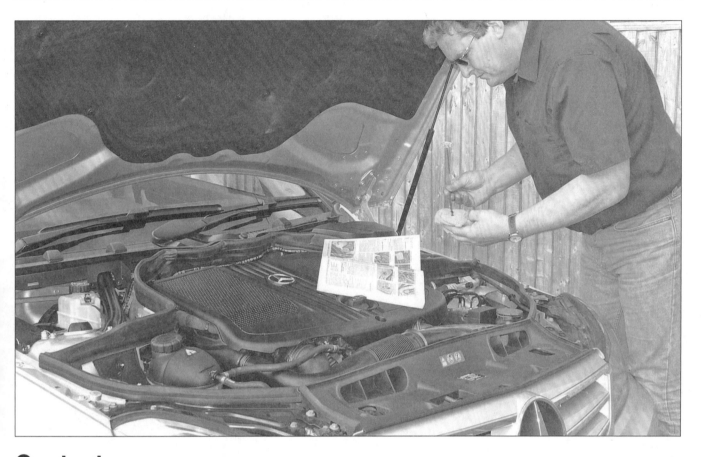

Contents

Section number

Air conditioning system check 10
Air filter element renewal 24
Antifreeze concentration check 12
Automatic transmission oil renewal 28
Auxiliary drivebelt check and renewal 6
Battery maintenance and charging 5
Brake fluid renewal 26
Braking system check 17
Coolant renewal 30
Door and bonnet check and lubrication 18
Driveshaft rubber gaiter check 14
Electrical system check 7
Engine compartment wiring check 9
Engine oil and filter renewal 4
Exhaust system check 15

Section number

Final drive oil renewal 29
Fuel filter renewal 25
Fuel sedimentor draining 20
Introduction 2
Maintenance schedule 1
Manual transmission oil renewal 27
Pollen filter renewal 19
Regular maintenance 3
Reset the service indicator 22
Road test 21
Roadwheels anti-seize grease 23
Seat belt check 11
Steering, suspension and roadwheel check 13
Underbody and fuel/brake line check 16
Underbonnet check for fluid leaks and hose condition 8

Degrees of difficulty

| Easy, suitable for novice with little experience | Fairly easy, suitable for beginner with some experience | Fairly difficult, suitable for competent DIY mechanic | Difficult, suitable for experienced DIY mechanic | Very difficult, suitable for expert DIY or professional |

Lubricants and fluids. . . . .   Refer to '*Weekly checks* '

Capacities
Engine oil (with filter) . . . .   6.5 litres
Cooling system. . . . .   10.0 litres
Fuel tank . . . .   59 or 66 litres model/specification dependent
Manual transmission . . . .   Refer to Chapter 7A Section 0
Automatic transmission . . . .   Refer to Chapter 7B Section 0
Final drive. . . . .   1.0 to 1.35 litres model/specification dependent

Cooling system
Protection at mixture of 50% anti-freeze and 50% water . . . .   -40°C

Braking system
Brake pad friction material minimum thickness (front and rear). . . . . . .   2.0 mm

Torque wrench settings

	Nm	lbf ft
Automatic transmission:		
Drain plug.	20	15
Engine oil drain plug:		
Metal plug.	30	22
Plastic plug.	5	3
Engine oil filter cap.	25	18
Manual transmission:		
Drain plug		
711 transmission.	33	24
716 transmission.	30	22
Filler plug	35	25
Roadwheel bolts.	130	96

1 Maintenance schedule

1 The maintenance intervals in this manual are provided with the assumption that you, not the dealer, will be carrying out the work. These are the minimum maintenance intervals recommended by us for cars driven daily. If you wish to keep your car in peak condition at all times, you may wish to perform some of these procedures more often. We encourage frequent maintenance, because it enhances the efficiency, performance and resale value of your car.

2 The C-Class is equipped with a time/condition dependent service interval display system (ASSYST PLUS – Active Service System). Owners may wish to follow the service schedule indicated by this system, or follow the schedule detailed below.

Note: *Two different engines are covered by this manual. The 2148 cc (Type 646) engine wash fitted until approximately June 2010, and can be identified by the timing chain at the front of the engine, and a single turbocharger. This was replaced by the 2143 cc (Type 651) engine, with the timing chain at the rear of the engine, and twin sequential turbochargers.*

3 If the car is driven in dusty areas, used to tow a trailer, or driven frequently at slow speeds (idling in traffic) or on short journeys, more frequent maintenance intervals are recommended.

Every 250 miles or weekly
☐ Refer to Weekly checks

Every 6000 miles or 6 months, whichever occurs first
☐ Renew the engine oil and filter (Section 4).

Note: *Frequent oil and filter changes are good for the engine. We recommend changing the oil at the mileage specified here, or at least twice a year if the mileage covered is less.*

Every 12 000 miles or 12 months, whichever occurs first
☐ In addition to the item listed in the previous service, carry out the following:
☐ Check the battery and clean the terminals (Section 5).
☐ Check the auxiliary drivebelt (Section 6).
☐ Check the electrical system (Section 7).
☐ Check under the bonnet for fluid leaks and hose condition (Section 8).
☐ Check the condition of all engine compartment wiring (Section 9).
☐ Check the condition of the air conditioning components (Section 10).

Every 12 000 miles or 12 months, whichever occurs first (continued)
☐ Check the seat belts (Section 11).
☐ Check the antifreeze concentration (Section 12).
☐ Check the steering, suspension and roadwheels (Section 13).
☐ Check the driveshaft rubber gaiters (Section 14).
☐ Check the exhaust system (Section 15).
☐ Check the underbody, and all fuel/brake lines (Section 16).
☐ Check the braking system (Section 17).
☐ Check the doors and bonnet, and lubricated their hinges and locks (Section 18).
☐ Road test (Section 21).
☐ Drain the fuel sedimentor (Section 20).
☐ Reset the service indicator (Section 22).

Every 24 months or 24 000 miles, whichever occurs first
☐ Remove the roadwheels, and apply anti-seize grease to the hubs (Section 23).
☐ Renew the air cleaner element (Section 24).
☐ Renew the fuel filter element (Section 25).
☐ Renew the pollen filter (Section 19).

Every 2 years, regardless of mileage
☐ Renew the brake fluid (Section 26).

Once at 37 000 miles
☐ Renew the manual transmission oil (Section 27).
☐ Renew the automatic transmission oil (Section 28).
☐ Renew the rear final drive oil (Section 29).

Every 10 years, regardless of mileage
☐ Renew the coolant (Section 30).

Front underbonnet view – 2148 cc (Type 646) engine

1 Engine oil filler cap
2 Engine oil level dipstick
3 Fuel filter
4 Engine oil filter cap
5 Air filter housing
6 Coolant filler cap
7 Battery (under cover)
8 Power steering reservoir cap
9 Brake/clutch fluid reservoir cap
10 Engine compartment fusebox
11 Screenwash reservoir cap

Front underbonnet view – 2143 cc (Type 651) engine

1 Engine oil filler cap
2 Engine oil level dipstick
3 Engine oil filter cap
4 Fuel filter
5 Air filter housing
6 Engine management ECM
7 Battery (under cover)
8 Coolant filler cap
9 Engine compartment fuse box
10 Brake/clutch fluid reservoir
11 Vacuum reservoir
12 Screenwash reservoir cap

Front underbody view (2148 cc engine shown – others are similar)

1 Engine oil drain plug
2 Transmission fluid drain/filler plug
3 Anti-roll bar
4 Torque strut
5 Cross strut
6 Track rod end
7 Brake caliper
8 Catalytic converter
9 Steering rack

Rear underbody view

1 Propeller shaft
2 Final drive drain plug
3 Final drive filler plug
4 Spring control arm
5 Driveshaft
6 Thrust arm
7 Parking brake cable
8 Brake hose
9 Anti-roll bar

2 Introduction

1 This Chapter is designed to help the home mechanic maintain his/her vehicle for safety, economy, long life and peak performance.

2 The Chapter contains a maintenance schedule, followed by Sections dealing specifically with each task in the schedule. Visual checks, adjustments, component renewal and other helpful items are included. Refer to the accompanying illustrations of the engine compartment and the underside of the vehicle for the locations of the various components.

3 Servicing your vehicle in accordance with the above recommendations and the following Sections will provide a planned maintenance programme, which should result in a long and reliable service life. This is a comprehensive plan, so maintaining some items, but not others at the specified service intervals, will not produce the same results.

4 As you service your vehicle, you will discover that many of the procedures can – and should – be grouped together, because of the particular procedure being performed, or because of the proximity of two otherwise-unrelated components to one another. For example, if the vehicle is raised for any reason, the exhaust can be inspected at the same time as the suspension and steering components.

5 The first step in this maintenance programme is to prepare yourself before the actual work begins. Read through all the

4.2 Undo the fasteners and remove the engine undershield

Sections relevant to the work to be carried out, then make a list and gather all the parts and tools required. If a problem is encountered, seek advice from a parts specialist, or a dealer service department.

3 Regular maintenance

1 If, from the time the vehicle is new, the routine maintenance schedule is followed closely, and frequent checks are made of fluid levels and high-wear items, as suggested throughout this manual, the engine will be kept in relatively good running condition, and the need for additional work will be minimised.

2 It is possible that there will be times when the engine is running poorly due to the lack of regular maintenance. This is even more likely if a used vehicle, which has not received regular and frequent maintenance checks, is purchased. In such cases, additional work may need to be carried out, outside of the regular maintenance intervals.

3 If engine wear is suspected, a compression test (refer to Chapter 2A Section 2, or Chapter 2B Section 2 as applicable) will provide valuable information regarding the overall performance of the main internal components. Such a test can be used as a basis to decide on the extent of the work to be carried out. If, for example, a compression test indicates serious internal engine wear, conventional maintenance as described in this Chapter will not greatly improve the performance of the engine, and may prove a waste of time and money, unless extensive overhaul work is carried out first.

4 The following series of operations are those most often required to improve the performance of a generally poor-running engine:

Primary operations

a) Clean, inspect and test the battery (see Weekly checks and Section 5).
b) Check all the engine-related fluids (refer to Weekly checks).
c) Check the condition and tension of the auxiliary drivebelt (Section 6).
d) Check the condition of all hoses, and check for fluid leaks (Section 8).

e) Renew the fuel filter (Section 25).
f) Check the glow plugs (Chapter 5B Section 2).
g) Check the condition of the air filter, and renew if necessary (Section 24).

5 If the above operations do not prove fully effective, carry out the following secondary operations:

Secondary operations

6 All items listed under Primary operations, plus the following:
a) Check the charging system (Chapter 5A Section 5).
b) Check the fuel system (Chapter 4A Section 9).

4 Engine oil and filter renewal

Note: A new engine oil drain plug sealing washer will be required.

1 Frequent oil and filter changes are the most important preventative maintenance procedures, which can be undertaken by the DIY owner. As engine oil ages, it becomes diluted and contaminated, which leads to premature engine wear.

2 Before starting this procedure, gather together all the necessary tools and materials. Also make sure that you have plenty of clean rags and newspapers handy, to mop-up any spills. Ideally, the engine oil should be warm, as it will drain better, and more built-up sludge will be removed with it. Take care, however, not to touch the exhaust or any other hot parts of the engine when working under the vehicle. To avoid any possibility of scalding, and to protect yourself from possible skin irritants and other harmful contaminants in used engine oils, it is advisable to wear gloves when carrying out this work. Access to the underside of the vehicle will be greatly improved if it can be raised on a lift, driven onto ramps, or jacked up and supported on axle stands as described in Vehicle jacking and support. Whichever method is chosen, make sure that the vehicle remains level, or if it is at an angle, so that the drain plug is at the lowest point. Where necessary, remove the undershield from under the engine (see illustration).

3 Remove the plastic covers from the top of the engine (see illustrations).

4.3a Pull up the front edge and remove the cover – 2148 cc engines

4.3b On 2143 cc engines, rotate the catch anti-clockwise...

4.3c ...and pull the cover forwards from its' mountings

4.4a Unscrew the oil filter cap using a special socket...

4.4b ...and lift the cap with the filter from place

4.6a Engine oil sump drain plug – 2148 cc engines...

4 Locate the oil filter/housing on the front left-hand side of the engine **(see illustrations)**. Place a wad of rag around the housing to absorb any spilt oil, and then unscrew the oil filter cap.

Note: *By removing the cap, the oil will drain from the housing into the sump.*

5 Pull the old filter from the cap and discard it.

6 Working under the vehicle, unscrew the sump drain plug about half a turn. Position the draining container under the drain plug, and then remove the plug completely **(see illustrations)**.

4.6b ...and 2143 cc engines

HAYNES HINT *If possible, try to keep the plug pressed into the sump while unscrewing it by hand the last couple of turns. As the plugs releases from the threads, move it away sharply, so that the stream of oil issuing from the sump runs into the container, nut up your sleeve.*

7 Recover the sealing washer from the drain plug.

8 Allow some time for the old oil to drain, noting that it may be necessary to reposition the container as the oil flow slows to a trickle. Remove the oil filler cap from the camshaft cover.

9 After all the oil has drained from the engine, wipe off the drain plug with a clean rag and renew the sealing washer **(see illustration)**. Clean the area around the drain plug opening,

then refit and tighten the plug to the specified torque.

10 Remove the old oil and all tools from under the car, then refit the undershield and lower the car to the ground.

11 Wipe out the oil filter housing and cap using a clean rag, then fit new O-rings to the cap **(see illustration)**.

12 Fit the new filter element into the cap, then refit and tighten the cap to the specified torque **(see illustrations)**.

13 Refit the plastic cover(s) to the top of the engine.

14 Remove the oil level dipstick then fill the engine, using the correct grade and type of oil (see Lubricants and fluids 0 5). An oil can spout or funnel may help to reduce spillage. Pour in half the specified quantity of oil first, and then wait a few minutes for the oil to run to the sump. Continue adding oil a small

quantity at a time until the level is up to the lower mark on the dipstick. Finally, bring the level up to the upper mark on the dipstick. Insert the dipstick, and refit the filler cap.

15 Start the engine and run it for a few minutes; check for leaks around the oil filter cap and the sump drain plug. Note that there may be a delay of a few seconds before the oil pressure warning light goes out when the engine is first started, as the oil circulates through the engine oil galleries and the new oil filter before the pressure builds-up.

16 Switch off the engine, and wait a few minutes for the oil to settle in the sump once more. With the new oil circulated and the filter completely full, recheck the level on the dipstick, and add more oil as necessary.

17 Dispose of the used engine oil safely, with reference to *General repair procedures* in the Reference section of this manual.

4.9 Renew the sump plug sealing washer

4.11 Renew the O-ring seals

4.12a Fit the new element into the cap

4.12b Tighten the cap to the specified torque

5 Battery maintenance and charging

Warning: Certain precautions must be followed when checking and servicing the battery. Hydrogen gas, which is highly flammable, is always present in the battery cells, so keep lighted tobacco and all other open flames and sparks away from the battery. The electrolyte inside the battery is actually dilute sulphuric acid, which will cause injury if splashed on your skin or in your eyes. It will also ruin clothes and painted surfaces. When disconnecting the battery, always detach the negative (earth) lead first and connect it last.

Note: *Before disconnecting the battery, refer to Battery disconnection in Chapter 5A Section 4.*

General

1 A routine preventive maintenance programme for the battery in your car is the only way to ensure quick and reliable starts. For general maintenance, refer to *Weekly checks* at the start of this manual. Also at the front of the manual is information on jump starting. For details of removing and installing the battery, refer to Chapter 5A Section 4.

Battery electrolyte level

2 On models not equipped with a sealed or 'maintenance-free' battery, check the electrolyte level of all six battery cells.
3 The level must be approximately 10 mm above the plates; this may be shown by maximum and minimum level lines marked on the battery's casing.
4 If the level is low, use a coin or screwdriver to release the filler/vent cap, and add distilled water. Do not overfill – this can actually render the battery useless. To improve access to the centre caps, it may be helpful to remove the battery hold-down clamp.
5 Install and securely retighten the cap, then wipe up any spillage.
Caution: Overfilling the cells may cause electrolyte to spill over during periods of heavy charging, causing corrosion or damage.

Charging

Warning: When batteries are being charged, hydrogen gas, which is very explosive and flammable, is produced. Do not smoke, or allow open flames, near a charging or a recently-charged battery. If the battery is being charged indoors, ensure this is done in a well-ventilated area. Wear eye protection when near the battery during charging.

Also, make sure the charger is unplugged before connecting or disconnecting the battery from the charger.
6 Slow-rate charging is the best way to restore a battery that's discharged to the point where it will not start the engine. It's also a good way to maintain the battery charge in a car that's only driven a few miles between starts. Maintaining the battery charge is particularly important in winter, when the battery must work harder to start the engine, and electrical accessories that drain the battery are in greater use.
7 Check the battery case for any instructions regarding charging the battery. Some maintenance-free batteries may require a particularly low charge rate or other special conditions, if they are not to be damaged.
8 It's best to use a one- or two-amp battery charger (sometimes called a 'trickle' charger), or a 'Smart/intelligent' charger. They are the safest, and put the least strain on the battery. For a faster charge, you can use a higher-amperage charger, but don't use one rated more than 1/10th the amp/hour rating of the battery (ie, no more than 5 amps, typically). Rapid boost charges that claim to restore the power of the battery in one to two hours are hardest on the battery, and can damage batteries not in good condition. This type of charging should only be used in emergency situations.
9 The average time necessary to charge a battery should be listed in the instructions that come with the charger. As a general rule, a trickle charger will charge a battery in 12 to 16 hours.

6 Auxiliary drivebelt check and renewal

Check

1 Due to its function and construction, the belt is prone to failure after a period of time, and should be inspected periodically to prevent problems.

2 The drivebelt is used to drive the coolant pump, alternator, power steering pump and air conditioning compressor.
3 To improve access for belt inspection, remove the cooling fan shroud as described in Chapter 3 Section 6.
4 With the engine stopped, using your fingers (and an electric torch if necessary), move along the belt, checking for cracks and separation of the belt plies. Also check for fraying and glazing, which gives the belt a shiny appearance. Both sides of the belt should be inspected, which means the belt will have to be twisted to check the underside. If necessary turn the engine using a spanner or socket on the crankshaft pulley bolt so that the whole of the belt can be inspected.
5 If the belt shows signs of damage, or significant deterioration, renew it as described in this Section.

Tension

6 The auxiliary drivebelt is tensioned by an automatic tensioner; regular checks are not required, and manual 'adjustment' is not possible.
7 If you suspect that a drivebelt is slipping and/or running slack, or that the tensioner is otherwise faulty, it and/or an idler pulley must be renewed.

Renewal

2148 cc engines

8 Unclip and remove the air intake duct between the bonnet slam panel, and the air filter housing.
9 Engage a socket with the tensioner body, and then lever the tensioner anti-clockwise to relieve the tension in the belt **(see illustration)**.
10 Hold the tensioner in position with the spanner/socket, and slide the belt from the pulleys. If necessary, the tensioner can be retained in its released position by inserting a suitable bolt or metal dowel (4 mm diameter) through the holes provided **(see illustration)**.
11 Fit the new belt around the pulleys, starting with the crankshaft pulley. Check that the belt is correctly seated on all the pulleys

6.9 Rotate the tensioner anti-clockwise

6.10 Use a 4 mm diameter rod to lock the tensioner in place

6.11 Auxiliary drivebelt routing – 2148 cc engines

6.14a Rotate the fasteners anti-clockwise…

6.14b …unclip the duct from the air filter…

6.14c …and the bonnet slam panel

6.15 Fit a socket to the lug and rotate the tensioner anti-clockwise

(see illustration). Where applicable, remove the metal dowel/bolt from the tensioner.

12 Release the spanner/socket, and allow the tensioner to move into position against the belt.

13 Refit the air intake ducting.

2143 cc engines

14 Remove the air intake duct between the bonnet slam panel and the air filter housing (see illustrations).

15 Rotate the tensioner anti-clockwise to relieve the tension in the belt (see illustration).

16 Hold the tensioner in position with the spanner/socket, and slide the belt from the pulleys. If necessary, the tensioner can be retained in its released position by inserting a suitable bolt or metal dowel (4 mm diameter) through the holes provided (see illustration).

17 Fit the new belt around the pulleys, starting with the crankshaft pulley. Check that the belt is correctly seated on all the pulleys (see illustration). Where applicable, remove the metal dowel/bolt from the tensioner.

18 Allow the tensioner to move into position against the belt.

19 The remainder of refitting is a reversal of removal.

6.16 Lock the tensioner in place using a 4 mm diameter bolt/rod

6.17 Auxiliary drivebelt routing – 2143 cc engines

7 Electrical system check

1 Check for satisfactory operation of the instrument panel, its illumination and warning lights, the switches and their function lights.
2 Check the horns for satisfactory operation.
3 Check all other electrical equipment for satisfactory operation.
4 If a fault is suspected, proceed as described in Chapter 12 Section 2.

8 Underbonnet check for fluid leaks and hose condition

1 Visually inspect the engine joint faces, gaskets and seals for any signs of water or oil leaks. Pay particular attention to the areas around the camshaft cover, cylinder head, oil filter and sump joint faces. Bear in mind that, over a period of time, some very slight seepage from these areas is to be expected – what you are really looking for is any indication of a serious leak. Should a leak be found, renew the offending gasket or oil seal by referring to the appropriate Chapters in this manual.
2 Also check the security and condition of all the engine-related pipes and hoses. Ensure that all cable-ties or securing clips are in place and in good condition. Clips that are broken or missing can lead to chafing of the hoses, pipes or wiring, which could cause more serious problems in the future.
3 Carefully check the radiator hoses and heater hoses along their entire length. Renew any hose which is cracked, swollen or deteriorated. Cracks will show up better if the hose is squeezed. Pay close attention to the hose clips that secure the hoses to the cooling system components. Hose clips can pinch and puncture hoses, resulting in cooling system leaks.
4 Inspect all the cooling system components

HAYNES HINT

A leak in the cooling system will usually show up as white-or antifreeze coloured deposits on the area adjoining the leak.

(hoses, joint faces, etc) for leaks. A leak in the cooling system will usually show up as white- or antifreeze-coloured deposits on the area adjoining the leak (see **Haynes Hint**). Where any problems of this nature are found on system components, renew the component or gasket with reference to Chapter 3.
5 Where applicable, inspect the automatic transmission fluid cooler hoses for leaks or deterioration.
6 With the vehicle raised, inspect the fuel tank and filler neck for punctures, cracks and other damage. The connection between the filler neck and tank is especially critical. Sometimes a rubber filler neck or connecting hose will leak due to loose retaining clamps or deteriorated rubber.
7 Carefully check all rubber hoses and metal fuel lines leading away from the petrol tank. Check for loose connections, deteriorated hoses, crimped lines, and other damage. Pay particular attention to the vent pipes and hoses, which often loop up around the filler neck and can become blocked or crimped. Follow the lines to the front of the vehicle, carefully inspecting them all the way. Renew damaged sections as necessary.
8 Closely inspect the metal brake pipes, which run along the vehicle underbody. If they show signs of excessive corrosion or damage they must be renewed.
9 From within the engine compartment, check the security of all fuel hose attachments and pipe unions, and inspect the fuel hoses and vacuum hoses for kinks, chafing and deterioration.
10 Check the condition of the power steering fluid hoses and pipes.

9 Engine compartment wiring check

1 With the car parked on level ground, apply the handbrake firmly and open the bonnet. Using an inspection light or a small electric torch, check all visible wiring within and beneath the engine compartment.
2 What you are looking for is wiring that is obviously damaged by chafing against sharp edges, or against moving suspension/transmission components and/ or the auxiliary drivebelt, by being trapped or crushed between carelessly-refitted components, or melted by being forced into contact with the hot engine castings, coolant pipes, etc. In almost all cases, damage of this sort is caused in the first instance by incorrect routing on reassembly after previous work has been carried out.
3 Depending on the extent of the problem, damaged wiring may be repaired by rejoining the break or splicing-in a new length of wire, using solder to ensure a good connection, and remaking the insulation with adhesive insulating tape or heat-shrink tubing, as appropriate. If the damage is extensive, given

the implications for the car's future reliability, the best long-term answer may well be to renew that entire section of the loom, however expensive this may appear.
4 When the actual damage has been repaired, ensure that the wiring loom is rerouted correctly, so that it is clear of other components, and not stretched or kinked, and is secured out of harm's way using the plastic clips, guides and ties provided.
5 Check all electrical connectors, ensuring that they are clean, securely fastened, and that each is locked by its plastic tabs or wire clip, as appropriate. If any connector shows external signs of corrosion (accumulations of white or green deposits, or streaks of 'rust'), or if any is thought to be dirty, it must be unplugged and cleaned using electrical contact cleaner. If the connector pins are severely corroded, the connector must be renewed; note that this may mean the renewal of that entire section of the loom – see your local Mercedes dealer for details.
6 If the cleaner completely removes the corrosion to leave the connector in a satisfactory condition, it would be wise to pack the connector with a suitable material which will exclude dirt and moisture, preventing the corrosion from occurring again; a Mercedes dealer may be able to recommend a suitable product.
7 Check the condition of the battery connections – remake the connections or renew the leads if a fault is found (see Chapter 5A Section 4). Use the same techniques to ensure that all earth points in the engine compartment provide good electrical contact through clean, metal-to-metal joints, and that all are securely fastened.

10 Air conditioning system check

1 The following maintenance checks will ensure that the air conditioner operates at peak efficiency:
a) Check the auxiliary drivebelt (see Section 6).
b) Check the system hoses for damage or leaks.
c) Inspect the condenser fins for leaves, insects and other debris. Use a clean paint brush to clean the condenser. The condenser is mounted in front of the radiator.
d) Check that the drain tube from the evaporator housing is clear – the hose is located under the drivers side of the facia, and connects the housing to the engine compartment bulkhead. Note that it is normal to have clear fluid (water) dripping from this while the system is in operation, to the extent that quite a large puddle can be left under the car when it is parked.
2 It's a good idea to operate the system for about 30 minutes at least once a month, particularly during the winter. Long

term non-use can cause hardening, and subsequent failure, of the seals.

3 Because of the complexity of the air conditioning system and the special equipment necessary to service it, in-depth fault diagnosis and repairs are not included in this manual.

4 The most common cause of poor cooling is simply a low system refrigerant charge. If a noticeable drop in cool air output occurs, the following quick check will help you determine if the refrigerant level is low.

5 Warm the engine up to normal operating temperature.

6 Place the air conditioning temperature selector at the coldest setting, and put the blower at the highest setting. Open the doors – to make sure the air conditioning system doesn't cycle off as soon as it cools the passenger compartment

7 With the compressor engaged – the clutch will make an audible click, and the centre of the clutch will rotate – feel the inlet and outlet pipes at the compressor. One side should be cold, and one hot. If there's no perceptible difference between the two pipes, there's something wrong with the compressor or the system. It might be a low charge – it might be something else. Take the car to a dealer service department or an automotive air conditioning specialist.

11 Seat belt check

1 Check the seat belts for satisfactory operation and condition. Inspect the webbing for fraying and cuts. Check that they retract smoothly and without binding into their reels.
2 Check that the seat belt mounting bolts are tight, and if necessary tighten them to the specified torque wrench setting (Chapter 11 Section 0).

12 Antifreeze concentration check

1 The cooling system should be filled with the recommended antifreeze and corrosion protection fluid. Over a period of time, the concentration of fluid may be reduced due to topping-up (this can be avoided by topping-up with the correct antifreeze mixture) or fluid loss. If loss of coolant has been evident, it is important to make the necessary repair before adding fresh fluid. The exact mixture of antifreeze-to-water which you should use depends on the relative weather conditions. The mixture should contain at least 40% anti-freeze, but not more than 70%. Consult the mixture ratio chart on the antifreeze container before adding coolant. Use antifreeze which meets the car manufacturer's specifications.

2 With the engine cold, carefully remove the cap from the expansion tank. If the engine is not completely cold, place a cloth rag over the cap before removing it, and remove it slowly to allow any pressure to escape.
3 Antifreeze checkers are available from car accessory shops. Draw some coolant from the expansion tank and observe how many plastic balls are floating in the checker. Usually, 2 or 3 balls must be floating for the correct concentration of antifreeze, but follow the manufacturer's instructions.
4 If the concentration is incorrect, it will be necessary to either withdraw some coolant and add antifreeze, or alternatively drain the old coolant and add fresh coolant of the correct concentration.

13 Steering, suspension and roadwheel check

Front suspension

1 Raise the front of the vehicle and support it securely on axle stands (see *Vehicle jacking and support*).
2 Visually inspect the balljoint dust covers and the steering linkage gaiters for splits, chafing or deterioration. Any wear of these components will cause loss of lubricant, together with dirt and water entry, resulting in rapid deterioration of the balljoints. Also check that the steering rack mountings are tightened to the specified torque settings (see Chapter 10).
3 Check the power steering fluid hoses for chafing or deterioration, and the pipe and hose unions for fluid leaks. Also check for signs of fluid leakage under pressure from the steering rack, which would indicate failed fluid seals within the steering rack.
4 Grasp the roadwheel at the 12 o'clock and 6 o'clock positions, and try to rock it **(see illustration)**. Very slight free play may be felt, but if the movement is appreciable, further investigation is necessary to determine the source. Continue rocking the wheel while an assistant depresses the footbrake. If the movement is now eliminated or significantly reduced, it is likely that the hub bearings are at fault. If the free play is still evident with the footbrake depressed, then there is wear in the suspension joints or mountings. Note that the front hub bearings are adjustable (See Chapter 10 Section 2).
5 Now grasp the wheel at the 9 o'clock and 3 o'clock positions, and try to rock it as before. Any movement felt now may again be caused by wear in the hub bearings or the steering track rod balljoints. If the inner or outer balljoint is worn, the visual movement will be obvious.
6 Using a large screwdriver or flat bar, check for wear in the suspension mounting bushes by levering between the relevant suspension component and its attachment point. Some

13.4 Check for wear in the hub bearings by grasping the wheel and trying to rock it

movement is to be expected as the mountings are made of rubber, but excessive wear should be obvious. Also check the condition of any visible rubber bushes, looking for splits, cracks or contamination of the rubber.
7 With the car standing on its wheels, have an assistant turn the steering wheel back-and-forth about an eighth of a turn each way. There should be very little lost movement between the steering wheel and roadwheels. If this is not the case, closely observe the linkage joints and mountings previously described, but in addition, check the steering column universal joint/coupling for wear, and the steering rack itself.

Rear suspension

8 Chock the front wheels, then jack up the rear of the vehicle and support securely on axle stands (see *Vehicle jacking and support*).
9 Working as described previously for the front suspension, check the rear hub bearings, the suspension bushes and the strut or shock absorber mountings (as applicable) for wear.

Shock absorber

10 Check for any signs of fluid leakage around the shock absorber body, or from the rubber gaiter around the piston rod. Should any fluid be noticed, the shock absorber is defective internally, and should be renewed.
Note: *Shock absorbers should always be renewed in pairs on the same axle.*
11 The efficiency of the shock absorber may be checked by bouncing the vehicle at each corner. Generally speaking, the body will return to its normal position and stop after being depressed. If it rises and returns on a rebound, the shock absorber is probably suspect. Examine also the shock absorber upper and lower mountings for any signs of wear.

Roadwheels

12 Periodically remove the roadwheels, and clean any dirt or mud from the inside and outside surfaces. Examine the wheel rims for signs of rusting, corrosion or other damage. Light alloy wheels are easily damaged by 'kerbing' whilst parking, and similarly, steel wheels may become dented or buckled. Specialist firms do exist who will repair alloy

14.1 Check the condition of the rubber gaiters on each end of the driveshafts

15.2a Check the security of the various exhaust brackets…

15.2b …and mountings

wheels, but sometimes renewal of the wheel is the only course of remedial action possible.
13 The balance of each wheel and tyre assembly should be maintained, not only to avoid excessive tyre wear, but also to avoid wear in the steering and suspension components. Wheel imbalance is normally signified by vibration through the car's bodyshell, although in many cases it is particularly noticeable through the steering wheel. Conversely, it should be noted that wear or damage in suspension or steering components may cause excessive tyre wear. Out-of-round or out-of-true tyres, damaged wheels and wheel bearing wear/maladjustment also fall into this category. Balancing will not usually cure vibration caused by such wear.
14 Wheel balancing may be carried out with the wheel either on or off the car. If balanced on the car, ensure that the wheel-to-hub relationship is marked in some way prior to subsequent wheel removal, so that it may be refitted in its original position.
15 At this time, also check the spare wheel for damage.

14 Driveshaft rubber gaiter check

1 With the vehicle raised and securely supported on stands, slowly rotate the rear roadwheel. Inspect the condition of the outer constant velocity (CV) joint rubber gaiters, squeezing the gaiters to open out the folds. Check for signs of cracking, splits or deterioration of the rubber, which may allow the grease to escape, and lead to water and grit entry into the joint. Also check the security and condition of the retaining clips. Repeat these checks on the inner CV joints **(see illustration)**. If any damage or deterioration is found, the gaiters should be renewed (see Chapter 8 Section 6).
2 At the same time, check the general condition of the CV joints themselves by first holding the driveshaft and attempting to rotate the wheel. Repeat this check by holding the inner joint and attempting to rotate the driveshaft. Any appreciable

movement indicates wear in the joints, wear in the driveshaft splines, or a loose driveshaft retaining nut.

15 Exhaust system check

1 With the engine cold, check the complete exhaust system from the engine to the end of the tailpipe. The exhaust system is most easily checked with the vehicle raised on a hoist, or suitably supported on axle stands, so that the exhaust components are readily visible and accessible.
2 Check the exhaust pipes and connections for evidence of leaks, severe corrosion and damage. Make sure that all brackets and mountings are in good condition, and that all relevant nuts and bolts are tight **(see illustrations)**. Leakage at any of the joints or in other parts of the system will usually show up as a black sooty stain in the vicinity of the leak.
3 Rattles and other noises can often be traced to the exhaust system, especially the brackets and mountings. Try to move the pipes and silencers. If the components are able to come into contact with the body or suspension parts, secure the system with new mountings. Otherwise separate the joints (if possible) and twist the pipes as necessary to provide additional clearance.

16 Underbody and fuel/brake line check

1 With the car raised and supported on axle stands (see *Vehicle jacking and support*), thoroughly inspect the underbody and wheel arches for signs of damage and corrosion. In particular, examine the bottom of the side sills, and any concealed areas where mud can collect. Also check the inside edges at the base of all doors.
2 Where corrosion and rust is evident, press and tap firmly on the panel with a screwdriver, and check for any serious corrosion which would necessitate repairs.
3 If the panel is not seriously corroded, clean

away the rust, and apply a new coating of underseal. Refer to Chapter 11 for more details of body repairs.
4 At the same time, inspect the PVC-coated lower body panels for stone damage and general condition.
5 Inspect all of the fuel and brake lines on the underbody for damage, rust, corrosion and leakage. Particularly check the rear brake pipes where they pass over the fuel tank. Also make sure that the pipes are correctly supported in their clips. Where applicable, check the PVC coating on the lines for damage.

17 Braking system check

Front brakes

1 Apply the handbrake, then jack up the front of the car and support it on axle stands (see *Vehicle jacking and support*). For better access to the brake calipers, remove the wheels.
2 Look through the inspection window in the caliper, and check that the thickness of the friction lining material on each of the pads is not less than the recommended minimum thickness given in the Specifications **(see illustration)**.
3 If it is difficult to determine the exact thickness of the pad linings, or if you are at all concerned about the condition of the pads, then remove them from the calipers for further inspection (refer to Chapter 9 Section 4).

17.2 Check the friction material thickness through the window in the caliper

17.7 Check the condition of the flexible hoses

4 Check the caliper on the other side in the same way.
5 If any one of the brake pads has worn down to, or below, the specified limit, all four pads at that end of the car must be renewed as a set.
6 Check both front brake discs with reference to Chapter 9 Section 6.
7 Before refitting the wheels, check all brake lines and flexible hoses with reference to Chapter 9 Section 3. In particular, check the flexible hoses in the vicinity of the calipers, where they are subjected to most movement. Bend them between the fingers and check that this does not reveal previously-hidden cracks, cuts or splits **(see illustration)**.
8 On completion, refit the wheels and lower the car to the ground. Tighten the wheel nuts to the specified torque.

Rear brakes

9 Chock the front wheels, then jack up the rear of the car and support on axle stands (see *Vehicle jacking and support*). Remove the rear wheels.
10 The procedure for checking the rear brakes is much the same as described in paragraphs 1 to 8 above.

Parking brake

11 With the car on a slight slope, firmly apply the parking brake lever, and check that it holds the car stationary, then release the lever and check that there is no resistance to movement of the car. If necessary, the parking brake should be adjusted as described in Chapter 9 Section 13.

19.3a Slide the locking catch to the right...

19.2 Prise off the clip at each end of the cover

18 Door and bonnet check and lubrication

1 Check that the doors, bonnet and tailgate/boot lid close securely. Check that the bonnet safety catch operates correctly. Check the operation of the door check straps.
2 Lubricate the hinges, door check straps, the striker plates and the bonnet catch sparingly with a little oil or grease.

19 Pollen filter renewal

1 Remove the passengers side lower facia panel as described in Chapter 11 Section 37.
2 Release the clip at each end of the filter cover **(see illustration)**.
3 Slide the locking catch to the right, and manoeuvre the pollen filter from place **(see illustrations)**.
4 Clean any debris from the filter housing.
5 Transfer the locking catch from the old filter to the new one.
6 Insert the new filter element into the housing, with the arrow on the base of the filter pointing towards the blower motor **(see illustration)**.
7 Slide the locking catch to the left, and secure the clip at each end of the filter housing.
8 The remainder of refitting is a reversal of removal.

19.3b ...and remove the pollen filter element

20 Fuel sedimentor draining

Note: *A filter drain port is only fitted to some models. None of the vehicles we examined were equipped with a drain port.*
1 Remove the plastic cover from the top of the engine.
2 A drain port is provided on the fuel filter housing to enable draining water from the filter. On some models the port is controlled by a screw valve, whilst on others, a plug is fitted to the port.
3 On models with a screw, attach a hose to the port, and position the other end of the hose in a suitable container. Slacken the screw.
4 On models with a plug, remove the plug and attach a hose to the port. Position the other end of the hose in a suitable container.
5 On all models, have an assistant switch on the ignition, and observe the flow of fluid from the hose. When clean fuel emerges, have the ignition switched off.
6 Tighten the port screw, and disconnect the hose, or disconnect the hose and refit the plug as applicable.
7 Refit the cover to the top of the engine.
8 Start the engine, and allow it to idle for at least 3 minutes. Check for leaks.

21 Road test

Instruments and electrical equipment

1 Check the operation of all instruments and electrical equipment.
2 Make sure that all instruments read correctly, and switch on all electrical equipment in turn, to check that it functions properly.

Suspension and steering

3 Check for any abnormalities in the steering, suspension, handling or road 'feel'.
4 Drive the vehicle, and check that there are no unusual vibrations or noises.

19.6 The arrow must point towards the blower motor

5 Check that the steering feels positive, with no excessive 'sloppiness', or roughness, and check for any suspension noises when cornering and driving over bumps.

Drivetrain

6 Check the performance of the engine, clutch (where applicable), gearbox/transmission, propeller shaft and driveshafts.
7 Listen for any unusual noises from the engine, clutch and gearbox/transmission.
8 Make sure that the engine runs smoothly when idling, and that there is no hesitation when accelerating.
9 Check that, where applicable, the clutch action is smooth and progressive, that the drive is taken up smoothly, and that the pedal travel is not excessive. Also listen for any noises when the clutch pedal is depressed.
10 On manual gearbox models, check that all gears can be engaged smoothly without noise, and that the gear lever action is smooth and not abnormally vague or 'notchy'.
11 On automatic transmission models, make sure that all gearchanges occur smoothly, without snatching, and without an increase in engine speed between changes. Check that all the gear positions can be selected with the vehicle at rest. If any problems are found, they should be referred to a Mercedes-Benz dealer.

Braking system

12 Make sure that the vehicle does not pull to one side when braking, and that the wheels do not lock when braking hard.
13 Check that there is no vibration through the steering when braking.
14 Check that the parking brake operates correctly without excessive movement of the foot pedal, and that it holds the vehicle stationary on a slope.
15 Test the operation of the brake servo unit as follows. With the engine off, depress the footbrake four or five times to exhaust the vacuum. Hold the brake pedal depressed, and then start the engine. As the engine starts, there should be a noticeable 'give' in the brake pedal as vacuum builds-up. Allow the engine to run for at least two minutes, and then switch it off. If the brake pedal is depressed now, it should be possible to detect a hiss

from the servo as the pedal is depressed. After about four or five applications, no further hissing should be heard, and the pedal should feel considerably harder.

22 Reset the service indicator

1 Close all doors, bonnet and tailgate, then turn the Ignition key to position 'I'

Models with the Luxury multifunction steering wheel

2 Repeatedly press the selection button until menu item 'Trip' is highlighted in the display, then within 5 seconds, press and hold down the 'accept/end phone call' button, and within 1 second, also press and hold down the 'OK' button for approximately 5 seconds.
3 The workshop menu will be displayed, scroll backwards/forwards until 'ASSYST PLUS' is highlighted, and confirm the selection by pressing the 'OK' button.
4 Scroll backwards/forwards to highlight 'Full Service', and confirm the selection with the 'OK' button.
5 Scroll backwards/forwards until 'Confirm Serv' is highlighted, and confirm the selection with the 'OK' button.
6 Where applicable, now select the specification of engine oil used using the scroll back/forwards buttons, and confirm your selection with the 'OK' button.
7 Scroll backwards/forwards until 'Yes' is highlighted, and confirm with the 'OK' button.
8 Scroll backwards/forwards until 'Confirmation' is highlighted, then confirm with the 'OK' button. If the process has been successful, 'Service carried out' will be displayed.
9 Press the 'Back/Voice Control System' button repeatedly until the standard display appears.
10 Turn the ignition off.

Models without the Luxury steering wheel

11 Press the 'System selection' button repeatedly until the standard display (total distance) appears in the multifunction display.

12 Press and hold the 'R' button, then within 1 second, press and hold the '+' button for approximately 5 seconds. The display should now show the system voltage.
13 Press the system select button repeatedly until 'Full Service' is shown in the display.
14 Press the 'R' button. The current service items will be displayed.
15 Press the system selection button repeatedly until 'Confirm service' appears in the display.
16 Press the 'R' button.
17 Where applicable, now select the specification of engine oil used and confirm your selection.
18 Press the '+' button. 'Reversal not possible' will be displayed.
19 Press the '+' button again. 'Fully service completed' will be displayed.
20 Press the 'System selection' button repeatedly until the standard display (total distance) is shown.
21 Turn the ignition off.

23 Roadwheels anti-seize grease

1 Slacken the roadwheel bolts, raise the front and rear of the vehicle and support it securely on axle stands (see *Vehicle jacking and support*). Remove the roadwheels.
2 Check the condition of the wheel hub spigots, and where necessary remove any dirt/rust etc.
3 Apply a little anti-seize grease to the wheel hub spigots.
4 Take this opportunity to examine the wheels/tyres for signs of damage etc.
5 Refit the roadwheels, but do not fully tighten the retaining bolts yet.
6 Lower the vehicle to the ground, and tighten the roadwheel bolts to the specified torque.

24 Air filter element renewal

2148 cc engines

1 Remove the plastic cover from the top of the engine (**see illustration 4.3a**).
2 Prise off the 6 clips around the edge of the filter housing cover (**see illustration**).
3 Release the retaining clip at the front edge and remove the air filter cover (**see illustration**).
4 Lift the filter element at the rear, and manoeuvre it from the housing.
5 Clear any debris from the filter housing.
6 Locate the new filter element into the housing, noting how the lug on the filter engages with the notch in the housing (**see illustrations**).
7 Remove the cover to the top of the engine.

24.2 Prise away the clips around the edge

24.3 Release the clip at the front and remove the cover

24.6a Fit the new element into the housing...

24.6b ...ensuring the lug engages with the notch

24.9 Depress the catches and slide up the harness clips

2143 cc engines

8 Pull the plastic cover on the top of the engine upwards to release it from the rubber mountings **(see illustration 4.3b and 4.3c)**.
9 Depress the catches and slide up the ECM wiring harness clips from the bracket on the top of the air cleaner housing **(see illustration)**.
10 Undo the 7 retaining bolts, and lift the filter housing cover **(see illustration)**.
11 Lift the filter element at the rear, and remove it from the housing **(see illustration)**.
12 Clear any debris from the filter housing.
13 Insert the new element into the housing, ensuring it locates correctly.
14 Refit the filter housing cover, and tighten the retaining bolts securely.
15 Slide the wiring harness clips back into place, and refit the cover to the top of the engine.

24.10 The cover is secured by 6 bolts around the edge, and one in the centre

24.11 Lift the cover and remove the element

---

25 Fuel filter renewal

Note: *Before carrying out the following procedure, read carefully the precautions given in Chapter 4A Section 1.*

2148 cc engines

1 Remove the plastic cover from the top of the engine **(see illustration 4.3a)**.
2 The fuel filter is located to the left-hand side of the cylinder head. To minimise fuel spillage, pad the surrounding area with absorbent rags.
3 Where applicable, disconnect the wiring plug from the water sensor on the top of the filter.
4 Release the securing clips and disconnect the fuel hoses from the top of the fuel filter. Note the fitted positions for refitting; one of the fuel hoses has a larger diameter than the other. Plug the ends of the fuel hoses to prevent dirt ingress **(see illustration)**.
5 Release the clamps at the side of the filter, and then withdraw the filter from its mounting bracket.
6 Remove the filter canister from the engine bay, keeping the mating face upwards to minimise fuel spillage.

7 Where applicable, transfer the water sensor from the old filter element to the new one.
8 Take the new fuel filter canister and fit it into the mounting bracket. Don't tighten the clamps at this stage.
9 Refit the fuel hoses to the top of the fuel filter in their correct positions (as noted on removal), making sure they are secure. Ensure the hoses are not kinked or under tension.
10 Tighten the filter retaining clamps.
11 Start and run the engine at idle and check around the fuel filter for fuel leaks. Note that the fuel pump is self-priming, but it may take a few seconds of cranking before the engine starts.
12 Raise the engine speed to about 2000 rpm several times, and then allow the engine to idle again. This should bleed the air bubbles

from the filter canister, but if the engine idle is at all rough or hesitant, repeat the action until the fuel system clears itself.
13 Refit the cover to the top of the engine.

2143 cc engines

14 Rotate the catch anti-clockwise, then pull the plastic cover on the top of the engine forwards from its rubber mountings (see illustration 4.3b and 4.3c).
15 Where applicable, disconnect the wiring plugs from the water sensor/heater on the top of the filter.
16 Release the clamps and disconnect the hoses from the top of the fuel filter **(see illustration)**. Plug the openings to prevent contamination. Take care not to damage the hoses, and not allow any debris to enter the fuel system.

25.4 Fuel hose clips and filter retaining clamps

25.16 Release the clamps and disconnect the hoses

25.18a Prise open the clamps...

25.18b ...and lift the filter from place

17 Release the cable tie securing the drain hose to the pipe (where fitted).

18 Prise open the clamps, and lift the filter from the mounting bracket **(see illustrations)**.

19 Install the new filter into the bracket, ensuring its correctly located, and pushed down fully into the bracket to prevent the engine cover may damage the pipes. Tighten the clamps.

20 Refit the hoses, and wiring plug (where applicable) to the filter, and secure with new clamps where necessary.

21 Start and run the engine at idle and check around the fuel filter for fuel leaks. Note that the fuel pump is self-priming, but it may take a few seconds of cranking before the engine starts.

22 Raise the engine speed to about 2000 rpm several times, and then allow the engine to idle again. This should bleed the air bubbles from the filter canister, but if the engine idle is at all rough or hesitant, repeat the action until the fuel system clears itself.

23 Refit the cover to the top of the engine.

26 Brake fluid renewal

⚠ *Warning: Brake hydraulic fluid can harm your eyes and damage painted surfaces, so use extreme caution when handling and pouring it. Do not use fluid that has been standing open for some time, as it absorbs moisture from the air. Excess moisture can cause a dangerous loss of braking effectiveness.*

1 The procedure is similar to that for the bleeding of the hydraulic system as described in Chapter 9 Section 2, except that the brake fluid reservoir should be emptied by syphoning, using a clean poultry baster or similar before starting, and allowance should

be made for the old fluid to be expelled when bleeding a section of the circuit.

2 Working as described in Chapter 9 Section 2, open the first bleed screw in the sequence, and pump the brake pedal gently until nearly all the old fluid has been emptied from the master cylinder reservoir.

Caution: Do not allow the fluid level to drop below the bottom of the reservoir.

3 Top-up to the MAX level with new fluid, and continue pumping until only the new fluid remains in the reservoir, and new fluid can be seen emerging from the bleed screw. Tighten the screw, and top the reservoir level up to the MAX level line.

4 Work through all the remaining bleed screws in the sequence until new fluid can be seen at all of them. Be careful to keep the master cylinder reservoir topped-up to above the MIN level at all times, or air may enter the system and greatly increase the length of the task.

5 When the operation is complete, check that all bleed screws are securely tightened, and that their dust caps are refitted. Wash off all traces of spilt fluid, and recheck the master cylinder reservoir fluid level.

6 Check the operation of the brakes before taking the car on the road.

27 Manual transmission oil renewal

1 Manual transmission oil renewal is described in Chapter 7A Section 2.

28 Automatic transmission oil renewal

1 Automatic transmission oil renewal is described in Chapter 7B Section 5.

29 Final drive oil renewal

1 Refer to Chapter 8 Section 2.

30 Coolant renewal

⚠ *Warning: Refer to Chapter 3 Section 1 and observe the warnings given. In particular, never remove the expansion tank filler cap when the engine is running, or has just been switched off, as the cooling system will be hot, and the consequent escaping steam and scalding coolant could cause serious injury. If the engine is hot, the electric cooling fan may start rotating even if the engine is not running, so be careful to keep hands, hair and loose clothing well clear when working in the engine compartment.*

Cooling system draining

⚠ *Warning: Wait until the engine is cold before starting this procedure.*

1 After allowing the engine to cool completely, cover the pressure cap with a wad of rag, and slowly turn the cap anti-clockwise to relieve the pressure in the cooling system (a hissing sound will normally be heard). Wait until any pressure remaining in the system is released, then continue to turn the cap until it can be removed.

2 Raise the front of the vehicle and support it securely on axle stands (see *Vehicle jacking and support*). Undo the fasteners and

30.2 Undo the fasteners each side, and remove the radiator undershield

30.3 Attach a hose to the outlet, then rotate the tap 90° anti-clockwise and pull it out slightly

remove the radiator undershield (see illustration).

3 Push a length of hose onto the radiator drain tap, then rotate the tap 1/4 turn anticlockwise, pull it out slightly, and allow the coolant to drain into a suitable container (see illustration). The drain tap is located at the left-hand end of the radiator.

4 Once the coolant has ceased flowing, tighten the drain tap and remove the hose.

Cooling system flushing

5 If coolant renewal has been neglected, or if the antifreeze mixture has become diluted, then in time, the cooling system may gradually lose efficiency, as the coolant passages become restricted due to rust, scale deposits, and other sediment. The cooling system efficiency can be restored by flushing the system clean.

6 The radiator should be flushed independently of the engine, to avoid unnecessary contamination.

Radiator flushing

7 Disconnect the top and bottom hoses and any other relevant hoses from the radiator, with reference to Chapter 3 Section 2.

8 Insert a garden hose into the radiator top inlet. Direct a flow of clean water through the radiator, and continue flushing until clean water emerges from the radiator bottom outlet.

9 If after a reasonable period, the water still does not run clear, the radiator can be flushed with a good proprietary cleaning agent. It is important that the manufacturer's instructions are followed carefully. If the contamination is particularly bad, remove the radiator, insert the hose in the radiator bottom outlet, and reverse-flush the radiator.

Antifreeze mixture

10 The antifreeze should always be renewed at the specified intervals. This is necessary

not only to maintain the antifreeze properties, but also to prevent corrosion, which would otherwise occur as the corrosion inhibitors become progressively less effective.

11 Always use a good quality antifreeze that meets Mercedes specifications. The quantity of antifreeze and levels of protection are indicated in the Specifications.

12 Before adding antifreeze, the cooling system should be completely drained, preferably flushed, and all hoses checked for condition and security.

13 After filling with antifreeze, a label should be attached to the expansion tank or header tank, stating the type and concentration of antifreeze used, and the date installed. Any subsequent topping-up should be made with the same type and concentration of antifreeze.

14 Do not use engine antifreeze in the windscreen/tailgate washer system, as it will cause damage to the vehicle paintwork. A screenwash additive should be added to the washer system in the quantities stated on the bottle.

Cooling system refilling

15 Before attempting to fill the cooling system, make sure that all hoses and clips are in good condition, and that the clips are tight. Note that an antifreeze mixture must be used all year round, to prevent corrosion of the engine components (see previous sub-Section).

16 Remove the pressure cap, and fill the system by slowly pouring the coolant into the expansion tank to prevent airlocks from forming.

17 If the coolant is being renewed, begin by pouring in a couple of litres of water, followed by the correct quantity of antifreeze, then top-up with more water.

18 Once the level in the expansion tank/header tank starts to rise, squeeze the radiator top and bottom hoses to help expel any trapped air in the system. Once all the air

is expelled, top-up the coolant level until the white level indicator is visible in the expansion tank filler neck (see illustration). Refit the pressure cap securely.

19 Start the engine and run it until the thermostat opens – the radiator top hose will begin to heat up as coolant flows through it of the radiator when this happens.

20 Check for leaks, particularly around disturbed components. Check the coolant level in the expansion tank/header tank, and top-up if necessary. Note that the system must be cold before an accurate level is indicated. If the pressure cap is removed while the engine is still warm, cover the cap with a thick cloth, and unscrew the cap slowly to gradually relieve the system pressure (a hissing sound will normally be heard). Wait until any pressure remaining in the system is released, then continue to turn the cap until it can be removed.

Airlocks

21 If, after draining and refilling the system, symptoms of overheating are found which did not occur previously, then the fault is almost certainly due to trapped air at some point in the system, causing an airlock and restricting

30.18 Add coolant until it's level with the indicator in the filler neck

the flow of coolant; usually, the air is trapped because the system was refilled too quickly.

22 If an airlock is suspected, first try gently squeezing all visible coolant hoses. A coolant hose which is full of air feels quite different to one full of coolant, when squeezed. After refilling the system, most airlocks will clear once the system has cooled, and been topped-up.

23 While the engine is running at operating temperature, switch on the heater and heater fan, and check for heat output. Provided there is sufficient coolant in the system, any lack of heat output could be due to an airlock in the system.

24 Airlocks can have more serious effects than simply reducing heater output – a severe airlock could reduce coolant flow around the engine. Check that the radiator top hose is hot when the engine is at operating temperature – a top hose which stays cold could be the result of an airlock (or a non-opening thermostat).

25 If the problem persists, stop the engine and allow it to cool down completely, before unscrewing the expansion tank filler cap or loosening the hose clips and squeezing the hoses to bleed out the trapped air. In the worst case, the system will have to be at least partially drained (this time, the coolant can be saved for re-use) and flushed to clear the problem.

Pressure cap check

26 Clean the pressure cap (expansion tank), and inspect the seal inside the cap for damage or deterioration. If there is any sign of damage or deterioration to the seal, fit a new pressure cap. If the cap is old, it is worth considering fitting a new one for peace of mind – they are not expensive. If the pressure cap fails, excess pressure will be allowed into the system, which may result in the failure of hoses, the radiator, or the heater matrix.

Chapter 2 Part A
2148 cc engine in-car repair procedures

Contents

Section number

Balancer shaft assembly – removal and refitting 13
Camshafts, camshaft housing and hydraulic tappets –
   removal, inspection and refitting 9
Compression test – description and interpretation 2
Crankshaft oil seals – renewal 15
Crankshaft pulley – removal and refitting. 5
Cylinder head – removal, inspection and refitting 10
Cylinder head cover – removal and refitting. 4
Cylinder head front cover – removal and refitting 16
Engine assembly/valve timing settings – general information
   and usage. 3

Section number

Engine oil sensor – renewal 18
Engine/transmission mountings – inspection and renewal 17
Flywheel/driveplate – removal, inspection and refitting 14
General information 1
Oil pump – removal, inspection and refitting 12
Sump – removal and refitting 11
Timing chain – inspection and renewal 7
Timing chain cover – removal and refitting. 6
Timing chain tensioner, sprockets and guides –
   removal, inspection and refitting. 8

Degrees of difficulty

Easy, suitable for novice with little experience 🔧	**Fairly easy,** suitable for beginner with some experience 🔧	**Fairly difficult,** suitable for competent DIY mechanic 🔧	**Difficult,** suitable for experienced DIY mechanic 🔧	**Very difficult,** suitable for expert DIY or professional 🔧

Specifications

General

Engine type.	4-cylinder in-line diesel, double overhead camshaft (DOHC)
Engine code	646.811 or 646.812
Bore	88.0 mm
Stroke.	88.3 mm
Capacity	2148 cc
Emissions standard	EU4
Firing order	1-3-4-2
Direction of crankshaft rotation	Clockwise (seen from the front of the vehicle)
Compression ratio	16.5 : 1
Compression pressures:	
New compression pressure	23.0 to 30.0 bar
Minimum compression pressure	17.0 bar (approximately)
Maximum difference between cylinders.	3.0 bar

Cylinder head bolts

Thread diameter	M12
Length when new (from under head)	102.0 mm
Maximum length.	104.0 mm

Lubrication system

Minimum system pressure at normal operating temperature:	
At idle speed.	0.7 bar
At 3200 rpm	2.5 bar

Balancer shaft assembly

Shaft circumferential backlash:	
Nominal dimension.	0.08 mm
Minimum.	0.05 mm
Maximum	0.13 mm

Torque wrench settings

	Nm	lbf ft
Balancer shaft housing-to-crankcase:		
Stage 1	25	17
Stage 2	45	33
Camshaft bearing cap bolts	9	6
Camshaft sprocket bolt (exhaust)	18	14
Centrifuge-to-camshaft sprocket	36	27
Cylinder head cover bolts:		
Middle bolt	7	5
Outer bolts	10	7
Connecting rod bolts*:		
Stage 1	5	3
Stage 2	25	17
Stage 3	Slacken 180°	
Stage 4	25	17
Stage 5	Angle-tighten a further 90°	
Crankshaft pulley bolt*:		
Stage 1	200	147
Stage 2	Angle-tighten a further 90°	
Stage 3	Angle-tighten a further 90°	
Crankshaft rear oil seal housing bolts	10	7
Cylinder head bolts*:		
Stage 1	15	11
Stage 2	60	44
Stage 3	Angle-tighten a further 90°	
Stage 4	Angle-tighten a further 90°	
Engine/transmission mountings:		
Engine mounting-to-crossmember	35	26
Bracket to engine mounting	50	37
Bracket to cylinder block	20	15
Rear bracket-to-transmission	50	37
Rear mounting-to-crossmember	50	37
Rear mounting to transmission bracket	28	20
Exhaust manifold-to-cylinder head	20	15
Exhaust manifold-to-turbocharger:		
Stage 1	20	15
Stage 2	Angle-tighten a further 90°	
Flywheel/driveplate bolts*:		
Stage 1	45	33
Stage 2	Angle-tighten a further 90°	
Front cover-to-cylinder head	14	10
Main bearing cap bolts:		
Stage 1	55	41
Stage 2	Angle-tighten a further 90°	
Oil filter cap	25	17
Oil pump bolts	19	14
Oil pump pick-up tube	10	7
Oil sensor	14	10
Oil separator-to-cylinder head cover	10	7
Sump drain plug	30	22
Sump:		
To crankcase:		
M6	10	7
M8	20	15
To transmission	40	30
To rear seal housing	10	7
Timing chain cover:		
M6	10	7
M8	20	15
Bolt plug:		
M10	10	7
M22	45	33
Timing chain tensioner	80	60
Turbocharger oil feed pipe:		
To turbocharger	20	9
To cylinder head	9	6
Turbocharger oil drain pipe bolt	9	6

*Do not re-use

1 General information

How to use this Chapter

1 This Part of the Chapter describes those repair procedures that can reasonably be carried out on the engine whilst it remains in the vehicle. If the engine has been removed from the vehicle and is being dismantled as described in Part C of this Chapter, any preliminary dismantling procedures can be ignored.

2 Note that whilst it may be possible physically to overhaul items such as the piston/connecting rod assemblies with the engine in the vehicle, such tasks are not usually carried out as separate operations and usually require the execution of several additional procedures (not to mention the cleaning of components and of oilways). For this reason, all such tasks are classed as major overhaul procedures and are described in Chapter 2C.

Engine description

3 The engines are of in-line double overhead camshaft design, mounted in-line ('north-south') at the front of the vehicle with the transmission mounted on the rear of the engine.

4 The crankshaft is supported in five main bearing within the cast iron cylinder block. Crankshaft endfloat is controlled by thrustwashers fitted on either side of No 3 main bearing.

5 The connecting rods are attached to the crankshaft by horizontally-split big-end bearings, and to the pistons by fully-floating gudgeon pins retained by circlips. The alloy pistons are fitted with three piston rings; two compression and one oil control.

6 The exhaust camshaft is driven from the crankshaft sprocket by a double-row chain, and the inlet camshaft is gear-driven from the exhaust camshaft. The camshaft also drives the fuel injection pump.

7 The camshaft is supported in bearings in the cylinder head, and actuates the valves directly, via hydraulic valve lifters.

8 The oil pump is chain-driven from the front of the crankshaft. An oil cooler is located on the oil filter housing at the left-hand front of the cylinder block.

Repair operations possible with the engine in the car

9 The following operations can be carried out with the engine in the car:

a) *Compression pressure – testing*
b) *Camshaft cover – removal and refitting.*
c) *Crankshaft pulley – removal and refitting.*
d) *Camshaft and hydraulic tappets – removal, inspection and refitting.*
e) *Cylinder head – removal and refitting.*
f) *Cylinder head and pistons* – decarbonising.*
g) *Sump – removal and refitting.*
h) *Oil pump – removal and refitting.*
i) *Crankshaft oil seals – renewal.*
j) *Engine mountings – inspection and renewal.*
k) *Flywheel/driveplate – inspection and renewal.*
l) *Timing chain – removal and refitting.*

Note: **Although it is possible to remove these components with the engine in place, for reasons of access and cleanliness it is recommended that the engine be removed.*

2 Compression test – description and interpretation

Compression test

Note: *A compression tester designed for diesel engines must be used for this test.*

1 When engine performance is down, a compression test can provide diagnostic clues as to the engine's condition. If the test is performed regularly, it can give warning of trouble before any other symptoms become apparent.

2 A compression tester specifically intended for diesel engines must be used, because of the higher pressures involved. The tester is connected to an adapter, which screws into the glow plug. It is unlikely to be worthwhile buying such a tester for occasional use, but it may be possible to borrow or hire one – if not, have the test performed by a garage.

3 Unless specific instructions to the contrary are supplied with the tester, observe the following points.

a) *The battery must be in a good state of charge, the air filter must be clean, and the engine should be at normal operating temperature.*
b) *All the glow plugs should be removed before starting the test (see Chapter 5B Section 3).*
c) *The starter should not be operated using the stop/start button, but by a switch/wiring placed between the battery positive terminal and the positive terminal of the starter solenoid.*

4 There is no need to hold the accelerator pedal down during the test, because the diesel engine air inlet is not throttled.

5 Crank the engine on the starter motor. After one or two revolutions, the compression pressure should build-up to a maximum figure, and then stabilise. Record the highest reading obtained.

6 Repeat the test on the remaining cylinders, recording the pressure in each.

7 The cause of poor compression is less easy to establish on a diesel engine than on a petrol one. The effect of introducing oil into the cylinders ('wet' testing) is not conclusive, because there is a risk that the oil will sit in the swirl chamber or in the recess in the piston crown instead of passing to the rings. However, the following can be used as a rough guide to diagnosis.

8 All cylinders should produce very similar pressures; if there is a large difference, then this indicates a fault. Note that the compression should build-up quickly in a healthy engine; low compression on the first stroke, followed by gradually increasing pressure on successive strokes, indicates worn piston rings. A low compression reading on the first stroke, which does not build-up during successive strokes, indicates leaking valves or a blown head gasket (a cracked head could also be the cause). Deposits on the undersides of the valve heads can also cause low compression.

9 A low reading from two adjacent cylinders is almost certainly due to the head gasket having blown between them; the presence of coolant in the engine oil will confirm this.

10 If the compression reading is unusually high, the combustion chambers are probably coated with carbon deposits. If this is the case, the cylinder head should be removed and decarbonised.

11 On completion of the test, refit the glow plugs.

Leakdown test

12 A leakdown test measures the rate at which compressed air fed into the cylinder is lost. It is an alternative to a compression test, and in many ways is better, since the escaping air provides easy identification of where a pressure loss is occurring (piston rings, valves or head gasket).

13 The equipment needed for leakdown testing is unlikely to be available to the home mechanic. If poor compression is suspected, have the test performed by a suitably-equipped garage.

3 Engine assembly/valve timing settings – general information and usage

⚠ **Warning: When turning the engine, do not turn the engine using the camshaft sprocket bolts, and do not turn the engine backwards (ie, anti-clockwise).**

1 Top Dead Centre (TDC) is the highest point in the cylinder that each piston reaches as it travels up and down when the crankshaft turns. Each piston reaches TDC at the end of the compression stroke and again at the end of the exhaust stroke, but for valve timing TDC refers to the No 1 piston position on the compression stroke. No 1 piston is at the timing chain end of the engine.

2 Positioning No 1 piston at TDC is an essential part of many procedures, such as timing chain removal and camshaft removal.

3 Remove the cylinder head cover as described in Section 4.

3.4 TDC (O/T) mark on the crankshaft pulley/vibration damper aligned with the pointer on the timing chain cover

3.5a Camshaft gear alignment marks...

3.5b ...aligned through the centre of the camshafts

4 Using a socket on the crankshaft pulley/ vibration damper hub bolt, turn the crankshaft clockwise until the O/T (TDC) mark on the crankshaft pulley/vibration damper is aligned with the pointer on the timing chain cover (see illustration). For access to the bolt, it may be necessary to remove the fan unit and radiator shroud as described in Chapter 3.

5 In this position the alignment indentations (two 1.5 mm dots) on the camshaft gears (timing chain side) should be next to each other and aligned with the centre points of the camshafts (see illustrations). The camshaft lobes on No 1 cylinder should be facing upwards.

6 If necessary, the camshafts can be locked in position. The inlet camshaft gear has a timing hole, which aligns with a hole in the camshaft front bearing cap, and a suitable close-fitting drill should be inserted to lock the camshaft (see illustration). Note: Do

not use this method to lock the engine, while slackening any retaining bolts.

7 With the camshafts aligned as described, No 1 piston is at TDC on its firing stroke.

4 Cylinder head cover – removal and refitting

Removal

1 Remove the air filter housing as described in Chapter 4A Section 2.

2 Unclip the wiring harness, then undo the retaining bolts and remove the heatshield from above the exhaust manifold (see illustration).

3 Disconnect the camshaft sensor wiring plug.

4 On models with a particulate filter, label

and disconnect the hoses from the differential pressure sensor at the rear of the cylinder head, then undo the bolts and move the sensor and retaining plate to one side.

5 Undo the bolts and remove the air filter rear mounting bracket (see illustration).

6 Remove the fuel injectors as described in Chapter 4A Section 11.

7 Undo the Torxs screws and remove the wiring duct from the cylinder head cover.

8 Gradually, evenly, undo the retaining bolts and remove the camshaft cover (see illustration). Discard the seals – new ones must be fitted.

Refitting

9 Clean the joint surfaces of the cover and cylinder head, then locate the new gaskets in the grooves in the camshaft cover (see illustrations).

3.6 Insert a drill bit to lock the camshaft

4.2 Remove the heatshield above the exhaust manifold

4.5 Air filter rear bracket bolts

4.8 Remove the camshaft cover

4.9a Fit a new camshaft cover gasket...

4.9b ...and fuel injector recess gaskets

5.3a The Mercedes crankshaft locking tool..

5.3b ...slides into the starter motor aperture to engage with the flywheel/ driveplate teeth

5.4 Remove the bolt and washer

10 Position the camshaft cover with gaskets on the cylinder head, then insert the bolts and finger-tighten them progressively. Do not fully tighten at this point as the fuel injectors will need to centralise in the cover.

11 Refit the fuel injectors and fuel lines and tighten the union nuts to the specified torque.

12 Tighten the camshaft cover bolts to their specified torque setting.

13 Complete the rest of the installation by reversing the removal procedure, referring to the relevant Chapters. When all components are refitted, start the engine and check carefully around the camshaft cover for any oil leaks.

5 Crankshaft pulley – removal and refitting

Removal

1 Working under the front of the vehicle, undo the retaining bolts and remove the engine undershield.

2 Remove the auxiliary drivebelt as described in Chapter 1 Section 6.

3 The crankshaft must now be held stationary while the pulley bolt is loosened. The bolt is tightened to a high torque. Mercedes-Benz technicians remove the starter motor (see Chapter 5A Section 9) and use a special tool (No. 602 589 00 40 00) which is bolted to the transmission and locks the flywheel **(see illustrations)**. It may be possible to insert a

5.7 Make sure the Woodruff key is located securely

wide-bladed screwdriver between the starter ring gear teeth to prevent the engine from turning.

4 Unscrew the crankshaft pulley bolt then slide the pulley from the front of the crankshaft. Note the location of the washers under the head of the bolt, as they need to be fitted in the same position on refitting **(see illustration)**. If the pulley is tight on the crankshaft, use a suitable puller to remove it. A two-legged puller, which locates in the pulley holes, is ideal.

5 If necessary, remove the Woodruff key from the groove in the nose of the crankshaft.

6 Examine the oil seal contact surface of the pulley/vibration damper for an excessive wear groove. If evident, it is permissible to position the oil seal slightly further into the timing chain cover so that it runs on the unworn area of the pulley. Alternatively, the pulley should be renewed. The oil seal in the timing cover must be renewed as a matter of course with reference to Section 15.

Refitting

7 Locate the Woodruff key in the groove in the nose of the crankshaft. Make sure that it is firmly pressed into position, and that its outer edge is parallel with the crankshaft so that the pulley/vibration damper will engage with it easily **(see illustration)**.

8 Wipe clean and lightly oil the seal contact surface of the pulley, and then slide it fully onto the crankshaft, engaging it with the Woodruff key.

6.8 Protect the radiator with a piece of board

9 Lightly oil the threads of the crankshaft pulley bolt and the washers, and then locate the washer(s) correctly onto the bolt, as noted on removal. Insert the bolt and tighten it to the specified torque while holding the crankshaft stationary as for removal. If necessary, refit the starter motor

10 Refit the auxiliary drivebelt with reference to Chapter 1 Section 6.

11 Refit the engine undershield

6 Timing chain cover – removal and refitting.

Note: *The timing chain cover is located between the cylinder head and the sump; take care not to damage any of these gaskets.*

Removal

1 Disconnect the battery negative lead as described in Chapter 5A Section 4.

2 Apply the parking brake, then jack up the front of the vehicle and support it on axle stands (see *Vehicle jacking and support*). Remove the engine compartment undershields.

3 Drain the engine oil from the sump and remove the oil filter as described in Chapter 1 Section 4.

4 Remove the cylinder head cover as described in Section 4.

5 Remove the air ducts from between the intercooler and intake manifold.

6 Remove the air ducts from the turbocharger to the intercooler.

7 Remove the cooling fan and shroud from the rear of the radiator as described in Chapter 3 Section 6.

8 Using a piece of thin plywood or similar, cover the radiator/condenser to protect it from any damage **(see illustration)**.

9 Refer to Section 3 and set the engine at TDC compression on No 1 cylinder. Ideally the crankshaft should be locked in this position during the removal of the timing chain cover. Mercedes-Benz technicians remove the starter motor and use a special tool to lock the teeth of the starter ring gear.

10 Drain the cooling system as described in Chapter 1 Section 30.

6.11 Timing chain tensioner

6.15 Disconnect the hoses from the coolant pump

11 With the engine set at TDC, slacken and remove the timing chain tensioner from the right-hand front of the engine (see illustration). Discard the sealing washer, as a new one will be required for refitting.
12 Remove the cover plate from the front of the cylinder head as described in Section 16.
13 Remove the high-pressure fuel pump as described in Chapter 4A Section 10.
14 Undo the retaining bolt, and remove the charge air pipes to, and from the intercooler.
15 Release the clamps and detach the coolant hoses from the coolant pump (see illustration).
16 Slacken the power steering pump pulley bolts, then remove the auxiliary drivebelt as described in Chapter 1 Section 6.
17 Remove the pulley, then unbolt the power steering pump and position it to one side. Do not disconnect the hydraulic pipes from the pump.
18 Disconnect the wiring plug, then unbolt the air conditioning compressor (where fitted), and position it to one side. Suspend the compressor from the bodywork with cable ties, etc. to prevent any strain on the refrigerant hoses. Do not disconnect the hoses.
19 Release the clamps and disconnect the coolant hoses from the oil cooler assembly.
20 Remove the alternator as described in Chapter 5A Section 6.
21 Remove the crankshaft pulley/vibration damper as described in Section 5.
22 Unscrew and remove the bolts securing the sump to the bottom of the timing chain

cover. Slacken the remaining sump bolts by 2 or 3 turns.
23 Working through the aperture in the top of the cylinder head, unscrew the two bolts securing the timing chain cover to the cylinder head (see illustration).
24 Unscrew the bolts and remove the timing chain cover from the front of the engine, taking care not to damage the front parts of the cylinder head gasket and sump gasket. If required, to ensure the bolts are refitted in their correct locations, make a drawing of their positions, or use a dab of paint on them to identify them. If the two location dowels are loose, remove them also.
25 With the timing chain cover removed, it is recommended that the crankshaft front oil seal be renewed with reference to Section 15.

Refitting

26 Commence refitting by thoroughly cleaning away all traces of old sealant from the mating faces of the timing chain cover

6.29 Apply a 2 mm bead of sealant on the inside of the bolt holes

and cylinder block. Also clean the areas of the cylinder head gasket and sump gasket which contact the timing chain cover.
27 Carefully check the condition of the cylinder head gasket. If the gasket has been damaged during the removal procedure, the cylinder head should be removed in order to renew the gasket, as described in Section 10.
28 Similarly, carefully check the condition of the sump gasket. If the gasket has been damaged during the removal procedure, the sump should be removed in order to renew the gasket, as described in Section 11.
29 Apply sealant (Loctite 5970) to the cylinder block mating face of the timing chain cover. Make sure that the two location dowels are correctly fitted (see illustration).
30 Coat the lips of the crankshaft oil seal with clean engine oil, then slide the cover into position over the crankshaft. Take care not to damage the oil seal lips and the cylinder head and sump gaskets as the cover is fitted.
31 Insert all the retaining bolts, including the two upper ones, in their original positions and hand-tighten them. First, progressively tighten the bolts securing the timing chain cover to the cylinder block to the specified torque, and then tighten the two upper bolts to the specified torque.
32 Insert the bolts securing the sump to the bottom of the timing chain cover. Progressively tighten all the sump bolts to the specified torque.
33 Complete the rest of the installation by reversing the removal procedure, referring to the relevant Chapters.
34 Refill the engine with the correct grade and quantity of oil, as described in Chapter 1 Section 4.
35 Reconnect the battery negative lead as described in Chapter 5A Section 4.
36 When all components are refitted, start the engine and check carefully around the front of the engine any oil leaks, or coolant leaks.
37 Refit the engine compartment undershield and lower the car to the ground.

7 Timing chain –
inspection and renewal

Inspection

1 Remove the camshaft cover as described in Section 4.
2 Using a socket on the crankshaft pulley/vibration damper hub bolt, turn the engine so that the whole length of the chain can be progressively viewed at the camshaft sprocket.
3 The chain should be renewed if the sprocket is worn or if the chain is worn (indicated by excessive lateral play between the links, and excessive noise in operation). Note that the rollers on a very badly worn chain may be slightly grooved. To avoid future problems, if

6.23 Timing chain cover upper retaining bolts

there is any doubt at all about the condition of the chain, renew it.

Renewal

Note: *This following procedure, uses a chain breaker/riveter to renew the chain without removing the front timing chain cover, a second person will be required to assist fitting the timing chain. Ensure that all tools are available, as well as a new chain and new connecting link before proceeding.*

Note: *If the chain needs to be renewed as a complete assembly, then remove the front timing chain cover as described in Section 6.*

4 Disconnect the battery negative lead as described in Chapter 5A Section 4.

5 If not already done, remove the cylinder head cover as described in Section 4.

6 Remove the air filter assembly as described in Chapter 4A Section 2.

7 Remove the cover plate from the front of the cylinder head as described in Section 16.

8 Remove the fan and shroud, as described in Chapter 3 Section 6.

9 Using a socket on the crankshaft pulley bolt, turn the engine until the timing marks are aligned, as described in Section 3.

10 Remove the timing chain tensioner as described in Section 8.

11 With the engine still in the TDC position, use a couple of cable-ties to keep the timing chain on the camshaft sprocket. Put some clean rag into the timing chain recess to prevent anything dropping down into the engine.

12 Use the chain breaker to press out one of the timing chain pins and split the timing chain.

13 Connect the new timing chain to the old chain and press the chain link pin back into position. **Note:** *Make sure the new chain is connected to the front part of the chain, as the engine has to be turned clockwise, in the direction of rotation to feed the chain around the sprockets.*

14 With the new chain connected securely to the old chain, take a firm hold of both ends of the chain and remove the cable-ties from the camshaft sprocket. Remove the clean rag from around the timing chain before turning the engine.

15 With the aid of an assistant, turn the engine in the direction of rotation. Keeping the timing chain taut feed it around the crankshaft sprocket, until the new chain comes all the way around to the camshaft sprocket.

16 Cable-tie both ends of the timing chain back to the camshaft sprocket, and refit the clean rag back into the timing chain recess.

17 Use the chain breaker to press out the timing chain pin and split the old timing chain from the new timing chain. **Note:** *Make sure the chain is pulled tight on the lower section of the engine, and the upper section slack to allow for the fitting of the chain tensioner.*

18 Check that the TDC marks on the crankshaft pulley and timing chain cover are aligned, and the marks on the camshaft and camshaft bearing caps are still aligned correctly.

19 Fit the new timing chain link, using the timing chain riveter to connect the two ends of the chain securely. Always read the instructions that come with the chain riveter, as there are many different types available. The link pins need to be riveted securely, to prevent the chain coming apart.

20 Remove the clean rag from the timing chain recess, and fit the timing chain tensioner, with reference to Section 8. With the tensioner now fitted, check the timing marks are still in line.

21 Rotate the engine two complete turns and check the timing marks come back in alignment. Refer to Section 3 to check timing mark alignment is correct.

22 Refit the cylinder head cover with reference to Section 4.

23 Refit the air cleaner assembly.

24 Reconnect the battery negative lead as described in Chapter 5A Section 4.

---

8   Timing chain tensioner, sprockets and guides – removal, inspection and refitting.

Timing chain tensioner

Removal

1 Set the engine to TDC on No 1 cylinder as described in Section 3.

2 Remove the air filter housing as described in Chapter 4A Section 2.

3 Remove the heat shield above the turbocharger.

4 Unscrew the tensioner from the right-hand side of the timing chain cover **(see illustration)**. Recover the sealing ring and discard; a new one will be required for refitting.

Inspection

5 Do not attempt to dismantle the tensioner assembly. If it is suspected that the tensioner is worn or faulty, the complete unit should be renewed.

Refitting

6 Locate a new sealing ring on the tensioner, then screw it into position in the cylinder head and tighten to the specified torque.

7 Refitting is the reversal of the removal procedure, referring to the relevant Chapters, where applicable. When all components are refitted, start the engine and check carefully around the tensioner for any oil leaks.

Camshaft sprocket

Removal

8 Refer to Section 3 and set the engine to TDC on No 1 cylinder. Lock the inlet camshaft as described by inserting a drill through the camshaft front bearing cap into the gear **(see illustration)**.

9 Remove the cover plate from the front of the cylinder head as described in Section 16.

10 Where fitted, undo the retaining bolt and remove the centrifuge from the exhaust camshaft sprocket.

11 Use a dab of paint or a marker pen to mark the timing chain and the exhaust camshaft sprocket in relation to each other. This will help ensure that the chain is refitted correctly and the valve timing maintained.

12 Remove the timing chain tensioner as described earlier in this Section.

13 Hold the exhaust camshaft (timing chain) sprocket stationary using a suitable tool located in the sprocket cut-outs, then loosen the bolts securing the sprocket to the camshaft **(see illustration)**. Do not rely only on the drill located in the inlet camshaft sprocket to hold the sprocket.

14 At this stage the crankshaft sprocket will still be at TDC, and the crankshaft must not be

8.4 Remove the timing chain tensioner

8.8 Lock the camshaft using a drill bit

8.13 Unbolt the sprocket from the camshaft

turned until the camshaft sprocket has been refitted. Use a length of wire to tie the upper part of the timing chain to the cylinder head to ensure the chain remains on the sprockets.

15 Remove the sprockets from their location dowel on the camshaft flange. Remove the timing chain sprocket from the timing chain, and if required remove the dowel from the flange in the end of the camshaft. **Note:** *The sprocket bolts must be renewed every time they are removed.*

Inspection

16 Examine the teeth on the sprockets for wear. Each tooth forms an inverted V. If worn, the side of each tooth under tension will be slightly concave in shape when compared with the other side of the tooth (ie, the teeth will have a hooked appearance). If the teeth appear worn, the sprocket must be renewed.

Refitting

17 Ensure that the camshaft and crankshaft timing marks are still aligned, as described in Section 3. If a new sprocket is being fitted, transfer the chain alignment mark from the old sprocket to the new.

18 Fit the location dowel to the hole in the exhaust camshaft flange.

19 Engage the sprocket with the chain, aligning the marks made on the chain and sprocket before removal, then locate the sprocket on the camshaft flange and engage it with the dowel.

20 Insert the bolts and tighten them to the specified torque while holding the sprocket stationary using the used tool for removal. Remove the wire used to tie the chain to the cylinder head.

21 Refit the centrifuge to the exhaust camshaft sprocket, and tighten the retaining bolt to the specified torque.

22 Refit the timing chain tensioner as described earlier in this Section.

23 Refit the front plate as described in Section 16.

24 Using a socket on the crankshaft pulley/vibration damper hub bolt, turn the crankshaft through two complete revolutions, and check that the crankshaft and camshaft timing marks are still aligned with No 1 piston at TDC, as described in Section 3.

25 Remove the inlet camshaft locking drill, then refit the cylinder head cover with reference to Section 4.

Crankshaft sprocket

Removal

Note: *A puller may be required to remove the sprocket.*

26 Remove the timing chain cover as described in Section 6. This procedure includes removal of the crankshaft pulley/vibration damper and Woodruff key, and the setting of the engine to its TDC position.

27 Remove the sump as described in Section 11.

28 Hold the oil pump sprocket on the oil pump stationary using a suitable tool engaged with the sprocket holes, then unscrew and remove the mounting bolts. Remove the sprocket from the oil pump drive flange and unhook the drive chain from the crankshaft sprocket on the front of the crankshaft. **Note:** *The oil pump chain drive sprocket is incorporated into the crankshaft sprocket.*

29 Remove the camshaft sprocket as described previously in this Section, however, in addition to marking the timing chain in relation to the camshaft sprocket, also mark it in relation to the injection pump sprocket and crankshaft sprocket. This is necessary to ensure the valve timing and injection pump timing is maintained, since it will also be difficult to ascertain the TDC position of the crankshaft with the timing chain cover removed.

30 Unhook the timing chain from the crankshaft sprocket and injection pump sprocket.

31 Slide the crankshaft sprocket from the front of the crankshaft. If it is tight, use a suitable puller, taking care not to damage the sprocket teeth. Alternatively, use two levers against the front of the cylinder block, positioning the levers diagonally opposite each other.

32 Recover the Woodruff key from the groove in the crankshaft.

Inspection

33 Examine the teeth on the sprockets for wear. Each tooth forms an inverted V. If worn, the side of each tooth under tension will be slightly concave in shape when compared with the other side of the tooth (ie, the teeth will have a hooked appearance). If the teeth appear worn, the sprocket must be renewed.

Refitting

34 Locate the Woodruff key in the crankshaft groove, making sure that the upper edge is parallel with the surface of the crankshaft.

35 Slide the crankshaft sprocket onto the front of the crankshaft and engage it with the Woodruff key. If necessary, use a suitable metal tube to tap it into position.

36 Engage the timing chain with the crankshaft sprocket and injection pump sprocket, making sure that the previously-made marks are aligned with each other, then pull the chain up through the aperture at the front of the cylinder head.

37 Refit the camshaft sprocket as described earlier in this Section, making sure that the previously-made marks on the chain and sprocket are aligned with each other. Check that the alignment marks are still correctly aligned.

38 Refit the oil pump drive chain and sprocket with reference to Section 12.

39 Refit the sump as described in Section 11.

40 Refit the timing chain cover and crankshaft pulley/vibration damper as described in Section 6.

Tensioner rail

Removal

41 Remove the cylinder head as described in Section 10.

42 Remove the timing chain cover as described in Section 6.

43 Remove the timing chain tensioner as described earlier in this Section.

44 Remove the tensioner rail from its pin.

Inspection

45 Examine the tensioner rail for signs of excessive wear, damage or cracks, and renew if necessary.

Refitting

46 Locate the tensioner rail on the pin.

47 Refit the timing chain tensioner as described previously in this Section.

48 Refit the timing chain cover as described in Section 6.

49 Refit the cylinder head as described in Section 10.

---

9 Camshafts, camshaft housing and hydraulic tappets – removal, inspection and refitting

Camshafts

Removal

1 Remove the exhaust camshaft sprocket as described in Section 8, making sure that the timing chain remains engaged with the crankshaft sprocket, using wire to tie it to one side.

2 The camshaft bearing caps are numbered from the timing chain end of the engine **(see illustration)**. Check the bearing caps to ensure that marks are present, and if necessary make suitable marks using quick-drying paint or a centre-punch.

3 The camshaft bearing cap bolts must now be slackened as follows, and the camshafts removed.

 Warning: It is absolutely essential to observe the correct sequence when slackening the camshaft bearing cap bolts, because the camshafts are very sensitive to fracturing.

9.2 Check the marking on the bearing caps

a) *Progressively slacken and then remove the bolts from bearing caps 1, 3 and 5.*
b) *Lift off bearing caps 1, 3 and 5, keeping them in order* **(see illustration)**. *Note that the bearing caps locate on dowels – if they are stuck, tap gently using a soft-faced mallet.*
c) *Progressively slacken the bearing cap bolts for bearing caps 2 and 4, in one-turn stages until all pressure on the camshaft is relieved. Take care not to allow uneven pressure on the camshaft as the bolts are unscrewed.*
d) *Lift off bearing caps 2 and 4, again keeping them in order.*
e) *Lift the inlet and exhaust camshafts from the camshaft housing and recover the thrustwashers from No 3 bearing location.*

Inspection

4 Thoroughly clean the camshafts and the housing/caps.
5 Examine the camshaft journals and cam lobes for any sign of scoring, wear grooves or pitting, and if apparent, renew the relevant camshaft. Any damage of this nature may be attributable to a blocked oil passage in the cylinder head, and careful examination should be carried out to determine the cause.
6 Examine the bearing surfaces in the camshaft housing and bearing caps for excessive wear and scoring. If evident, renew the components together with the camshafts.

Refitting

7 Lubricate the camshaft journals and the bearing locations in the camshaft housing/caps with clean engine oil **(see illustration)**. Also lubricate the hydraulic tappets.
8 Locate the inlet camshaft in the left-hand side of the camshaft housing, and then locate the exhaust camshaft in the right-hand side, at the same time engaging the gears at the fronts of the camshafts so that the timing marks are aligned **(see illustrations)**, see Section 3.
9 Locate the bearing caps in position over the camshafts and tighten the securing bolts according to the following information, ensuring that the bearing caps are fitted to their original locations.

9.3 Note the position of the bearing caps

9.8a Lower the camshaft into position...

9.7 Lubricate the camshaft bearing housing

9.8b ...and align the timing marks

> ⚠ *Warning: It is absolutely essential to observe the correct sequence when tightening the camshaft bearing cap bolts, in order to avoid damage to the camshaft.*
a) *Fit bearing caps 2 and 4, then insert the bolts, and tighten them progressively in one-turn stages to the specified torque. Take care not to allow uneven pressure on the camshaft as the bolts are tightened.*
b) *Fit bearing caps 1, 3 and 5, then insert the bolts, and tighten them progressively in one-turn stages to the specified torque.*

Camshaft lower housing and hydraulic tappets

Removal

10 Remove the camshafts as described

earlier in this Section. This procedure includes removal of the cylinder head cover and cylinder head front cover.
11 Obtain a container with 16 compartments and number the compartments to indicate the location of the hydraulic tappets. Remove each hydraulic tappet in turn from the camshaft housing and store them in the container **(see illustration)**.
12 Lift the camshaft lower housing from the cylinder head **(see illustration)**.

Inspection

13 Clean the camshaft housing and cylinder head and check for damage and wear.
14 The operation of the removed hydraulic tappets can be checked as follows.
a) *Press down firmly on the top of each tappet, using a blunt instrument such as a wooden hammer handle, for approximately 10 seconds.*
b) *Note how far the piston moves when depressed.*
c) *Repeat the operation for all the tappets in turn.*
d) *If any one tappet can be depressed more easily than the others, renew it.*
15 Check the hydraulic tappets and the bores in the camshaft lower housing for wear and scoring. If any serious damage or wear is evident, the camshaft housing and tappets must be renewed.

Refitting

16 Locate the lower housing back into position on the cylinder head.

9.11 Remove the hydraulic tappets, noting their fitted positions

9.12 Remove the camshaft lower housing

9.17 Lubricate the hydraulic tappets with clean engine oil

10.10 Remove the turbocharger oil feed pipe

17 Lubricate the hydraulic tappet bores in the camshaft housing with clean engine oil, then locate each hydraulic tappet in its original position in the housing (see illustration).

18 Complete the rest of the installation by reversing the removal procedure, referring to the relevant Chapters. When all components are refitted, start the engine and check carefully around the cylinder head cover for any oil leaks.

10 Cylinder head – removal, inspection and refitting

Note: *New cylinder head bolts may be required – see text.*

Removal

1 Ensure that the engine is cold before attempting to remove the cylinder head.

2 Apply the parking brake, then jack up the front of the vehicle and support it on axle stands (see *Vehicle jacking and support*).

3 Disconnect the battery negative lead as described in Chapter 5A Section 4.

4 Raise the bonnet to the fully open position.

5 Drain the engine oil and coolant as described in Chapter 1 Section 4.

6 Remove the glow plugs as described in Chapter 5B Section 3.

7 Remove the camshafts, hydraulic tappets and lower housing, as described in Section 9.

8 Remove the thermostat housing from the right-hand side front of the cylinder head, as described in Chapter 3 Section 4.

9 Remove the inlet manifold as described in Chapter 4A Section 15.

10 Undo the retaining bolts and remove the oil feed pipe to the turbocharger from the cylinder head (see illustration).

11 Undo the retaining bolts from the turbocharger to the exhaust manifold (see illustration).

12 Undo the retaining nut from the exhaust mounting bracket at the rear of the exhaust manifold (see illustration).

13 Using a socket through the cylinder head aperture, unscrew and remove the two bolts securing the timing chain cover to the cylinder head (see illustration 6.23).

14 Make a final check to ensure that all relevant hoses and wires have been disconnected from the cylinder head.

15 Progressively loosen the cylinder head bolts, working in the reverse order to the tightening sequence (see illustration 10.32). Remove all cylinder head bolts.

16 Release the cylinder head from the cylinder block and locating dowels by rocking it. Do not prise between the mating faces of the cylinder head and block, as this may damage the gasket faces.

17 With the aid of an assistant, carefully lift the cylinder head, complete with exhaust manifold, from the block, and manoeuvre it out from the engine compartment.

10.11 Turbo-to-manifold retaining bolts

10.12 Exhaust mounting bracket

18 Recover the cylinder head gasket.
19 If necessary, remove the exhaust manifold from the cylinder head.

Inspection

20 Refer to Chapter 2C Section 6 for details of the cylinder head dismantling and reassembly.
21 The mating faces of the cylinder head and block must be perfectly clean before refitting the head. Use a scraper to remove all traces of gasket and carbon, and also clean the tops of the pistons. Take particular care with the cylinder head, as the metal is easily damaged. Also make sure that debris is not allowed to enter the oil and water passages. Using adhesive tape and paper, seal the water, oil and bolt holes in the cylinder block. To prevent carbon entering the gap between the pistons and bores, smear a little grease in the gap. After cleaning each piston, rotate the crankshaft so that the piston moves down the bore, and then wipe out the grease and carbon with a cloth rag.
22 Check the block and head for nicks, deep scratches and other damage. If very slight, they may be removed from the cylinder block carefully with a file. More serious damage may be repaired by machining, but this is a specialist job.
23 If warpage of the cylinder head is suspected, use a straight-edge to check it for distortion, with reference to Chapter 2C Section 7.
24 Clean out the bolt holes in the block using a pipe cleaner or thin rag and a screwdriver. Make sure that all oil and water is removed, otherwise there is a possibility of the block being cracked by hydraulic pressure when the bolts are tightened.
25 Examine the bolt threads and the threads in the cylinder block for damage. If necessary, use the correct size tap to chase out the threads in the block.
26 The manufacturers recommend that the cylinder head bolts are measured, to determine whether renewal is necessary; however, some owners may wish to renew all the bolts as a matter of course.
27 Measure the length of each bolt from the base of the head to the end of the shank. If the bolt length is greater than the maximum specified, the bolts should be renewed.
28 Reassemble the cylinder head with reference to Chapter 2C Section 8. Where applicable, refit the exhaust manifold together with a new gasket.

Refitting

29 Locate the new cylinder head gasket on the block, making sure that it is the correct way up and positioned over the location dowels.
30 With the aid of an assistant, lower the cylinder head carefully onto the block.
31 Oil the threads and the cylinder head contact faces of the cylinder head bolts, then insert them and screw them into the cylinder

A bolts securing the cylinder head to the timing chain cover

10.32 Cylinder head bolt (B) tightening sequence

block by hand. Ensure that the bolts are fitted to their correct locations as noted on removal.
32 Tighten the cylinder head bolts in the order shown **(see illustration)**, and in the stages given in the Specifications – ie, tighten all bolts to the Stage 1 torque, then tighten all bolts to the Stage 2 torque, and so on.
33 Tighten the two bolts securing the timing chain cover to the cylinder head at the front of the engine.
34 The remainder of refitting is a reversal of removal, noting the following points:
a) *Refill the cooling system and refill the engine with oil as described in Chapter 1.*
b) *Reconnect the battery negative lead as described in Chapter 5A Section 4.*
c) *When all components have been refitted, start the engine and check carefully around the engine for any oil or coolant leaks.*

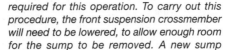

11 Sump – removal and refitting

Removal

Note: *A suitable hoist and lifting tackle will be required for this operation. To carry out this procedure, the front suspension crossmember will need to be lowered, to allow enough room for the sump to be removed. A new sump gasket will be required on refitting.*
1 Apply the parking brake, then jack up the

front of the vehicle and support it on axle stands (see *Vehicle jacking and support*). Remove both front road wheels.
2 Drain the engine oil as described in Chapter 1 Section 4. On completion, renew the sealing washer, then refit the drain plug and tighten to the specified torque.
3 Attach a suitable hoist to the engine and take the weight of the engine.
4 Unscrew the bolts from the bottom of the engine mountings at each side of the engine.
5 Lower the front suspension crossmember with reference to Chapter 10 Section 10.
6 Remove the cooling fan and shroud from the rear of the radiator, with reference to Chapter 3 Section 6.
7 Refer to Chapter 4A Section 19 and detach the exhaust downpipe from the turbocharger, then unbolt the exhaust mounting from the transmission and support the exhaust on an axle stand.
8 Detach the hydraulic pipe bracket from the sump **(see illustration)**.
9 Disconnect the wiring from the oil level and temperature sensors. If necessary, the sensor may be removed from the sump.
10 Undo the bolt and remove the engine oil level dipstick guide tube. Renew the O-ring seal.
11 Remove the charge air pipe from beneath the sump.
12 Remove the bracket for the starter/alternator wiring loom **(see illustration)**.
13 On automatic transmission models, detach the fluid pipes from the transmission and sump.

11.8 Undo the bolts securing the bracket to the sump

11.12 Remove the wiring loom bracket

11.18a Note the points where sealant is located on the gasket

11.18b Fit the sump using a new gasket

11.19 Sump bolt locations

| 1 M6x20 | 2 M6x40 | 3 M6x80 | 4 M6x90 | 5 M8x40 | 6 M10x40 |

14 Where applicable, remove the sump sound insulation material.

15 Unscrew the bolts securing the transmission to the rear of the sump, then unscrew the remaining sump-to-engine bolts and lower the sump from the cylinder block. Note the location of the bolts as some are of different lengths. Where applicable, recover the gasket. If the sump is stuck, use a hide or wooden mallet to tap its sides in order to release it. Do not drive a screwdriver between the sump and cylinder block as this may damage the mating surfaces.

16 It is recommended that the oil and oil filter are renewed whenever the sump is removed.

Before refitting the sump, it is a good idea to remove the oil filter in order to allow the oil to drain from the cylinder block oil gallery and internal oilways.

Refitting

17 Thoroughly clean the mating surfaces of the sump and cylinder block.

18 Place the gasket onto the sump and align it with the bolt holes in the cylinder block (see illustrations).

19 With the sump in place, insert all of the bolts finger-tight (see illustration). Make sure all bolts are fitted in the correct position as noted on removal.

20 The bolts can now be tightened securing the transmission to the sump to the specified torque. This will ensure the rear of the sump is correctly aligned with the transmission, as if it is not aligned correctly, vibration and noise may occur.

21 Tighten the remaining sump bolts to the specified torque.

22 Complete the rest of the installation by reversing the removal procedure, referring to the relevant Chapters.

23 When all components are refitted, start the engine and check carefully around the sump for any oil leaks.

12 Oil pump – removal, inspection and refitting

Removal

1 Remove the sump as described in Section 11.

2 The sprocket must be disengaged from the chain as the oil pump is being removed.

3 Unscrew the mounting bolts, withdraw the oil pump from the bottom of the crankcase, and recover the O-ring seal (see illustration).

4 Press against the chain tensioner and disengage the sprocket from the chain as the pump is being removed (see illustration).

12.3 Oil pump mounting bolts

12.4 Press against the chain tensioner

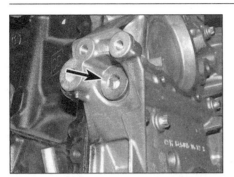

12.6 Relief valve retaining plug

Inspection

5 With the exception of the oil pressure relief valve components, the oil pump is a sealed unit. To remove the oil pressure relief valve components, proceed as follows.

6 Unscrew the relief valve plug, in the side of the timing chain cover **(see illustration)**. Take care, as the plug will be pushed out by the spring pressure when it reaches the end of the threads. **Note:** *if a sealing ring is present it will need to be renewed on refitting.*

7 Withdraw the spring, guide pin and piston, noting the orientation of the piston.

8 Thoroughly clean all components, and examine them for wear and damage. If there is any sign of excessive wear or damage, renew the appropriate component(s) – pay particular attention to the spring.

9 Also clean the oil pump intake strainer thoroughly, however, do not immerse the oil pump in cleaning solvent.

10 Examine the drive chain for wear and damage. If necessary, renew the chain as described later in this Section.

11 Reassemble the oil pressure relief valve using a reversal of the dismantling procedure, lubricating each component with fresh engine oil before fitting. Tighten the relief valve plug to the specified torque.

12 With the oil pump upright, pour fresh engine oil into the upper aperture while turning the pump shaft slowly. This will prime the oil pump so that normal oil pressure will be resumed as soon as possible after starting the engine.

Refitting

13 Check that the sprocket is engaged with the drive chain correctly and then locate the oil pump onto the crankcase. Insert the mounting bolts and tighten the bolts to the specified torque.

14 Refit the sump as described in Section 11.

13 Balancer shaft assembly – removal and refitting

Removal

Note: *Prior to removing the balancer shaft assembly, Mercedes-Benz recommend that the circumferential backlash of the balancer shafts is measured, and if excessive, is corrected using different thickness spacers between the assembly and the crankcase. Ir order to lock the shafts and measure the backlash, MB special tools No. 646 589 00 21 00 will be needed. However, in order simply remove and refit the unit, a home-made locking tool will suffice – details in the text.*

1 Remove the oil sump as described in Section 11.

2 Remove the oil pump as described in Section 12.

3 Set the engine at TDC on No. 1 cylinder as described in Section 3, with the off-centre holes in the ends of the balancer shafts pointing to the right-hand (drivers) side of the vehicle **(see illustration)**.

Caution: Observe the oil pump drive chain whilst rotating the crankshaft and prevent it from jamming

4 If the balancer shaft assembly is simply to be removed, and refitted, lock the shafts in this position using steel strip bolted to the end of the shafts using the holes provided.

5 If the balancer shaft circumferential backlash needs to be checked, obtain the Mercedes-Benz special tools No. 646 589 00 21 00, and follow the instructions provided.

13.10 Balancer shaft assembly retaining bolt tightening sequence

6 Working in the reverse of the sequence shown in illustration 13.11, gradually slacken and remove the shaft assembly retaining bolts.

7 Detach the balancer shaft assembly from the base of the engine.

Refitting

8 Examine the balancer shaft assembly for excessive wear or signs of damage. The assembly is a sealed unit, if defective it must be replaced as a whole.

9 Check that the engine is still set at TDC on cylinder No.1, and ensure the balancer shafts are set as described earlier in this section.

10 Manoeuvre the balancer shaft assembly into position on the crankcase, then insert the retaining bolts and tighten them to the specified torque in the sequence shown **(see illustration)**.

11 The remainder of refitting is a reversal of removal.

14 Flywheel/driveplate – removal, inspection and refitting

Removal

1 Remove the manual transmission (Chapter 7A Section 6), or automatic transmission (Chapter 7B Section 6).

2 On manual transmission models, remove the clutch as described in Chapter 6 Section 5.

3 The flywheel/driveplate must be held stationary while the mounting bolts are loosened. To do this, have an assistant insert a wide-bladed screwdriver in the starter ring gear teeth through the access hole in the rear of the sump. Mercedes-Benz technicians use a special tool incorporating serrations which engage with the ring gear teeth **(see illustration 5.3a)**. Alternatively, make up a tool as shown **(see illustration)** and bolt it to a starter motor mounting hole.

4 Unscrew the mounting bolts, then lift the flywheel/driveplate from the rear of the

13.3 The off-centre holes in the end of the shafts must point to the right-hand (drivers) side

14.3 Lock the flywheel in position

14.4a Remove the flywheel/driveplate

14.4b Location dowel

14.9a Turn the flywheel secondary element anti-clockwise and mark the limit of its travel on the starter ring gear teeth ...

14.9b ... then turn the secondary element clockwise, and mark its travel limit again

14.11 Attach a length of steel strip to the flywheel secondary element (drive surface)

14.12 The spigot bearing is in the centre of the flywheel

crankshaft **(see illustrations)**. Note that the location dowel ensures the flywheel/driveplate can only be fitted in one position.

5 On automatic transmission models recover the locking plates from each side of the driveplate.

Inspection

6 If the flywheel-to-clutch mating surface is deeply scored, cracked or otherwise damaged, then the flywheel must be renewed, unless it is possible to have it surface ground. Seek the advice of a Mercedes-Benz dealer or engine reconditioning specialist.

7 If the ring gear is badly worn or has missing teeth, then it must be renewed. This job is best left to a Mercedes-Benz dealer or engine reconditioning specialist.

8 On vehicles with dual mass flywheels, check the rotational and lateral movement as follows.

9 In order to check the rotational movement, lock the flywheel in place as previously described. Rotate the flywheel secondary element (drive surface) by hand anti-clockwise, mark its position in relation to the primary flywheel element (bolted to the crankshaft), then rotate it by hand clockwise and mark its position. Bear in mind, that the free rotational movement is being measured here – do not use excessive force to rotate the secondary element. Mark the limits of the rotational movement in relation to the number of flywheel starter ring gear teeth **(see illustrations)**.

10 If the number of starter ring gear teeth travelled by the flywheel secondary element

exceeds 2 (flywheel manufacturer LUK), the flywheel may need replacing.

11 In order to check the lateral movement of the flywheel, attach a length of steel strip to the flywheel secondary element (drive surface), and mount a DTI gauge so that it measures in-line with the transmission mounting flange holes **(see illustration)**. Pull the steel strip away from the flywheel, zero the DTI gauge, then push the strip towards the flywheel and read off the measurement. The maximum permissible amount of lateral movement specified by Mercedes-Benz is 2.5 mm (flywheel manufacturer LUK). If the dimension measured exceeds this, the flywheel may need replacing.

12 Check the condition of the spigot bearing in the centre of the flywheel or in the end of the crankshaft, and renew if necessary **(see illustration)**.

13 It is recommended that the flywheel/driveplate securing bolts are renewed whenever removed.

Refitting

14 Commence refitting by cleaning the mating faces of the crankshaft and flywheel/driveplate.

15 Make sure that the location dowel is in position in the end of the crankshaft. On automatic transmission models, fit the locking plate onto the crankshaft.

16 Locate the flywheel/driveplate onto the crankshaft, then insert the new mounting bolts (and further locking plate on automatic transmission models) and hand-tighten them.

17 Lock the flywheel/driveplate using the method employed during removal, then tighten the securing bolts progressively in a diagonal sequence to the specified torque first, then tighten all the bolts by the specified angle.

18 The remainder of refitting is a reversal of removal.

15 Crankshaft oil seals – renewal

Front oil seal

1 Remove the crankshaft pulley/vibration damper and inspect it as described in Section 5.

2 Measure and note the fitted depth of the oil seal in the timing chain cover.

3 Prise the oil seal from the cover using a hooked instrument. Alternatively, drill a small hole in the oil seal, and use a self-tapping screw and a pair of pliers to remove it.

Caution: Take great care not to damage the crankshaft surface.

4 Clean the seal location in the timing cover, and also clean the oil seal contact surface on the crankshaft pulley/vibration damper. Examine the seal contact surface of the pulley/vibration damper for an excessive wear groove. If evident, refer to Section 5.

5 Press the new seal into the timing chain cover (open end first) to the previously-noted depth, using a suitable tube or socket. Do

15.8 Rear crankshaft oil seal/housing bolts

not apply any lubricant to the seal or the crankshaft.

6 Refit the crankshaft pulley/vibration damper as described in Section 5.

Rear oil seal

Note: *The rear oil seal is integral with the oil seal housing and should be renewed whenever it is removed.*

7 Remove the flywheel/driveplate as described in Section 14.

8 Unscrew the retaining bolts and remove the oil seal/housing from the cylinder block **(see illustration)**. Take care not to damage the sump gasket.

9 New oil seal/housings are supplied with a plastic sleeve on the inside of the seal to aid refitting of the seal over the end of the crankshaft. DO NOT remove the plastic fitting sleeve until the oil seal housing is in its fitted position.

10 Ensure that the cylinder block mating face of the oil seal housing is free from all traces of old sealant, oil and grease, and then apply a 1.5 to 2.5 mm thick bead of silicone sealant (A 001 989 89 20 10 Loctite 574 or equivalent) to the oil seal housing. Note that the sealant should be run around the inside of the bolt holes in the oil seal housing. It must be fitted within 10 minutes of applying the sealant. Also apply sealant at the area where the sump, oil seal housing and cylinder block meet.

11 Fit the new oil seal housing over the crankshaft and onto the cylinder block, keeping the plastic sleeve in position.

12 Fit the retaining bolts and tighten them to the specified torque setting.

13 Remove the plastic fitting sleeve from the new oil seal housing.

14 Refit the flywheel/driveplate (Section 14).

16 Cylinder head front cover – removal and refitting

Removal

1 Disconnect the battery negative lead as described in Chapter 5A Section 4.

2 Remove the cylinder head cover, as described in Section 4.

3 Remove the vacuum pump as described in Chapter 9 Section 19.

4 Remove the high-pressure fuel pump as described in Chapter 4A Section 10.

5 Position the engine at TDC for No 1 cylinder as described in Section 3.

6 Remove the chain tensioner as described in Section 8.

7 Clamp the hose leading to the oil separator on the front of the cylinder head, then undo the retaining screws and pull the separator fowards. Renew the gasket.

8 Undo the retaining bolts and pull the front cover forwards from place.

Refitting

9 Ensure the cylinder head and cover mating surfaces are clean.

10 Apply sealant (MB No. A 003 989 98 20, Loctite 5970 or equivalent) to the area where the front cover contacts the cylinder head.

11 Position the front cover over the locating dowels, insert the retaining bolts and tighten them to the specified torque.

12 The remainder of refitting is a reversal of removal.

17 Engine/transmission mountings – inspection and renewal

Inspection

1 Three engine/transmission mountings are used, one on either side of the engine, and one under the rear of the transmission.

2 For improved access, raise the front of the vehicle and support it securely on axle stands (see *Vehicle jacking and support*).

3 Check the condition of the mounting rubber to see if it is cracked, hardened or separated from the metal at any point. Renew the mounting if any such damage or deterioration is evident. The mountings contain hydraulic oil, and must be renewed if oil leakage is evident.

4 Check the mounting bolts are tight.

5 Using a large screwdriver or metal bar, check for wear in the mounting by carefully levering against it to check for free play. Where this is not possible, enlist the aid of an assistant to move the engine/transmission back-and-forth, or from side-to-side, while you observe the mounting. If excessive free play is found, check first that the fasteners are correctly secured, and then renew any worn components as required.

Renewal

Front engine mountings

6 Support the engine, either using a hoist and lifting tackle connected to the engine lifting brackets, or by positioning a jack and interposed block of wood under the sump. Ensure that the engine is adequately supported before proceeding.

7 Depending on which engine mounting requires removal, it may be necessary to remove the alternator or turbocharger to make access easier. See the relevant Chapters to remove any other components.

8 Unscrew the bolts securing the mountings to the engine crossmember.

9 Raise the engine a little, then undo the bolts securing the mounting brackets to the engine.

10 Fit the new mountings, and tighten the fasteners to the specified torque.

Rear engine/transmission mounting

11 Raise the front of the vehicle and support it securely on axle stands (see *Vehicle jacking and support*).

12 Support the transmission using a jack and interposed block of wood.

13 Unbolt the mounting bracket from the underbody, then unscrew the bolts securing the mounting rubber to the rear of the transmission. Lower the bracket together with the mounting from the underbody **(see illustrations)**.

17.13a Unscrew the rear mounting bolts...

17.13b ...and the lower mounting bracket bolts...

17.13c ...then manoeuvre it from position

14 The mounting rubber can then be unbolted from the bracket.

15 Refitting is a reversal of removal, making sure that the earth cable (where fitted) is bolted to the transmission **(see illustration)**.

18 Engine oil sensor – renewal

1 Raise the front of the vehicle and support it securely on axle stands (see *Vehicle jacking and support*). Undo the fasteners and remove the engine undershield.

2 Drain the engine oil as described in Chapter 1 Section 4.

3 Disconnect the wiring plug from the oil sensor on the base of the sump **(see illustration)**.

17.15 Earth cable fitted to the rear mounting

18.3 Engine oil sensor

4 Undo the retaining bolts and withdraw the sensor from the sump. Renew the O-ring seal.

5 Refitting is a reversal of removal, tightening the sensor retaining bolts to the specified torque.

Chapter 2 Part B
2143 cc engine in-car repair procedures

Contents

Section number

Camshafts, rocker arms and hydraulic tappets – removal,
  inspection and refitting................................... 9
Compression test – description and interpretation 2
Crankshaft oil seals – renewal 14
Crankshaft pulley – removal and refitting...................... 5
Cylinder head – removal, inspection and refitting 10
Cylinder head cover – removal and refitting.................... 4
Engine assembly/valve timing settings – general information
  and usage... 3
Engine oil sensors – renewal 16

Section number

Engine/transmission mountings – inspection and renewal 15
Flywheel/driveplate – removal, inspection and refitting 13
General information 1
Oil pump – removal, inspection and refitting 12
Sump – removal and refitting 11
Timing chain – inspection and renewal 7
Timing chain cover – removal and refitting.................... 6
Timing chain tensioner and sprockets – removal, inspection
  and refitting... 8

Degrees of difficulty

Easy, suitable for novice with little experience	Fairly easy, suitable for beginner with some experience	Fairly difficult, suitable for competent DIY mechanic	Difficult, suitable for experienced DIY mechanic	Very difficult, suitable for expert DIY or professional

Specifications

General

Engine type..	4-cylinder in-line diesel, double overhead camshaft (DOHC)
Engine code	651.911
Bore	83.0 mm
Stroke	99.0 mm
Capacity	2143 cc
Emissions standard	EU5
Firing order..	1-3-4-2
Direction of crankshaft rotation	Clockwise (seen from the front of the vehicle)
Compression ratio	16.2 : 1
Compression pressures:	
New compression pressure	23.0 to 30.0 bar
Minimum compression pressure	17.0 bar (approximately)
Maximum difference between cylinders....................	3.0 bar

Cylinder head bolts

Thread diameter...	M12
Length when new (from under head)	226.0 ± 0.5 mm
Maximum length...	227.5 mm

Lubrication system

Minimum system pressure at normal operating temperature:

At idle speed..	0.9 bar
At 3750 rpm	3.0 bar

Torque wrench settings	Nm	lbf ft
Auxiliary drivebelt tensioner to major assembly carrier:		
M8	20	15
M10	45	33
Auxiliary drivebelt pulley bolts:		
M8	25	17
M10	45	33
Balancer shaft drive gear bolt:		
Stage 1	50	37
Stage 2	Angle-tighten a further 90°	
Camshaft bearing cap bolts	9	6
Camshaft sprocket bolts (left-hand thread):		
Stage 1	55	41
Stage 2	Angle-tighten a further 90°	
Connecting rod bolts*:		
Initial tightening after cracking (new rods):		
Stage 1	5	3
Stage 2	25	17
Stage 3	Angle-tighten a further 180°	
Subsequent tightening (used rods):		
Stage 1	5	3
Stage 2	25	17
Stage 3	Angle-tighten a further 90°	
Crankcase coolant drain plug	30	22
Crankshaft pulley bolts*:		
M12 x 56 mm:		
Stage 1	80	60
Stage 2	Angle-tighten a further 90°	
M12 x 129 mm:		
Stage 1	80	60
Stage 2	Angle-tighten a further 90°	
Stage 3	Angle-tighten a further 90°	
Cylinder head bolts* (see text):		
Stage 1	10	7
Stage 2	50	37
Stage 3	Angle-tighten a further 90°	
Stage 4	Angle-tighten a further 90°	
Stage 5	Angle-tighten a further 90°	
Stage 6	Angle-tighten a further 90°	
Cylinder head to timing cover M8	20	15
Cylinder head cover bolts	9	6
Engine/transmission mountings:		
Engine mounting-to-crossmember	35	26
Bracket to engine mounting	50	37
Bracket to crankcase:		
Stage 1	20	15
Stage 2	Angle-tighten a further 90°	
Rear engine support bracket to floor assembly (M10 x 22 mm)	65	48
Rear mounting to transmission	50	37
Rear mounting to support bracket	28	20
Exhaust manifold nut:		
Steel manifold	30	22
Cast manifold:		
Stage 1	15	11
Stage 2	35	26
Flywheel/driveplate bolts*:		
Stage 1	45	33
Stage 2	Angle-tighten a further 90°	
High-pressure fuel pump drive gear bolts	20	15
Intermediate gears to crankcase	80	60
Main bearing cap bolts:		
Stage 1	45	33
Stage 2	Angle-tighten a further 180°	
Major assembly carrier to crankcase:		
M6	9	6
M8	20	15
Oil filter cap	25	17

Torque wrench settings (continued)

	Nm	lbf ft
Oil filter housing:		
M6	10	7
M8	20	15
Oil level sensor.	9	6
Oil pump bolts:		
M6:		
Stage 1	8	5
Stage 2	Angle-tighten a further 90°	
M8	34	25
Oil pump pick-up tube:		
Stage 1	6	4
Stage 2	Angle-tighten a further 90°	
Oil pump regulating valve.	5	3
Oil spray nozzle	6	4
Oil spray nozzle control valve.	20	15
Oil temperature sensor.	26	19
Oil valve at crankcase	5	3
Sump drain plug:		
Metal plug.	30	22
Plastic plug	5	3
Sump:		
Upper section to crankcase:		
M6	10	7
M8	22	16
Upper section to timing cover	20	15
Lower section to upper section	10	7
Sump support to crankcase.	60	44
Timing chain cover bolts	20	15
Timing chain tensioner to cylinder head	80	60
Turbocharger oil feed pipe:		
To turbocharger:		
Stage 2	9	6
Stage 2	Angle-tighten a further 90°	
Feed pipe union nut	22	16
Turbocharger oil drain pipe bolt	9	6

*Do not re-use

---

1 General information

How to use this Chapter

1 This Part of the Chapter describes those repair procedures that can reasonably be carried out on the engine whilst it remains in the vehicle. If the engine has been removed from the vehicle and is being dismantled as described in Part C of this Chapter, any preliminary dismantling procedures can be ignored.

2 Note that whilst it may be possible physically to overhaul items such as the piston/ connecting rod assemblies with the engine in the vehicle, such tasks are not usually carried out as separate operations and usually require the execution of several additional procedures (not to mention the cleaning of components and of oilways). For this reason, all such tasks are classed as major overhaul procedures and are described in Chapter 2C.

Engine description

3 The engines are of in-line double overhead camshaft design, mounted in-line ('north-south') at the front of the vehicle with the transmission mounted on the rear of the engine.

4 The crankshaft is supported in five main bearing within the cast iron cylinder block. Crankshaft endfloat is controlled by thrustwashers fitted on either side of No 3 main bearing.

5 The connecting rods are attached to the crankshaft by horizontally-split big-end bearings, and to the pistons by fully-floating gudgeon pins retained by circlips. The alloy pistons are fitted with three piston rings; two compression and one oil control.

6 In contrast to the earlier 2143 cc engine, the oil pump, vacuum pump, twin balancer shafts and high-pressure fuel pump are gear-driven from the crankshaft at the rear of the engine. Also at the rear of the engine, a simplex timing chain from the high-pressure fuel pump gear drives both camshafts.

7 The camshaft is supported in bearings in the cylinder head, and actuates the valves via roller-rocker arms, with the clearances maintained by hydraulic valve lifters.

8 In order for this engine to reach Euro 5 emissions level, several innovative features have been incorporated into the design. These include a coolant pump whose output is regulated, so that when cooling is not required (cold starts etc.), no coolant is circulated, and piston cooling jets which only spray the underside of the pistons with oil when combustion temperatures reach a pre-determined level. Both of these features will reduce the load on the engine, particularly at low temperature, thus reducing fuel consumption and emissions.

Repair operations possible with the engine in the car

9 The following operations can be carried out with the engine in the car:
a) Compression pressure – testing
b) Cylinder head cover – removal and refitting.
c) Crankshaft pulley – removal and refitting.
d) Camshaft and hydraulic tappets – removal, inspection and refitting.

e) Cylinder head – removal and refitting.
f) Cylinder head and pistons* – decarbonising.
g) Sump – removal and refitting.
h) Crankshaft oil seals – renewal.
i) Engine mountings – inspection and renewal.
j) Flywheel/driveplate – inspection and renewal.
k) Timing chain – removal and refitting.
Note: *Although it is possible to remove these components with the engine in place, for reasons of access and cleanliness it is recommended that the engine be removed.*

---

2 Compression test –
description and interpretation

Compression test

Note: *A compression tester designed for diesel engines must be used for this test.*
1 When engine performance is down, a compression test can provide diagnostic clues as to the engine's condition. If the test is performed regularly, it can give warning of trouble before any other symptoms become apparent.
2 A compression tester specifically intended for diesel engines must be used, because of the higher pressures involved. The tester is connected to an adapter, which screws into the glow plug. It is unlikely to be worthwhile buying such a tester for occasional use, but it may be possible to borrow or hire one – if not, have the test performed by a garage.
3 Unless specific instructions to the contrary are supplied with the tester, observe the following points.
a) The battery must be in a good state of charge, the air filter must be clean, and the engine should be at normal operating temperature.
b) All the glow plugs should be removed before starting the test (see Chapter 5B Section 3).
c) The starter should not be operated using the stop/start button, but by a switch/ wiring placed between the battery positive

terminal and the positive terminal of the starter solenoid.
4 There is no need to hold the accelerator pedal down during the test.
5 Crank the engine on the starter motor. After one or two revolutions, the compression pressure should build-up to a maximum figure, and then stabilise. Record the highest reading obtained.
6 Repeat the test on the remaining cylinders, recording the pressure in each.
7 The cause of poor compression is less easy to establish on a diesel engine than on a petrol one. The effect of introducing oil into the cylinders ('wet' testing) is not conclusive, because there is a risk that the oil will sit in the swirl chamber or in the recess in the piston crown instead of passing to the rings. However, the following can be used as a rough guide to diagnosis.
8 All cylinders should produce very similar pressures; if there is a large difference, then this indicates a fault. Note that the compression should build-up quickly in a healthy engine; low compression on the first stroke, followed by gradually increasing pressure on successive strokes, indicates worn piston rings. A low compression reading on the first stroke, which does not build-up during successive strokes, indicates leaking valves or a blown head gasket (a cracked head could also be the cause). Deposits on the undersides of the valve heads can also cause low compression.
9 A low reading from two adjacent cylinders is almost certainly due to the head gasket having blown between them; the presence of coolant in the engine oil will confirm this.
10 If the compression reading is unusually high, the combustion chambers are probably coated with carbon deposits. If this is the case, the cylinder head should be removed and decarbonised.
11 On completion of the test, refit the glow plugs.

Leakdown test

12 A leakdown test measures the rate at which compressed air fed into the cylinder is lost. It is an alternative to a compression test,

and in many ways is better, since the escaping air provides easy identification of where a pressure loss is occurring (piston rings, valves or head gasket).
13 The equipment needed for leakdown testing is unlikely to be available to the home mechanic. If poor compression is suspected, have the test performed by a suitably-equipped garage.

---

3 Engine assembly/valve
timing settings – general
information and usage

⚠ *Warning: When turning the engine, do not turn the engine using the camshaft sprocket bolts, and do not turn the engine backwards (ie, anti-clockwise).*

1 Top Dead Centre (TDC) is the highest point in the cylinder that each piston reaches as it travels up and down when the crankshaft turns. Each piston reaches TDC at the end of the compression stroke and again at the end of the exhaust stroke, but for valve timing TDC refers to the No 1 piston position on the compression stroke. No 1 piston is at the front end of the engine.
2 Positioning No 1 piston at TDC is an essential part of many procedures, such as timing chain removal and camshaft removal.
3 Rotate the fastener at the front anti-clockwise, then pull the cover on the top of the engine forwards to remove it **(see illustration 4.1a and 4.1b)**.
4 Unscrew the oil filler cap, then disconnect the wiring plug, undo the retaining bolt and remove the camshaft position sensor **(see illustration)**.
5 Using a socket on the crankshaft pulley/ vibration damper hub bolt, turn the crankshaft clockwise until the O° (OT TDC) mark on the crankshaft pulley/vibration damper is aligned with the pointer on the crankcase **(see illustration)**. **Note:** *Although not absolutely necessary, a special tool (No. 651 589 00 40 00) is available from Mercedes that locates over the crankshaft pulley bolts, allowing the engine to be rotated with ease* **(see illustration)**.

3.4 Undo the Torx bolt and pull out the camshaft position sensor

3.5a TDC (OT) mark on the crankshaft pulley/vibration damper aligned with the pointer on the crankcase

3.5b The Mercedes special tool locates over the pulley bolts

3.6a The marks on the intake bearing cap and camshaft should align...

3.6b ...and the pointer with the edge of the exhaust position sensor 'window'

3.8 Slide the locking tools down over the flats of the camshaft flanges

Caution: Don't turn the crankshaft anti-clockwise as this may damage the timing chain/tensioner.

6 In this position the alignment indentations on the intake camshaft and bearing cap should align, along with the mark on the index wheel and position sensor 'window' for the exhaust camshaft **(see illustrations)**. If the marks are not aligned, rotate the crankshaft one complete revolution clockwise, and check again.

7 If necessary, the camshafts can be locked in position, although this is only necessary if the camshafts, sprockets or cylinder head are to be removed. Remove the cylinder head cover as described in Section 4, then undo the bolts and remove the camshaft bearing caps at the rear of the camshafts, adjacent to the timing chain.

8 With the camshaft aligned as previously described, it should be possible to slide the Mercedes locking tools down over the machined sections at the rear of each camshaft **(see illustration)**.

Note: *Engines up to 31/12/11 use tools No. 651 589 01 40 00, whilst engines after this date use tools No. 651 589 09 40 00.*

4 Cylinder head cover – removal and refitting

Removal

1 Rotate the fastener anti-clockwise, and pull the cover on the top of the engine forwards **(see illustrations)**.
2 Remove the air filter housing as described in Chapter 4A Section 2.
3 Disconnect the wiring plugs from the fuel filter, fuel rail pressure sensor, etc, then release the clips and move the wiring harness duct to one side.
4 Remove the injectors as described in Chapter 4A Section 11.
5 Undo the banjo bolt, and disconnect the fuel return pipe from the fuel rail **(see illustration)**. Plug the openings to prevent contamination. Be prepared for fuel spillage. New sealing washers will be required.
6 Undo the retaining bolts around the edges

and in the centre, then carefully remove the cylinder head cover. Note that the bolts are retained in the cover seal. Discard the rubber seal, a new one must be fitted.

Refitting

7 Clean the joint surfaces of the cover and cylinder head, then locate the new seal in the grooves in the cylinder head cover **(see illustration)**.
8 Position the cylinder head cover on the cylinder head, then tighten the bolts progressively to their specified torque.
9 Complete the rest of the installation by reversing the removal procedure, referring to the relevant Chapters. When all components are refitted, start the engine and check carefully around the camshaft cover for any oil leaks.

4.1a Rotate the fastener anti-clockwise...

4.1b ...then pull the cover forwards from its' mountings

4.7 Locate the new seal in the cover grooves

5 Crankshaft pulley – removal and refitting

Removal

1 Working under the front of the vehicle, undo the retaining bolts and remove the engine undershield.
2 Remove the auxiliary drivebelt as described in Chapter 1 Section 6.
3 The crankshaft must now be held stationary while the pulley bolts are loosened. The bolts are tightened to a high torque. Mercedes-Benz technicians use a tool (No. 651 589 00 40 00) that locates over 3 of the retaining bolts, allowing the crankshaft to be held, whilst the remaining bolt is slacked **(see illustration**

4.5 Undo the fuel return banjo bolt

3.5b). In the absence of this tool, counterhold the pulley bolts using a length of angle iron **(see illustration)**.

4 Unscrew the crankshaft pulley bolts then slide the pulley from the front of the crankshaft. Note that new bolts will be required.

Refitting

5 Wipe clean the pulley, and then slide it fully onto the crankshaft, aligning the locating dowel **(see illustration)**.

6 Insert the new bolts and tighten them to the specified torque while holding the crankshaft stationary as for removal.

7 Refit the auxiliary drivebelt with reference to Chapter 1 Section 6.

8 Refit the engine undershield

6 Timing chain cover – removal and refitting

1 As the timing chain cover is located at the rear of the engine, removal is only possible once the engine has been removed. Consequently, the procedure is described in Chapter 2C Section 9.

7 Timing chain – inspection and renewal

Inspection

1 Remove the cylinder head cover as described in Section 4.

2 Using a socket on the crankshaft pulley/ vibration damper hub bolt, turn the engine clockwise so that the whole length of the chain can be progressively viewed at the camshaft sprocket.

3 The chain should be renewed if the sprocket is worn or if the chain is worn (indicated by excessive lateral play between the links, and excessive noise in operation). Note that the rollers on a very badly worn chain may be slightly grooved. To avoid future problems, if there is any doubt at all about the condition of the chain, renew it.

5.3 Pulley can be counterheld with a length of angle-iron located between the bolt heads

Renewal

Note: *This following procedure, uses a chain breaker/riveter to renew the chain without removing the timing chain cover, a second person will be required to assist fitting the timing chain. Ensure that all tools are available, as well as a new chain and new connecting link before proceeding.*

4 Two methods for chain renewal are described below. The first (recommended by Mercedes) involves splitting the original chain, joining it to the new one, then rotating the crankshaft and camshafts in unison, and 'feeding' the new chain around the various sprockets. The old chain is then removed, and the two ends of the new one joined with a 'soft' rivet link. In practice, even with an assistant, we found this method involved a considerable risk of damage due to the difficulty of rotating the shafts in unison, and maintaining chain tension. As the shafts are rotated, the chain would attempt jump teeth, and then be prone to jamming in the timing cover.

5 The second method is to remove the camshafts completely, then split the original chain, and join it to the new one. The crankshaft is then rotated, 'feeding' the chain around the fuel pump sprocket until the two ends of the new chain can be joined by a 'soft' rivet link. The camshafts are then refitted. This method eliminates any possibility of accidental valve-to-piston contact. After careful consideration, although it involves

5.5 Align the dowel with the hole in the crankshaft

slightly more dismantling, this is our preferred method of chain renewal.

Method 1

Note: *After-market timing chain replacement tool kits are available from various manufacturers. Try searching for AST or Laser tools.*

6 If not already done, remove the cylinder head cover as described in Section 4.

7 Using a socket on the crankshaft pulley bolt, turn the engine until the timing marks are aligned, as described in Section 3..

8 Remove the timing chain tensioner as described in Section 8.

9 Position the chain guide (supplied in the kit) on the cylinder head and secure it with 3 bolts. This will help prevent the timing chain from jumping on the sprockets. Put some clean rag into the timing chain recess to prevent anything dropping down into the engine.

10 Use the chain breaker to press out one of the timing chain pins and split the timing chain **(see illustration)**. Take care not to drop the pin.

11 Examine the new timing chain. The chain rollers may have lubrication holes on one side. These holes must point outwards – ie. when connecting the new chain to the old chain, the holes must point upwards **(see illustration)**.

12 Connect the new timing chain to the old chain using the temporary pin and spring link supplied in the tools kit **(see illustration)**. **Note:** *Make sure the new chain is connected to the old chain above the intake camshaft*

7.10 Press out one of the timing chain pins

7.11 The lubrication holes in the chain rollers must point outwards

7.12 Using the temporary link supplied in the tool kit, join the new chain to the old one

7.18a Join the ends of the new chain with the 'soft' rivet link and side plate supplied...

7.18b ...then use the tool to securely spread the ends of the link

sprocket, as the engine has to be turned clockwise, in the direction of rotation to feed the chain around the sprockets.

13 With the new chain connected securely to the old chain, take a firm hold of both ends of the chain. Remove the clean rag from around the timing chain before turning the engine.

14 With the aid of an assistant, turn the engine in the direction of rotation. At the same time as turning the crankshaft, have the assistant rotate the exhaust camshaft at the same rate to maintain camshaft synchronisation, and chain tension. If the tension is not maintained, it may jam. Rotate the crankshaft/camshaft until the new chain comes all the way around to the intake camshaft sprocket. Try to keep tension on the chain as it's pulled over the intake camshaft sprocket.

15 Refit the clean rag back into the timing chain recess.

16 Remove the temporary connecting link and split the old timing chain from the new timing chain. **Note:** *Make sure the chain is pulled tight on the left-hand side of the engine, and the right-hand side slack to allow for the fitting of the chain tensioner.*

17 Check that the TDC marks on the crankshaft pulley and timing chain cover are aligned, and the marks on the camshaft and camshaft bearing caps are still aligned correctly.

18 Fit the new timing chain link, using the timing chain riveter to connect the two

ends of the chain securely. Always read the instructions that come with the chain riveter, as there are many different types available. The link pins need to be riveted securely, to prevent the chain coming apart **(see illustrations)**.

19 Remove the clean rag from the timing chain recess, and fit the timing chain tensioner, with reference to Section 8. With the tensioner now fitted, check the timing marks are still in line.

20 Rotate the engine two complete turns and check the timing marks come back in alignment. Refer to Section 3 to check timing mark alignment is correct.

21 Remove the chain guide tool from the cylinder head.

22 Refit the cylinder head cover with reference to Section 4.

Method 2

23 Remove camshafts as described in Section 9.

24 Use the chain breaker to press out one of the timing chain pins and split the timing chain **(see illustration 7.10)**.

25 Examine the new timing chain. The chain rollers may have lubrication holes on one side. These holes must point outwards – ie. when connecting the new chain to the old chain, the holes must point upwards **(see illustration 7.11)**.

26 Connect the new timing chain to the old chain using the temporary pin and spring link supplied in the tools kit. **Note:** *As the*

crankshaft must be turned clockwise, ensure the new chain is connected to the old chain on the tension side (intake side).

27 With the aid of an assistant, turn the crankshaft in the direction of rotation (clockwise). At the same time as turning the crankshaft, have the assistant maintain some tension on both ends of the chain to prevent it jamming in the timing cover as the chain is 'fed' around the fuel pump sprocket. Rotate the crankshaft until the new chain comes all the way around.

28 Remove the temporary connecting link and split the old timing chain from the new timing chain.

29 Check that the TDC marks on the crankshaft pulley and timing chain cover are aligned.

30 Fit the new timing chain link, using the timing chain riveter to connect the two ends of the chain securely. Always read the instructions that come with the chain riveter, as there are many different types available. The link pins need to be riveted securely, to prevent the chain coming apart **(see illustration 7.18a and 7.18b)**.

31 Refit the camshafts as described in Section 9.

8 Timing chain tensioner and sprockets – removal, inspection and refitting.

Timing chain tensioner

Removal

1 Set the engine to TDC on No 1 cylinder as described in Section 3.

2 Remove the air filter housing as described in Chapter 4A Section 2.

3 Undo the 3 retaining bolts and remove the headshield over the EGR pipe **(see illustration)**.

4 Undo the bolts and remove the EGR pipe **(see illustration)**. Renew the gaskets.

5 On models with stop/start function, remove the rear bolt and gently push the starter heatshield down a little to access the chain tensioner **(see illustration)**.

6 Unscrew the tensioner from the right-hand

8.3 EGR pipe heatshield bolts

8.4 Remove the EGR pipe

8.5 Undo the bolt and push the heatshield downwards slightly

8.6 Remove the timing chain tensioner

side of the timing chain cover using a 27 mm socket or spanner **(see illustration)**- be prepared for oil spillage. Recover the sealing ring and discard; a new one will be required for refitting.

Inspection

7 Do not attempt to dismantle the tensioner assembly. If it is suspected that the tensioner is worn or faulty, the complete unit should be renewed.

Refitting

8 Compress the tensioner using hand pressure alone to expel any oil within, then locate a new sealing ring on the tensioner, then slowly screw it into position and tighten to the specified torque.
9 Refitting is the reversal of the removal procedure, referring to the relevant Chapters, where applicable. When all components are refitted, start the engine and check carefully around the tensioner for any oil leaks.

Camshaft sprockets

Removal

10 Refer to Section 3 and set the engine to TDC on No 1 cylinder. Lock the camshafts as described.
11 Use a dab of paint or a marker pen to mark the timing chain and the camshaft sprockets in relation to each other. This will help ensure that the chain is refitted correctly and the valve timing maintained.
12 Remove the timing chain tensioner as described earlier in this Section.

13 Hold the camshafts stationary using an open-ended spanner on the machined section of the flange at the rear, then loosen the bolts securing the sprockets to the camshafts. **Note:** *The sprocket bolts have a left-hand thread. Rotate the bolts clockwise to slacken them.*
14 At this stage the crankshaft sprocket will still be at TDC, and the crankshaft must not be turned until the camshaft sprockets have been refitted. Use a length of wire to tie the upper part of the timing chain to the cylinder head to ensure the chain remains on the fuel pump sprocket.
15 Fully unscrew the retaining bolts and remove the sprockets from the timing chain.

Inspection

16 Examine the teeth on the sprockets for wear. Each tooth forms an inverted V. If worn, the side of each tooth under tension will be slightly concave in shape when compared with the other side of the tooth (ie, the teeth will have a hooked appearance). If the teeth appear worn, the sprockets must be renewed.

Refitting

17 Ensure that the camshafts are still locked in place and that the crankshaft timing marks are still aligned, as described in Section 3. If a new sprocket is being fitted, transfer the chain alignment mark from the old sprocket to the new.
18 Engage the sprockets with the chain, aligning the marks made on the chain and sprockets before removal, then locate the sprockets on the camshaft flange.
19 Insert the sprocket retaining bolts, but only finger tighten them at this stage – the sprockets must be free to rotate independently of the camshafts. Remove the wire used to tie the chain to the cylinder head.
20 Refit the timing chain tensioner as described earlier in this Section.
21 Now tighten the camshaft sprocket retaining bolts to their specified torque. Note that the bolts have a left-hand thread.
22 Check that the crankshaft pulley mark is still aligned with the crankcase pointer, then remove the camshaft locking tools, refit the bearing caps and tighten the bolts to the specified torque.

23 Using a socket on the crankshaft pulley/vibration damper hub bolts, turn the crankshaft through two complete revolutions, and check that the crankshaft and camshaft timing marks are still aligned with No 1 piston at TDC, as described in Section 3.
24 Refit the cylinder head cover as described in Section 4.

Fuel pump sprocket

25 Removal of the fuel pump drive gear/ sprocket is only possible once the engine has been removed. Refer to Chapter 2C Section 10.

<table>
<tr><td>**9**</td><td>**Camshafts, rocker arms and hydraulic tappets** – removal, inspection and refitting</td></tr>
</table>

Camshafts

Removal

1 Set the engine at TDC on No. 1 cylinder as described in Section 3.
2 Remove the cylinder head cover as described in Section 4.
3 Using permanent marker or paint, make alignment marks between the timing chain and the camshaft sprockets to aid refitting **(see illustration)**.
4 Remove the chain tensioner as described in Section 8.
5 The camshaft bearing caps are marked A to K, starting at the No. 1 (front) cap on the exhaust side. The cylinder head is also marked to indicate the positions of the caps **(see illustrations)**. Check the bearing caps to ensure that marks are present, and if necessary make suitable marks using quick-drying paint.
6 The camshaft bearing cap bolts must now be slackened evenly, half-a-turn at a time.

> ⚠ *Warning: It is absolutely essential to release the camshaft bearing caps evenly, and gradually, because the camshafts are very sensitive to fracturing.*

7 With the bolts removed, lift off the bearing caps, keeping them in order. Note that the bearing caps locate on dowels – if they are

9.3 Paint alignment marks between the chain and sprockets

9.5a No.1 exhaust cap is marked 'A' – as is the cylinder head...

9.5b ...the last cap is marked 'K' – intake camshaft shaft, No. 5 cap

9.8 Secure the chain from slipping down the cover

9.15 Lubricate the bearing locations and rocker arms

9.17 Position the lobes of No.1 cylinder camshaft as shown

stuck, tap them gently using a soft-faced mallet.

8 Lift the camshafts from place, unhooking the sprockets from the timing chain as they are removed. Take precautions to prevent the chain from slipping down the cover – secure it using cable ties etc **(see illustration)**.

9 If required, unscrew the bolts and remove the sprockets from the camshafts.

Caution: The camshaft sprockets bolts have a left-hand thread! Rotate the bolts clockwise to remove them.

Inspection

10 Thoroughly clean the camshafts and the housing/caps.

11 Examine the camshaft journals and cam lobes for any sign of scoring, wear grooves or pitting, and if apparent, renew the relevant camshaft. Any damage of this nature may be attributable to a blocked oil passage in the cylinder head, and careful examination should be carried out to determine the cause.

12 Examine the bearing surfaces in the camshaft housing and bearing caps for excessive wear and scoring. If evident, renew the components together with the camshafts.

Refitting

13 If removed, locate the sprockets on the camshafts, and finger tighten the retaining bolts. It must be just possible to rotate the sprockets independently of the camshafts.

14 Ensure the crankshaft is still positioned

at TDC on No.1 cylinder as described in Section 3.

15 Lubricate the camshaft journals and the bearing locations in the camshaft housing/ caps with clean engine oil **(see illustration)**. Also lubricate the rocker arms.

16 Hook the intake camshaft sprocket into the timing chain, aligning the previously made marks, where applicable.

17 Position the intake camshaft in the housing with the top of the camshaft lobes of No. 1 cylinder (at the front of the engine – not the timing chain end) facing approximately upwards **(see illustration)**.

18 Refit the intake camshaft bearing caps to their original positions, then insert the retaining bolts, and tighten them gradually, evenly, half-a-turn at a time to their specified torque.

Caution: It's essential that the camshafts are installed with as little stress as possible on their structure. They are fragile and are easily fractured.

19 If the position of the camshaft is correct, with the No.1 cylinder camshaft lobes pointing approximately upwards, the tip of the machined section on the camshaft flange should align with the mark on the No.5 bearing cap (adjacent to the timing chain) **(see illustration)**. If necessary, use an open-ended spanner on the machined section, and rotate the camshaft slightly until the tip aligns with the mark.

20 Fit the exhaust camshaft using the exact same procedure. The camshaft lobes above

No.1 cylinder should be pointing upwards, and slightly towards each other **(see illustration)**.

21 Refit the timing chain tensioner as described in Section 8.

22 Check the crankshaft pulley TDC mark is still aligned with the pointer on the crankcase, and the tip of the hexagonal sections on the camshafts are still aligned with the marks on the No.5 bearing caps **(see illustration)**.

23 Temporarily refit the cylinder head cover, and check the intake and exhaust camshaft alignment marks are correct as described in Section 3.

24 Remove the cylinder head cover, and lock the camshafts in place as described in Section. If the locking tools are not available, prevent the camshafts from rotating using an open-ended spanner on their hexagonal sections, then tighten the sprocket retaining bolts to their specified torque. **Note:** *The sprocket bolts have a left-hand thread! Rotate them anti-clockwise to tighten.*

25 Once again, check the crankshaft and camshaft are still aligned as described in Section 3.

26 Wit the alignment correct, refit the cylinder head cover as described in Section 4.

Rocker arms and hydraulic tappets

Removal

27 Remove the camshafts as described earlier in this Section.

28 Obtain a container with 16 compartments

9.19 The mark on the bearing cap must align with the tip of the machined section of the flange

9.20 The lobes above No.1 cylinder should be positioned as shown

9.22 The marks on the bearing caps should align with the tips of the camshaft flanges

9.28a Remove each rocker arm

9.28b Using a magnet to lift out the hydraulic tappets

9.32 Refit the hydraulic tappets to their original locations

and number the compartments to indicate the location of the rocker arms and hydraulic tappets. Lift each rocker arm and hydraulic tappet in turn and store them in the container **(see illustrations)**.

Inspection

29 The operation of the removed hydraulic tappets can be checked as follows.
a) *Press down firmly on the top of each tappet, using hand pressure alone – don't use any tools as the surface of the tappets is easily damaged.*
b) *It should not be possible to compress the tappet using normal hand pressure, and only slightly using strong hand pressure.*
c) *Repeat the operation for all the tappets in turn.*
d) *If any one tappet can be depressed more easily than the others, renew it.*

30 Check the hydraulic tappets and the bores in the cylinder head for wear and scoring. If any serious damage or wear is evident, the cylinder head and tappets must be renewed.
31 Examine the rocker arms for wear or damage. Note that the rocker arms will probably wear at the same rate as the surface of the camshaft lobes. If the rockers are worn, the camshafts are probably worn too.

Refitting

32 Lubricate the hydraulic tappet bores in the cylinder head with clean engine oil, then locate each hydraulic tappet in its original position **(see illustration)**.
33 The remainder of refitting is a reversal of removal.

10 Cylinder head – removal, inspection and refitting

Note: *New cylinder head bolts may be required – see text.*

Removal

1 Ensure that the engine is cold before attempting to remove the cylinder head.
2 Apply the parking brake, then jack up the front of the vehicle and support it on axle stands (see *Vehicle jacking and support*).
3 Disconnect the battery negative lead as described in Chapter 5A Section 4.
4 Raise the bonnet to the fully open position.
5 Drain the engine oil and coolant as described in Chapter 1 Section 4 and Chapter 1 Section 30.

10.7a Remove the air filter housing front bracket...

10.7b ...and rear bracket

6 Remove the air filter housing as described in Chapter 4A Section 2.
7 Unclip the wiring loom, undo the bolts and remove the air filter brackets from the cylinder head **(see illustrations)**. Disconnect and unclip the wiring plug, then move the rear bracket to one side, along with the particulate pressure sensor.
8 Detach the rear lifting eye bracket from the cylinder head, and move it to one side along with the oil level dipstick tube **(see illustration)**.
9 Undo the bolts securing the turbocharger to the exhaust manifold **(see illustration)**. Note that new bolts will be required.
10 Unscrew the upstream temperature sensor from the exhaust manifold **(see illustration)**.
11 With reference to Chapter 1 Section 25, remove the fuel filter assembly.

10.8 Move the rear lifting eye bracket to one side

10.9 Turbocharger-to-manifold bolts

10.10 Use a second spanner to counterhold the union

10.12 Disconnect the output stage wiring plug

10.13 Glow plug output stage retaining bolts

10.15a Disconnect the earth lead...

10.15b ...and undo the mounting bolts

10.18 Remove the EGR cooler bracket

10.19 Fuel pipes bracket bolt

12 Disconnect the glow plug output stage wiring plug and unclip the wiring harness **(see illustration)**.

13 Disconnect the remaining output stage wiring plug, undo the 2 bolts and remove the unit **(see illustration)**.

14 Lift the clip and slide the coolant pump vacuum switch from the output stage bracket.

15 Disconnect the earth lead, undo the mounting bolts and move the glow plug output stage bracket to one side **(see illustrations)**.

16 Remove the EGR valve as described in Chapter 4B Section 2.

17 Note their fitted positions, disconnect the various wiring plugs, undo the retaining bolt and move the wiring harness and guide on the top of the engine to one side.

18 Undo the retaining bolts and remove the EGR cooler mounting bracket **(see illustration)**.

19 Undo the bolt and move the fuel pipes to one side **(see illustration)**.

20 Remove the thermostat as described in Chapter 3 Section 4.

21 Release the clamp and disconnect the coolant hose from the fuel filter housing.

22 Undo the union nuts and remove the high-pressure fuel pipe between the pump and fuel (common) rail. Note that new high-pressure fuel pipes will be needed upon reassembly.

23 Remove the camshafts, rocker arms and hydraulic tappets as described in Section 9.

24 Undo the 2 bolts securing the coolant housing to the rear of the cylinder head, and

the 2 bolts securing the support bracket **(see illustrations)**.

25 Disconnect the wiring plug, undo the 2 bolts and move the fuel pipe assembly to one side **(see illustration)**.

10.24a Coolant housing-to-cylinder head bolts

10.25 Fuel pipe retaining bolts

26 Undo the bolts and remove the left-hand lifting eye from the cylinder head.

27 Undo the bolt securing the fuel pressure switch to the intake manifold **(see illustration)**.

10.24b Support bracket bolts

10.27 Pressure switch retaining bolt

10.28a Undo the bolt in the left-hand rear corner...

10.28b ...and the bolts in the timing chain tunnel

10.43 Measure from the base of bolt head to the end of the shank

28 Undo the 3 bolts securing the cylinder head to the timing chain cover (see illustrations).

29 Make a final check to ensure that all relevant hoses and wires have been disconnected from the cylinder head.

30 Progressively loosen the cylinder head bolts, working in the reverse order to the tightening sequence (see illustration 10.49). Remove all cylinder head bolts.

31 Release the cylinder head from the cylinder block and locating dowels by rocking it. Do not prise between the mating faces of the cylinder head and block, as this may damage the gasket faces.

32 With the aid of an assistant, carefully lift the cylinder head, complete with exhaust manifold, from the block, and manoeuvre it out from the engine compartment.

33 Recover the cylinder head gasket.

34 Secure the timing chain to the tensioner rail using a cable tie or similar.

35 If necessary, remove the exhaust manifold from the cylinder head.

Inspection

36 Refer to Chapter 2C Section 6 for details of the cylinder head dismantling and reassembly.

37 The mating faces of the cylinder head and block must be perfectly clean before refitting the head. Use a scraper to remove all traces of gasket and carbon, and also clean the tops of the pistons. Take particular care with the cylinder head, as the metal is easily damaged. Also make sure that debris is not allowed to enter the oil and water passages. Using adhesive tape and paper, seal the water, oil and bolt holes in the cylinder block. To prevent carbon entering the gap between the pistons and bores, smear a little grease in the gap. After cleaning each piston, rotate the crankshaft so that the piston moves down the bore, and then wipe out the grease and carbon with a cloth rag.

38 Check the block and head for nicks, deep scratches and other damage. If very slight, they may be removed from the cylinder block carefully with a file. More serious damage may be repaired by machining, but this is a specialist job.

39 If warpage of the cylinder head is suspected, use a straight-edge to check it for distortion, with reference to Chapter 2C Section 7.

40 Clean out the bolt holes in the block using a pipe cleaner or thin rag and a screwdriver. Make sure that all oil and water is removed, otherwise there is a possibility of the block being cracked by hydraulic pressure when the bolts are tightened.

41 Examine the bolt threads and the threads in the cylinder block for damage. If necessary, use the correct size tap to chase out the threads in the block.

42 The manufacturers recommend that the cylinder head bolts are measured, to determine whether renewal is necessary; however, some owners may wish to renew all the bolts as a matter of course.

43 Measure the length of each bolt from the base of the head to the end of the shank (see illustration). If the bolt length is greater than the maximum specified, the bolts should be renewed.

44 Reassemble the cylinder head with reference to Chapter 2C Section 8. Where applicable, refit the exhaust manifold together with a new gasket.

Refitting

45 Apply a little silicone sealant (Loctite 5970) to the joints between the cylinder head and the timing cover (see illustration).

46 Locate the new cylinder head gasket on the block, making sure that it is the correct way up and positioned over the location dowels (see illustration).

10.45 Apply a thin bead of sealant to the cylinder head-to-timing cover joints

10.46 Position the gasket over the location dowels

10.48 Lubricate the underside of the bolt heads and the threads

6389 Fig.02b-10.49 HAYNES

10.49 Cylinder head bolt (B) tightening sequence

A Bolts securing the cylinder head to the timing chain cover

47 With the aid of an assistant, lower the cylinder head carefully onto the block.

48 Oil the threads and the cylinder head contact faces of the cylinder head bolts, then insert them and screw them into the cylinder block by hand **(see illustration)**. Ensure that the bolts are fitted to their correct locations as noted on removal.

49 Tighten the cylinder head bolts in the order shown **(see illustration)**, and in the stages given in the Specifications – ie, tighten all bolts to the Stage 1 torque, then tighten all bolts to the Stage 2 torque, and so on.

50 Tighten the 3 bolts securing the timing chain cover to the cylinder head at the front of the engine.

51 The remainder of refitting is a reversal of removal, noting the following points:

a) Refill the cooling system and refill the engine with oil as described in Chapter 1.

b) Reconnect the battery negative lead as described in Chapter 5A Section 4.

c) When all components have been refitted, start the engine and check carefully around the engine for any oil or coolant leaks.

11 Sump – removal and refitting

Removal

Note: *A suitable hoist and lifting tackle will be required for this operation. To carry out this procedure, the front suspension crossmember will need to be lowered, to allow enough room for the sump to be removed. A new sump gasket will be required on refitting.*

1 Remove the engine cover as described in Section 4.

2 Remove the flywheel/driveplate as described in Section 13.

3 Drain the engine oil as described in Chapter 1 Section 4. On completion, renew the sealing washer, then refit the drain plug and tighten to the specified torque.

4 Attach a suitable hoist to the engine and take the weight of the engine.

5 Unscrew the bolts from the bottom of the engine mountings at each side of the engine.

6 Lower the front suspension crossmember with reference to Chapter 10 Section 10.

7 Undo the retaining bolts and remove the engine oil level dipstick guide tube **(see illustration)**. Renew the O-ring seal.

8 Disconnect the oil sensor wiring plug.

9 Undo the retaining bolts and remove the lower section of the sump **(see illustration)**. Renew the sump seal.

10 Remove the bolts securing the upper section of the sump to the timing cover **(see illustration)**.

11.7 Renew the oil level dipstick guide tube O-ring seal

11.9 Don't overlook the bolt in the centre of the sump lower section

11.10 Remove the timing cover-to-sump bolts

11.11a Sump bolt details

A M6 x 16 mm   B M6 x 65 mm   C M8 x 45 mm   D Screw 'feedthroughs'

11.11b Screw-in 8 mm bolts to gently force the sump from the crankcase

11 Undo the bolts securing the upper section of the sump to the crankcase, then screw-in four M8 mm bolts into the 'feedthrough' holes and gradually force the sump from the crankcase **(see illustrations)**. Be sure to screw-in the bolts evenly and gradually. Do not drive a screwdriver between the sump and crankcase as this may damage the mating surfaces.

11.12 Oil pick-up tube bolts

12 Undo the bolts and remove the oil pump pick-up tube **(see illustration)**. Renew the O-ring seal.

Refitting

13 Thoroughly clean the mating surfaces of the sump and cylinder block, then refit the oil pick-up tube with a new O-ring seal, and

11.13 Renew the pick-up tube O-ring seal

tighten the bolts to the specified torque **(see illustration)**.
14 Apply a 2.0 mm continuous bead of silicone sealant (MB recommend Loctite 5970) to the upper section of the sump as shown **(see illustration)**.
15 Manoeuvre the upper section of the sump into position, then insert the retaining bolts **(see illustration 11.11a)**, and gradually tighten them to the specified torque. Note that the bolts must be tightened within 7 minutes of the sealant being applied, or it will begin to harden.
16 Place the new seal onto the lower section of the sump, then manoeuvre it into position, inset the retaining bolts and tighten them to the specified torque **(see illustration)**.
17 Complete the rest of the installation by reversing the removal procedure, referring to the relevant Chapters.
18 When all components are refitted, start the engine and check carefully around the sump for any oil leaks.

11.14 Apply a 2 mm diameter bead of sealant as shown

11.16 Renew the lower section seal

13.3 Remove the crankshaft position sensor

13.5a Unscrew the flywheel/driveplate bolts

13.5b Note the locating dowel and hole

12 Oil pump – removal, inspection and refitting

1 Removal of the oil pump is only possible once the timing cover has been removed. Removal of this cover is only possible with the engine removed.
2 Consequently, oil pump removal, inspection and refitting is described in Chapter 2C Section 11.

13 Flywheel/driveplate – removal, inspection and refitting

Removal

1 Remove the manual transmission (Chapter 7A Section 6), or automatic transmission (Chapter 7B Section 6).
2 On manual transmission models, remove the clutch as described in Chapter 6 Section 5.
3 Undo the retaining bolt and withdraw the crankshaft position sensor (see illustration).
4 The flywheel/driveplate must be held stationary while the mounting bolts are loosened. To do this, counterhold the crankshaft using a socket on the crank pulley bolts, or refit a few of the clutch pressure plate bolts, and counterhold the flywheel/driveplate with a suitable bar (see illustration 5.3).
5 Unscrew the mounting bolts, then lift the flywheel/driveplate from the rear of the crankshaft (see illustrations). Note that the location dowel ensures the flywheel/driveplate can only be fitted in one position. Discard the flywheel bolts, new ones must be fitted.

Inspection

6 If the flywheel-to-clutch mating surface is deeply scored, cracked or otherwise damaged, then the flywheel must be renewed, unless it is possible to have it surface ground. Seek the advice of a Mercedes-Benz dealer or engine reconditioning specialist.
7 If the ring gear is badly worn or has missing teeth, then it must be renewed. This job is best left to a Mercedes-Benz dealer or engine reconditioning specialist.

13.9a Turn the flywheel secondary element anti-clockwise and mark the limit of its travel on the starter ring gear teeth ...

8 On vehicles with dual mass flywheels, check the rotational and lateral movement as follows.
9 In order to check the rotational movement, lock the flywheel in place as previously described. Rotate the flywheel secondary element (drive surface) by hand anti-clockwise, mark its position in relation to the primary flywheel element (bolted to the crankshaft), then rotate it by hand clockwise and mark its position. Bear in mind, that the free rotational movement is being measured here – do not use excessive force to rotate the secondary element. Mark the limits of the rotational movement in relation to the number of flywheel starter ring gear teeth (see illustrations).
10 If the number of starter ring gear teeth travelled by the flywheel secondary element exceeds 8 (flywheel manufacturer SACHS or LUK), the flywheel may need replacing.

13.11 Attach a length of steel strip to the flywheel secondary element (drive surface)

13.9b ... then turn the secondary element clockwise, and mark its travel limit again

11 In order to check the lateral movement of the flywheel, attach a length of steel strip to the flywheel secondary element (drive surface), and mount a DTI gauge so that it measures in-line with the transmission mounting flange holes (see illustration). Pull the steel strip away from the flywheel, zero the DTI gauge, then push the strip towards the flywheel and read off the measurement. The maximum permissible amount of lateral movement specified by Mercedes-Benz is 2.5 mm (flywheel manufacturer LUK), or 10.0 mm (flywheel manufacturer SACHS). If the dimension measured exceeds this, the flywheel may need replacing.
12 Check the condition of the spigot bearing in the centre of the flywheel or in the end of the crankshaft, and renew if necessary (see illustration).

13.12 The spigot bearing is in the centre of the flywheel

13 It is recommended that the flywheel/driveplate securing bolts are renewed whenever removed.

Note: *On vehicles equipped with an LUK dual mass flywheel, a centrifugal-force pendulum is incorporated into the design to further increase the damping capacity at low engine speeds, and prolong service life. A characteristic of this design is that when operated/shaken by hand, the flywheel will emit a pronounced rattle. This is not a fault, and is not grounds for replacement.*

Refitting

14 Commence refitting by cleaning the mating faces of the crankshaft and flywheel/driveplate.

15 Make sure that the location dowel is in position in the end of the crankshaft.

16 Locate the flywheel/driveplate onto the crankshaft, then insert the new mounting bolts and hand-tighten them.

17 Lock the flywheel/driveplate using the method employed during removal, then tighten the securing bolts progressively in a diagonal sequence to the specified torque.

18 The remainder of refitting is a reversal of removal.

14 Crankshaft oil seals – renewal

Front oil seal

1 Remove the crankshaft pulley/vibration damper and inspect it as described in Section 5.

2 Measure and note the fitted depth of the oil seal in the crankcase **(see illustration)**.

3 Prise the oil seal from the cover using a hooked instrument. Alternatively, drill a small hole in the oil seal, and use a self-tapping screw and a pair of pliers to remove it **(see illustrations)**.

Caution: Take great care not to damage the crankshaft surface.

4 Clean the seal location in the crankcase, and also clean the oil seal contact surface on the crankshaft.

5 Press the new seal into the crankcase (open end first) to the previously-noted depth, using a suitable tube or socket. Do not apply any lubricant to the seal or the crankshaft. Generic insertion tools are available that locate over the end of the crankshaft. The seal is then located over the tool, and slid squarely into place.

6 Refit the crankshaft pulley/vibration damper as described in Section 5.

Rear oil seal

7 Remove the flywheel/driveplate as described in Section 13.

8 Prise the oil seal from the cover using a screwdriver/hooked instrument **(see illustration)**.

9 Clean the seal location in the crankcase, and also clean the oil seal contact surface on the crankshaft. The new seal must be installed without lubricant.

10 Fit the new oil seal housing over the crankshaft and into the timing cover. Generic insertion tools are available, that located over

the end of the crankshaft. The seal is then located over the tool, and slid squarely into place **(see illustration)**.

11 The seal must be fitted so it's rear edge is flush with the edge of the timing cover **(see illustration)**.

12 Refit the flywheel/driveplate (Section 13).

15 Engine/transmission mountings – inspection and renewal

Inspection

1 Three engine/transmission mountings are used, one on either side of the engine, and one under the rear of the transmission.

2 For improved access, raise the front of the vehicle and support it securely on axle stands (see *Vehicle jacking and support*).

3 Undo the fasteners and remove the engine undertray.

4 Check the condition of the mounting rubber to see if it is cracked, hardened or separated from the metal at any point. Renew the mounting if any such damage or deterioration is evident. The mountings contain hydraulic oil, and must be renewed if oil leakage is evident.

5 Check the mounting bolts are tight.

6 Using a large screwdriver or metal bar, check for wear in the mounting by carefully levering against it to check for free play. Where this is not possible, enlist the aid of an assistant to move the engine/transmission back-and-forth, or from side-to-side, while

14.2 Note the fitted depth of the seal

14.3a Carefully drill a small hole…

14.3b …screw in a self-tapping screw, and pull out the seal

14.8 Take care not to damage the crankshaft surface when removing the seal

14.10 The insertion tool fits inside the seal, over the end of the crankshaft

14.11 The seal must be flush with the timing cover

15.15 Crossmember and rear mounting bolts

you observe the mounting. If excessive free play is found, check first that the fasteners are correctly secured, and then renew any worn components as required.

Renewal

Front engine mountings

7 Support the engine, either using a hoist and lifting tackle connected to the engine lifting brackets, or by positioning a jack and interposed block of wood under the sump. Ensure that the engine is adequately supported before proceeding.
8 Depending on which engine mounting requires removal, it may be necessary to catalytic converter/diesel particulate filter as described in Chapter 4B Section 2.
9 Unscrew the bolts securing the mountings to the engine crossmember.
10 Raise the engine a little, then undo the

bolts securing the mounting brackets to the engine.
11 Fit the new mountings, and tighten the fasteners to the specified torque.

Rear engine/transmission mounting

12 Raise the front of the vehicle and support it securely on axle stands (see *Vehicle jacking and support*).
13 Remove the fasteners and remove the undertray beneath the transmission.
14 Support the transmission using a jack and interposed block of wood.
15 Unbolt the crossmember from the underbody, then unscrew the bolts securing the mounting to the rear of the transmission. Lower the crossmember together with the mounting from the underbody **(see illustration)**.
16 The mounting can then be unbolted from the bracket if required.
17 Refitting is a reversal of removal.

16 Engine oil sensors – renewal

Level sensor

1 Raise the front of the vehicle and support it securely on axle stands (see *Vehicle jacking and support*). Undo the fasteners and remove the engine undershield.
2 Drain the engine oil as described in Chapter 1 Section 4.
3 Disconnect the wiring plug from the oil sensor on the base of the sump **(see illustration)**.

4 Undo the retaining bolts and withdraw the sensor from the sump. Renew the O-ring seal.
5 Refitting is a reversal of removal, tightening the sensor retaining bolts to the specified torque.

Temperature sensor

6 The oil temperature sensor is located on the left-hand side of the crankcase at the rear **(see illustration)**.
7 Raise the front of the vehicle and support it securely on axle stands (see *Vehicle jacking and support*). Undo the fasteners and remove the engine undershield.
8 Disconnect the wiring plug from the sensor, then unscrew it from the crankcase. Be prepared for oil spillage. Renew the sealing washer.
9 Insert the sensor with a new sealing ring, and tighten it to the specified torque.
10 The remainder of refitting is a reversal of removal.

Oil pump regulating valve

11 The oil pump regulating valve is located on the left-hand side of the crankcase, at the rear **(see illustration)**.
12 Raise the front of the vehicle and support it securely on axle stands (see *Vehicle jacking and support*). Undo the fasteners and remove the engine undershield.
13 Disconnect the wiring plug from the sensor, then unscrew the valve from place. Renew the O-ring seal.
14 Refitting is a reversal of removal. Tighten the sensor to the specified torque.

16.3 Engine oi level sensor

16.6 Oil temperature sensor

16.11 Oil pump regulating valve

Notes

Chapter 2 Part C
General engine removal and overhaul procedures

Contents

Section number

Crankshaft – inspection 16
Crankshaft – refitting 20
Crankshaft – removal 13
Cylinder block/crankcase – cleaning and inspection. 14
Cylinder head – dismantling. 6
Cylinder head – reassembly 8
Cylinder head and valves – cleaning and inspection 7
Engine – initial start-up after overhaul 22
Engine – removal, separation and refitting. 4
Engine overhaul – dismantling sequence. 5
Engine overhaul – general information 2

Section number

Engine overhaul – reassembly sequence. 18
Engine removal – methods and precautions 3
General information 1
Main and big-end bearings, and bearing cap bolts – inspection. . . . 17
Oil pump (2143 cc engine only) – removal, inspection and refitting. . 11
Piston rings – refitting 19
Piston/connecting rod assemblies – refitting 21
Piston/connecting rod assembly – cleaning and inspection 15
Piston/connecting rod assembly – removal 12
Timing cover – removal and refitting 9
Timing gears – removal and refitting 10

Degrees of difficulty

Easy, suitable for novice with little experience 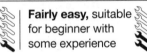	Fairly easy, suitable for beginner with some experience	Fairly difficult, suitable for competent DIY mechanic	Difficult, suitable for experienced DIY mechanic	Very difficult, suitable for expert DIY or professional

Specifications

Note: *At the time of writing, some specifications for certain engines were not available. Where the relevant specifications are not given here, refer to your Mercedes dealer for further information.*

Cylinder head
Maximum gasket face distortion . . . .   0.08 mm
Cylinder head height:
   646 (2148 cc) engines . . . .   N/A
   651 (2143 cc) engines . . . .   134.35 to 134.65 mm
Wear limit after machining:
   646 (2148 cc) engines . . . .   N/A
   651 (2143 cc) engines . . . .   134.15 mm

Valves

	Intake	Exhaust
Valve stem diameter:		
646 (2148 cc) engines	N/A	N/A
651 (2143 cc) engines	5.960 to 5.975 mm	5.955 to 5.970 mm

Crankshaft
Endfloat:
   All engines . . . .   0.10 to 0.30 mm

Pistons

	646 (2148 cc) engines	651 (2143 cc) engines
Ring end gap:		
1st compression ring	0.22 to 0.37 mm	0.27 to 0.37 mm
2nd compression ring	0.80 to 1.00 mm	0.80 to 1.0 mm
Oil control ring	0.20 to 0.40 mm	0.20 to 0.40 mm

1 General information

1 Included in this Part of Chapter 2 are details of removing the engine from the car and general overhaul procedures for the cylinder head, cylinder block/crankcase and all other engine internal components.

2 The information given ranges from advice concerning preparation for an overhaul and the purchase of parts, to detailed step-by-step procedures covering removal, inspection, renovation and refitting of engine internal components.

3 After Section 9, all instructions are based on the assumption that the engine has been removed from the car. For information concerning in-car engine repair, as well as the removal and refitting of those external components necessary for full overhaul, refer to Part A or B of this Chapter, as applicable, and to Section 6. Ignore any preliminary dismantling operations described in Parts A or B that are no longer relevant once the engine has been removed from the car.

2 Engine overhaul – general information

1 It is not always easy to determine when, or if, an engine should be completely overhauled, as a number of factors must be considered.

2 High mileage is not necessarily an indication that an overhaul is needed, while low mileage does not preclude the need for an overhaul. Frequency of servicing is probably the most important consideration. An engine which has had regular and frequent oil and filter changes, as well as other required maintenance, should give many thousands of miles of reliable service. Conversely, a neglected engine may require an overhaul very early in its life.

3 Excessive oil consumption is an indication that piston rings, valve seals and/or valve guides are in need of attention. Make sure that oil leaks are not responsible before deciding that the rings and/or guides are worn. Perform a compression test, as described in Part A or B of this Chapter (as applicable), to determine the likely cause of the problem.

4 Check the oil pressure with a gauge fitted in place of the oil pressure switch, and compare it with that specified in Part A or B. If it is extremely low, the main and big-end bearings, and/or the oil pump, are probably worn out.

5 Loss of power, rough running, knocking or metallic engine noises, excessive valve gear noise, and high fuel consumption may also point to the need for an overhaul, especially if they are all present at the same time. If a complete service does not remedy the

situation, major mechanical work is the only solution.

6 A full engine overhaul involves restoring all internal parts to the specification of a new engine. During a complete overhaul, the pistons and the piston rings are renewed, and the cylinder bores are reconditioned. New main and big-end bearings are generally fitted; if necessary, the crankshaft may be reground, to compensate for wear in the journals. The valves are also serviced as well, since they are usually in less-than-perfect condition at this point. Always pay careful attention to the condition of the oil pump when overhauling the engine, and renew it if there is any doubt as to its serviceability. The end result should be an as-new engine that will give many trouble-free miles.

Note: *Critical cooling system components such as the hoses, thermostat and coolant pump should be renewed when an engine is overhauled. The radiator should be checked carefully, to ensure that it is not clogged or leaking. Also, it is a good idea to renew the oil pump whenever the engine is overhauled.*

7 Before beginning the engine overhaul, read through the entire procedure, to familiarise yourself with the scope and requirements of the job. Overhauling an engine is not difficult if you follow carefully all of the instructions, have the necessary tools and equipment, and pay close attention to all specifications. It can, however, be time-consuming. Plan on the car being off the road for a minimum of two weeks, especially if parts must be taken to an engineering works for repair or reconditioning. Check on the availability of parts and make sure that any necessary special tools and equipment are obtained in advance. Most work can be done with typical hand tools, although a number of precision measuring tools are required for inspecting parts to determine if they must be renewed. Often the engineering works will handle the inspection of parts and offer advice concerning reconditioning and renewal.

Note: *Always wait until the engine has been completely dismantled, and until all components (especially the cylinder block/ crankcase and the crankshaft) have been inspected, before deciding what service and repair operations must be performed by an engineering works. The condition of these components will be the major factor to consider when determining whether to overhaul the original engine, or to buy a reconditioned unit. Do not, therefore, purchase parts or have overhaul work done on other components until they have been thoroughly inspected. As a general rule, time is the primary cost of an overhaul, so it does not pay to fit worn or sub-standard parts.*

8 As a final note, to ensure maximum life and minimum trouble from a reconditioned engine, everything must be assembled with care, in a spotlessly-clean environment.

3 Engine removal – methods and precautions

1 If you have decided that the engine must be removed for overhaul or major repair work, several preliminary steps should be taken.

2 Locating a suitable place to work is extremely important. Adequate workspace, along with storage space for the car, will be needed. If a workshop or garage is not available, at the very least, a flat, level, clean work surface is required.

3 Cleaning the engine compartment and engine/transmission before beginning the removal procedure will help keep tools clean and organised.

4 An engine hoist will also be necessary. Make sure the equipment is rated in excess of the weight of the engine (and transmission if both are being removed). Safety is of primary importance, considering the potential hazards involved in lifting the engine out of the car.

5 If this is the first time you have removed an engine, an assistant should ideally be available. Advice and aid from someone more experienced would also be helpful. There are many instances when one person cannot simultaneously perform all of the operations required when lifting the engine out of the vehicle.

6 Plan the operation ahead of time. Before starting work, arrange for the hire of or obtain all of the tools and equipment you will need. Some of the equipment necessary to perform engine removal and installation safely and with relative ease (in addition to an engine hoist) is as follows: a heavy duty trolley jack, complete sets of spanners and sockets (see *Tools and working facilities*), wooden blocks, and plenty of rags and cleaning solvent for mopping-up spilled oil, coolant and fuel. If the hoist must be hired, make sure that you arrange for it in advance, and perform all of the operations possible without it beforehand. This will save you money and time.

7 Plan for the car to be out of use for quite a while. An engineering works will be required to perform some of the work, which the do-it-yourselfer cannot accomplish without special equipment. These places often have a busy schedule, so it would be a good idea to consult them before removing the engine, in order to accurately estimate the amount of time required to rebuild or repair components that may need work.

8 Always be extremely careful when removing and refitting the engine. Serious injury can result from careless actions. Plan ahead and take your time, and a job of this nature, although major, can be accomplished successfully.

9 On all models, the engine is removed by lifting the assembly out from above the vehicle, once the transmission has been removed.

4 Engine – removal, separation and refitting

Removal

1 Ensure the transmission is in Neutral.

2 Raise the front of the vehicle and support it securely on axle stands (see *Vehicle jacking and support*). Undo the fasteners and remove the engine/transmission undershields.

3 Disconnect the battery negative lead as described in Chapter 5A Section 4.

4 Remove the plastic cover from the top of the engine.

5 Remove the air filter assembly and intake ducts as described in Chapter 4A Section 2.

6 On 651 (2143 cc) engines, undo the bolts and remove the air filter assembly rear mounting bracket from the cylinder head **(see illustration)**.

7 Remove the radiator cooling fan as described in Chapter 3 Section 6.

8 Release the clamps and remove the charge air hoses from the intercooler.

9 On models with traditional hydraulic power steering, syphon out the fluid, then disconnect the hoses, undo the bolts and remove the power steering pump fluid reservoir. Release the wiring harness retaining clip where applicable.

10 On 2148 cc engines, disconnect the fluid hoses from the power steering pump.

11 Drain the engine oil and coolant as described in Chapter 1 Section 4 and Chapter 1 Section 30.

12 Release the clamps and disconnect the coolant hoses from the radiator, thermostat housing and coolant pump.

13 Disconnect the hoses, undo the retaining bolt(s) and remove the coolant expansion tank. Disconnect the sensor wiring plug as the tank is withdrawn.

14 Remove the auxiliary drivebelt as described in Chapter 1 Section 6.

15 Disconnect the following wiring plugs, noting their locations and harness routing **(see illustrations)**:
a) *2148 cc engines – ECM wiring plug as described in Chapter 4A Section 13.*
b) *Wiring plug adjacent to the ECM.*
c) *Alternator and starter motor connections at the left-hand power distribution box/ battery positive clamp, then unclip the harness from the inner wing (where applicable). Where applicable, lift the rubber sealing strip, and lift the starter wiring harness from the engine compartment bulkhead.*
d) *Power steering pump (2148 cc engines)*

16 Disconnect the vacuum pipe from the brake servo unit on 2148 cc engines, or at the left-hand side of the engine on 2143 cc engines **(see illustration)**.

17 Disconnect the wiring plug, then unbolt the air conditioning compressor, and secure it to the side of the engine compartment with

4.6 Remove the air filter rear mounting bracket – 2143 cc engines

wire/string/cable ties, etc. There's no need to disconnect the refrigerant pipes. Note the wiring harness bracket on the rearmost bolt.

18 Where applicable, undo the bolt securing the power steering fluid pipe to the sump.

19 Remove the particulate filter and catalytic converter (where applicable) as described in Chapter 4B Section 3.

20 Remove the exhaust system as described in Chapter 4A Section 19.

21 Remove the exhaust mounting bracket from the transmission.

22 Remove the transmission as described in Chapter 7A Section 6 or Chapter 7B Section 6.

23 Disconnect the heater hose(s) at the engine compartment bulkhead **(see illustration)**.

4.15a Pull up the sealing strip...

4.15b ...and slide up the starter wiring harness

4.15c Where applicable, prise out the orange catch...

4.15d ...and disconnect the wiring plug from the starter lead/positive battery clamp

4.16 Squeeze together the release buttons, and disconnect the vacuum pipe to the servo – 2143 cc engine shown

4.23 Prise out the wire clip a little, and disconnect the heater hose(s)

4.24 Apply clamps, then disconnect the fuel feed and return pipes underneath the engine compartment on the left-hand side

4.28 Guide the engine forwards and upwards

24 Mark the fuel supply and return pipes to aid refitting, then disconnect them **(see illustration)**. Plug the openings to prevent contamination.
25 Undo the bolt securing the power steering pipe to the engine sump (where applicable).
26 Attach a hoist to the engine lifting eyes, and take the weight of the engine.
27 Unscrew the lower bolts from the engine front mountings.
28 With the help of an assistant, lift and tilt the engine to withdraw it from the engine compartment, taking care not to damage the surrounding components and wiring **(see illustration)**. It will be necessary to move the hoist forwards and guide the engine up through the engine compartment, taking care not to damage the surrounding components. Move the hoist forwards and lower the engine assembly to the ground.

Refitting

29 Before refitting the engine, check the condition of the engine mountings. In particular, check if they are compressed, are damaged or split, or have signs of oil leakage. If necessary, renew them with reference to Chapter 2A Section 17 or Chapter 2B Section 15.
30 The reconnection and refitting procedures are a reversal of removal, noting the following additional information.
a) Tighten all nuts and bolts to the specified torque wrench settings, where given.
b) On automatic transmission models, adjust the selector rod as described in Chapter 7B Section 3.
c) On manual transmission models, bleed the clutch hydraulic system as described in Chapter 6 Section 4.
d) Reconnect the propeller shaft to the flange on the rear of the transmission with reference to Chapter 8 Section 7.
e) Refill the power steering fluid reservoir with fresh fluid and bleed the system as described in Chapter 10 Section 24.

f) Ensure that all wiring, hoses and brackets are positioned and routed as noted before removal.
g) On completion, refill the engine with oil, and refill the cooling system as described in Chapter 1.

5 Engine overhaul – dismantling sequence

1 It is much easier to dismantle and work on the engine if it is mounted on a portable engine stand. These stands can often be hired from a tool hire shop. Before the engine is mounted on a stand, the flywheel/driveplate should be removed, so that the stand bolts can be tightened into the end of the cylinder block/crankcase.
2 If a stand is not available, it is possible to dismantle the engine with it blocked up on a sturdy workbench, or on the floor. Be extra careful not to tip or drop the engine when working without a stand.
3 If you are going to obtain a reconditioned engine, all the external components around the engine must be removed first, so that they can be transferred to the new engine (just as they will if you are doing a complete engine overhaul yourself). These components include the following.
a) Ancillary unit mounting brackets (oil filter, alternator, power steering pump, engine mountings, crankcase breather housing, etc).
b) Thermostat and housing (Chapter 3 Section 4).
c) Dipstick tube.
d) All electrical switches and sensors.
e) Inlet and exhaust manifolds (Chapter 4A Section 15).
f) Injectors and fuel pipes (Chapter 4A Section 11).
Note: When removing the external components from the engine, pay close

attention to details that may be helpful or important during refitting. Note the fitted position of gaskets, seals, spacers, pins, washers, bolts, and other small items.
4 If you are obtaining a 'short' engine (which consists of the engine cylinder block/crankcase, crankshaft, pistons and connecting rods all assembled), then the cylinder head(s), sump, oil pump, and timing chain will have to be removed also.
5 If you are planning a complete overhaul, the engine can be dismantled, and the internal components removed, in the order given below, referring to Part A or B of this Chapter unless otherwise stated.
a) Inlet and exhaust manifolds (Chapter 4A Section 15).
b) Timing chain, sprockets and tensioner (646 (2148 cc) engine only).
c) Cylinder head.
d) Flywheel/driveplate.
e) Sump.
f) Oil pump.
g) Piston/connecting rod assemblies.
h) Balance shaft assembly.
i) Crankshaft.
6 Before beginning the dismantling and overhaul procedures, make sure that you have all of the correct tools necessary. Refer to Tools and working facilities for further information.

6 Cylinder head – dismantling

Note: New and reconditioned cylinder heads are available from the manufacturer, and from engine overhaul specialists. Be aware that some specialist tools are required for the dismantling and inspection procedures, and new components may not be readily available. It may therefore be more practical and economical for the home mechanic to purchase a reconditioned head, rather than

6.4a Remove the valve cap...

6.4b ...and spring

6.5 Lift off the spring seat

dismantle, inspect and recondition the original head. A valve spring compressor tool will be required for this operation.

1 Remove the cylinder head as described in Chapter 2A Section 10 or Chapter 2B Section 10.

2 Remove the exhaust manifold as described in Chapter 4A Section 15.

3 Remove the glow plugs as described in Chapter 5B Section 3.

4 Using a valve spring compressor, compress the spring on each valve in turn until the split collets can be removed. Release the compressor, and lift off the spring cap and spring **(see illustrations)**. If, when the valve spring compressor is screwed down, the spring cap refuses to free and expose the split collets, gently tap the top of the tool, directly over the spring cap, with a light hammer. This will free the retainer.

5 Using a pair of pliers or special removal tool, carefully extract the valve stem oil seal from the top of the guide, then lift off the spring seat **(see illustration)**.

6 Withdraw the valve through the combustion chamber **(see illustration)**.

7 It is essential that each valve is stored with its collets, cap, spring, and spring seat. The valves should also be kept in their correct sequence, unless they are so badly worn that they are to be renewed. If they are going to be kept and used again, place each valve assembly in a labelled polythene bag or similar small container **(see illustration)**. Label each bag No 1 inlet, No 1 exhaust, No 2 inlet, No 2

exhaust, etc, noting that No 1 valve is nearest to the timing chain end of the engine.

---

7 Cylinder head and valves – cleaning and inspection

1 Thorough cleaning of the cylinder head and valve components, followed by a detailed inspection, will enable you to decide how much valve service work must be carried out during the engine overhaul. **Note:** *If the engine has been severely overheated, it is best to assume that the cylinder head is warped – check carefully for signs of this.*

Cleaning

2 Scrape away all traces of old gasket material from the cylinder head.

3 Scrape away the carbon from the combustion chambers and ports, then wash the cylinder head thoroughly with paraffin or a suitable solvent.

4 Scrape off any heavy carbon deposits that may have formed on the valves, then use a power-operated wire brush to remove deposits from the valve heads and stems.

Inspection

Note: *Be sure to perform all the following inspection procedures before concluding that the services of a machine shop or engine overhaul specialist are required. Make a list of all items that require attention.*

Cylinder head

5 Inspect the head very carefully for cracks, evidence of coolant leakage, and other damage. If cracks are found, a new cylinder head should be obtained.

6 Use a straight-edge and feeler blade to check that the cylinder head gasket surface is not distorted **(see illustration)**. If it is, it may be possible to have it machined, provided that the cylinder head is not reduced to less than the specified height.

7 Examine the valve seats in each of the combustion chambers. If they are severely pitted, cracked, or burned, they will need to be renewed or recut by an engine overhaul specialist. If they are only slightly pitted, this can be removed by grinding-in the valve heads and seats with fine valve-grinding compound, as described later in this Section.

8 Check the valve guides for wear by inserting the relevant valve, and checking for side-to-side motion of the valve. A very small amount of movement is acceptable. If the movement seems excessive, remove the valve. Measure the valve stem diameter (see later in this Section), and renew the valve if it is worn. If the valve stem is not worn, the wear must be in the valve guide, and the guide must be renewed. The renewal of new valve guides should be entrusted to a Mercedes-Benz dealer or engine overhaul specialist, who will have the necessary tools available.

9 If renewing the valve guides, the valve seats

6.6 Remove the valves from the combustion chamber

6.7 Store the valve components in a labelled bag

7.6 Use a straight-edge and feeler blade to check the cylinder head gasket face for distortion

7.12 Measure the valve stem diameter with a micrometer

should be recut or reground only after the guides have been fitted.

10 Examine the camshaft bearing surfaces in the cylinder head and the bearing caps for signs of wear or damage. If the bearings are excessively worn, consult a Mercedes-Benz dealer, or an engine overhaul specialist for further advice.

Valves

⚠️ **Warning: The exhaust valves on most petrol and diesel engines are filled with sodium to improve their heat transfer. Sodium is a highly reactive substance, and will ignite or explode spontaneously on contact with water (including water vapour in the air). These valves must NOT be disposed of as ordinary scrap. Seek advice from a Mercedes-Benz dealer when disposing of the valves.**

11 Examine the head of each valve for pitting, burning, cracks, and general wear. Check the valve stem for scoring and wear ridges. Rotate the valve, and check for any obvious indication that it is bent. Look for pits or excessive wear on the tip of each valve stem. Renew any valve that shows any such signs of wear or damage.

12 If the valve appears satisfactory at this stage, measure the valve stem diameter at several points using a micrometer **(see illustration)**. Any significant difference in the readings obtained indicates wear of the valve stem. Should any of these conditions be apparent, the valve(s) must be renewed.

8.1 Lubricate the stems of the valves before inserting them

13 If the valves are in satisfactory condition, they should be ground (lapped) into their respective seats, to ensure a smooth, gas-tight seal. If the seat is only lightly pitted, or if it has been recut, fine grinding compound should be used to produce the required finish. Coarse valve-grinding compound should not be used, unless a seat is badly burned or deeply pitted. If this is the case, the cylinder head and valves should be inspected, to decide whether seat recutting, or even the renewal of the valve or seat insert (where possible) is required.

14 Valve grinding is carried out as follows. Place the cylinder head upside-down on a bench.

15 Smear a trace of (the appropriate grade of) valve-grinding compound on the seat face, and press a suction grinding tool onto the valve head. With a semi-rotary action, grind the valve head to its seat, lifting the valve occasionally to redistribute the grinding compound. A light spring placed under the valve head will greatly ease this operation.

16 If coarse grinding compound is being used, work only until a dull, matt even surface is produced on both the valve seat and the valve, then wipe off the used compound, and repeat the process with fine compound. When a smooth unbroken ring of light grey matt finish is produced on both the valve and seat, the grinding operation is complete. Do not grind-in the valves any further than absolutely necessary, or the seat will be prematurely sunk into the cylinder head.

17 When all the valves have been ground-in, carefully wash off all traces of grinding

compound using paraffin or a suitable solvent, before reassembling the cylinder head.

Valve components

18 Examine the valve springs for signs of damage and discoloration. Compare the length of the valve springs with that of a new component, where possible, and if necessary renew the springs.

19 Stand each spring on a flat surface, and check it for squareness. If any of the springs are damaged, distorted or have lost their tension, obtain a complete new set of springs. It is normal to renew the valve springs as a matter of course if a major overhaul is being carried out.

20 Renew the valve stem oil seals regardless of their apparent condition.

Hydraulic tappets

21 Refer to Chapter 2A Section 9 or Chapter 2B Section 9 for further details.

---

8 Cylinder head – reassembly

---

1 Lubricate the stems of the valves, and insert the valves into their original locations **(see illustration)**. If new valves are being fitted, insert them into the locations to which they have been ground.

2 Refit the spring seat.

3 Working on the first valve, dip the new valve stem seal in fresh engine oil. New seals are normally supplied with protective sleeves, which should be fitted to the tops of the valve stems to prevent the collet grooves from damaging the oil seals. If no sleeves are supplied, wind a little thin tape round the top of the valve stems to protect the seals. Carefully locate the seal over the valve and onto the guide. Take care not to damage the seal as it is passed over the valve stem. Use a suitable socket or tube to press the seal firmly onto the guide **(see illustrations)**. Remove the sleeve from the valve stem.

4 Locate the valve spring on top of the seat, then refit the spring cap. On engines where the spring is tapered, make sure that the large diameter end of the spring locates on the seat.

8.3a Locate the protective sleeve on the valve stem...

8.3b ...then oil the new valve stem seal...

8.3c ...and press it onto the valve guide

8.5 Fit the split collets

9.3a Undo the bolts in the timing chain tunnel (camshafts removed for clarity)…

9.3b …and the bolt in the left-hand rear corner

9.6a Timing cover bolts accessible from the rear…

5 Fit the compressor tool, then compress the valve spring and locate the split collets in the recess in the valve stem **(see illustration)**. Release the compressor, then repeat the procedure on the remaining valves.
6 With all the valves installed, support the cylinder head on blocks of wood and, using a hammer and interposed block of wood, tap the end of each valve stem to settle the components.
7 Refit the glow plugs as described in Chapter 5B Section 3.
8 Refit the exhaust manifold as described in Chapter 4A Section 15.
9 Refit the cylinder head(s) as described in Part A or Part B of this Chapter.

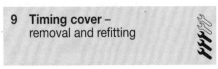

9 **Timing cover –**
removal and refitting

Note: *This procedure applies only to the type 651 (2143 cc) engine.*

Removal

1 Remove the flywheel/driveplate as described in Chapter 2B Section 13.
2 Remove the cylinder head cover as described in Chapter 2B Section 4.
3 Undo the 3 bolts securing the rear of the cylinder head to the timing cover **(see illustrations)**.
4 Disconnect the hose, then disconnect

9.6b …and right-hand side of the engine

the wiring plug at the top of the timing cover.
5 Undo the retaining bolts and move the fuel pipe assembly to one side.
6 Unscrew the bolts and carefully prise the timing cover from place **(see illustrations)**.
Caution: Do not prise between the cylinder head and the timing cover – the mating surfaces and cylinder head gasket are easily damaged.

9.6c Leverage points are provided between the timing cover and crankcase

9.8 Apply a 2.0 mm bead of sealant as indicated by the thick, black line

A M8 x 90 mm
B M8 x 60 mm
C M8 x 30 mm
D M8 x 60 mm
E M8 x 30 mm

9.9 Timing cover bolts details

Refitting

7 Clean the mating surfaces of the timing cover, cylinder head and crankcase, removing all traces of sealant, oil and dirt. Take care not to damage/scratch the sealing surfaces – use a non-abrasive cleaner, then prise the crankshaft oil seal from the cover.

8 Apply a continuous 2.0 mm bead of silicone sealant (MB recommend Loctite 5970) to the timing cover as shown **(see illustration)**.
Note: *The timing cover must be refitted within 7 minutes of the sealing being applied as it will start to harden.*

10.3 Make alignment marks between the gears

9 Manoeuvre the timing cover into position, then insert the retaining bolts **(see illustration)** and tighten them to the torque specified in Chapter 2B Section 0.
10 The remainder of refitting is a reversal of removal, noting the following points:
a) *Fit a new crankshaft rear oil seal as described in Chapter 2B Section 14, prior to refitting the flywheel/driveplate.*
b) *Upon completion, check for oil leaks prior to venturing onto the road.*

10 Timing gears – removal and refitting

Note: *These procedures only applies to the type 651 (2413 cc) engine.*

Intermediate gears

Removal

1 Set the engine at TDC on No.1 cylinder as described in Chapter 2B Section 3.
2 Remove the timing cover as described in Section 9.
3 Using paint or permanent marker, make alignment marks between the intermediate gears and the crankshaft gear, balance shaft

gears, oil/vacuum pump and fuel pump gears **(see illustration)**.
4 Undo the retaining bolts and gently pull the gears from place **(see illustration)**.
5 Examine the gears for signs of damage, wear or deterioration, and replace if necessary.

Refitting

6 Ensure the engine is still set to TDC on No.1 cylinder.
7 Slide one of the intermediate gears into position as far as the backlash compensator element **(see illustration)**. Align the previously made marks where applicable, allowing for the marks to be slightly out (in a clockwise direction) due to the spring-loaded design of the backlash compensator element.
8 Using a plastic tool, apply slight anti-clockwise pressure to the backlash compensator element, whilst at the same time, pressing the gear into place **(see illustration)**.
9 If the gear is correctly installed, there should be zero clearance between the backlash compensator element of the intermediate gear and the adjoining gears.
10 Insert the retaining bolt and tighten it to the specified torque, then repeat this procedure on the remaining intermediate gear.

10.4 Undo the bolt and pull the gear from place

10.7 Slide the gear into place, aligning the marks (see text)

10.8 Use a plastic tool to move the backlash compensator element anti-clockwise slightly

10.12 The faint line on the balance shaft should align with the raised lug on the housing

10.20 Timing chain side rail (2) and bearing pin (1)

10.21 Fuel pump drive gear retaining bolts

11 If the basic timing position of the camshafts has been lost, set the camshaft timing as described in Chapter 2B Section 3.

12 If the basic timing position of the balancer shafts have been lost, remove the lower section of the sump and oil pick-up tube and baffle plate (see Chapter 2B Section 11), then with the engine set to TDC on No.1 cylinder (Chapter 2B Section 3), The mark on each balancer shaft must align with the corresponding marks on the housing **(see illustration)**.

Note: *On the accompanying illustration, the mark on the shaft is shown slightly mis-aligned with the raised lug. This is because due to lighting conditions etc., it was impossible to photograph with the mark/lug accurately aligned.*

13 If the balancer shaft timing is not correct, the shaft gear retaining bolts must be slackened, and Mercedes special tool No. 651 589 02 63 00 slid into place over the corresponding sections of the shafts, locking them in the correct position (with the previously described marks aligned), whilst the gear retaining bolts are tightened to the specified torque. In the absence of these tools, we suggest that the engine is taken to a suitably equipped dealer/repairer and have them set the position of the shafts.

14 The remainder of refitting is a reversal of removal.

Fuel pump drive gear

Removal

15 Set the engine at TDC on No.1 cylinder as described in Chapter 2B Section 3.

16 Remove the timing cover as described in Section 9.

17 Remove the sump as described in Chapter 2B Section 11.

18 Remove the timing chain tensioner as described in Chapter 2B Section 8.

19 Referring to the description earlier in this Section, remove the intermediate drive gear between the crankshaft and the fuel pump.

20 Thread a suitable bolt into the end of the timing chain side rail bearing pin, attach a slide-hammer to the pin and pull it from place **(see illustration)**.

21 Undo the retaining bolts, detach the fuel pump drive gear from the pump shaft, and disengage it from the timing chain **(see illustration)**.

Refitting

22 Refitting is a reversal of removal.

11 Oil pump (2143 cc engine only) – removal, inspection and refitting

Removal

1 Set the engine at TDC on No.1 cylinder as described in Chapter 2B Section 3.

2 Remove the timing cover as described in Section 9.

3 Remove the vacuum pump as described in Chapter 9 Section 19.

4 Remove the lower section of the sump as described in Chapter 2B Section 11.

5 Undo the bolts and remove the oil pump pick-up tube. Renew the O-ring seal.

6 Remove the intermediate gear between the crankshaft and oil pump drive gear as described in Section 10.

7 Undo the 2 retaining bolts and withdraw the oil pump assembly from the crankcase **(see illustration)**.

Inspection

8 It would appear at the time of writing that the oil pump is only available as a complete assembly. Consequently, no dismantling

11.7 Oil pump retaining bolts

of the pump is recommend. If the pump is faulty, the complete assembly may need to be replaced. Consult a Mercedes-Benz dealer or specialist.

Refitting

9 Prior to fitting the oil pump, fill it with clean engine oil.

10 Manoeuvre the pump into the crankcase, then insert the retaining bolts and tighten them to the specified torque.

11 The remainder of refitting is a reversal of removal.

12 Piston/connecting rod assembly – removal

1 Remove the cylinder head, flywheel/driveplate, sump and oil pump (2148 cc engines only) as described in Chapter 2A or Chapter 2B as applicable. Where fitted, remove the oil pick-up tube and baffle plate from the base of the crankcase.

2 If there is a pronounced wear ridge at the top of any bore, it may be necessary to remove it with a scraper or ridge reamer, to avoid piston damage during removal. Such a ridge indicates excessive wear of the cylinder bore.

3 Check the connecting rods and big-end caps for identification marks. Both rods and caps should be marked with the cylinder number on the inlet manifold side of each assembly. Note that No 1 cylinder is at the timing chain end of the engine on 2148 cc engines, but at the front of the engine on 2143 cc models. If no marks are present, using a hammer and centre-punch, paint or similar, mark each connecting rod and big-end bearing cap with its respective cylinder number on the flat-machined surface provided – note on which side of the connecting rods the marks are made.

4 Similarly, check the piston crowns for a direction marking. An arrow on each piston crown should point towards the timing chain end of the engine. On some engines, this mark may be obscured by carbon build-up, in which case the piston crown should be

13.2 Crankshaft rear oil seal housing

13.7 Main bearing cap bolts

14.7 Piston oil spray jet

cleaned to check for a mark. In some cases, the direction arrow may have worn off, in which case a suitable mark should be made on the piston crown using a scriber – do not deeply score the piston crown, but ensure that the mark is easily visible.

5 Turn the crankshaft to bring piston No 1 to BDC (bottom dead centre).

6 Unscrew the bolts from No 1 piston big-end bearing cap. Take off the cap, and recover the bottom half bearing shell. If the bearing shells are to be re-used, tape the cap and the shell together.

7 Using a hammer handle, push the piston up through the bore, and remove it from the top of the cylinder block. Take care not to damage the piston cooling oil spay jets in the cylinder block as the piston/connecting rod assembly is removed. Recover the bearing shell, and tape it to the connecting rod for safekeeping.

8 Loosely refit the big-end cap to the connecting rod, and secure with the bolts – this will help to keep the components in their correct order.

9 Remove No 4 piston assembly in the same way before turning the crankshaft.

10 Turn the crankshaft as necessary to bring the remaining pistons to BDC, and remove them in the same manner.

13 Crankshaft – removal

1 Remove the sump, the timing chain cover, timing chain, crankshaft sprocket, and the flywheel/driveplate, as described in Part A or B of this Chapter.

2 On 2148 cc engines, unbolt the crankshaft rear oil seal housing from the cylinder block **(see illustration)**.

3 On 2143 cc engines, unbolt and remove the front cover from the crankshaft, then unbolt the baffle plate from the crankcase (where fitted).

4 Remove the pistons and connecting rods, as described in Section 12. If no work is to be done on the pistons and connecting rods, there is no need to remove the cylinder head, or to push the pistons out of the cylinder

bores. The pistons should just be pushed far enough up the bores so that they are positioned clear of the crankshaft journals.

5 Check the crankshaft endfloat as described in Section 16, then proceed as follows.

2148 cc engines

6 The crankshaft main bearing caps should be numbered from 1, starting from the front of the engine. If the bearing caps are not marked, mark them accordingly using a centre-punch. Note the orientation of the markings to ensure correct refitting.

7 Unscrew and remove the main bearing cap retaining bolts, and lift off each bearing cap **(see illustration)**. Recover the lower bearing shells, and tape them to their respective caps for safe-keeping.

8 Recover the lower endfloat control thrustwasher halves from either side of the No.3 bearing cap, noting their positions.

2143 cc engines

9 Undo the main bearing/balancer shaft housing bolts, and carefully remove the housing, noting the position of the thrustwashers from either side of the No.3 or No.4 bearing location (depending on production date).

10 Recover the lower bearing shells, and tape them to their locations in the housing for safe keeping.

All engines

11 Lift the crankshaft from the crankcase.

12 Recover the upper bearing shells from the cylinder block, and tape them to their respective caps for safe-keeping. Similarly, recover the upper thrustwasher halves, noting their orientation.

14 Cylinder block/crankcase – cleaning and inspection

Cleaning

1 Remove all external components, brackets and electrical switches/sensors from the block. Note the position of any mounting brackets before removal. For complete

cleaning, the core plugs should ideally be removed. Drill a small hole in the plugs, and then insert a self-tapping screw into the hole. Pull out the plugs by pulling on the screw with a pair of grips, or by using a slide hammer.

2 Scrape all traces of gasket from the cylinder block/crankcase, taking care not to damage the gasket/sealing surfaces.

3 Where applicable, remove the oil gallery plugs, and use new plugs when the engine is reassembled.

4 If the castings are extremely dirty, they should be steam-cleaned.

5 After the castings have been steam-cleaned, clean all oil holes and oil galleries one more time. Flush all internal passages with warm water until the water runs clear. Dry thoroughly, and apply a light film of oil to all mating surfaces, to prevent rusting. Also oil the cylinder bores. If you have access to compressed air, use it to speed up the drying process, and to blow out all the oil holes and galleries.

⚠️ **Warning: Wear eye protection when using compressed air.**

6 If the castings are not very dirty, you can do an adequate cleaning job with hot (as hot as you can stand!), soapy water and a stiff brush. Take plenty of time, and do a thorough job. Regardless of the cleaning method used, be sure to clean all oil holes and galleries very thoroughly, and to dry all components well. Protect the cylinder bores as described above, to prevent rusting.

7 Where applicable, the piston oil spray jets can be removed from the cylinder block for cleaning, however on 2148 cc engines, a special tool is required and it is recommended that an engine overhaul specialist carry out the work **(see illustration)**. The tool for removing the jets consists of an adapter, which engages the base of the jet, and a slide hammer screwed into the adapter. Renew any jets which show signs of damage. Check the oil spray hole and oil passages for blockage.

8 All threaded holes must be clean, to ensure accurate torque readings during reassembly. To clean the threads, run the correct-size tap into each of the holes to remove rust, corrosion, thread sealant or sludge, and to restore damaged threads **(see illustration)**. If possible, use compressed air to clear the holes of debris produced by this operation.

9 Ensure that all threaded holes in the cylinder block are dry.

10 After coating the mating surfaces of the new core plugs with suitable sealant, fit them to the cylinder block. Make sure that they are driven in straight and seated correctly, or leakage could result.

11 Where applicable, fit the new oil gallery plugs.

12 If the engine is not going to be reassembled right away, cover it with a large plastic bag to keep it clean; protect all mating surfaces and the cylinder bores as described above, to prevent rusting.

Inspection

13 Visually check the cylinder block/crankcase for cracks and corrosion. Look for stripped threads in the threaded holes. If there has been any history of internal water leakage, it may be worthwhile having an engine overhaul specialist check the cylinder block/crankcase with special equipment. If defects are found, have them repaired if possible, or renew the assembly.

14 Check each cylinder bore for scuffing and scoring. Check for signs of a wear ridge at the top of the cylinder, indicating that the bore is excessively worn.

15 If the cylinder walls are badly scored or scuffed, then the cylinders will have to be rebored by a suitably qualified specialist, and new oversize pistons will have to be fitted. A Mercedes-Benz dealer or engineering workshop will normally be able to supply suitable oversize pistons when carrying out the reboring work.

16 Inspect the upper surface of the cylinder block for damage. Use a straight-edge and feeler blade to check that the cylinder head gasket surface is not distorted. Note also that on in-line diesel engines, the piston protrusion must be checked whenever the cylinder head surface is machined.

17 After checking the cylinder block/crankcase, refit the items removed.

Piston protrusion

18 When inspecting the cylinder block, the piston protrusion should be checked – this is particularly important if the cylinder head face has been machined. If the piston protrusion is too great, the pistons may hit the swirl chambers when the engine is running, causing expensive damage.

19 Measure the protrusion of the piston from the sealing face of the cylinder head (a dial gauge should be used if possible). If the protrusion is greater than the specified maximum, consult a Mercedes-Benz dealer or an engine-reconditioning specialist for advice – it is likely that the cylinder block will have to be renewed.

14.8 Clean damaged threads using a tap

15 Piston/connecting rod assembly – cleaning and inspection

Cleaning

1 Before the inspection process can begin, the piston/connecting rod assemblies must be cleaned, and the original piston rings removed from the pistons.

2 Carefully expand the old rings over the top of the pistons. The use of two or three old feeler blades will be helpful in preventing the rings dropping into empty grooves **(see illustration)**. Be careful not to scratch the piston with the ends of the ring. The rings are brittle, and will snap if they are spread too far. They are also very sharp – protect your hands and fingers. Note that the third ring incorporates an expander. Always remove the rings from the top of the piston. Keep each set of rings with its piston if the old rings are to be re-used. Note which way up each ring is fitted to ensure correct refitting.

3 Scrape away all traces of carbon from the top of the piston. A hand-held wire brush (or a piece of fine emery cloth) can be used, once the majority of the deposits have been scraped away.

4 Remove the carbon from the ring grooves in the piston, using an old ring. Break the ring in half to do this (be careful not to cut your fingers – piston rings are sharp). Be careful to remove only the carbon deposits – do not remove any metal, and do not nick or scratch the sides of the ring grooves.

5 Once the deposits have been removed, clean the piston/connecting rod assembly with paraffin or a suitable solvent, and dry thoroughly. Make sure that the oil return holes in the ring grooves are clear.

Inspection

6 If the pistons and cylinder bores are not damaged or worn excessively, and if the cylinder block does not need to be rebored, the original pistons can be refitted. Measure the piston diameters, and check that they are within limits for the corresponding bore diameters. If the piston-to-bore clearance is

15.2 Use an old feeler gauge blade to help remove the piston rings

excessive, the block will have to be rebored, and new pistons and rings fitted. Normal piston wear shows up as even vertical wear on the piston thrust surfaces, and slight looseness of the top ring in its groove. New piston rings should always be used when the engine is reassembled. Note that the piston and bore size grades are stamped on the piston crowns, and on the adjacent cylinder head mating face of the cylinder block.

7 Carefully inspect each piston for cracks around the skirt, around the gudgeon pin holes, and at the piston ring 'lands' (between the ring grooves).

8 Look for scoring and scuffing on the piston skirt, holes in the piston crown, and burned areas at the edge of the crown. If the skirt is scored or scuffed, the engine may have been suffering from overheating, and/or abnormal combustion, which caused excessively high operating temperatures. The cooling and lubrication systems should be checked thoroughly. Scorch marks on the sides of the pistons show that blow-by has occurred. A hole in the piston crown, or burned areas at the edge of the piston crown, indicates that abnormal combustion (pre-ignition, knocking or detonation) has been occurring. If any of the above problems exist, the causes must be investigated and corrected, or the damage will occur again. The causes may include a faulty fuel injector.

9 Corrosion of the piston, in the form of pitting, indicates that coolant has been leaking into the combustion chamber and/or the crankcase. Again, the cause must be corrected, or the problem may persist in the rebuilt engine.

10 New pistons can be purchased from a Mercedes-Benz dealer or motor factor.

11 Examine each connecting rod carefully for signs of damage, such as cracks around the big-end and small-end bearings. Check that the rod is not bent or distorted. Damage is highly unlikely, unless the engine has been seized or badly overheated. Detailed checking of the connecting rod assembly can only be carried out by a Mercedes-Benz dealer or engine repair specialist with the necessary equipment.

12 The gudgeon pins are of the floating

15.13a Prise out the circlips…

15.13b …then press out the gudgeon pin and separate the connecting rod

16.2 Check the crankshaft end float using a dial test indicator (DTI)

type, secured in position by two circlips. The pistons and connecting rods can be separated as follows.

13 Using a small screwdriver, prise out the circlips, and push out the gudgeon pin **(see illustrations)**. Hand pressure should be sufficient to remove the pin. Identify the piston and rod to ensure correct reassembly. Discard the circlips – new ones must be used on refitting.

14 Examine the gudgeon pin and connecting rod small-end bearing for signs of wear or damage. It should be possible to push the gudgeon pin through the connecting rod bush by hand, without noticeable play. Wear can be cured by renewing both the pin and bush. Bush renewal, however, is a specialist job – press facilities are required, and the new bush must be reamed accurately.

15 The connecting rods themselves should not be in need of renewal, unless seizure or some other major mechanical failure has occurred. Check the alignment of the connecting rods visually, and if the rods are not straight, take them to an engine overhaul specialist for a more detailed check.

16 Examine all components, and obtain any new parts from your Mercedes-Benz dealer. If new pistons are purchased, they will be supplied complete with gudgeon pins and circlips. Circlips can also be purchased individually.

17 Position the piston in relation to the connecting rod as noted on removal.

18 Apply a smear of clean engine oil to the gudgeon pin. Slide it into the piston and through the connecting rod small-end. Check that the piston pivots freely on the rod, then secure the gudgeon pin in position with two new circlips. Ensure that each circlip is correctly located in its groove in the piston.

16 Crankshaft – inspection

Checking crankshaft endfloat

1 If the crankshaft endfloat is to be checked, this must be done when the crankshaft is still installed in the cylinder block/crankcase, but is free to move.

2 Check the endfloat using a dial gauge

in contact with the end of the crankshaft. Push the crankshaft fully one way, and then zero the gauge. Push the crankshaft fully the other way, and check the endfloat. The result can be compared with the specified amount, and will give an indication as to whether new thrustwasher halves are required **(see illustration)**. Note that all thrustwashers must be of the same thickness.

3 If a dial gauge is not available, feeler blades can be used. First push the crankshaft fully towards the flywheel/driveplate end of the engine, and then use feeler blades to measure the gap between the web of No 3 crankpin and the thrustwasher halves.

Inspection

4 Clean the crankshaft using paraffin or a suitable solvent, and dry it, preferably with compressed air if available. Be sure to clean the oil holes with a pipe cleaner or similar probe, to ensure that they are not obstructed.

5 Check the main and big-end bearing journals for uneven wear, scoring, pitting and cracking.

6 Big-end bearing wear is accompanied by distinct metallic knocking when the engine is running (particularly noticeable when the engine is pulling from low speed) and some loss of oil pressure.

7 Main bearing wear is accompanied by severe engine vibration and rumble – getting progressively worse as engine speed increases – and again by loss of oil pressure.

8 Check the bearing journal for roughness by running a finger lightly over the bearing surface. Any roughness (which will be accompanied by obvious bearing wear) indicates that the crankshaft requires regrinding (where possible) or renewal.

9 If the crankshaft has been reground, check for burrs around the crankshaft oil holes (the holes are usually chamfered, so burrs should not be a problem unless regrinding has been carried out carelessly). Remove any burrs with a fine file or scraper, and thoroughly clean the oil holes.

10 Have the crankshaft inspected and measured by a Mercedes Benz dealer or engine reconditioning specialist. They will be able to advise of any reconditioning work needed, and supply the appropriate replacement bearings etc.

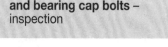

17 Main and big-end bearings, and bearing cap bolts – inspection

Bearings

1 Even though the main and big-end bearings should be renewed during the engine overhaul, the old bearings should be retained for close examination, as they may reveal valuable information about the condition of the engine. The bearing shells are graded by thickness.

2 Bearing failure can occur due to lack of lubrication, the presence of dirt or other foreign particles, overloading the engine, or corrosion. Regardless of the cause of bearing failure, the cause must be corrected before the engine is reassembled to prevent it from happening again.

3 When examining the bearing shells, remove them from the cylinder block/crankcase, the connecting rods and the connecting rod big-end bearing caps. Lay them out on a clean surface in the same general position as their location in the engine. This will enable you to match any bearing problems with the corresponding crankshaft journal. Do not touch any shell's bearing surface with your fingers while checking it, or the delicate surface may be scratched.

4 Dirt and other foreign matter get into the engine in a variety of ways. It may be left in the engine during assembly, or it may pass through filters or the crankcase ventilation system. It may get into the oil, and from there into the bearings. Metal chips from machining operations and normal engine wear are often present. Abrasives are sometimes left in engine components after reconditioning, especially when parts are not thoroughly cleaned using the proper cleaning methods. Whatever the source, these foreign objects often end up embedded in the soft bearing material, and are easily recognised. Large particles will not embed in the bearing, and will score or gouge the bearing and journal. The best prevention for this cause of bearing failure is to clean all parts thoroughly, and keep everything spotlessly clean during engine assembly. Frequent and regular engine oil and filter changes are also recommended.

5 Lack of lubrication (or lubrication breakdown) has a number of interrelated causes. Excessive heat (which thins the oil), overloading (which squeezes the oil from the bearing face) and oil leakage (from excessive bearing clearances, worn oil pump or high engine speeds) all contribute to lubrication breakdown. Blocked oil passages, which may be the result of misaligned oil holes in a bearing shell, will also oil-starve a bearing, and destroy it. When lack of lubrication is the cause of bearing failure, the bearing material is wiped or extruded from the steel backing of the bearing. Temperatures may increase to the point where the steel backing turns blue from overheating.

6 Driving habits can have a definite effect on bearing life. Full-throttle, low-speed operation (labouring the engine) puts very high loads on bearings, tending to squeeze out the oil film. These loads cause the bearings to flex, which produces fine cracks in the bearing face (fatigue failure). Eventually, the bearing material will loosen in pieces, and tear away from the steel backing.

7 Short-distance driving leads to corrosion of bearings, because insufficient engine heat is produced to drive off the condensed water and corrosive gases. These products collect in the engine oil, forming acid and sludge. As the oil is carried to the engine bearings, the acid attacks and corrodes the bearing material.

8 Incorrect bearing installation during engine assembly will lead to bearing failure as well. Tight-fitting bearings leave insufficient bearing running clearance, and will result in oil starvation. Dirt or foreign particles trapped behind a bearing shell result in high spots on the bearing, which lead to failure.

9 Do not touch any shell's bearing surface with your fingers during reassembly; there is a risk of scratching the delicate surface, or of depositing particles of dirt on it.

10 As mentioned at the beginning of this Section, the bearing shells should be renewed as a matter of course during engine overhaul; to do otherwise is false economy.

Bolts

11 It's strongly recommended that the main, and big-end bearing cap bolts are renewed regardless of their apparent condition.

18 Engine overhaul – reassembly sequence

1 Before reassembly begins, ensure that all new parts have been obtained, and that all necessary tools are available. Read through the entire procedure to familiarise yourself with the work involved, and to ensure that all items necessary for reassembly of the engine are at hand. In addition to all normal tools and materials, thread-locking compound will be needed. A suitable tube of liquid sealant (Loctite 5970 or equivalent) will also be required for the joint faces that are fitted without gaskets.

2 In order to save time and avoid problems, engine reassembly can be carried out in the following order, referring to Part A or B of this Chapter unless otherwise stated. Where applicable, use new gaskets and seals when refitting the various components.
a) Crankshaft.
b) Piston/connecting rods.
c) Oil pump.
d) Sump.
e) Flywheel/driveplate.
f) Cylinder head.
g) Timing chain, tensioner and sprockets (2148 cc engines).
h) Intermediate gears and timing cover (2143 cc engines).
i) Engine external components.

3 At this stage, all engine components should be absolutely clean and dry, with all faults repaired. The components should be laid out (or in individual containers) on a completely clean work surface.

19 Piston rings – refitting

1 Before fitting new piston rings, the ring end gaps must be checked as follows.
2 Lay out the piston/connecting rod assemblies and the new piston ring sets, so that the ring sets will be matched with the same piston and cylinder during the end gap measurement and subsequent engine reassembly.
3 Insert the top ring into the first cylinder, and push it down the bore using the top of the piston. This will ensure that the ring remains square with the cylinder walls. Position the ring near the bottom of the cylinder bore, at the lower limit of ring travel. Note that the top and second compression rings are different. The second ring is easily identified by the step on its lower surface.
4 Measure the end gap using feeler blades.
5 Repeat the procedure with the ring at the top of the cylinder bore, at the upper limit of its travel **(see illustration)**, and compare the measurements with the figures given in the Specifications.
6 If the gap is too small (unlikely if genuine Mercedes-Benz parts are used), it must

be enlarged, or the ring ends may contact each other during engine operation, causing serious damage. Ideally, new piston rings providing the correct end gap should be fitted. As a last resort, the end gap can be increased by filing the ring ends very carefully with a fine file. Mount the file in a vice equipped with soft jaws, slip the ring over the file with the ends contacting the file face, and slowly move the ring to remove material from the ends. Take care, as piston rings are sharp, and are easily broken.
7 With new piston rings, it is unlikely that the end gap will be too large. If the gaps are too large, check that you have the correct rings for your engine and for the particular cylinder bore size.
8 Repeat the checking procedure for each ring in the first cylinder, and then for the rings in the remaining cylinders. Remember to keep rings, pistons and cylinders matched up.
9 Once the ring end gaps have been checked and if necessary corrected, the rings can be fitted to the pistons.
10 Fit the piston rings using the same technique as for removal. Fit the bottom (oil control) ring first, and work up. When fitting the oil control ring, first insert the wire expander, then fit the ring with its gap positioned 180° from the protruding wire ends of the expander. Ensure that the rings are fitted the correct way up – the top surface of the rings is normally marked TOP **(see illustration)**. Arrange the gaps of the top and second compression rings 120° either side of the oil control ring gap, but make sure that none of the rings gaps are positioned over the gudgeon pin hole. **Note:** *Always follow any instructions supplied with the new piston ring sets – different manufacturers may specify different procedures. Do not mix up the top and second compression rings, as they have different cross-sections.*

20 Crankshaft – refitting

1 If the original crankshaft is in good condition and is being refitted, new main bearing shells, which are the same size as the removed shells, should be fitted.

19.5 Measure the piston ring end-gaps

19.10 Fit the oil control ring expander

20.4 Ensure that the tab on each bearing shell engages with the notch in the cap

20.7 Fit the upper thrustwasher halves

20.10a Locate the main bearing shells in the caps...

20.10b ...and lubricate them with clean engine oil

20.11a Fit the thrustwasher half to then main bearing cap (use a little grease to hold the washer in place)

20.11b Fit the No 3 main bearing cap

2 If the crankshaft has been reground, undersize bearing shells must be fitted. The engine-reconditioning specialist normally supplies the appropriate shells.

3 Clean the backs of the bearing shells, and the bearing locations in both the cylinder block/crankcase and the main bearing caps.

4 Press the bearing shells into their locations, ensuring that the tab on each shell engages in the notch in the cylinder block/crankcase or bearing cap **(see illustration)**. Take care not to touch any shell's bearing surface with your fingers. If the original bearing shells are being used for the check, ensure that they are refitted in their original locations. Note that the bearings shells with oil grooves fit in the cylinder block, and the plain bearing shells fit in the bearing caps.

5 Where applicable, ensure that the oil spray jets are fitted to the cylinder block.

6 Liberally lubricate each bearing shell in the cylinder block/crankcase and cap with clean engine oil.

7 Fit the upper thrustwasher halves to the appropriate bearing location in the cylinder block as follows **(see illustration)**.

● 2148 cc engines – No.3 main bearing.
● 2143 cc engines – No.3 or No.4 main bearing (depending on production date).

8 Ensure that any oil grooves in the thrustwasher halves face out towards the crankshaft journals.

9 The crankshaft can now be lowered into position.

2148 cc engines

10 Lubricate the lower bearing shells in the main bearing caps with clean engine oil. Make sure that the locating lugs on the shells engage with the corresponding recesses in the caps **(see illustrations)**.

11 Fit the main bearing caps to their correct locations, ensuring that they are fitted the correct way round. Ensure that the thrustwasher halves are in place on the appropriate bearing cap **(see illustrations)**.

12 Lightly lubricate the bolt threads, then fit the main bearing cap bolts. Where applicable, ensure that the oil pick-up pipe support bracket is in place on the relevant bolts, as noted before removal. Tighten the bolts by hand only at this stage.

13 Progressively tighten the main bearing cap bolts to the specified torque, starting with the centre bearing cap and working outwards. Observe the tightening stages given in the Specifications **(see illustration)**. If the bolts are angle-tightened, it is recommended that an angle-measuring gauge be used during this stage of the tightening, to ensure accuracy. If a gauge is not available, use a dab of white paint to make alignment marks between the bolt and bearing cap prior to tightening; the marks can then be used to check that the bolt has been rotated sufficiently during tightening.

14 Check that the crankshaft rotates freely.

15 Fit a new crankshaft rear oil seal to the housing, then refit the housing, using a new gasket, or suitable sealant, as applicable.

16 Refit the piston/connecting rod assemblies.

2143 cc engines

17 Locate the lower bearing shells in the balance shaft housing/main bearing bridge, and lubricate them with clean engine oil.

18 Install the thrustwashers each side of the No.3 or No.4 (depending on production date) bearing position in the housing/bridge. Ensure the oil grooves in the washer point outwards towards the crankshaft collars.

19 Gently lower the housing/bridge into position, then insert the retaining bolts and tighten them to the specified torque, starting at the middle and working outwards progressively.

20 The remainder of refitting is a reversal of removal.

20.13 Use an angle-tightening gauge

21 Piston/connecting rod assemblies – refitting

Note: *A piston ring compressor tool will be required for this operation. Note that the following procedure assumes that the main bearing caps are in place.*

1 If the big-end journals on the crankshaft are in good condition, new big-end bearing shells, which are the same size as the removed shells, should be fitted.

2 If the crankshaft has been reground, undersize bearing shells must be fitted. The engine-reconditioning specialist normally supplies the appropriate shells.

3 Clean the backs of the bearing shells, and the bearing locations in both the connecting rod and bearing cap.

4 Press the bearing shells into their locations, ensuring that the tab on each shell engages in the notch in the connecting rod and cap **(see illustrations)**. Take care not to touch the bearing surface of the shell with your fingers.

5 Lubricate the cylinder bores, the pistons, and piston rings, then lay out each piston/connecting rod assembly in its respective position **(see illustrations)**.

6 Start with assembly No 1. Make sure that the piston rings are still spaced as described in Section 17, and then clamp them in position with a piston ring compressor **(see illustration)**.

7 Insert the piston/connecting rod assembly into the top of cylinder No 1. Ensure that the arrow on the piston crown points towards the front of the engine, and that the identifying marks on the connecting rods and big-end caps are positioned as noted before removal. Using a block of wood or hammer handle against the piston crown, tap the assembly into the cylinder until the piston crown is flush with the top of the cylinder **(see illustration)**. Where applicable, take care not to damage the piston cooling oil spray jets as the piston/connecting rod assemblies are refitted.

8 Ensure that the bearing shell is still correctly installed. Liberally lubricate the crankpin and both bearing shells. Taking care not to mark the cylinder bores or damage the piston oil

21.4a Insert the bearing shells in the conrod...

21.4b ...and big-end cap

21.5a Lubricate the pistons, rings...

21.5b ...and cylinder bores

jets (where fitted), pull the piston/connecting rod assembly down the bore and onto the crankpin. Refit the big-end bearing cap **(see illustration)**. Note that the bearing shell locating tabs must abut each other. On some engines, the caps and rods are 'fractured' to ensure improved component location. Ensure the matching pair (cap and rod) are fitted together.

9 Lightly lubricate the bolt threads, then screw the big-end bearing cap bolts by hand into position in the connecting rods.

10 Progressively tighten the bolts to the specified torque and angle, observing the two tightening stages given in the Specifications. It is recommended that an angle-measuring gauge is used to angle-tighten the bolts. If a gauge is not available, use a dab of white paint to make alignment marks between the bolt and bearing cap prior to tightening; the

marks can then be used to check that the bolt has been rotated sufficiently during tightening.

11 Once the bearing cap bolts have been correctly tightened, rotate the crankshaft and check that it turns freely. Some stiffness is to be expected if new components have been fitted, but there should be no signs of binding or tight spots.

12 Refit the remaining piston/connecting rod assemblies in the same way.

22 Engine – initial start-up after overhaul

1 Refit the remainder of the engine components in the correct order listed in this Chapter. Refit the engine to the vehicle as described in the relevant Section of this

21.6 Fit a piston ring compressor

21.7 Insert the piston into the cylinder bore

21.8 Refit the big-end bearing caps

Chapter. Double-check the engine oil and coolant levels, and make a final check that everything has been reconnected. Make sure that there are no tools or rags left in the engine compartment.

2 Reconnect the battery negative lead as described in Chapter 5A Section 4.

3 Disconnect the injector harness wiring plug at the right-hand rear of the engine compartment.

4 Turn the engine using the starter motor until the oil pressure warning lamp goes out.

5 If the lamp fails to extinguish after several seconds of cranking, check the engine oil level and oil filter security. Assuming these are correct, check the security of the oil pressure switch cabling – do not progress any further until you are satisfied that oil is being pumped around the engine at sufficient pressure.

6 Reconnect the injector wiring plug.

7 Start the engine, but be aware that as fuel system components have been disturbed, the cranking time may be a little longer than usual.

8 While the engine is idling, check for fuel, water and oil leaks. Don't be alarmed if there are some odd smells and the occasional plume of smoke as components heat up and burn off oil deposits.

9 Assuming all is well; keep the engine idling until hot water is felt circulating through the top hose.

10 After a few minutes, recheck the oil and coolant levels, and top-up as necessary.

11 There is no need to retighten the cylinder head bolts once the engine has been run following reassembly.

12 If new pistons, rings or crankshaft bearings have been fitted, the engine must be treated as new, and run-in for the first 600 miles. Do not operate the engine at full-throttle, or allow it to labour at low engine speeds in any gear. It is recommended that the engine oil and filter are changed at the end of this period.

Chapter 3
Cooling, heating and ventilation systems

Contents

Section number

Air conditioning system – general information and precautions 9
Air conditioning system components – removal and refitting 10
Coolant pump – removal and refitting 5
Cooling fan assembly – removal and refitting 6
Cooling system electronic components – testing, removal
    and refitting. 7

Section number

Cooling system hoses – disconnection and renewal. 2
General information and precautions. 1
Heating and ventilation system components – removal and refitting 8
Radiator – removal, inspection and refitting. 3
Thermostat – removal, testing and refitting 4

Degrees of difficulty

Easy, suitable for novice with little experience	**Fairly easy,** suitable for beginner with some experience	**Fairly difficult,** suitable for competent DIY mechanic	**Difficult,** suitable for experienced DIY mechanic	**Very difficult,** suitable for expert DIY or professional

Specifications

System
Type . . . . Pressurised, pump-assisted with front mounted radiator and ECM controlled cooling fan

Thermostat

Operating temperatures	Starts to open	Fully open
2148 cc engines	80° C	100° C
2143 cc engine	ECM controlled	

Expansion tank
Cap pressure . . . . 1.4 bar

Air conditioning system
Refrigerant R134a
All models. . . . . 590 to 640g
Lubricating oil. . . . . MB 362.0 A 001 989 08 03

Torque wrench settings

	Nm	lbf ft
Auxiliary drivebelt guide pulley bolts:		
2148 cc engine.	35	26
2143 cc engine:		
M8	25	18
M10	45	33
Coolant pump:		
2148 cc engines:		
M6.	14	11
M8.	20	15
2143 cc engines	20	15
Facia crossmember-to-vehicle body nut/bolts	25	18
Thermostat housing:		
2148 cc engines	8	5
2143 cc engines	10	7
Compressor mounting bolts.	20	15

1 General information and precautions

General information

1 The cooling system is of pressurised type, comprising a pump, an aluminium crossflow radiator, an electric cooling fan, and a thermostat. The system functions as follows. Cold coolant from the radiator passes through the hose to the coolant pump, where it is pumped around the cylinder block and head passages. After cooling the cylinder bores, combustion surfaces and valve seats, the coolant reaches the underside of the thermostat, which is initially closed. The coolant passes through the heater and is returned through the cylinder block to the coolant pump.

2 When the engine is cold, the coolant circulates only through the cylinder block, cylinder head(s), expansion tank and heater. On 2148 cc engines, when the coolant reaches a predetermined temperature, the thermostat opens and the coolant passes through to the radiator. As the coolant circulates through the radiator, it is cooled by the inrush of air when the car is in forward motion. Airflow is supplemented by the action of the electric fan as necessary. Upon reaching the bottom of the radiator, the coolant is now cooled and the cycle is repeated. On 2143 cc engines, the action of the thermostat is controlled by a heating element within the housing, which itself is controlled by the ECM.

3 The coolant pump is mounted externally on the front of the engine, and is driven by the auxiliary drivebelt. On 2143 cc engine a regulating valve within the pump controls the flow of coolant to the various circuits – the electrically operated valve is controlled by the ECM.

4 Coolant temperature information for the gauge mounted in the instrument panel, and for the fuel system, is provided by temperature sensors mounted in the thermostat housing, left-hand coolant passage or in the cylinder head, depending on model. A coolant level switch is fitted to bottom of the radiator expansion tank on some models.

5 An electric cooling fan is fitted and serves a dual purpose, regulating both the engine

coolant temperature and that of the air conditioning refrigerant in the condenser (which is mounted in front of the radiator). Partly because of these two roles, the fan is controlled via an electronic unit.

6 All models have a remote-mounted coolant expansion tank, which is located on the left-hand side of the engine compartment and collects the coolant, which is displaced from the system as it expands due to the rise in temperature. The displaced coolant is returned to the radiator as the system cools.

7 The vehicle interior heater operates by means of coolant from the engine cooling system. Coolant flow through the heater matrix is regulated by solenoid valves, which are controlled by a temperature sensor at the front of the heater unit. Temperature control is by blending cool air from outside the vehicle (or from the air conditioning system) with the warm air from the heater matrix, in the desired ratio.

Precautions

⚠ *Warning: Do not attempt to remove the pressure cap, or disturb any part of the cooling system, while the engine is hot, as there is a high risk of scalding. If the pressure cap must be removed before the engine and radiator have fully cooled (even though this is not recommended), the pressure in the cooling system must first be relieved. Cover the cap with a thick layer of cloth, to avoid scalding, and slowly unscrew the pressure cap until a hissing sound is heard (be prepared to refit the cap quickly if bubbling noises are heard and hot coolant starts to come out). When the hissing stops, indicating that the pressure has reduced, slowly unscrew the pressure cap until it can be removed; if more hissing sounds are heard, wait until they have stopped before unscrewing the cap completely. At all times, keep your face well away from the pressure cap opening, and protect your hands.*

⚠ *Warning: Do not allow antifreeze to come into contact with your skin, or with the painted surfaces of the vehicle. Rinse off spills immediately with plenty of water. Never leave antifreeze lying around in an open container, or in a puddle in the driveway or*

on the garage floor. Children and pets are attracted by its sweet smell, but antifreeze can be fatal if ingested.

⚠ *Warning: The cooling fan could cut in even if the engine is not running (if the ignition is on). Be careful to keep your hands, hair, and any loose clothing well clear when working in the engine compartments.*

2 Cooling system hoses – disconnection and renewal

⚠ *Warning: Never work on the cooling system when it is hot. Release any pressure from the system by loosening the expansion tank cap, having first covered it with a cloth to avoid any possibility of scalding.*

1 The number, routing and pattern of hoses will vary according to model, but the same basic procedure applies. Before commencing work, make sure that the new hoses are to hand, along with new hose clips if needed. It is good practice to renew the hose clips at the same time as the hoses.

2 Drain the cooling system as described in Chapter 1 Section 30, saving the coolant if it is fit for re-use. Squirt a little penetrating oil onto the hose clips if they are corroded.

3 Release the hose clips from the hose concerned. The clip most commonly used on the Mercedes-Benz is the spring clip, which is released by squeezing its tags together with pliers, at the same time working the clip away from the hose stub **(see illustration)**. The worm-drive clip is released by turning its screw anti-clockwise **(see illustration)**. The 'sardine-can' clips are not re-usable, and are best cut off with snips or side cutters.

4 Unclip any wires, cables or other hoses, which may be attached to the hose being removed. Make notes for reference when reassembling, if necessary.

5 Release the hose from its stubs with a twisting motion. Be careful not to damage the stubs on delicate components such as the radiator, or thermostat housings. If the hose is stuck fast, the best course is often to cut it off using a sharp knife, but again be careful not to damage the stubs.

6 Before fitting the new hose, smear the stubs with washing-up liquid or a suitable rubber lubricant to aid fitting. Do not use oil or grease, which may attack the rubber.

7 Fit the hose clips over the ends of the hose, and then fit the hose over its stubs. Work the hose into position. When satisfied, locate and tighten the hose clips.

8 Refill the cooling system as described in Chapter 1 Section 30. Run the engine, and check that there are no leaks.

9 Recheck the tightness of the hose clips on any new hoses after a few hundred miles.

10 Top-up the coolant level if necessary (see *Weekly checks*).

2.3a Spring type hose clips...   **2.3b ...and worm-drive hose clips**

3.4 Radiator undertray right-hand fasteners

3.5 Prise out the wire clips a little, and pull the hoses from the intercooler

3.7a Prise out the wire clip a little, then pull the coolant hose from the left-hand side...

3.7b ...the right-hand side...

3.7c ...and the top right-hand corner of the radiator

3.8 Lift the clip each side securing the intercooler to the radiator

3 Radiator – removal, inspection and refitting

Removal

1 Drain the cooling system as described in Chapter 1 Section 30.
2 Remove the plastic cover from the top of the engine.
3 Remove the cooling fan assembly as described in Section 6.
4 Release the fasteners and remove the undertray beneath the radiator **(see illustration)**.
5 Release the clamps and disconnect the charge air hoses to and from the intercooler **(see illustration)**.
6 Lift the radiator/condenser/intercooler assembly, and move it towards the engine.
7 Disconnect the wiring plugs from the radiator, then release the clips and disconnect the coolant hoses from the radiator **(see illustrations)**.
8 Unclip the intercooler from the radiator and manoeuvre it from place **(see illustration)**. Release any wiring harnesses from the intercooler air ducting as it becomes accessible.
9 On automatic transmission models, disconnect the fluid cooling pipes from the radiator. Plug the openings to prevent contamination.
10 Squeeze together the clip each side, and

lower the condenser from the radiator **(see illustration 10.31)**.
11 Lift the radiator upwards from place, and recover the rubber mountings from the base **(see illustration)**.

Inspection

12 If the radiator was removed because of clogging (causing overheating) then try reverse flushing using a garden hose or, in severe cases, use a radiator cleanser strictly in accordance with the manufacturer's instructions.
13 Use a soft brush and an air line or garden hose to clear the radiator matrix of leaves, insects etc.
14 Major leaks or extensive damage should be repaired by a specialist, or the radiator should be renewed or exchanged for a reconditioned unit.

3.11 Recover the rubber mountings at the base of the radiator

15 Examine the mounting rubbers for signs of damage or deterioration and renew if necessary.

Refitting

16 Refitting the radiator is the reverse sequence to removal, noting the following points:
a) *Ensure that the lower mounting lugs properly engage with the rubber mountings, and that (where applicable) the locating studs are pressed fully home.*
b) *Make sure that the radiator and fan shroud retaining clips are a secure fit.*
c) *After fitting, fill the cooling system as described in Chapter 1 Section 30.*
d) *On automatic transmission models, check the transmission fluid level as described in Chapter 7B Section 5.*

4 Thermostat – removal, testing and refitting

Removal

1 Drain the coolant as described in Chapter 1 Section 30.
2 Remove the plastic cover from the top of the engine.

2148 cc engines

3 Disconnect the temperature sensor wiring plug.

4.4 Engine cover mounting bracket bolt

4.5 Disconnect the hoses from the thermostat housing

4.6 Remove the shield inform the housing

4.7 Disconnect the pressure sensor wiring plug

4.8 Thermostat housing bolts

4 Undo the bolt and remove the engine cover mounting bracket (see illustration).

5 Release the clamps and disconnect the coolant hoses from the thermostat housing (see illustration).

6 Unbolt the shield from in front of the thermostat housing (see illustration).

7 Disconnect the wiring plug from the pressure sensor on the end of the fuel (common) rail (see illustration).

8 Unclip the wiring harness to improve access, then undo the retaining bolts and remove the thermostat (see illustration). Renew the seal. No further dismantling of the thermostat is recommended. If faulty, the complete unit must be replaced.

2143 cc engines

9 Release the clamps and remove the intake hose upstream of the air filter assembly.

10 Disconnect the wiring plugs from the temperature sensor and heating element at the thermostat housing (see illustration).

11 Note their fitted locations, then disconnect the various coolant hoses from the thermostat housing (see illustrations).

12 Undo the retaining bolts and remove the thermostat housing (see illustrations). Note that no attempt must be made to remove the heating element from the housing – if defective the complete housing must be renewed.

4.10 Temperature sensor and heating element wiring plugs

4.11a Disconnect the various hoses...

4.11b ...from the thermostat housing

4.12a Undo the bolts at the front...

4.12b ...and top of the thermostat housing

Testing

Note: *This information applies only to the 2148 cc engine.*

13 If the thermostat remains in the open position at room temperature, then it is faulty and the complete housing assembly must be renewed.

14 To test it fully, suspend the (closed) thermostat housing on a length of string in a container of cold water, with a thermometer beside it.

15 Heat the water and check the temperature at which the thermostat begins to open. Compare this value with that specified. Continue to heat the water until the thermostat is fully open. Allow the thermostat to cool down and check that it closes fully.

16 If the thermostat does not open and close as described, if it sticks in either position, or if it does not open at the specified temperature, then it must be renewed.

Refitting

17 Refitting is a reversal of removal, but note the following additional points:

a) *Clean all mating surfaces thoroughly before reassembly.*
b) *Renew the thermostat housing seal/gasket regardless of condition (where applicable).*
c) *Renew the hose O-ring seals if they show signs of deterioration.*
d) *Tighten all bolts to their specified torque wrench settings (where given).*
e) *Ensure the coolant hose clips are positioned so that they do not foul any*

5.3a Prise out the plastic caps...

other component, then tighten them securely.
f) *Refill the cooling system as described in Chapter 1 Section 30.*

5 Coolant pump – removal and refitting

Removal

1 Drain the cooling system as described in Chapter 1 Section 30.
2 Remove the auxiliary drivebelt as described in Chapter 1 Section 6.

2148 cc engines

3 Remove the plastic caps and remove the belt guide pulleys from the oil filter lower housing and coolant pump **(see illustrations)**.

5.3b ...and remove the guide pulleys

4 Release the clamps and disconnect the coolant hoses from the pump.
5 Undo the retaining bolts and remove the heat shield adjacent to the pump.
6 Loosen and remove the bolts securing the coolant pump, noting their locations, as they are of different lengths and sizes **(see illustration)**.
7 Withdraw the pump, and recover the gasket **(see illustration)**. Discard the gasket, as a new one will be required when refitting.

2143 cc engines

8 Release the clamps and disconnect the various coolant hoses from the pump **(see illustrations)**.
9 Undo the bolt and remove the belt guide pulley from beneath the pump **(see illustration)**.
10 Undo the bolts and remove the support bracket beneath the pump **(see illustration)**.

5.6 Note the different sizes of the coolant pump retaining bolts

5.7 Renew the coolant pump gasket

5.8a Disconnect the hoses on the right-hand side of the pump...

5.8b ...and the hose to the thermostat housing

5.9 Remove the belt guide pulley

5.10 Remove the support bracket

5.11 Pull the vacuum hose from the pump

5.13a Coolant pump retaining bolts

5.13b Renew the pump seal

5.14 Undo the bolts and detach the coolant pipe

6.3a Rotate the centre fastener 90° anti-clockwise...

6.3b ...and release the 3 clips at the rear of the panel – 1 in the centre, and 1 each side

11 Disconnect the vacuum hose from the top of the pump (see illustration).
12 Detach the harness clip from the base of the pump, and move it to one side.
13 Undo the retaining bolts and manoeuvre the coolant pump from place (see illustrations). Pull the turbocharger bypass flap linkage downwards to facilitate pump removal. Renew the seal.
14 If required, undo the bolts and detach the coolant pipe from the pump (see illustration). Renew the O-ring seal.

Refitting

15 Carefully clean the coolant pump and cylinder block mating surfaces, removing all traces of the old gasket or sealant. Take care to avoid scoring the surfaces, as this will cause leakage.
16 Refit the coolant pump by following the removal procedure in reverse, noting these points:
a) Fit a new gasket when refitting the pump.
b) Tighten the pump bolts in a diagonal sequence to the correct torque, noting the different figures for the different size bolts used.
c) Refit the auxiliary drivebelt as described in Chapter 1 Section 6.
d) On completion, refill the cooling system as described in Chapter 1 Section 30.

6 Cooling fan assembly – removal and refitting

Removal

1 Remove the plastic cover from the top of the engine.
2 Unclip the air intake duct from air filter and cold air intake.
3 Release the clips and remove the cold air intake duct/panel from the bonnet slam panel (see illustrations).
4 Where fitted, remove the plastic covers above each headlight (see illustration).
5 Remove the radiator 'holders' each side (see illustration).

6.4 Prise up the centre pins, and lift the covers from place

6.5 Prise up the radiator 'holder' each side

6.6a Undo the bolts in the centre...

6.6b ...and the bolts each side

6 Undo the retaining bolts and remove the centre reinforcement panel **(see illustrations)**. Unclip the bonnet release cable as the panel is withdrawn.

7 Unclip the upper air ducting retaining lug from the fan assembly **(see illustration)**.

8 Where fitted, unclip the coolant hose from the brackets on the fan shroud.

9 Working at the left-hand side of the shroud, disconnect the fan motor wiring plug, and unclip the harness.

10 Where fitted, disconnect the vacuum pipe and wiring plug from the radiator shutters adjuster **(see illustration)**.

11 Press the catches each side apart and unclip the lower air duct from the underside of the fan unit **(see illustration)**.

12 On automatic transmission models, undo the bolt securing the oil cooler pipes to the fan unit.

13 Where applicable, unclip the coolant hose from the fan unit.

14 Manoeuvre the fan shroud upwards from place **(see illustration)**. Take great care not to damage the radiator during this procedure.

15 If required, prise up the cover, release the wiring harness, undo the screws and remove the fan motor **(see illustration)**.

Refitting

16 Refitting is a reversal of removal.

7 Cooling system electronic components – testing, removal and refitting

Engine coolant temperature sensor (ECT)

Testing

1 The engine coolant temperature sensor monitors the temperature of the coolant as it leaves the engine. The sensor is a 'thermistor', i.e. the resistance of the sensor changes as the temperature changes. The signal from the sensor is used by the engine management ECM (electronic control module) to regulate fuel injection quantity and timing, glow plugs, cooling fan operation, and the temperature gauge in the instrument cluster. Should the sensor fail, the ECM will adopt a pre-determined substitute value, and illuminate the MIL (malfunction indicator lamp) on the instrument cluster. No specific test values are available for the sensor. Consequently, testing is limited to inspecting the wiring and connectors to the sensor. Further

6.7 Release the clips each side and remove the upper air ducting

6.10 Disconnect the vacuum pipe and wiring plug

6.11 Press the catches apart to release them

6.14 Manoeuvre the fan shroud upwards

6.15 Fan motor retaining screws

7.4a Coolant temperature sensor on the thermostat housing – 2148 cc engines

7.4b The coolant temperature sensor is clipped into the thermostat housing – 2143 cc engines

7.9 The switch-over valve is located at the front of the engine

7.13 Coolant level sensor

8.5a Gently prise the panel rearwards...

8.5b ...to release the clips

investigation can only be carried out by the use of dedicated test equipment. Consult your Mercedes-Benz dealer or fuel injection specialist. Testing by any other means could result in ECM damage.

Removal

2 Drain the cooling system as described in Chapter 1 Section 30.

3 Remove the plastic cover from the top of the engine.

4 Disconnect the coolant temperature sensor wiring plug **(see illustrations)**.

5 Pull out the retaining clip and withdraw the sensor. Discard the sealing ring – a new one must be fitted.

Refitting

6 Refit the sensor with a new O-ring seal, and secure it with the retaining clip.

7 The remainder of refitting is a reversal of

8.6 Use a screwdriver to depress the clips and pull the panel from place

removal. Top up the coolant as described in Chapter 1 Section 30.

Coolant pump switch-over valve

Note: *This valve is only fitted to the 2143 cc engine*

.8 Remove the plastic cover from the top of the engine.

9 Disconnect the wiring plug from the switch-over valve **(see illustration)**.

10 Disconnect the vacuum hoses, release the clip and remove the valve.

11 Refitting is a reversal of removal.

Coolant level sensor

Testing

12 The level sensor is fitted to the base of the coolant expansion tank. Should a sensor fail, testing is only possible using Mercedes test equipment.

8.7 Undo the screws at the top of the panel

Removal and refitting

13 The sensor is integral with the coolant expansion tank **(see illustration)**. If the sensor is faulty, the complete assembly may need to be replaced. Check with a Mercedes dealer or parts specialist.

8 Heating and ventilation system components – removal and refitting

Heater control panel

Removal

1 Securely apply the handbrake, then move the selector lever (on automatic transmission models) to the rearmost position.

2 Disconnect the battery negative lead as described in Chapter 5A Section 4.

3 On vehicles from 2012 model year, remove the radio/audio unit as described in Chapter 12 Section 16.

Vehicles up to 28/02/11

4 Open the ashtray cover.

5 Carefully prise the surround panel from the control panel **(see illustrations)**.

6 Press the 2 clips at the top of the panel downwards a little, pull the control panel rearwards and disconnect the wiring plugs **(see illustration)**.

Vehicles from 01/03/11

7 Undo the 2 screws at the top of the control panel **(see illustration)**.

8.12 Starting at the front, pull up the door sill trim panel

8.13 Pull the lower A-pillar trim panel rearwards

8.14 Passengers side lower facia panel retaining screws

8 Manoeuvre the heater control panel rearwards, disconnecting the wiring plugs as they become accessible.

Refitting

9 Refitting is a reversal of removal.
10 If a new panel has been fitted, it will need to be reset using Mercedes-Benz diagnostic equipment. Entrust this task to a Mercedes-Benz dealer or suitably equipped specialist.

Heater blower motor

Removal

11 Move the passengers sear fully rearwards.
12 Pull up the door sill trim panel **(see illustration)**.
13 Pull away the weatherstrip at the front of the door opening, then pull the lower A-pillar trim panel rearwards and remove it **(see illustration)**.

14 Undo the 3 retaining screws and remove the passengers side lower facia panel **(see illustration)**. Disconnect any wiring plugs as the panel is withdrawn.
15 On vehicles from 01.06.10, remove the glove box as described in Chapter 11 Section 35.
16 Disconnect the blower motor wiring plug **(see illustration)**. Unclip any wiring harness from the motor casing.
17 Twist the blower motor to align the two marks, then manoeuvre it from place **(see illustrations)**.

Refitting

18 Refitting is a reversal of removal.

Heater blower motor control unit

19 Remove the passengers side lower facia panel as described in 'Heater blower motor' earlier in this Section.

Vehicles up to 31.05.10

20 Disconnect the wiring plug from the control unit, and slide the connector from placer.
21 Rotate the control unit anti-clockwise and remove it **(see illustration)**.

Vehicles from 01.06.10

22 Disconnect the wiring plugs from the control unit **(see illustration)**.
23 Undo the 2 retaining screws and remove the control unit.

All vehicles

24 Refitting is a reversal of removal.

Heater matrix

Removal

25 Remove the heater/air conditioning housing as described in this Section, and remove the insulation from the front of the housing **(see illustration)**.

8.16 Disconnect the wiring plug and unclip the harness

8.17a Lift the tab slightly...

8.17b ...and align the two marks

8.21 Rotate the control unit anti-clockwise

8.22 Blower motor control unit

8.25 Remove the insulation

8.26 Disconnect the power and earth cables

8.27 Matrix retaining bracket screw

8.28a Undo the screws...

26 On models with an auxiliary electrical heating element, disconnect the power and earth cables and move them to one side **(see illustration)**.

27 Undo the bolt and remove the matrix retaining bracket **(see illustration)**.

28 Undo the screws, remove the rubber seal, then remove the clamping bracket around the pipes **(see illustrations)**.

29 Release the clamps securing the pipes to the matrix **(see illustration)**. Renew the pipe seals.

30 Remove the heater matrix pipes **(see illustration)**.

31 Lift out the heater matrix, taking care not to damage the sealing tape **(see illustration)**.

Refitting

32 Refitting is a reversal of removal. Top up the cooling system as described in Chapter 1 Section 30.

8.28b ...peel away the rubber seal...

Heater/air conditioning housing

33 On models with air conditioning, have the refrigerant circuit evacuated by a Mercedes Benz dealer or suitably equipped specialist.

8.28c ...and remove the clamping bracket

34 Remove the wiper motor linkage assembly Chapter 12 Section 14.

35 Drain the cooling system as described in Chapter 1 Section 30, or apply clamps to the coolant hoses at the engine compartment bulkhead.

36 Working at the rear of the engine compartment, disconnect the heater hoses, undo the retaining nuts, and pull the refrigerant pipes from the connection at the bulkhead **(see illustration)**. Plug the openings to prevent contamination. Renew the pipe seals.

37 Remove the entire facia as described in Chapter 11 Section 37.

38 Working on the passengers side, disconnect the wiring plugs, unclip and remove the media interface control unit **(see illustration)**.

39 Note the routing, then release all wiring harnesses from the crossmember.

8.29 Slide off the pipe clamps

8.30 Pull the pipes upwards from the matrix

8.31 Lift the heater matrix from the housing

8.36 Refrigerant pipe connection retaining nuts, and heater/coolant hose retaining clips

8.38 Disconnect the media interface control unit wiring plugs

8.41 Remove the insulation mats

8.42 Unclip the air duct and the cooling fan

8.44a Undo the rear bolt...

40 Disconnect the wiring plug(s) and release the wiring harnesses from the air conditioning/heater housing.
41 Remove the insulation mat from the rear of the housing, then move the insulation at the drivers end of the crossmember down into the footwell **(see illustration)**.
42 On models from 01.03.11, detach the air duct from the steering column bracket, then slide the media unit cooling fan from its bracket **(see illustration)**.
43 Unclip the wiring harness from the steering column, then undo the bolts and gently lower the steering column into the footwell.
44 Undo the rear mounting bolt, then slacken the front mounting bolt securing the parking brake bracket to the vehicle body **(see illustrations)**. Pivot the bracket rearwards to disengage it from the facia crossmember.
45 Undo the Torx screw at the top securing

8.44b ...and slacken the front parking brake bracket bolt

8.45 Remove the screw at the top of the housing

the air conditioning/heater housing to the crossmember **(see illustration)**.
46 Undo the 3 nuts securing the housing to the crossmember **(see illustrations)**.
47 The crossmember is now secured by 3 bolts in the instrument cluster area, 2 bolts

at each end, and 1 bolt in the centre/lower section. Make alignment marks between the facia crossmember and the A-pillars, and centre console bracket, then undo the bolts/nuts and move the crossmember rearwards a little **(see illustrations)**.

8.46a Undo the 2 nuts in the centre...

8.46b ...and nut on the passengers side

8.47a The facia crossmember is secured by 3 bolts in the instrument cluster area...

8.47b ...a bolt in the centre/lower section...

8.47c ...2 bolts at the passengers end...

8.47d ...and 2 bolts at the drivers end

8.49 Disconnect the drain hose each side of the housing

8.50 Undo the nut and disconnect the positive lead

8.56 The heating water circulation pump is located on the right-hand side of the engine compartment

48 With the help of an assistant, manoeuvre the crossmember from place.

49 Disconnect the water drain hoses from the air conditioning/heater housing **(see illustration)**.

50 Note their fitted positions, then disconnect any wiring plugs from the housing as necessary, and release the relevant harnesses. On models with an auxiliary electric heater, undo the nut and disconnect the positive lead at the passengers side lower A-pillar **(see illustration)**.

51 Disconnect the left-, and right-hand rear air ducts from the housing.

52 Make a final check to ensure all wiring, and air ducts have been disconnected from the housing.

53 With the help of an assistant, lift and pull the heater/air conditioning housing from place, unclipling the wiring harness as the housing is withdrawn.

Refitting

54 Check the condition of the seals between the heater/air conditioning housing and the vehicle body. Renew where necessary.

55 Refitting is a reversal of removal, noting the following points:

a) *Tighten all fasteners to their specified torque where given.*

b) *Align the facia crossmember with previously made marks.*

c) *Top up the cooling system as described in Chapter 1 Section 30.*

d) *Have the air conditioning refrigerant circuit recharged by a Mercedes-Benz dealer or suitably equipped specialist.*

Heating water circulation pump

Removal

56 The heating water circulation pump is located adjacent to the coolant expansion tank **(see illustration)**. Apply clamps to the pump coolant hoses.

57 Disconnect the pump wiring plug.

58 Pull the pump out of the holder, and disconnect the hoses.

Refitting

59 Refitting is a reversal of removal.

Auxiliary electrical heating element

Removal

60 Remove the heater matrix as described previously in this Section.

61 Undo the 3 screws and detach the servo motor from the top of the housing **(see illustration)**. There's no need to disconnect the wiring plug.

62 LIft up the foam seal each side, undo the 2 screws, release the 4 clips and move the flap assembly on top of the housing rearwards slightly to provide clearance for the element to side upwards from place **(see illustrations)**.

63 Disconnect the wiring plug on the top of the element.

64 Undo the 2 screws and slide the element upwards from the housing **(see illustration)**.

Refitting

65 Refitting is a reversal of removal.

8.61 Undo the screws and pull the servo motor from place

8.62a Remove the screw each side under the foam seals

8.62b Prise off the clips around the circumference...

8.62c ...and move the flap assembly rearwards

8.64 Undo the screws and remove the element

9.4a Refrigerant circuit service ports – 2148 cc engines...

9.4b ...and 2143 cc engines

9 Air conditioning system – general information and precautions

1 An air conditioning system is fitted as standard equipment on high-specification models, and was available as an optional extra on lower-specification models. In conjunction with the heater, the system enables any reasonable air temperature to be achieved inside the car, it also reduces the humidity of the incoming air, aiding demisting even when cooling is not required.

2 The refrigeration circuit of the air conditioning system functions in a similar way to a domestic refrigerator. A compressor, belt-driven from the crankshaft pulley, draws refrigerant in its gaseous state from an evaporator. The refrigerant heats up as a result of being compressed, but is then passed through a condenser (mounted in front of the engine radiator) where it loses heat and enters its liquid state. After dehydration, the refrigerant is passed through an evaporator (mounted alongside the heater/ventilation unit) where it is allowed to expand and reverts to being gas. This change of state has the effect of absorbing heat from the air passing over the evaporator fins, reducing its temperature. This cool air is mixed with warm air from the heater unit to achieve the desired cabin temperature. The refrigerant is directed back to the compressor and the cycle is then repeated.

3 Various subsidiary controls and sensors protect the system against excessive temperature and pressures. Additionally, engine idle speed is increased when the system is in use to compensate for the additional load imposed by the compressor. Electronic sensors detect the rotational speed differential between the engine and the compressor – if this becomes too great (due to a malfunctioning compressor), the compressor clutch is disengaged, to preserve the drivebelt.

4 The refrigerant circuit service ports are

located in the engine compartment **(see illustrations)**.

Note: *The air conditioning electronic control system can only be tested using dedicated equipment. For this reason, it is recommended that problems with the operation of the air conditioning system are referred to a Mercedes-Benz dealer for diagnosis.*

⚠ **Warning: The refrigeration circuit contains pressurised liquid refrigerant. The refrigerant is potentially dangerous, and should only be handled by qualified persons. Refrigerant that is allowed to come into contact with the skin will cause severe frostbite. It is not itself poisonous, but in the presence of a naked flame (including inhalation through a lighted cigarette), it forms a poisonous gas. Uncontrolled discharging of the refrigerant is dangerous and is also extremely damaging to the environment. For these reasons, disconnection of any part of the system without specialised knowledge and equipment is not recommended.**

Caution: Do not allow refrigerant lines to be exposed to temperatures in excess of 110°C, for example during welding or paint-drying operations.

Caution: Do not operate the air conditioning system if it is known to be short of refrigerant, or component damage may result.

10 Air conditioning system components – removal and refitting

⚠ **Warning: Refer to the previous Section before proceeding. Before carrying out any of the procedures detailed below, the air conditioning system MUST be professionally discharged by a garage or air conditioning specialist.**

Note: *The car may be driven once the system has been discharged, but the air conditioning system should NOT be switched on, as this*

will cause damage to the compressor. The safest option is to have the system discharged where the car is to be worked on, and not move the car until the system has been recharged. With air conditioning becoming an increasingly common fitment, mobile air conditioning specialists are becoming more widespread.

Evaporator

Removal

1 Remove the heater/air conditioning housing as described in Section 8.

2 Undo the 2 retaining bolts and remove the expansion valve **(see illustration 10.56)**. Renew the O-ring seals.

3 Disconnect the wiring plugs from the blower motor and control unit, and unclip the wiring harness from the lower housing.

4 Remove the seal around the refrigerant pipes, and the pipe clamp **(see illustration 8.28a, 8.28b and 8.28c)**.

5 On models with an auxiliary electrical heating element, disconnect the power supply and earth connections and release the cables from the clips **(see illustration 8.26)**.

6 Undo the 5 screws and remove the upper section of the blower motor housing **(see illustration)**.

10.6 Undo the screws and remove the upper housing

10.7a Remove the screw beside the blower motor...

10.7b ...two screws in the centre section...

10.7c ...prise away the various clips around its edge...

10.7d ...and lift away the front section of the housing

7 The front section of the housing is secured by 3 screws, and numerous clips around its circumference **(see illustrations)**. Undo the screws, prise away the clips and separate the halves of the housing.

8 Lift the evaporator from the housing **(see illustration)**.

Refitting

9 Refitting is a reversal of removal, noting the following points:

a) *Renew the refrigerant circuit O-ring seals* **(see illustration)**.

b) *Apply a little refrigerant oil to the seals prior to reassembly.*

c) *Have the refrigerant circuit recharged and leak tested by a Mercedes Benz dealer or suitably equipped specialist.*

Receiver/drier

Removal

10 Remove the air intake ducting from the front of the engine.

11 Remove the left-, and right-hand retaining clips (with the brackets) from the bonnet slam panel.

12 Gently push the radiator and condenser forwards a little to access the top of the receiver/drier.

13 Undo the screw plug from the top of the condenser.

14 Insert the removal tool (supplied with the Mercedes-Benz repair kit) into the top of the receiver/drier, then rotate the tool back and forth whilst pulling up at the same time.

The receiver/drier insert should release from the housing. Plug the opening to prevent contamination.

Refitting

15 Refitting is a reversal of removal, noting the following points:

a) *Renew the refrigerant circuit O-ring seals.*

b) *Apply a little refrigerant oil to the seals prior to reassembly.*

c) *Have the refrigerant circuit recharged and leak tested by a Mercedes Benz dealer or suitably equipped specialist.*

Condenser

Removal

16 Raise the front of the vehicle and support it securely on axle stands (see *Vehicle jacking and support*). Undo the fasteners and remove the undertray beneath the radiator.

17 Unclip and remove the air intake ducting from the front of the engine.

18 Remove the plastic expansion rivets and swivel the covers above each headlight to one side **(see illustration 6.4)**.

19 Release the fasteners and remove the bonnet slam panel above the condenser **(see illustration 6.6a and 6.6b)**.

20 Where applicable, release the fasteners and remove the Distronic control unit from in front of the condenser.

21 Unclip the lower air duct beneath condenser and swivel it downwards.

22 Release the clamps and disconnect both charge air hoses from the intercooler.

23 Where applicable, remove the bolt securing the power steering pipe to the base of the cooling fan cowling.

24 Lift the intercooler and condenser slightly and carefully move them rearwards a little.

25 Disconnect the outside temperature sensor wiring plug and unclip the harness.

26 Release the clips each side and remove the intercooler **(see illustration 3.8)**.

27 Disconnect the refrigerant pressure sensor wiring plug **(see illustration)**.

28 Undo the bolts and disconnect the refrigerant pipes from the condenser **(see illustrations)**. Renew the pipes seals. Plug the openings to prevent contamination.

29 Where applicable, unclip the power

10.8 Separate the halves of the housing and lift the evaporator from place

10.9 Renew all refrigerant circuit O-ring seals

10.27 Refrigerant pressure sensor

10.28a Disconnect the refrigerant pipe at the right-hand side of the condenser...

10.28b ...and at the base

10.31 Squeeze together the clips each side of the condenser

steering fluid cooler from the mountings on the condenser.

30 On models with automatic transmission, unclip the fluid cooler from the mountings on the condenser.

31 Release the clips each side of the condenser, and lower it from place (see illustration).

Refitting

32 Refitting is a reversal of removal, noting the following points:

a) Renew the refrigerant circuit O-ring seals.

b) Apply a little refrigerant oil to the seals prior to reassembly.

c) If a new condenser is to be fitted, renew the receiver/drier as described in this Section.

d) Upon completion, have the refrigerant circuit recharged and leak tested by a Mercedes Benz dealer or suitably equipped specialist.

e) On models equipped with the Distronic system, the control unit may need to be initialised before it will function correctly, using Mercedes-Benz diagnostic equipment. Entrust this task to a dealer or suitably equipped repairer.

Compressor

Removal

33 Raise the front of the vehicle and support it securely on axle stands (see Vehicle jacking and support). Undo the fasteners and remove the engine undershield.

34 Disconnect the battery negative lead as described in Chapter 5A Section 4.

35 Remove the auxiliary drivebelt as described in Chapter 1 Section 6.

2148 cc engines

36 Disconnect the charge air temperature sensor wiring plug.

37 Working underneath the vehicle, disconnect the charge air hose from the intercooler, then remove the retaining bolt, and remove the charge air pipe along with the hose (see illustration).

38 Disconnect the lower pressure refrigerant pipe at the separation point at the top of the engine compartment (see illustration). Plug

the openings to prevent contamination, and renew the O-ring seals.

39 Support the compressor (it is a heavy unit) and remove the mounting bolts. Depending on the exact type of compressor, and on the engine to which it is fitted, there will be either three or four mounting bolts. Lift the compressor and move it forward to access the refrigerant lines and wiring connector.

40 Disconnect the wiring plug from the compressor.

41 If the compressor is being removed as part of another procedure (such as engine removal), it is sufficient to remove the mounting bolts and tie the compressor up to one side without disconnecting the refrigerant lines. If the compressor is being removed completely, proceed as follows.

42 Unscrew the unions on the two pipes on the compressor, and disconnect them.

10.37 Undo the bolt and remove the charge air pipe

10.46 Compressor wiring plug

Recover the O-ring seals – new ones must be used when refitting. Cover the pipe ends, to prevent the entry of foreign matter.

43 Manoeuvre the compressor upwards from the engine compartment.

2143 cc engines

44 Remove the plastic cover from the top of the engine.

45 Remove the intake hose upstream of the air cleaner assembly.

46 Disconnect the wiring plug from the compressor (see illustration).

47 Undo the retaining bolts and disconnect the refrigerant pipes from the top of the compressor (see illustration). Renew the pipe O-ring seals. Plug the openings to prevent contamination.

48 Undo the 3 mounting bolts and manoeuvre the compressor from place.

10.38 Depress the clip, open the cover and disconnect the refrigerant pipe

10.47 Undo the bolts and disconnect the pipes

All engines

49 It is advisable to cover the openings on the compressor while it is removed, to reduce oil loss and to prevent foreign matter from entering.

Refitting

50 Refitting is a reversal of removal, noting the following points:
a) *Renew the refrigerant circuit O-ring seals.*
b) *Apply a little refrigerant oil to the seals prior to reassembly.*
c) *Upon completion, have the refrigerant circuit recharged and leak tested by a Mercedes-Benz dealer or suitably equipped specialist.*

Sunlight sensor

51 Using a blunt, flat-bladed tool, carefully prise the trim panel from the centre of the facia **(see illustration)**. Disconnect the sensor wiring plug as it becomes accessible.
52 Note its fitted position, release the clips and remove the sensor from the panel.
53 Refitting is a reversal of removal.

Expansion valve

Removal

54 Remove the wiper motor and linkage as described in Chapter 12 Section 14.
55 Undo the retaining nuts and disconnect

10.51 Carefully prise up the facia panel

the refrigerant pipes from the bulkhead connection **(see illustration 8.37)**. Renew the O-ring seals. Plug the openings to prevent contamination.
56 Undo the 2 retaining bolts and remove the expansion valve **(see illustration)**. Renew the O-ring seals. Plug the openings to prevent contamination.

Refitting

57 Refitting is a reversal of removal, noting the following points:
a) *Renew the refrigerant circuit O-ring seals.*
b) *Apply a little refrigerant oil to the seals and valve retaining bolts prior to reassembly.*

10.56 Expansion valve retaining bolts

c) *Have the refrigerant circuit recharged and leak tested by a Mercedes Benz dealer or suitably equipped specialist.*

Humidity/pollution sensor

Note: *Only on models with Comfort air conditioning*
58 Undo the fasteners and remove the cover in the left-hand, rear corner of the engine compartment.
59 Working through the aperture, rotate the sensor approximately 10° – 30° anti-clockwise and withdraw it from place. Disconnect the wiring plug as the sensor is withdrawn.
60 Refitting is a reversal of removal.

Chapter 4 Part A
Fuel and exhaust systems

Contents

Section number

Accelerator pedal – removal and refitting. 5
Air cleaner assembly – removal and refitting 2
Common fuel rail – removal and refitting 12
Engine management control system components –
  removal and refitting. 13
Exhaust system – general information and component renewal 19
Fuel injection pump – removal and refitting. 10
Fuel injection system – general information. 6
Fuel injection system – testing and adjustment. 9
Fuel injectors – removal and refitting 11

Section number

Fuel level sensors/pump – removal and refitting 4
Fuel pipes and fittings – general information and disconnection. . . . 8
Fuel system – priming and bleeding. 7
Fuel tank – removal and refitting 3
General information and precautions. 1
Intercooler – removal and refitting 18
Manifolds – removal and refitting. 15
Throttle body – removal and refitting 14
Turbocharger – examination and overhaul. 17
Turbocharger – removal and refitting 16

Degrees of difficulty

Easy, suitable for novice with little experience	Fairly easy, suitable for beginner with some experience	Fairly difficult, suitable for competent DIY mechanic	Difficult, suitable for experienced DIY mechanic	Very difficult, suitable for expert DIY or professional

Specifications

System type . . . . Direct injection common rail with high-pressure delivery pump and Electronic Diesel Control

Injection pressures:
  2148 cc engines . . . . upto 1600 bar
  2143 cc engines . . . . upto 2000 bar
Turbocharging:
  2148 cc engines . . . . Single variable vane geometry turbocharger
  2143 cc engines . . . . Two-stage turbocharging with fixed geometry

Torque wrench settings	Nm	lbf ft
Camshaft position sensor:		
2148 cc engines	11	8
2143 cc engines	8	6
Common (fuel) rail:		
Mounting bolts	14	10
Fuel return banjo bolt:		
2148 cc engines	20	15
2143 cc engines	25	18
Crankshaft position sensor	8	6
Combustion chamber pressure sensor-to-cylinder head (2143 cc engines):		
Stage 1	5	3
Stage 2	Angle-tighten a further 90°	
Exhaust manifold-to-cylinder head: *		
2148 cc engines	30	22
2143 cc engines:		
Steel manifold.	30	22
Cast iron manifold:		
Stage 1	15	10
Stage 2	35	26
Exhaust temperature sensor (2143 cc engines)	45	33

Torque wrench settings (continued)	**Nm**	**lbf ft**
Fuel injector clamp bolts: *		
2148 cc engines:		
Stage 1	7	5
Stage 2	Angle-tighten a further 90°	
Stage 3	Angle-tighten a further 90°	
2143 cc engines:		
Stage 1	15	10
Stage 2	Angle-tighten a further 90°	
Stage 3	Angle-tighten a further 90°	
Fuel injection pump:		
2148 cc engines	15	10
2143 cc engines	20	15
Fuel injection pump coupling flange nut (2143 cc engines)	70	52
Fuel temperature sensor:		
2148 cc engines	23	17
2143 cc engines	15	10
Intake manifold:		
2148 cc engines	16	11
2143 cc engines	15	10
High-pressure fuel pipe unions:		
Stage 1	7	5
Stage 2	33	25
High pressure pump union nuts	33	25
Common fuel rail union nuts	27	19
Injector union nuts	33	25
Knock sensor(s)	20	15
Rear axle retaining bolts: *		
Stage 1	80	59
Stage 2	Slacken	
Stage 3	80	59
Stage 4	Angle-tighten a further 90°	
Stop plate-to-body bolts	28	21
Throttle body bolts:		
2148 cc engines	10	7
2143 cc engines	9	6
Turbocharger – 2148 cc engines:		
Turbocharger-to-exhaust manifold:		
Stage 1	20	15
Stage 2	Angle-tighten a further 90°	
Turbocharger oil feed banjo bolt:		
To-turbocharger	18	14
To-cylinder head	10	7
Turbocharger oil return	10	7
Turbocharger support bracket:		
To-turbocharger	30	22
To-cylinder block	20	15
Turbochargers – 2143 cc engines:		
Exhaust manifold-to-turbocharger: *		
Stage 1	20	15
Stage 2	Angle-tighten a further 90°	
Low pressure turbocharger-to-high pressure turbocharger:		
Stage 1	20	15
Stage 2	Angle-tighten a further 90°	
Oil pipe connections	18	14
Oil return pipe to crankcase	10	7
Oil supply pipe-to-turbocharger:		
Stage 1	10	7
Stage 2	Angle-tighten a further 90°	
Rear/centre support bracket-to-turbocharger/crankcase	20	15
Turbocharger retaining bracket-to turbocharger/crankcase:		
Stage 1	20	15
Stage 2	Angle-tighten a further 90°	

*Do not re-use

1 General information and precautions

General information

1 The operation of the fuel injection system is described in more detail in Section 6.
2 Fuel is drawn from a tank under the rear of the vehicle, by a tank-mounted pump, through the pipework, and through fuel filter/water separator/heater into the high-pressure injection pump.

2148 cc engines

3 The high-pressure injection pump is driven by a timing chain at the end of the inlet camshaft, and supplies very high pressure fuel to the common fuel rail, which is connected to each individual injector. The injectors are operated by solenoids controlled by the ECM, based on information supplied by various sensors. The multi-hole injectors are capable of multiple pre-, and post-injections per stroke. The engine ECM also controls the pre-heating side of the system – refer to Chapter 5B for more details.

2143 cc engines

4 These engines are equipped with a second generation Dephi common rail system, incorporating piezo crystal injectors, and a high-pressure pump which is gear-driven at the rear of the engine via in intermediate gear by the crankshaft. All functions of the system are controlled by the engine management ECM.

All engines

5 The EDC (electronic diesel control) system fitted, incorporates a 'drive by wire' system, where the traditional accelerator cable is replaced by an accelerator pedal position sensor. The position and rate-of-change of the accelerator pedal is reported by the position sensor to the ECM, which then adjusts the fuel injectors to deliver the required amount of fuel, and optimum combustion efficiency.
6 Fuel level in the tank is determined by 2 level sensors – on each side of the saddle tank. The right-hand side sensor is fitted to in the in-tank pump module.
7 The exhaust system incorporates a turbocharger(s), EGR and on some models, a diesel particulate filter. Further detail of the emission control systems can be found in Chapter 4B.
8 2143 cc engines are equipped with two-stage turbocharging. A small diameter, high-pressure, low inertia turbocharger provides enhanced boost pressure/response at low engine speeds. As the air flow/engine speed increases, a system of bypass valves and ducting forces the intake air into the larger, low-pressure turbocharger. This provides a greater volume of pressurised air flow, thus boosting engine output further. The result is high engine output over the entire engine speed/load range, with a linear torque curve.

Precautions

9 When working on diesel fuel system components, scrupulous cleanliness must be observed, and care must be taken not to introduce any foreign matter into fuel lines or components.
10 After carrying out any work involving disconnection of fuel lines, it is advisable to check the connections for leaks; pressurise the system by cranking the engine several times.
11 Electronic control units are very sensitive components, and certain precautions must be taken to avoid damage to these units as follows.
12 When carrying out welding operations on the vehicle using electric welding equipment, the battery and alternator should be disconnected.
13 Although the underbonnet-mounted modules will tolerate normal underbonnet conditions, they can be adversely affected by excess heat or moisture. If using welding equipment or pressure-washing equipment in the vicinity of an electronic module, take care not to direct heat, or jets of water or steam, at the module. If this cannot be avoided, remove the module from the vehicle, and protect its wiring plug with a plastic bag.
14 Before disconnecting any wiring, or removing components, always ensure that the ignition is switched off.
15 Do not attempt to improvise ECM fault diagnosis procedures using a test lamp or multi-meter, as irreparable damage could be caused to the module.
16 After working on fuel injection/engine management system components, ensure that all wiring is correctly reconnected before reconnecting the battery or switching on the ignition.

2 Air cleaner assembly – removal and refitting

Removal

2148 cc engines

1 Remove the plastic cover on the top of the engine **(see illustration)**.
2 Remove the intake hose upstream of the air filter housing **(see illustrations)**.
3 Where applicable, disconnect the breather hose from the oil separator on the cylinder head cover.
4 Disconnect the wiring plugs from the breather hose heater element (where fitted), hot film mass air flow sensor, and air pressure sensor **(see illustration)**.

2.1 Pull up the engine cover

2.2a Rotate the fasteners anti-clockwise…

2.2b …release the clip at the air filter…

2.2c …and the clip at the air intake

2.4 Disconnect the wiring plugs from the air flow sensor and air pressure sensor

2.5 Release the air outlet pipe clamp

2.6a Pull the air filter housing upwards...

2.6b ...then forwards to release the mountings

5 Release the clamp and remove the air outlet pipe from the air filter housing (**see illustration**).

6 Pull up the front edge of the air filter housing, the pull it forwards from its rubber mountings (**see illustrations**).

2143 cc engines

7 Disconnect the battery negative lead as described in Chapter 5A Section 4.

8 Rotate the catch anti-clockwise and pull the plastic cover on the top of the engine forwards from its rubber mountings (**see illustrations**).

9 Remove the air intake duct upstream of the air filter housing (**see illustrations**).

2.8a Rotate the catch anti-clockwise...

2.8b ...then pull the cover forwards from its' mountings

2.9a Undo the fastener...

2.9b ...unclip the intake duct from the air cleaner...

2.9c ...and bonnet panel

2.10a Release the clamp at the air filter...

2.10b ...slide out the locking catch, disconnect the breather hose heater plug...

2.10c ...disconnect the pressure sensor plug...

2.10d ...and release the clamp at the turbocharger

10 Disconnect the pressure sensor, breather hose heater plug, breather hose, release the clamps and disconnect the air duct downstream of the air filter housing **(see illustrations)**.

11 Lever over the locking catches and disconnect the ECM wiring plugs **(see illustration 13.23)**, then unclip the wiring harnesses from the ECM.

12 Slide out the locking catch, and disconnect the wiring plug from the mass air flow sensor at the front of the air filter housing.

13 Pull up the front edge of the air filter housing upwards, then forwards from its mountings **(see illustration)**.

Caution: Take care not to bend the air filter housing excessively.

Refitting

14 Refitting is a reversal of removal.

3 Fuel tank – removal and refitting

Removal

Note: *Removal of the fuel tank is an involved procedure that requires the removal of the complete rear axle.*

1 The fuel tank must be emptied before the operation can be started. This is best achieved by waiting until the tank is almost empty through the course of normal driving.

2 Raise the rear of the vehicle and support it securely on axle stands (see *Vehicle jacking and support*).

3 Disconnect the battery negative lead as described in Chapter 5A Section 4.

4 Remove the rear seat cushion as described in Chapter 11 Section 31.

5 Fold back the insulation, undo the screws and remove the left-, and right-hand access covers above the fuel tank **(see illustration 4.2)**.

6 Disconnect the wiring plugs from the sensor/pump covers.

7 Undo the fuel tank centre mounting nuts, between the access covers **(see illustration)**.

8 Undo the bolts and remove the crossmember beneath the propeller shaft.

9 Release the fasteners and remove both sections of the rear underfloor panelling.

10 Remove the complete exhaust system as described in Section 19.

11 Undo the fasteners and remove the heatshields above the exhaust system location.

12 Remove the propeller shaft as described in Chapter 8 Section 7.

13 Release the fasteners and remove the heatshield from beneath the fuel tank.

14 With reference to Chapter 9 Section 15, unhook the parking brake cable from the centre joining piece.

15 Remove the rear coils springs as described in Chapter 10 Section 14.

16 Detach the rear shock absorbers from the lower control arms as described in Chapter 10 Section 13.

17 Note their fitted positions, then disconnect the various wiring plugs from the rear ABS wheel speed sensors, brake pad wear sensors, ride height sensors, damper valve units, as applicable. Unclip the wiring harnesses from the rear axle assembly.

18 Disconnect the brake hoses from the calipers, and unclip them from the rear axle.

19 Support the rear axle assembly with suitable jack(s), undo the retaining bolts and with the aid of an assistant, gently lower the axle assembly. Note that new retaining bolts will be required.

20 Release the fasteners and remove the right-hand rear wheelarch liner.

21 Undo the nut securing the earth lead to the filler neck **(see illustration)**.

22 Disconnect the drain hose from the filler neck.

2.13 Pull the housing upwards at the front, then forwards

3.7 Undo the mounting nuts between the access covers

3.21 Undo the nut and disconnect the earth lead

3.27a Undo the bolt at the upper end of the filler neck...

3.27b ...and the bolt securing the neck to the inner wing

3.28 Fuel tank retaining straps rear nuts

4.2 Undo the fasteners and remove both access covers

4.3 Depress the release buttons, disconnect the hoses and the wiring plug

of thread-locking compound, apply a little before fitting.

c) *Prior to refitting the rear axle, it's essential that the captive threads in the body are cleaned using the correct size tap.*

---

4 Fuel level sensors/pump – removal and refitting

Removal

1 Remove the rear seat cushion as described in Chapter 11 Section 31. The fuel pump is located under the right-hand cover, whilst level sensors are located under both covers.
2 Fold back the insulation material, undo the retaining screws and remove both the left- and right-hand tank access covers **(see illustration)**.
3 Note their fitted positions, then disconnect the wiring plug and hoses from the sensor covers **(see illustration)**.
4 The retaining rings must now be loosened and removed. To do this, Mercedes-Benz technicians use a special tool (No. 001 589 00 07 00), which engages the holes in the ring **(see illustrations)**. Alternative after-market

23 Unclip the rubber filler neck boot from the rear inner wing.
24 Unclip the fuel supply and return pipes from the vehicle floor in front of the fuel tank, then disconnect them at the fittings. Plug the openings to prevent contamination. Be prepared for fuel spillage.
25 Undo the fasteners and remove the heatshield beneath the fuel tank.
26 Support the fuel tank with a suitable jack. Use a sheet of plywood (or similar) interposed between the jack head and tank to prevent damage.

27 Undo the bolts securing the fuel filler neck **(see illustrations)**.
28 Undo the nuts and detach the fuel tank retaining straps **(see illustration)**.
29 With the help of an assistant, lower the fuel tank and manoeuvre it from position.

Refitting

30 Refitting is a reversal of removal, noting the following points:
a) *Renew all self-locking nuts.*
b) *Renew the rear axle retaining bolts. If the new bolts do not already have a coating*

4.4a Make alignment marks between the cover, ring and tank...

4.4b ...then slacken and remove the retaining ring – note that the ring maybe very tight!

4.5a Lift the sensor cover...

4.5b ...squeeze together the clips, disconnect the hose from the cover...

4.5c ...then depress the clip...

4.5d ...and slide out the transfer hose fitting

4.6 Tie a length of string/wire to the end of the transfer hoses

4.10 Release the clips and slide up the sensor

fuel tank cap removal tools are readily available. Make alignment marks between the cover, retaining ring and tank to aid reassembly.

5 Note its fitted position, then lift the left-hand sensor cover, and disconnect the fuel pipes **(see illustrations)**. Carefully manoeuvre the assembly from place, taking care not to damage the delicate float arm.

6 Tie a length of string/wire to the end of the transfer hoses in the left-hand tank opening to aid refitting **(see illustration)**. The string/wire will be pulled through as the right-hand sensor/pump is withdrawn.

7 Lift the right-hand cover from the tank, along with the pump, level sensor and transfer pipes. Take care not to damage the float arm.

8 Untie the string/wire from the transfer pipes and leave it in place to aid refitting.

9 Disconnect the level sensor wiring plug from the underside of the cover, and unhook the wiring.

10 Release the clips and slide the level sensor from place **(see illustration)**.

11 If required, the resistance of the fuel level sensor can be checked using a multi-meter. On full deflection (full tank) we recorded approximately 50 ohms, and on zero deflection (empty tank) we recorded approximately 990 ohms **(see illustration)**. If the resistance of the sensor(s) varies significantly from these measurements, it may be faulty.

Refitting

12 Refitting is a reversal of removal, noting the following points:
a) Renew the sensor/pump cover seals **(see illustration)**.

b) Tighten the retaining rings to their specified torque.
c) Align the marks between the covers and the tank.

---

5 Accelerator pedal – removal and refitting

Removal

1 Undo the 2 retaining nuts, disconnect the wiring plug and remove the pedal **(see illustration)**. No dismantling of the pedal assembly is recommended.

Refitting

2 Refitting is a reversal of removal.

4.11 Measure the fuel tank level sensor resistance with a multi-meter

4.12 Renew the cover seals

5.1 Pedal assembly retaining nuts

6 Fuel injection system – general information

1 The system is under the overall control of the Common rail Diesel Injection (CDI) system, which also controls the pre-heating system (see Chapter 5B).

2 Fuel is supplied from the rear-mounted fuel tank, via an electrically powered lift pump, and fuel filter, to the fuel injection pump. The fuel injection pump supplies fuel under high pressure to the common fuel rail. The fuel rail provides a reservoir of fuel under pressure ready for the injectors to deliver direct to the combustion chamber. The individual fuel injectors, which when operated, allow the high pressure fuel to be injected. The injectors are controlled by the ECM. The fuel injection pump purely provides high pressure fuel. The timing and duration of the injection is controlled by the ECM based, on the information received from the various sensors. In order to increase combustion efficiency and reduce combustion noise (diesel 'knock'), a small amount of fuel can be injected before, and after the main injection takes place – this is known as Pre-, Pilot-, or Post-injection.

3 Additionally, the control module activates the pre-heating system, and the exhaust gas recirculation (EGR) system (see Chapter 5B).

4 The system uses the following sensors:

d) Crankshaft sensor – informs the ECM of the crankshaft speed and position.

e) Coolant temperature sensor – informs the ECM of engine temperature.

f) Mass airflow sensor(s) – informs the ECM of the mass and temperature of air entering the intake tract.

g) Air intake sensor(s) – informs the ECM of the intake air temperature.

h) Wheel speed sensors – informs the ECM of the vehicle speed.

i) Accelerator pedal position sensor – informs the ECM of throttle position, and the rate of throttle opening/closing.

j) Fuel high-pressure sensor – informs the ECM of the pressure of the fuel in the common rail.

k) Manifold absolute pressure sensor –

informs the ECM of the pressure in the intake manifold.

l) Fuel temperature sensor – informs the ECM of the fuel supply temperature.

m) Camshaft position sensor – informs the ECM of the camshaft position so that the engine firing sequence can be established.

n) Stop-light switch – informs the ECM when the brakes are being applied.

o) Exhaust gas temperature sensor – informs the ECM of the temperature of the exhaust gases.

p) Exhaust gas pressure sensor – informs the ECM of the back pressure in the exhaust system.

q) O2 sensors – informs the ECM of the oxygen content in the exhaust gases – fitted upstream, and downstream of the catalytic converter.

5 On all models, a "drive-by-wire" throttle control system is used. No traditional cable is fitted, instead an accelerator pedal position sensor informs the ECM of the pedal position and rate of change.

6 The signals from the various sensors are processed by the ECM, and the optimum fuel quantity and injection timing settings are selected for the prevailing engine operating conditions.

7 A catalytic converter and an exhaust gas recirculation (EGR), and on some models, a diesel particulate filter system is fitted, to reduce harmful exhaust gas emissions. Details of this and other emissions control system equipment are given in Chapter 4B.

8 If there is an abnormality in any of the readings obtained from any sensor, the ECM enters its back-up mode. In this event, the ECM ignores the abnormal sensor signal, and assumes a pre-programmed value which will allow the engine to continue running (albeit at reduced efficiency). If the ECM enters this back-up mode, the warning light on the instrument panel will come on, and the relevant fault code will be stored in the ECM memory.

9 If the warning light comes on, the vehicle should be taken to a Mercedes dealer or specialist at the earliest opportunity. A complete test of the CDI system can then be carried out, using a special electronic test unit which is simply plugged into the system's diagnostic connector (see illustration). The connector is located under the driver's side of the facia.

6.9 Pull open the cover to access the diagnostic connector

7 Fuel system – priming and bleeding

1 The fuel system fitted to the diesel engines in the range, is designed to be self-priming. After disturbing an element of the fuel system, switch the ignition on for approximately 15 seconds before operating the starter and attempting to start the engine. This should

allow the in-tank pump to fill the high-pressure tank. Only operate the starter for a maximum of 10 seconds at a time to prevent overheating. It may take several attempts before the engine starts.

8 Fuel pipes and fittings – general information and disconnection

1 Disconnect the cable from the negative battery terminal (see Chapter 5A Section 4) before proceeding.

2 The fuel supply pipe connects the fuel pump in the fuel tank to the fuel filter on the engine.

3 Whenever you're working under the vehicle, be sure to inspect all fuel and evaporative emission pipes for leaks, kinks, dents and other damage. Always replace a damaged fuel pipe immediately.

4 If you find signs of dirt in the pipes during disassembly, disconnect all pipes and blow them out with compressed air. Inspect the fuel strainer on the fuel pump pick-up unit for damage and deterioration.

Steel tubing

5 It is critical that the fuel pipes be replaced with pipes of equivalent type and specification.

6 Some steel fuel pipes have threaded fittings. When loosening these fittings, hold the stationary fitting with a spanner while turning the union nut.

Plastic tubing

⚠ Warning: When removing or installing plastic fuel tubing, be careful not to bend or twist it too much, which can damage it. Also, plastic fuel tubing is NOT heat resistant, so keep it away from excessive heat.

7 When replacing fuel system plastic tubing, use only original equipment replacement plastic tubing.

Flexible hoses

8 When replacing fuel system flexible hoses, use original equipment replacements, or hose to the same specification.

9 Don't route fuel hoses (or metal pipes) within 100 mm of the exhaust system or within 280 mm of the catalytic converter. Make sure that no rubber hoses are installed directly against the vehicle, particularly in places where there is any vibration. If allowed to touch some vibrating part of the vehicle, a hose can easily become chafed and it might start leaking. A good rule of thumb is to maintain a minimum of 8.0 mm clearance around a hose (or metal pipe) to prevent contact with the vehicle underbody.

Disconnecting Fuel pipe Fittings

10 Typical fuel pipe fittings:

8.10a Two-tab type fitting; depress both tabs with your fingers, then pull the fuel pipe and the fitting apart

8.10b On this type of fitting, depress the two buttons on opposite sides of the fitting, then pull it off the fuel pipe

8.10c Threaded fuel pipe fitting; hold the stationary portion of the pipe or component (A) while loosening the union nut (B) with a flare-nut spanner

8.10d Plastic collar-type fitting; rotate the outer part of the fitting

8.10e Metal collar quick-connect fitting; pull the end of the retainer off the fuel pipe and disengage the other end from the female side of the fitting ...

8.10f ... insert a fuel pipe separator tool into the female side of the fitting, push it into the fitting and pull the fuel pipe off the pipe

8.10g Some fittings are secured by lock tabs. Release the lock tab (A) and rotate it to the fully-opened position, squeeze the two smaller lock tabs (B) ...

8.10h ... then push the retainer out and pull the fuel pipe off the pipe

8.10i Spring-lock coupling; remove the safety cover, install a coupling release tool and close the tool around the coupling ...

8.10j ... push the tool into the fitting, then pull the two pipes apart

8.10k Hairpin clip type fitting: push the legs of the retainer clip together, then push the clip down all the way until it stops and pull the fuel pipe off the pipe

9 Fuel injection system – testing and adjustment

Testing

1 If a fault appears in the fuel injection system, first ensure that all the system wiring connectors are securely connected and free from corrosion. Ensure that the fault is not due to poor maintenance; ie, check that the air cleaner filter element is clean, that the cylinder compression pressures are correct (see Chapter 2A Section 2 or), and that the engine breather hoses are clear and undamaged (see Chapter 4B).
2 If the engine will not start, check the condition of the glow plugs (see Chapter 5B Section 2).
3 If these checks fail to reveal the cause of the problem, the vehicle should be taken to a Mercedes Benz dealer or specialist for testing using special electronic equipment which is plugged into the diagnostic connector (see Section 6). The tester should locate the fault quickly and simply, avoiding the need to test all the system components individually, which is time-consuming, and also carries a risk of damaging the ECM.

Adjustment

4 The engine idle speed, and maximum speed are all controlled by the ECM. Whilst in theory it is possible to check the settings, if they are found to be in need of adjustment, the car will have to be taken to a suitably-equipped Mercedes-Benz dealer or specialist. They will have access to the necessary diagnostic equipment required to test and (where possible) adjust the settings.

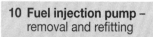

10 Fuel injection pump – removal and refitting

Warning: Observe the precautions in Section 1 before working on any component in the fuel system.

10.4 Slide up the locking clips and disconnect the wiring plugs from the pump

Removal

1 Remove the plastic cover from the top of the engine.

2148 cc engines

2 If improved access is required, remove the cooling fan shroud as described in Chapter 3 Section 6.
3 Undo the bolts and remove the heatshield (where fitted) adjacent to the injection pump.
4 Disconnect the wiring plugs from the fuel temperature sensor and the quantity control valve **(see illustration)**.
5 Release the clamp and disconnect the fuel supply/return hoses from left-hand side of the pump. Be prepared for fuel spillage. Plug the openings to prevent contamination.
6 Remove the support bracket bolt, then undo the unions securing the high-pressure fuel pipe to the pump and the common rail **(see illustration)**. Take care not to bend or squeeze the pipe. Plug the openings to prevent contamination.
7 Undo the 3 retaining bolts,and remove the high-pressure fuel pump from the front of the cylinder head. As the pump is removed, retrieve the drivegear from the end of the shaft.
8 Recover the O-ring seal from the rear of the injection pump and discard it – a new one must be used on refitting.
9 Mercedes Benz insist that no further dismantling of the pump is to be carried out. If a fault is suspected, have the pump inspected by a Mercedes Benz dealer or specialist.

10.6 High pressure pipe support bracket bolt

2143 cc engines

10 Raise the vehicle and support it securely on axle stands (see *Vehicle jacking and support*). Undo the fasteners and remove the undertray beneath the engine.
11 Remove the throttle body as described in Section 14.
12 Undo the 2 bolts and move the wiring harness bracket above the left-hand engine mounting to one side.
13 Undo the 2 bolts and remove the mounting plate for the mixing chamber.
14 Release the clamps and remove the charge air hose from the intercooler to the duct alongside the left-hand side of the engine.
15 Disconnect the wiring plug from the air temperature sensor on the charge air duct **(see illustration 13.30b)**.
16 Undo the retaining bolt at the front, then manoeuvre the charge air duct rearwards from place **(see illustration)**.
17 Disconnect the wiring plugs from the fuel quantity control valve and the fuel temperature sensor.
18 Disconnect the vacuum pipe from the vacuum pump **(see illustration)**.
19 Undo the bolts securing the high-pressure fuel pipe support brackets.
20 Using a second spanner to counterhold, undo the union nuts securing the high-pressure fuel pipe to the pump and fuel rail **(see illustration)**. Be prepared for fuel spillage. Plug the openings as they become accessible.

10.16 Charge air duct retaining bolt

10.18 Squeeze together the clips each side and disconnect the vacuum hose

10.20 Pump-to-fuel rail upper union and clamp bolt

10.21 Fuel supply hose and quantity valve wiring plug

10.22a Fuel pump lower retaining bolt...

10.22b ...and upper retaining bolts (one hidden)

21 Disconnect the remaining fuel hose from the pump **(see illustration)**. Plug the openings to prevent contamination. Be prepared for fuel spillage.

22 Undo the 3 retaining bolts, unhook the wiring harness from the EGR pipe bracket, and detach the high-pressure pump **(see illustrations)**. Note that the retaining bolts and the O-ring seal must be renewed.

23 With the exception of drive gear removal, Mercedes Benz insist that no further dismantling of the pump is to be carried out. If a fault is suspected, have the pump inspected by a Mercedes Benz dealer or specialist.

Refitting

24 Refitting is a reversal of removal, noting the following points:

a) *Ensure the mating surfaces of the pump and cylinder head are clean.*

b) *Apply a little clean engine oil to the new pump O-ring seal prior to refitting.*

c) *All high-pressure fuel pipes must be fitted 'without tension'.*

d) *Tighten all fasteners to their specified torque, where given.*

e) *Upon completion, switch the ignition on for at least 15 seconds to circulate fuel through the pump. Failure to do so may damage the pump.*

11 Fuel injectors –
removal and refitting

 Warning: Exercise extreme caution when working on the fuel injectors. Never expose the hands or any part of the body to injector spray, as the high working pressure can cause the fuel to penetrate the skin, with possibly fatal results. You are strongly advised to have any work which involves testing the injectors under pressure carried out by a dealer or fuel injection specialist. Refer to the precautions given in Section 1 of this Chapter before proceeding.

Note: *Take care not to allow dirt into the fuel rail, injectors or fuel pipes during this procedure. Keep the fuel pipes and injectors identified for position to ensure correct refitting. As the fuel pipes are removed, plug the ends of the pipes, injectors and fuel rail to prevent dirt ingress.*

Removal

1 Remove the plastic cover from the top of the engine.

2148 cc engines

2 Remove the insulation material above the injectors **(see illustration)**.

3 Using a second spanner to counterhold,

11.2 Lift away the insulation material

11.5a Prise out the clips...

undo the unions securing the high-pressure fuel pipes to the injectors and common fuel rail **(see illustration)**.

4 Undo any nuts/bolts securing the pipe retaining brackets and manoeuvre the pipes from place. Take care not to bend or squeeze the pipes. Plug all openings to prevent contamination.

5 Release the catches and disconnect the fuel return hoses from the top of each injector **(see illustrations)**.

6 Squeeze together the retaining clips and disconnect the wiring plugs from each injector.

7 Slacken and remove the injector clamp mounting bracket retaining bolts from

11.3 Undo the unions of the common rail-to-injector pipes

11.5b ...and pull the return pipes upwards

11.7a Undo the retaining bolts...

11.7b ...and remove the clamp brackets

11.8 Withdraw each injector from the cylinder head

11.9 Pull up the collar to cover the 'white' mark, and disconnect the hoses

11.10 Remove the pipes between the common rail and the injectors

11.11 Slide out the clip and disconnect the wiring plug

between the injectors **(see illustrations)**. Discard the mounting bolts, as new ones will be required when refitting.

8 If required use a slide hammer/puller to withdraw the injectors from the cylinder head, making sure it is in the vertical position **(see illustration)**. Recover the sealing rings/washers and discard. New ones must be used for refitting. **Note:** *If the injectors are to be refitted, it's essential that they're refitted to their original locations. Mark the injectors with permanent marker (or similar) to indicate the cylinder number.*

2143 cc engines

9 Disconnect the fuel return hoses from the top of the injectors **(see illustration)**. Be prepared for fuel spillage. Plug the openings to prevent contamination.

Note: *When the white marking on the return fitting*

is visible, the connection is locked. If the marking is not visible, the connection is not secure.

10 Undo the union nuts and remove the high-pressure fuel injection pipes between the common fuel rail and the injectors **(see illustration)**. Note that Mercedes insist that new pipes are fitted. Plug all openings as they become accessible.

11 Release the clips and disconnect the wiring plugs from each injector **(see illustration)**. Unclip the harness guide and move it to one side.

12 Slacken and remove the injector clamp retaining bolts from each injector **(see illustration)**. Discard the bolts, as new ones will be required when refitting.

13 Withdraw the injectors and clamps from the cylinder head. If necessary, use a slide hammer/puller to withdraw the injectors, making sure it is in the vertical position **(see**

illustration). Recover the sealing rings/washers and discard. New ones must be used for refitting. **Note:** *If the injectors are to be refitted, it's essential that they're refitted to their original locations. Mark the injectors with permanent marker (or similar) to indicate the cylinder number.*

Caution: If a impact extractor (slide hammer) is used to release the injectors, damage to the injectors is likely, and replacements will be required.

Refitting

14 Thoroughly clean the injectors and their locating holes in the cylinder head. Use a bottle brush (or similar) and and vacuum cleaner to remove all traces of carbon/debris from the area.

15 Renew the sealing washers at the base of each injector **(see illustration)**.

11.12 Injector clamp retaining bolt

11.13 Withdrawn the injector and clamp from the cylinder head

11.15 Renew the injector sealing washers

11.17 Make a note of the injector numbers

12.8 Common rail retaining bolt locations

12.9 The harness duct is secured by various clips

16 Apply special grease (Mercedes No. A 001 898 42 51 10) to the injector bodies to prevent them seizing in place.

17 Make a note of any numbers on the injectors **(see illustration)**. If new injectors are being fitted, a control unit adaption must be carried out using Mercedes-Benz diagnostic equipment (or equivalent). These numbers will be needed during the adaption process.

18 Fit the injectors in to the holes in the cylinder heads. If the original injectors are being refitted, they must be fitted into their original locations. Note that on 2143 cc engines, the retaining brackets must be fitted at the same time as the injectors are inserted.

19 On 2148 cc engines, refit the injector retaining brackets.

20 Fit the new high-pressure fuel pipes, and tighten the unions to their specified torque. The pipes must be installed 'without tension'.

21 Insert the injector retaining bolts and tighten them to the specified torque.

22 The remainder of refitting is a reversal of removal, noting the following points:
a) *Tighten all fasteners to their specified torque where given.*
b) *Lubricate the return (leak-off) pipe rubber seals prior to refitting.*
c) *If new injectors have been fitted, carry out the control unit adaption using Mercedes-Benz diagnostic equipment (or similar). Entrust this task to a dealer or suitably equipped specialist.*

12 Common fuel rail – removal and refitting

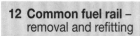

Removal

1 Remove the plastic cover from the top of the engine.

2148 cc engines

2 Remove the insulation material above the injectors **(see illustration 11.2)**.

3 Using a second spanner to counterhold, undo the unions securing the high-pressure fuel pipes to the injectors and common fuel rail, and from the common rail to the injection pump.

4 Undo the retaining bolts and detach the wiring harness cable duct.

5 Release the cable ties, and disconnect the wiring plugs from the common rail pressure sensor and pressure regulator valve.

6 Remove the exhaust back pressure sensor as described in Section 13.

7 Disconnect the fuel return pipe from the rail. Plug the openings to prevent contamination. Renew the sealing rings.

8 Undo the retaining bolts and withdraw the fuel rail from the top of the engine **(see illustration)**.

2143 cc engines

9 Disconnect the wiring plugs from the fuel filter, fuel rail pressure sensor, fuel quantity control valve, etc, then release the clips and move the wiring harness duct to one side **(see illustration)**.

10 Undo the union nuts and remove the high-pressure fuel injection pipes between the common fuel rail and the injectors **(see illustration 11.10)**. Take care not to bend or squeeze the pipes. Plug all openings as they become accessible. Mark the pipes with paint (or similar) to indicate their fitted positions.

11 Undo the banjo bolt, and disconnect the fuel return pipe from the fuel rail **(see illustration)**. Plug the openings to prevent contamination. Be prepared for fuel spillage. New sealing washers will be required.

12 Slacken the common rail mounting bolts, then undo the union securing the high-pressure pipe from the pump to the rail, and remove the pipe support brackets.

13 Completely remove the mounting bolts, and withdraw the common rail.

Refitting

14 Refitting is a reversal of removal, noting the following points:
a) *Examine the condition of the rigid, high-pressure fuel pipes. If they show any sign of wear or damage, particularly at the tapered seats at each end, renew them. It may be prudent to renew them regardless of condition.*
b) *Tighten all fasteners to their specified torque where given.*
c) *Check the fuel system for leaks prior to refitting the engine cover.*

13 Engine management control system components – removal and refitting

1 Disconnect the battery negative lead, as described in Chapter 5A Section 4, then wait at least 5 minutes for any residual electrical energy to dissipate.

Crankshaft sensor

2 Remove the plastic cover from the top of the engine.

3 Raise the front of the vehicle and support it securely on axle stands (see *Vehicle jacking and support*). Release the fasteners and remove the engine undershield **(see illustration)**.

4 The sensor if fitted to the left-hand

12.11 Fuel return pipe banjo bolt

13.3 Engine/transmission undershield fasteners

13.5 Crankshaft position sensor wiring plug

13.11 Mass air flow sensor/intake air temperature sensor

13.14 Slide out the locking catch and disconnect the mass air flow sensor wiring plug

side of the cylinder block, adjacent to the transmission bell housing. Where fitted, undo the bolt and remove the sensor heatshield.

5 Disconnect the sensor wiring plug **(see illustration)**.

6 Undo the retaining bolt and withdraw the sensor.

7 Refitting is a reversal of removal, tightening the sensor retaining bolt to the specified torque.

Coolant temperature sensor

8 Removal of the sensor is described in Chapter 3 Section 7.

Accelerator pedal position sensor

9 The sensor is integral with the accelerator pedal assembly, see Section 5.

Mass airflow/Intake air temperature sensor

10 Remove the plastic cover from the top of the engine.

2148 cc engines

11 Undo the fasteners and detach the mass airflow/intake temperature sensor from the air cleaner housing **(see illustration)**.

12 Refitting is a reversal of removal.

2143 cc engines

13 Slacken the clamps and remove the air intake hose from the front of the air filter housing.

14 Disconnect the wiring plug from the mass air flow sensor **(see illustration)**.

15 Undo the screws and remove the outlet duct from the housing. Note that the mass airflow sensor and the integral air intake temperature sensor can only be replaced complete with the air outlet ducting.

16 Refitting is a reversal of removal.

Stop-light switch

17 The engine control module receives a signal from the stop-light switch which indicates when the brakes are being applied. Stop-light switch removal and refitting details can be found in Chapter 9 Section 17.

Engine electronic control module (ECM)

Caution: Electronic Control Units (ECMs) contain components that are sensitive to the levels of static electricity generated by a person during normal activity. Once the multiway harness connector has been unplugged, the exposed ECM connector pins can freely conduct stray static electricity to these components, damaging or even destroying them – the damage will be invisible and may not manifest itself immediately. Expensive repairs can be avoided by observing the following basic handling rules:

a) Handle a disconnected ECM by its case only; do not allow fingers or tools to come into contact with the pins.

b) When carrying an ECM, earth yourself from time to time, by touching a metal object such as an unpainted water pipe, this will discharge any potentially damaging static that may have built-up.

c) Do not leave the ECM unplugged from its connector for any longer than is absolutely necessary.

Note: *If the ECM is to be renewed, prior to removal, Mercedes Benz diagnostic equipment (or equivalent) must be connected to the diagnostic plug and the stored data in the ECM retrieved. This information is essential for correctly programming the replacement ECM. Entrust this task to a Mercedes dealer or suitably equipped specialist.*

2148 cc engines

18 Unclip and remove the cover from the rear, left-hand corner of the engine compartment **(see illustration)**.

19 Release the wiring harness cable ties, then unlock and disconnect the wiring plugs from the ECM **(see illustration)**.

20 Undo the 2 retaining bolts and remove the ECM **(see illustration)**.

21 Refitting is a reversal of removal. Note that if a new ECM has been fitted, it must be configured/programmed using Mercedes diagnostic equipment (or equivalent).

2143 cc engines

22 Remove the plastic cover from the top of the engine.

23 Unlock and disconnect the wiring

13.18 Release the clips and remove the cover

13.19 As the locking catches are slid out, the wiring plugs will disconnect

13.20 ECM retaining bolts

13.23 Pivot over the locking catches to disconnect the wiring plugs

13.24 ECM retaining bolts

13.27 Fuel temperature sensor – 2148 cc engines

plugs from the ECM, then unclip the wiring harnesses **(see illustration)**.

24 Undo the 4 retaining bolts and remove the ECM **(see illustration)**.

25 Refitting is a reversal of removal. Note that if a new ECM has been fitted, it must be configured/programmed using Mercedes diagnostic equipment (or equivalent).

Fuel temperature sensor

26 Remove the plastic cover from the top of the engine.

27 The fuel temperature sensor is located the injection pump. Disconnect the sensor wiring plug **(see illustration)**.

28 Ensure that the area around the sensor is scrupulously clean, then unscrew the sensor from the pump. Renew the sealing ring.

29 Refitting is a reversal of removal, tightening the sensor to the specified torque.

Charge air temperature sensor

30 The charge air temperature sensor is located in the charge air duct adjacent to the air conditioning compressor at the front, left-hand side of the engine **(see illustrations)**.

31 Disconnect the wiring plug, then squeeze together the side of the retaining clips and pull the sensor from the duct. Renew the O-ring seal.

32 Refitting is a reversal of removal.

Camshaft position sensor

33 Remove the plastic cover from the top of the engine.

13.30a Charge air temperature sensor – 2148 cc engines...

13.30b ...and 2143 cc engines

34 Disconnect the camshaft position sensor wiring plug **(see illustrations)**.

35 Undo the retaining bolt and withdrawn the sensor from place. Renew the sensor sealing ring.

36 Refitting is a reversal of removal, tightening the sensor retaining bolt to the specified torque.

37 Refit the engine top cover.

Knock sensor

2148 cc engines

38 Remove the starter motor as described in Chapter 5A Section 9.

39 Undo the 3 retaining bolts and remove the intake port shut-off motor from the underside of the intake manifold.

40 Disconnect the wiring plug, undo the retaining bolt and withdraw the knock sensor.

41 Refitting is a reversal of removal. It's

essential that the sensor retaining bolt is tightened to the specified torque.

2143 cc engines

42 Two knock sensors are fitted to these engines. Both on the left-hand side of the cylinder block, below the intake manifold.

43 To remove the sensor for cylinders 1 and 2, remove the EGR cooler as described in Chapter 4B Section 2. There's no need to disconnect the coolant hoses from the cooler, simply move it to one side.

44 To remove the sensor for cylinders 3 and 4, remove the EGR valve as described in Chapter 4B Section 2.

45 Disconnect the wiring plug, then undo the bolt and remove the sensor **(see illustration)**.

46 Refitting is a reversal of removal. It's essential that the sensor retaining bolt is tightened to the specified torque.

13.34a Slide out the locking clip and disconnect the camshaft position sensor – 2148 cc engine

13.34b Camshaft position sensor – 2143 cc engine

13.45 Knock sensors (cylinder head removed for clarity)

13.49 Fuel filter retaining clamps

13.50 Depress the wiring plug clip

14 Throttle body –
removal and refitting

13.54 Pull the weatherstrip from the door pillar

13.55 Fuel pump control unit

Boost pressure sensor

2148 cc engines

47 Remove the plastic cover from the top of the engine.
48 Unclip the vacuum switch assembly from above the fuel filter location.
49 Release the clamps and slide the fuel filter upwards from its bracket **(see illustration)**. Move the filter to one side without disconnecting the hoses.
50 Depress the clip and disconnect the sensor wiring plug **(see illustration)**.
51 Undo the Torx bolt and pull the sensor from the manifold.
52 Refitting is a reversal of removal.

Fuel pump control unit

Note: *If the control unit is to be renewed,*

prior to removal, Mercedes-Benz diagnostic equipment (or equivalent) must be connected to the diagnostic plug and the stored data in the control unit retrieved. This information is essential for correctly programming the replacement control unit. Entrust this task to a Mercedes dealer or suitably equipped specialist.
Note: *Only fitted to 2143 cc (651 type) engines*
53 Remove the rear seat cushion as described in Chapter 11 Section 31.
54 Carefully pull the rubber weatherstrip from the right-hand rear door pillar, and pull the side panel to one side **(see illustration)**.
55 Disconnect the wiring plugs and remove the control unit **(see illustration)**.
56 Refitting is a reversal of removal.

Removal

2148 cc engines

1 Remove the plastic cover from the top of the engine.
2 Raise the front of the vehicle and support it securely on axle stands (see *Vehicle jacking and support*). Release the fasteners and remove the engine undershield.
3 Undo the top bolt, slacken the lower bolt and move the top of the engine oil level dipstick guide tube to one side.
4 Undo the 3 retaining bolts, release the fuel pipes (no need to disconnect) and position the support brace to one side.
5 Release the clamps and disconnect the EGR pipe from the throttle body.
6 Remove the fuel filter as described in Chapter 1 Section 25.
7 Undo the bolts and remove the EGR cooler bracket.
8 Undo the 5 retaining bolts and manoeuvre the intake manifold upwards from place. Renew the seals.
9 Disconnect the throttle valve actuator wiring plug.
10 Undo the 4 retaining bolts and remove the throttle body. Renew the throttle body seals.

2143 cc engines

11 Remove the plastic cover on the top of the engine.
12 Unhook the coolant hose from the holder **(see illustration)**.
13 Mark their fitted positions, then disconnect the various hoses from the vacuum reservoir **(see illustration)**.
14 Undo the retaining bolts and remove the vacuum reservoir **(see illustration)**.
15 Undo the mounting bolts, swivel the EGR cooler upwards and place to one side with the coolant hoses still attached.
16 Undo the bolts and remove the EGR pipe to the intake manifold. New seals will be required.

14.12 Unclip the coolant hose

14.13 Disconnect the vacuum hoses

14.14 Vacuum reservoir retaining bolts

17 Disconnect the wiring plug, detach the various brackets, then undo the bolts and remove the mixing chamber **(see illustrations)**.

18 Disconnect the throttle valve wiring plug, and remove the throttle body **(see illustrations)**. Renew the seal.

Refitting

19 Refitting is a reversal of removal, tightening the fasteners to their specified torque where given.

15 Manifolds – removal and refitting

Intake manifold

1 Disconnect the battery negative lead as described in Chapter 5A Section 4.
2 Remove the plastic cover from the top of the engine.
3 Drain the cooling system as described in Chapter 1 Section 30.

2148 cc engines

4 Remove the common fuel rail as described in Section 12.
5 Unclip the hoses, then unclip the fuel filter and move it to one side, with the hoses still attached.
6 Remove the EGR cooler as described in Chapter 4B Section 2.
7 Undo the upper bolt, slacken the lower bolt and move the top of the engine oil level dipstick guide tube to one side.
8 Undo the bolts and remove the EGR cooler support bracket.
9 Undo the bolts and remove the EGR pipe. New seals will be required.
10 Remove the mixing chamber.
11 Undo the bolt and disconnect the EGR pipe from the cylinder head.
12 Working under the vehicle, disconnect the wiring plugs from the glow plug output stage.
13 Undo the retaining bolts and remove the glow plug output stage.
14 Check to ensure all wiring/hoses that would impede the removal of the manifold have been released, then undo the retaining bolts and manoeuvre the intake manifold from place. Renew the manifold seals.
15 Refitting is a reversal of removal, tightening all fasteners to their specified torque.

2143 cc engines

16 Remove the fuel filter as described in Chapter 1 Section 25.
17 Remove the EGR valve as described in Chapter 4B Section 2.
18 At the rear, left-hand corner of the engine, undo the bolts securing the fuel supply and return pipes bracket, and move it to one side **(see illustration)**.
19 Disconnect the coolant hose from the outlet **(see illustration)**.

14.17a Throttle body-to-mixing chamber bolts (3 arrowed – 1 hidden), and lower mounting bolt

14.17b Mixing chamber-to-manifold bolts

14.18a Slide out the locking clip and disconnect the wiring plug

14.18b Renew the throttle body seal

20 Unclip the fuel hose, then undo the bolts and remove the fuel filter housing. A new seal will be required.
21 Undo the clamp bolts, then undo the unions and remove the high-pressure fuel pipe between the fuel rail and the pump. Plug the openings to prevent contamination.
22 Make a final check to ensure all wiring/hoses that may impeded manifold removal have been disconnected.
23 Gradually, evenly, undo the retaining bolts and lift the intake manifold from place. Renew the manifold seal.
24 Refitting is a reversal of removal, noting the following points:
a) *Tighten all fasteners to their specified torque, where given.*
b) *Top up the cooling system as described in Chapter 1 Section 30.*

c) *Check for leaks before refitting the engine cover/undershield.*

Exhaust manifold

2148 cc engines

25 Remove the turbocharger as described in Section 16.
26 Undo the retaining nuts and remove the exhaust manifold. Renew the self-locking nuts and the manifold gasket.
27 Ensure the manifold and cylinder head mating surfaces are clean, then check the condition/security of the mounting studs. Renew as necessary.
28 Refit the manifold and tighten the new retaining nuts to the specified torque.
29 Refit the turbocharger as described in Section 16.

15.18 Fuel pipes bracket bolts

15.19 Disconnect the coolant hose above the intake manifold

15.32 Move the actuator unit to one side

15.36 Counterhold the sensor union in the manifold

15.38 Disconnect the EGR pipe from the manifold

15.42 Exhaust manifold nuts tightening sequence

2143 cc engines

30 Remove the air filter housing as described in Section 2.

31 Undo the bolt/nut securing the catalytic converter to the cylinder head.

32 Disconnect the vacuum hose, undo the bolts/nut and remove the boost pressure control flap actuator unit along with its bracket **(see illustration)**. Don't disconnect the operating rod from the flap.

33 Undo the bolts and remove the heat shield above the exhaust manifold.

34 Undo the nuts and remove the bracket under the rear of the manifold.

35 Undo the screws and remove the 'holder' beneath the rear of the manifold.

36 Disconnect the wiring plug, release the harness from the clips, then unscrew the temperature sensor from the manifold **(see illustration)**.

37 Undo the bolts and remove the heat shield over the EGR pipe at the rear of the manifold.

38 Undo the bolts securing the EGR pipe to the rear of the manifold **(see illustration)**. A new gasket will be required.

39 Undo the bolts securing the manifold to the turbocharger **(see illustration 16.25)**. Note that new bolts will be required.

40 Undo the nut and press the heat shield above the starter downwards a little.

41 Undo the nuts and manoeuvre the exhaust manifold from place. Note that new nuts and a new gasket will be required.

42 Refitting is a reversal of removal. Tighten the new manifold nuts to their specified torque in the sequence shown **(see illustration)**.

16 Turbocharger – removal and refitting

Removal

2148 cc engines

1 Remove the air filter housing as described in Section 2.

2 Remove the heatshield above the turbocharger **(see illustration)**.

3 Raise the front of the vehicle and support it securely on axle stands (see *Vehicle jacking and support*). Undo the fasteners and remove the engine undershield.

4 Release the clamp securing the catalytic converter/particulate filter to the turbocharger **(see illustration)**.

5 Undo the bolts securing the catalytic converter/particulate filter to the brackets on the transmission and cylinder block.

6 Undo the retaining bolt, unclip the wiring harness, and remove the charge air pipe upstream of the intercooler.

7 Undo the banjo bolts and remove the turbocharger oil feed pipe **(see illustration)**. Renew the sealing washers.

8 Undo the retaining bolts and remove the support bracket beneath the turbocharger.

9 Disconnect the wiring plugs from the boost pressure control motor and exhaust

16.2 Undo the bolts and remove the heatshield with the brackets

16.4 Slacken the clamp bolt

16.7 Remove the turbocharger oil feed pipe

16.9 Disconnect the boost pressure control motor wiring plug

16.14a Disconnect the vacuum hoses…

16.14b …from the actuators…

16.14c …and the housing

16.18 Undo the banjo bolts and separate the pipe at the union

16.22 Remove the bracket above the alternator location

gas temperature sensor upstream of the turbocharger **(see illustration)**.

10 Remove the bolts securing the turbocharger to the exhaust manifold. Note that if Torx bolts are fitted, they must be replaced by 12-point star bolts.

11 Manoeuvre the turbocharger upwards from position, complete with the oil drain tube. Be prepared for oil spillage. Renew the drain tube O-ring seal.

12 If required, undo the bolts and detach the oil drain tube from the underside of the turbocharger.

2143 cc engines

13 Remove the air cleaner assembly as described in Section 2.

14 Disconnect the vacuum hoses from the boost pressure control flap actuators and housing **(see illustrations)**.

15 Disconnect the wiring plugs from the turbocharger temperature sensor, unclip the wiring harness, then undo the bolts and remove the air cleaner assembly front mounting bracket.

16 Unscrew the temperature sensor from the manifold flange.

17 Disconnect the wiring plug from the glow plug output stage.

18 Remove the turbocharger oil supply pipe **(see illustration)**. Plug the openings to prevent contamination.

19 Raise the front of the vehicle and support it securely on axle stands (see 'Vehicle jacking

and support'). Undo the fasteners and remove the engine undershield.

20 With reference to Section 19, remove the catalytic converter/particulate filter.

21 Remove the alternator as described in Chapter 5A Section 6.

22 Undo the bolts and remove the bracket above the alternator location **(see illustration)**.

23 Working underneath the vehicle, undo the bolts and remove the turbocharger oil return pipes assembly **(see illustration)**. Renew the seals.

24 Undo the retaining bolts and remove the turbocharger front and remove support brackets **(see illustrations)**.

25 Undo the bolts securing the exhaust

16.23 Oil return pipe bolts

16.24a Remove the front…

16.24b …and rear support brackets

16.25 Manifold-to-turbocharger bolts

18.7 Prise out the clips and disconnect the air hoses from each side of the intercooler

18.9 Lift the clip each side securing the intercooler to the radiator

manifold to the turbocharger assembly **(see illustration)**. Note than new bolts will be required.

26 Manoeuvre the turbocharger upwards from place. Renew the gasket between the exhaust manifold and turbocharger.

27 No further dismantling of the turbocharger assembly is recommended.

Refitting

28 The remainder of refitting is a reversal of removal, noting the following points:
a) *Tighten all fasteners to their specified torque where given.*
b) *Renew all seals disturbed during the removal procedure.*
c) *We consider it prudent to change the engine oil and filter following turbocharger renewal.*
d) *Ensure the charge air ducts are clean and free from debris prior to refitting.*
e) *Check for correct operation and fluid leaks.*

17 Turbocharger – examination and overhaul

1 With the turbocharger removed, inspect the housing for cracks or other visible damage.

2 Spin the turbine(s) or the compressor wheel(s) to verify that the shaft is intact and to feel for excessive shake or roughness. Some play is normal since in use the shaft is 'floating' on a film of oil. Check that the wheel vanes are undamaged.

3 The wastegate and actuator are integral with the turbocharger, and cannot be checked or renewed separately. Consult a Mercedes Benz dealer or other specialist if it is thought that the wastegate may be faulty.

4 If the exhaust or induction passages are excessively oil-contaminated, the turbo shaft oil seals have probably failed (On the induction side, this will also have contaminated the intercooler, where applicable, which if necessary should be flushed with a suitable solvent). It's normal to find a little oil residue in the ducts/intercooler due to the crankcase ventilation system.

5 Check the condition of the air duct sealing rings and renew if necessary.

6 No DIY repair of the turbo is possible. A new unit may be available on an exchange basis.

18 Intercooler – removal and refitting

Removal

1 Raise the front of the vehicle and support it securely on axle stands (see *Vehicle jacking and support*). Undo the fasteners and remove the engine undershield.

2 Remove the plastic cover on the top of the engine.

3 Remove the air intake duct at the front of the engine.

4 Remove the cooling fan and shroud as described in Chapter 3 Section 6.

5 Disconnect the wiring plug from the outside temperature sensor, and unclip the wiring harness.

6 Unclip the refrigerant pressure sensor wiring from the air duct.

7 Disconnect the intercooler intake and outlet hoses **(see illustration)**.

8 Raise the cooling module, and move it back towards the engine.

9 Unclip the intercooler on both sides, and manoeuvre it downwards from place **(see illustration)**. Unclip any wiring harnesses from the intercooler air ducting as it becomes accessible.

Refitting

10 Ensure the intercooler and air ducts are free from oil and debris. If the induction passages are excessively oil-contaminated, the turbo shaft oil seals may have failed, although it's normal to find a little oil residue in the ducts/intercooler due to the crankcase ventilation system.

11 Check the condition of the air duct sealing rings, and renew if necessary. Do not apply grease or lubricant to the new seals.

12 Refit the intercooler, reversing the removal procedure.

19 Exhaust system – general information and component renewal

General information

1 The exhaust system consists of a catalytic converter/particulate filter, a centre section and a rear section incorporating the silencer. The front section of the system is rigidly bolted to the engine and transmission, whilst the rear section is supported on rubber mountings.

2 The rear silencer is integral with the tailpipe, and is secured to the front pipes by means of clamping rings.

Removal

3 Each exhaust section can be removed individually or, alternatively, the complete system can be removed at a unit.

4 Before removing any part of the system, raise the vehicle and support it securely on axle stands (see *Vehicle jacking and support*). Where necessary, undo the fasteners and remove the engine/transmission undershield.

Rear silencer

5 Slacken the clamp at the connection securing the rear pipe/silencer to the connecting pipe.

6 Unhook the rubber mountings, and with the help of an assistant, manoeuvre the rear silencer/pipe assembly from under the vehicle.

Connecting pipe

7 Slacken the clamps securing the connecting pipe to the rear pipe and catalytic converter/particulate filter.

8 Undo the bolts/nuts securing the connecting pipe support bracket.

9 Manoeuvre the connecting pipe from place. *Caution: Take great care not to excessively bend or twist the flexible section of the exhaust pipe – it's easily damaged.*

Catalytic converter/particulate filter

2148 cc engines

10 Remove the air filter housing as described in Section 2.

11 Undo the bolts and remove the heatshield above the turbocharger.

19.12 Undo the bolts and remove the air filter rear mounting bracket

19.13 Remove the bracket above the catalytic converter

19.15 Slacken the bolt and slide the clamp along the pipe

19.16 Slacken the clamp bolt – viewed from underneath

19.17 Lower catalytic converter mounting nut

19.18 Upper mounting bracket nut location

12 Undo the bolts and remove the air filter housing rear mounting bracket **(see illustration)**.

13 Undo the bolt and remove the bracket above the catalytic converter **(see illustration)**.

14 Working underneath the vehicle, trace the oxygen sensor wiring back to the plug and disconnect it. Slide the connector from the bracket.

15 Release the clamp and disconnect the exhaust pipe from the lower catalytic converter **(see illustration)**.

16 Release the clamp securing the lower catalytic converter to the upper converter **(see illustration)**.

17 Undo the mounting nut and manoeuvre the lower catalytic converter from place **(see illustration)**.

18 Undo the nut securing the upper catalytic converter upper mounting bracket **(see illustration)**.

19 Release the clamp at the turbocharger outlet pipe, and manoeuvre the upper catalytic converter from place **(see illustration)**.

2143 cc engines

Catalytic converter

20 During removal and refitting access is extremely limited.

21 Remove the particulate filter as described later in this Section.

22 Disconnect the hose from the differential pressure sensor, and release the hose from the clamp **(see illustration)**.

23 Disconnect the oxygen sensor wiring plug and unclip the wiring from the rear air cleaner bracket.

24 Working underneath the vehicle, undo the screw and remove the heatshield around the

19.19 Turbocharger-to-catalytic converter clamp bolt

19.24 Undo the screw and unclip the heatshield

top of the steering column lower shaft **(see illustration)**.

25 Unscrew and remove the steering column lower shaft upper universal joint pinch bolt **(see illustration)**.

19.22 The differential pressure sensor is located on the rear of the air filter mounting bracket at the back of the engine

19.25 Steering column lower shaft upper joint pinch bolt

19.27 Catalytic converter-to-cylinder head bracket nut

19.30 Move the shaft to one side, and remove the catalytic converter

19.33 Detach the rear air filter mounting bracket

19.34 Disconnect the outer hose from the pressure sensor

19.36 Slacken the bolt and slide the clamp along

26 Gently push the steering column upwards from the coupling.

Caution: Don't rotate the steering wheel or column once the lower shaft has been disconnected.

27 Undo the nut securing the top of the catalytic converter to the cylinder head bracket, then slacken the nuts securing the bracket to the cylinder head **(see illustration)**.
28 Slacken the clamp securing the catalytic converter to the turbocharger.
29 Unscrew the temperature sensor from the base of the catalytic converter.
30 Move the lower steering column shaft to one side, and carefully manoeuvre the catalytic converter downwards from place **(see illustration)**.

Particulate filter

31 Raise the front of the vehicle and support it securely on axle stands (see *Vehicle jacking and support*). Release the fasteners and remove the engine undershield.
32 Remove the air filter assembly as described in Section 2.
33 Undo the bolts and detach the rear air filter mounting bracket from the cylinder head **(see illustration)**.
34 Release the clamps and disconnect the outer rubber hose from the particulate pressure sensor on the rear of the air filter bracket **(see illustration)**.
35 Undo the bolt and release the clamp securing the hoses to the air filter bracket, then undo the bolt and release the clamp securing the pressure take off pipes to the catalytic converter.
36 Working underneath the vehicle, slacken the bolt and remove the clamp securing the

exhaust pipe to the particulate filter **(see illustration)**.
37 Undo the bolt and remove the clamp securing the particulate filter to the catalytic converter **(see illustration)**.
38 Slacken the mounting nuts and slide the exhaust system rearwards a little **(see illustration)**.
39 Remove the 2 nuts securing the filter to the mounting bracket, and manoeuvre it from place **(see illustration)**.

Refitting

40 Each section is refitted by reversing the removal sequence, noting the following points:

f) *Inspect the rubber mountings for signs of damage or deterioration, and renew as necessary.*
g) *It's essential that the system if fitted 'free of tension'.*
h) *Prior to tightening the exhaust system fasteners to the specified torque, ensure that all rubber mountings are correctly located, and that there is adequate clearance between the exhaust system and vehicle underbody.*
i) *If a new particulate filter has been fitted, upon completion an engine management ECM 'adjustment' must be carried out using Mercedes-Benz STAR diagnostic equipment (or equivalent).*

19.37 Undo the bolt and remove the clamp

19.38 Slacken the mounting nuts at the front of the exhaust pipe

19.39 Undo the nuts securing the filter to the bracket

Chapter 4 Part B
Emission control systems

Contents

Section number

Catalytic converter – general information and precautions 3
Engine emission control systems – testing and component renewal   2

Section number

General information 1

Degrees of difficulty

Easy, suitable for novice with little experience	Fairly easy, suitable for beginner with some experience	Fairly difficult, suitable for competent DIY mechanic	Difficult, suitable for experienced DIY mechanic	Very difficult, suitable for expert DIY or professional

Specifications

Emissions level:
2148 cc engine (type 646) EU4
2143 cc engine (type 651) EU5

Torque wrench settings	Nm	lbf ft
EGR cooler:		
M6	10	7
M8	20	15
EGR valve.	10	7

1 General information

1 All diesel engine models are also designed to meet strict emission requirements. All models are fitted with a crankcase emission control system, a catalytic converter/ particulate filter, and an exhaust gas recirculation (EGR) system.
2 The emission control systems function as follows.

Crankcase emission control

3 To reduce the emission of unburned hydrocarbons from the crankcase into the atmosphere, the engine is sealed and the blow-by gases and oil vapour are drawn from inside the crankcase, through a wire mesh oil separator, into the intake tract to be burned by the engine during normal combustion.

Exhaust emission control

4 To minimise the level of exhaust pollutants released into the atmosphere, all models are fitted with a catalytic converter and a diesel particulate filter incorporated into the front section of the exhaust pipe.
5 The catalytic converter consists of a canister containing a fine mesh impregnated with a catalyst material, over which the hot exhaust gases pass. The catalyst speeds up the oxidation of harmful carbon monoxide, unburned hydrocarbons and soot, effectively reducing the quantity of harmful products released into the atmosphere via the exhaust gases.

Particulate filter

6 This device is designed to trap carbon particulates produced by the combustion process. The particle filter is fitted downstream of the catalytic converter. In order to prevent the filter blocking, pressure and temperature sensors are fitted to the filter. Under the normal, high-speed driving conditions, the soot particles are burnt off in the filter by the high temperature of the exhaust gases. However, where the driving conditions are such that the exhaust gases are not sufficiently high, the engine management system injects fuel into the cylinders after the point of combustion. These are called post-injections, and raise the temperature of the exhaust gases, causing the soot particles in the filter to be burnt off.
7 On some models, an additive known as Adblue is added to the fuel to help clean the particulate filter. For more information concerning Adblue, consult your vehicle handbook or Mercedes Dealer.

Exhaust gas recirculation (EGR) system

8 This system is designed to recirculate small quantities of exhaust gas into the intake tract, and therefore into the combustion process. This process reduces the level of unburnt hydrocarbons present in the exhaust gas before it reaches the catalytic converter. The system is controlled by the engine management system ECM, using the information from its various sensors, via the EGR valve which is fitted to the metal pipe connecting the intake and exhaust manifolds. On all models, the exhaust gasses are cooled prior to entering the intake manifold by passing through a cooler mounted on the side of the EGR valve. Engine coolant circulates through the cooler.

2 Engine emission control systems – testing and component renewal

Crankcase emission control

Testing

1 The components of this system require no attention other than to check that the hose(s) are clear and undamaged at regular intervals. If the system is thought to be faulty, renew the crankcase pressure limiting valve as follows.

Oil separator

2148 cc engines

2 The oil separator is integral with the cylinder head cover. Removal of the cover is described in Chapter 2A Section 4.

2143 cc engines

3 The oil separator is incorporated into the cylinder head cover. Removal of the cover is described in Chapter 2B Section 4.
4 Refitting is a reversal of removal. Tighten the retaining bolts securely.

Exhaust emission control

Testing

5 The performance of the catalytic converter or diesel particulate filter can be checked only by using Mercedes Benz diagnostic equipment (or equivalent). Entrust this task to a dealer or suitable equipped specialist.
6 Before assuming that the catalytic

converter/particulate filter is faulty, it is worth checking whether the problem is not due to a faulty injector(s). Refer to your Mercedes Benz dealer for further information.

Catalytic converter and particulate filter – renewal

7 Refer to Chapter 4A Section 19 for removal and refitting details.

Exhaust gas recirculation (EGR) system

Testing

8 Comprehensive testing of the system can only be carried out using specialist electronic equipment which is connected to the injection system diagnostic wiring connector (see Chapter 4A).

EGR cooler – renewal

9 Drain the coolant as described in Chapter 1 Section 30.

2148 cc engines

10 Remove the upper bolt, and slacken the oil level dipstick guide tube lower bolt.
11 Slacken the lower bolt, and remove the upper bolts securing the EGR cooler support bracket. Move the support bracket to one side a little.
12 Release the clamps and disconnect the coolant hoses from the EGR cooler.
13 Undo the EGR cooler retaining bolts and remove the upper support bracket.
14 Manoeuvre the EGR cooler from place. Renew the gasket.

15 Refitting is a reversal of removal.

2143 cc engines

16 Remove the plastic cover from the top of the engine.
17 Unclip the coolant hose, then mark their fitted positions, and disconnect the various vacuum hoses from the vacuum reservoir **(see illustration)**.
18 Undo the bolts and remove the vacuum reservoir **(see illustration)**.
19 Apply clamps to the EGR cooler hoses, then disconnect the hoses **(see illustration)**.
20 Undo the retaining bolts, and remove the EGR cooler **(see illustrations)**. Renew the gasket.
21 Refitting is a reversal of removal.

All engines

22 Refitting is a reversal of removal.

Exhaust gas recirculation (EGR) valve – renewal

2148 cc engines

23 Undo the fasteners and remove the plastic cover from the top of the engine.
24 Disconnect the EGR valve wiring plug **(see illustration)**.
25 Undo the retaining bolts and remove the EGR valve. Renew the O-ring seal.

2143 cc engines

26 Remove the EGR cooler as described earlier in this Section.
27 Undo the bolts and remove the EGR pipe

2.17 Disconnect the hoses from the vacuum reservoir

2.18 Vacuum reservoir bolts

2.19 Release the clips and disconnect the hoses

2.20a Remove the front, lower bolt...

2.20b ...followed by the 3 upper, and 3 lower bolts at the rear

2.24 EGR valve wiring plug

2.27 Remove the pipe between the mixing chamber and EGR valve

2.28 Mixing chamber retaining bolts

2.29 Fuel pipe bracket retaining bolts

2.34 EGR valve lower retaining bolts

between the mixing chamber and the EGR valve **(see illustration)**. Renew the gaskets.

28 Remove the mixing chamber **(see illustration)**.

29 Disconnect the vacuum solenoid wiring plug, then undo the 2 screws securing the fuel supply and return pipes bracket **(see illustration)**.

30 Slacken the upper bolt, undo the lower bolt and remove the shield over the fuel supply pipe.

31 Release the clamp, then disconnect the fuel supply hose from the high-pressure pump and move it one side. Be prepared for fuel spillage.

32 Prise the wiring harness clips from place, then undo the 4 bolts and move the wiring harness bracket to one side.

33 Disconnect the EGR valve wiring plug and vacuum hose.

34 Undo the 4 retaining bolts and remove the EGR valve **(see illustration)**. Renew the seal/gasket.

All engines

35 Refitting is a reversal of removal.

3 Catalytic converter – general information and precautions

1 The catalytic converter is a reliable and simple device which needs no maintenance

in itself, but there are some facts of which an owner should be aware if the converter is to function properly for its full service life.

a) *DO NOT use fuel or engine oil additives – these may contain substances harmful to the catalytic converter.*

b) *DO NOT continue to use the car if the engine burns oil to the extent of leaving a visible trail of blue smoke.*

c) *Remember that the catalytic converter operates at very high temperatures. DO NOT, therefore, park the car in dry undergrowth, over long grass or piles of dead leaves after a long run.*

d) *Remember that the catalytic converter is FRAGILE – do not strike it with tools during servicing work.*

Notes

Chapter 5 Part A
Starting and charging systems

Contents

Section number

Alternator – removal and refitting............................. 6
Alternator – testing and overhaul............................. 7
Battery – disconnection, removal and refitting............... 4
Battery – testing and charging............................... 3
Charging system – testing 5

Section number

Electrical fault finding – general information 2
General information and precautions.......................... 1
Starter motor – removal and refitting........................ 9
Starter motor – testing and overhaul 10
Starting system – testing 8

Degrees of difficulty

Easy, suitable for novice with little experience	**Fairly easy,** suitable for beginner with some experience	**Fairly difficult,** suitable for competent DIY mechanic	**Difficult,** suitable for experienced DIY mechanic	**Very difficult,** suitable for expert DIY or professional

Specifications

System type .... 12-volt, negative earth
Alternator .... 140 to 180 A @ 25°C
Battery charge condition:
  Poor .... 12.5 volts
  Normal .... 12.6 volts
  Good .... 12.7 volts

Torque wrench settings	Nm	lbf ft
Alternator bolts..	20	15
Starter motor bolts.....................................	40	30

1 General information and precautions

General information

1 The engine electrical system consists mainly of the charging and starting systems. Because of their engine-related functions, these components are covered separately from the body electrical devices such as the lights, instruments, etc (which are covered in Chapter 12). Refer to Chapter 5B for information on the pre-heating system.
2 The electrical system is of the 12-volt negative earth type.
3 The battery is of the low maintenance or "maintenance-free" (sealed for life) type and is charged by the alternator, which is belt-driven from the crankshaft pulley.
4 The starter motor is of the pre-engaged type incorporating an integral solenoid. On

starting, the solenoid moves the drive pinion into engagement with the flywheel ring gear before the starter motor is energised. Once the engine has started, a one-way clutch prevents the motor armature being driven by the engine until the pinion disengages from the flywheel.

Precautions

5 Further details of the various systems are given in the relevant Sections of this Chapter. While some repair procedures are given, the usual course of action is to renew the component concerned. The owner whose interest extends beyond mere component renewal should obtain a copy of the "Automotive Electrical & Electronic Systems Manual", available from the publishers of this manual.
6 It is necessary to take extra care when working on the electrical system to avoid damage to semi-conductor devices (diodes and transistors), and to avoid the risk of personal injury. In addition to the precautions

given in "Safety first!" at the beginning of this manual, observe the following when working on the system:
7 Always remove rings, watches, etc before working on the electrical system. Even with the battery disconnected, capacitive discharge could occur if a component's live terminal is earthed through a metal object. This could cause a shock or nasty burn.
8 Do not reverse the battery connections. Components such as the alternator, electronic control units, or any other components having semi-conductor circuitry could be irreparably damaged.
9 If the engine is being started using jump leads and a slave battery, connect the batteries positive-to-positive and negative-to-negative (see *Jump starting* at the beginning of this manual. This also applies when connecting a battery charger.
10 Never disconnect the battery terminals, the alternator, any electrical wiring or any test instruments when the engine is running.

11 Do not allow the engine to turn the alternator when the alternator is not connected.

12 Never "test" for alternator output by "flashing" the output lead to earth.

13 Never use an ohmmeter of the type incorporating a hand-cranked generator for circuit or continuity testing.

14 Always ensure that the battery negative lead is disconnected when working on the electrical system.

15 Before using electric-arc welding equipment on the car, disconnect the battery, alternator and components such as the fuel injection/ignition electronic control unit to protect them from the risk of damage.

2 Electrical fault finding – general information

1 Refer to Chapter 12 Section 2.

3 Battery – testing and charging

Standard and low maintenance battery – testing

1 If the vehicle covers a small annual mileage, it is worthwhile checking the specific gravity of the electrolyte every three months to determine the state of charge of the battery. Use a hydrometer to make the check and compare the results with the following table. Note that the specific gravity readings assume an electrolyte temperature of 15°C (60°F); for every 10°C (18°F) below 15°C (60°F) subtract 0.007. For every 10°C (18°F) above 15°C (60°F) add 0.007.

Ambient temperature	Above 25°C (77°F)	Below 25°C (77°F)
Fully charged	1.210 to 1.230	1.270 to 1.290
70% charged	1.17 to 1.190	1.230 to 1.250
Discharged	1.050 to 1.070	1.110 to 1.130

2 If the battery condition is suspect, first check the specific gravity of electrolyte in each cell. A variation of 0.040 or more between any cells indicates loss of electrolyte or deterioration of the internal plates.

3 If the specific gravity variation is 0.040 or more, the battery should be renewed. If the cell variation is satisfactory but the battery is discharged, it should be charged as described later in this Section.

Maintenance-free battery – testing

4 In cases where a "sealed for life" maintenance-free battery is fitted, topping-up and testing of the electrolyte in each cell is not possible. The condition of the battery can therefore only be tested using a battery condition indicator or a voltmeter.

5 Models may be fitted with a "Delco" type maintenance-free battery, with a built-in charge condition indicator. The indicator is located in the top of the battery casing, and indicates the condition of the battery from its colour. If the indicator shows green, then the battery is in a good state of charge. If the indicator turns darker, eventually to black, then the battery requires charging, as described later in this Section. If the indicator shows clear/yellow, then the electrolyte level in the battery is too low to allow further use, and the battery should be renewed. Do not attempt to charge, load or jump start a battery when the indicator shows clear/yellow.

6 If testing the battery using a voltmeter, connect the voltmeter across the battery and compare the result with those given in the Specifications under "charge condition". The test is only accurate if the battery has not been subjected to any kind of charge for the previous six hours. If this is not the case, switch on the headlights for 30 seconds, then wait four to five minutes before testing the battery after switching off the headlights. All other electrical circuits must be switched off, so check that the doors and tailgate are fully shut when making the test.

7 If the voltage reading is less than 12.2 volts, then the battery is discharged, whilst a reading of 12.2 to 12.4 volts indicates a partially discharged condition.

8 If the battery is to be charged, remove it from the vehicle (Section 4) and charge it as described later in this Section.

Standard and low maintenance battery – charging

Note: *The following is intended as a guide only. Always refer to the manufacturer's recommendations (often printed on a label attached to the battery) before charging a battery.*

9 Charge the battery at a rate of 3.5 to 4 amps and continue to charge the battery at this rate until no further rise in specific gravity is noted over a four hour period.

10 Alternatively, a trickle charger charging at the rate of 1.5 amps can safely be used overnight.

11 Specially rapid "boost" charges which are claimed to restore the power of the battery in 1 to 2 hours are not recommended, as they can cause serious damage to the battery plates through overheating.

12 While charging the battery, note that the temperature of the electrolyte should never exceed 37.8°C (100°F).

Maintenance-free battery – charging

Note: *The following is intended as a guide only. Always refer to the manufacturer's recommendations (often printed on a label attached to the battery) before charging a battery.*

13 This battery type takes considerably longer to fully recharge than the standard type, the time taken being dependent on the extent of discharge, but it can take anything up to three days.

14 A constant voltage type charger is required, to be set, when connected, to 13.9 to 14.9 volts with a charger current below 25 amps. Using this method, the battery should be usable within three hours, giving a voltage reading of 12.5 volts, but this is for a partially discharged battery and, as mentioned, full charging can take considerably longer.

15 If the battery is to be charged from a fully discharged state (condition reading less than 12.2 volts), have it recharged by your Mercedes Benz dealer or local automotive electrician, as the charge rate is higher and constant supervision during charging is necessary.

Caution: Do not charge AGM batteries above 14.8 volts, or the battery may be damaged.

16 The battery can only be charged by connecting the charger positive lead to the battery positive terminal, and the charger negative lead to the vehicle earth connection. Do not connect a battery charger negative lead directly to the battery terminal. These vehicles are fitted with an Battery Sensor, which monitors the flow of current to and from the battery. If it calculates the state of the battery is getting low, it will ask the various car electrical systems to shut down certain electrical consumers. Eventually, the control unit/sensor may decide the battery state is so poor it decides the starting system must be disabled. Consequently, if a battery charger is connected directly to the terminals of the battery, even though the battery may be completely recharged, the system may still believe the battery state to be poor, as it has registered no current passing into the battery. Therefore, even though the battery is charged, the starter circuit may still be disabled.

4 Battery – disconnection, removal and refitting

Battery

Main battery

Disconnection

1 Ensure that all electrical consumers are switched off, all windows are closed, and the alarm is disarmed. Remove the remote control from the vehicle, and wait at least 2 minutes for the electrical systems to 'power down'.

2 On models equipped with 'Keyless GO', remove the transmitter key from the vehicle, and store it at least 2m away, out of transmitter range.

4.3a Release the three clips…

4.3b …and lift up the cover

4.5 Slacken the nut and pull the negative terminal clamp from the battery post

Models with the battery in the engine compartment

3 Release the 3 retaining clips and remove the plastic cover from the left-hand rear corner of the engine compartment **(see illustrations)**.

Models with the battery in the luggage compartment

4 Open the tailgate and lift out the luggage compartment floor panel.

All models

5 Slacken the nut and disconnect the negative terminal clamp from the battery **(see illustration)**. Position the negative lead in such a way that it cannot accidentally touch the battery terminal.
6 If required, lift up the plastic cover, slacken the nut and disconnect the positive terminal clamp from the battery **(see illustration)**.

Removal

7 Disconnect the battery as described previously in this Section.
8 Unscrew the bolt and remove the battery retaining clamp then lift the battery out of the engine compartment **(see illustration)**. Disconnect the vent pipe as the battery is withdrawn.

Refitting

9 Refitting is a reversal of removal, but smear petroleum jelly on the terminals when reconnecting the leads, and always reconnect

4.6 Disconnect the positive terminal clamp in the same manner

the positive lead first, and the negative lead last.
10 After reconnection, the following procedures may need to be carried out:

Set time in instrument cluster

11 Refer to the owners handbook.

Reset the electric windows

12 Operate the window switch to fully close the window, then hold the switch in this position for approximately 1 second. Repeat this procedure for each window.

Folding mirrors

13 Reset the folding exterior mirrors function as follows:

4.8 Battery retaining clamp bolt

a) *Turn the ignition switch to position I.*
b) *Briefly press the centre mirror-fold switch.*
c) *Turn off the ignition.*

Additional battery

14 On some models, an additional battery is fitted. Lift out the luggage compartment floor, followed the by storage tray where fitted.
15 Prise up the centre pins, lever out the plastic expansion rivets and remove the plastic cover over the battery (where fitted) **(see illustrations)**.
16 Undo the bolt and disconnect the battery negative lead **(see illustration)**.
17 Undo the bolt and disconnect the battery positive lead.

4.15a Prise up the centre pins, lever out the expansion rivets…

4.15b …and lift out the cover

4.16 Negative lead bolt

4.18 Battery clamp retaining nut

18 Undo the retaining nut and lift open the battery clamp **(see illustration)**.
19 Disconnect the vent pipe and manoeuvre the battery from place.
20 Refitting is a reversal of removal.

5 Charging system – testing

1 Refer to the warnings given in "Safety first!" and in Section 1 of this Chapter before starting work.
2 If the ignition warning light fails to illuminate when the ignition is switched on, first check the alternator wiring connections for security. If the light still fails to illuminate, check the

6.4a Remove the upstream air duct...

continuity of the warning light feed wire from the alternator to the instrument. If all is satisfactory, the alternator maybe at fault and should be renewed or taken to an auto-electrician for testing and repair. Bear in mind that the E-Class is equipped with a sophisticated self-diagnosis system, and any fault detected by the system will generate a fault code. Use Mercedes Benz diagnostic equipment (or equivalent) connected to the vehicles diagnostic plug (see Chapter 4A Section 6) to interrogate the ECM, read the code, and investigate the fault recorded.
3 If the ignition warning light illuminates when the engine is running, stop the engine and check that the drivebelt is correctly tensioned (see Chapter 1 Section 6) and that the alternator connections are secure. If all is so far satisfactory, have the alternator checked by an auto-electrician for testing and repair.
4 If the alternator output is suspect even though the warning light functions correctly, the regulated voltage may be checked as follows.
5 Connect a voltmeter across the battery terminals and start the engine.
6 Increase the engine speed until the voltmeter reading remains steady; the reading should be approximately 12 to 13 volts, and no more than 14 volts.
7 Switch on as many electrical accessories (eg, the headlights, heated rear window and heater blower) as possible, and check that the

6.4b ...and the downstream duct

alternator maintains the regulated voltage at around 13 to 14 volts.
8 If the regulated voltage is not as stated, the fault may be due to worn brushes, weak brush springs, a faulty voltage regulator, a faulty diode, a severed phase winding or worn or damaged slip rings. The alternator should be renewed or taken to an auto-electrician for testing and repair.

6 Alternator – removal and refitting

Removal

1 Raise the front of the vehicle and support it securely on axle stands (see *Vehicle jacking and support*). Undo the fasteners and remove the engine undershield.
2 Disconnect the battery negative lead as described in Section 4.

2148 cc engines

3 Remove the plastic cover from the top of the engine.
4 Release and remove the air intake ducts, upstream and downstream of the air cleaner housing **(see illustrations)**.
5 Remove the auxiliary drivebelt as described in Chapter 1 Section 6.
6 Undo the bolts and remove the noise damper upstream of the intercooler.
7 Disconnect the wiring from the alternator.
8 Undo the 4 mounting bolts, and manoeuvre the alternator downwards from place **(see illustration)**.

2143 cc engines

9 Remove the cooling fan shroud as described in Chapter 3 Section 6.
10 Remove the auxiliary drivebelt as described in Chapter 1 Section 6.
11 Remove the air duct between the intercooler and the turbocharger.
12 Unclip the wiring harness, then undo the bolts and remove the alternator upper mounting bracket **(see illustration)**.

6.8 Alternator upper mounting bolts

6.12 Remove the alternator upper mounting bracket

6.13a Pull off the plastic cap, unscrew the nut and disconnect the battery lead

6.13b Slide out the locking clip and disconnect the wiring plug

6.14 Alternator lower mounting bolts

13 Disconnect the wiring from the alternator **(see illustrations)**.

14 Undo the mounting bolts and lower the alternator from place **(see illustration)**.

Refitting

15 Refitting is the reverse of removal tightening all mounting bolts to their specified torque settings (where given). Ensure the drivebelt is correctly refitted and tensioned as described in Chapter 1 Section 6.

7 Alternator – testing and overhaul

1 If the alternator is thought to be suspect, it should be removed from the vehicle and taken to an auto-electrician for testing. Most auto-electricians will be able to supply and fit brushes at a reasonable cost. However, check on the cost of repairs before proceeding as it may prove more economical to obtain a new or exchange alternator.

8 Starting system – testing

Note: *Refer to the precautions given in Safety first! and in Section 1 of this Chapter before starting work.*

1 If the starter motor fails to operate when the ignition key is turned to the appropriate position, the following possible causes may be responsible.

a) *The battery is faulty.*
b) *The electrical connections between the switch, solenoid, battery and starter motor are somewhere failing to pass the necessary current from the battery through the starter to earth.*
c) *The solenoid is faulty.*
d) *The starter motor is mechanically or electrically defective.*

2 To check the battery, switch on the headlights. If they dim after a few seconds, this indicates that the battery is discharged – recharge (see Section 3) or renew the battery. If the headlights glow brightly, operate the ignition switch and observe the lights. If they

dim, then this indicates that current is reaching the starter motor; therefore the fault must lie in the starter motor. If the lights continue to glow brightly (and no clicking sound can be heard from the starter motor solenoid), this indicates that there is a fault in the circuit or solenoid – see following paragraphs. If the starter motor turns slowly when operated, but the battery is in good condition, then this indicates that either the starter motor is faulty, or there is considerable resistance somewhere in the circuit.

3 If a fault in the circuit is suspected, disconnect the battery leads (including the earth connection to the body), the starter/solenoid wiring and the engine/ transmission earth strap. Thoroughly clean the connections, and reconnect the leads and wiring, then use a voltmeter or test lamp to check that full battery voltage is available at the battery positive lead connection to the solenoid, and that the earth is sound. Smear petroleum jelly around the battery terminals to prevent corrosion – corroded connections are amongst the most frequent causes of electrical system faults

4 If the battery and all connections are in good condition, check the circuit by disconnecting the trigger wire from the solenoid terminal. Connect a voltmeter or test lamp between the wire end and a good earth (such as the battery negative terminal), and check that the wire is live when the ignition switch is turned to the 'start' position. If it is, then the circuit is sound – if not the circuit wiring can be checked as described in Chapter 12 Section 2.

5 The solenoid contacts can be checked by connecting a voltmeter or test lamp between the battery positive feed connection on the starter side of the solenoid and earth. When the ignition switch is turned to the 'start' position, there should be a reading or lighted bulb, as applicable. If there is no reading or lighted bulb, the solenoid is faulty and should be renewed.

6 If the circuit and solenoid are proved sound, the fault must lie in the starter motor. Begin checking the starter motor by removing it and having the brushes checked. If the fault does not lie in the brushes, the motor windings must be faulty. In this event, it may be possible to have the starter motor overhauled

by a specialist, but check on the availability and cost of spares before proceeding, as it may prove more economical to obtain a new or exchange motor.

9 Starter motor – removal and refitting

Removal

2148 cc engines

1 The starter motor is bolted to the transmission bellhousing, at the rear of the engine on the left-hand side. Access is best achieved from under the front of the car.

2 Disconnect the battery negative lead as described in Section 4.

3 Raise the front of the vehicle and support it securely on axle stands (see *Vehicle jacking and support*). Undo the fasteners and remove the engine undershield.

4 Disconnect the wiring from the starter. Where necessary unbolt the wiring harness bracket **(see illustration)**.

5 Undo the mounting bolts, and lower the starter motor from place. In order to access the upper mounting bolt, use Torx socket and long extensions accross the top of the gearbox.

2143 cc engines

6 The starter is fitted to the right-hand side of the cylinder block.

9.4 Disconnect the wiring from the front of the starter motor, and unbolt the harness bracket

9.10 Remove the heatshield above the starter

9.11a Undo the nut, disconnect the wiring…

7 Disconnect the battery negative lead as described in Section 4.

8 Raise the front of the vehicle and support it securely on axle stands as described in *Vehicle jacking and support*. Undo the fasteners and remove the engine/transmission undershield.

9 Remove the catalytic converter/particulate filter as described in Chapter 4A Section 19.

10 Undo the bolts and remove the heat shield over the starter motor **(see illustration)**. Unclip the vacuum pipe from the rear of the heatshield.

11 Disconnect the wiring from the starter motor **(see illustrations)**.

12 Remove the turbocharger rear support bracket **(see illustration)**.

13 Undo the mounting bolts and lower the

starter motor from place. Note that we found it easier to unscrew the upper mounting bolt using a series of extension rods, working over the top of the transmission.

Refitting

14 Refitting is a reversal of removal tightening the mounting bolts to the specified torque. Ensure all wiring is correctly routed and its retaining nuts are securely tightened.

9.11b …pull away the cap, undo the nut and disconnect the battery lead

9.12 Turbocharger rear support bracket

10 Starter motor – testing and overhaul

1 If the starter motor is thought to be suspect, it should be removed from the vehicle and taken to an auto-electrician for testing. Most auto-electricians will be able to supply and fit brushes at a reasonable cost. However, check on the cost of repairs before proceeding as it may prove more economical to obtain a new or exchange motor.

Chapter 5 Part B
Pre-heating system

Contents

Section number

General information 1
Glow plug output stage – removal and refitting 4

Section number

Glow plugs – removal, inspection and refitting 3
Pre-heating system – testing 2

Degrees of difficulty

Easy, suitable for novice with little experience	Fairly easy, suitable for beginner with some experience	Fairly difficult, suitable for competent DIY mechanic	Difficult, suitable for experienced DIY mechanic	Very difficult, suitable for expert DIY or professional

Specifications

Torque wrench settings	Nm	lbf ft
Glow plugs:		
M8	10	7
M10	18	13

1 General information

1 To assist cold starting, diesel-engined models are fitted with a preheating system, which comprises glow plugs (one per cylinder), a glow plug output stage, a facia-mounted warning lamp, a coolant temperature sensor and the associated electrical wiring.

2 The glow plugs are miniature electric heating elements, encapsulated in a ceramic case with a probe at one end and electrical connection at the other. Each combustion chamber has one glow plug threaded into it. When the glow plug is energised, it heats up rapidly causing the temperature of the air charge drawn into each of the combustion chambers to rise. The glow plug probe is positioned directly in line with the incoming spray of fuel from the injectors. Hence the fuel passing over the glow plug probe is also heated, allowing its optimum combustion temperature to be achieved more readily. In addition, small particles of the fuel passing over the glow plugs are ignited and this helps to trigger the combustion process.

3 A warning light informs the driver that pre-heating is taking place. The lamp extinguishes when sufficient pre-heating has taken place to allow the engine to be started, but power will still be supplied to the glow plugs for a further period until the engine is started. If no attempt is made to start the engine, the power supply to the glow plugs is switched off to prevent battery drain and glow plug burn-out.

4 The system employs post-glowing (after-heating), which operates as follows. After the engine has been started, the glow plugs continue to operate for a further period of time. This helps to improve fuel combustion whilst the engine is warming-up, resulting in quieter, smoother running and reduced exhaust emissions. The duration of the after-heating period is dependent on the coolant temperature.

2 Pre-heating system – testing

1 Full testing of the system can only be carried out using specialist diagnostic equipment which is connected to the engine management system diagnostic wiring connector (see Chapter 4A Section 6). If the pre-heating system is thought to be faulty, some preliminary checks of the glow plug operation may be made as described in the following paragraphs.

Caution: Do not apply battery voltage (12v) to the glow plugs – they may be damaged by the voltage.

2 To locate a faulty glow plug, first operate the pre-heating system to allow the glow plugs to reach working temperature, then disconnect the battery negative lead as described in Chapter 5A Section 4.

3 Refer to Section 3, and remove the supply cable from No 2 glow plug terminal. Measure the electrical resistance between the glow plug terminal and the engine earth. A reading of anything more than a few Ohms indicates that the glow plug is defective.

4 As a final check, remove the glow plugs and inspect them visually, as described in Section 3.

Note: *Hairline cracks may cause the ceramic probe to fail, and yet be impossible to detect.*

5 If no problems are found, take the vehicle to a Mercedes Benz dealer or suitably equipped specialist for testing using the appropriate diagnostic equipment.

3.3 Squeeze together the sides and pull the connector from the glow plug

3.8 Release the various clips and move the harness duct to one side

3.9 The glow plugs are located beneath the common fuel rail

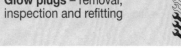

3   Glow plugs – removal, inspection and refitting

Removal

Caution: The glow plugs are very delicate, and easily damaged – handle with care.

1 Disconnect the battery negative lead as described in Chapter 5A Section 4.

2148 cc engines

2 Remove the plastic cover on the top of the engine.

3 Disconnect the glow plug wiring connectors **(see illustration)**.

4 Clean the area around the glow plugs to prevent contamination, then using a deep socket, unscrew and remove them.

5 If the torque required to remove a glow plug exceeds 25 Nm, Mercedes recommend to bring the engine upto operating temperature and trying again. Bear in mind that if the hexagonal section of the plug breaks off, the plug will then need to be drilled out, which may involve cylinder head removal.

2143 cc engines

6 Remove the plastic cover on the top of the engine.

4.3 The output stage is above the starter motor

7 Remove the fuel filter as described in Chapter 1 Section 25. There's no need to disconnect the hoses from the filter – place the filter to one side.

8 Disconnect the wiring plugs from the fuel filter, fuel rail pressure sensor, etc, then release the clips and move the wiring harness duct to one side **(see illustration)**.

9 Squeeze together the sides, and disconnect the glow plug wiring connectors **(see illustration)**.

10 Clean the area around the glow plugs to prevent contamination, then using a deep socket, unscrew and remove them.

11 If the torque required to remove a glow plug exceeds 25 Nm, Mercedes recommend to bring the engine upto operating temperature and trying again. Bear in mind that if the hexagonal section of the plug breaks off, the plug will then need to be drilled out, which may involve cylinder head removal.

Inspection

12 Inspect the glow plugs for signs of damage. Burnt or eroded glow plug tips can be caused by a bad injector spray pattern. Have the injectors checked if this sort of damage is found.

Caution: The glow plugs may be damaged if battery voltage (12v) is applied to them.

4.6 Glow plug output stage retaining bolts

Refitting

13 Thoroughly clean the glow plugs, and the glow plug seating areas in the cylinder head.

14 Apply a thin smear of anti-seize compound to the glow plug threads, then refit the glow plug and tighten it to the specified torque.

15 Reconnect the wiring to the glow plug. The connectors are a push-fit.

16 The remainder of refitting is a reversal of removal.

4   Glow plug output stage – removal and refitting

Removal

1 Disconnect the battery negative lead as described in Chapter 5A Section 4.

2148 cc engines

2 Raise the front of the vehicle and support it securely on axle stands (see *Vehicle jacking and support*). Undo the fasteners and remove the engine/transmission undershield.

3 The glow plug output stage is located on the left-hand side of the engine/transmission **(see illustration)**. Undo the retaining bolts, lower the output stage, and disconnect the wiring plugs.

2143 cc engines

4 The glow plug output stage is located at the front of the engine. Remove the plastic cover from the top of the engine.

5 Disconnect the wiring plugs from the output stage.

6 Undo the 2 retaining bolts and remove the output stage **(see illustration)**. Note the earth connection under the mounting bolt.

Refitting

7 Refitting is a reversal of removal.

Chapter 6
Clutch

Contents

	Section number		Section number
Clutch assembly – removal, inspection and refitting	5	Clutch slave cylinder – removal, inspection and refitting	3
Clutch hydraulic system – bleeding	4	General information and precautions	1
Clutch master cylinder – removal and refitting	2	Release bearing – renewal	6

Degrees of difficulty

Easy, suitable for novice with little experience	**Fairly easy,** suitable for beginner with some experience	**Fairly difficult,** suitable for competent DIY mechanic	**Difficult,** suitable for experienced DIY mechanic	**Very difficult,** suitable for expert DIY or professional

Specifications

Type	Self-adjusting, single dry plate with diaphragm spring, hydraulically-operated
Friction plate	
Diameter	240 or 260 mm
Lining thickness:	
New (approximate)	3.6 to 4.0 mm
Service limit	2.6 to 3.0 mm

Torque wrench settings	Nm	lbf ft
Brake servo-to-pedal pivot bolt*	20	15
Pedal assembly retaining nuts	20	15
Pressure plate retaining bolts:		
Stage 1	16	12
Stage 2	25	18
Slave cylinder mounting bolt:		
716 transmission	10	7
711 transmission	8	6

*Do not re-use

1 General information and precautions

1 All models are fitted with a single dry plate clutch system. The main components consist of a friction disc, pressure plate (or cover), hydraulic master cylinder and release bearing/slave cylinder.

2 The clutch pressure plate is bolted to the rear face of the flywheel, and the friction disc is located between the pressure plate and the flywheel friction surface. The friction disc is splined to the transmission input shaft and is free to slide along the splines. Friction lining material is riveted to each side of the disc, and the disc hub incorporates cushioning springs to absorb transmission shocks and ensure a smooth take-up of drive. The pressure plate incorporates an internal diaphragm spring mounted on a fulcrum ring. When the inner fingers of the spring are depressed, the outer perimeter draws the pressure plate away from the friction disc.

3 The release bearing is part of the slave cylinder and is operated by the clutch pedal, using hydraulic pressure. The pedal acts on the hydraulic master cylinder pushrod, and hydraulic pressure operates the slave cylinder, which incorporates the release bearing.

4 When the clutch pedal is depressed, the release bearing is pushed forwards, to bear against the centre of the diaphragm spring, thus pushing the centre of the diaphragm spring inwards.

5 When the clutch pedal is released, the diaphragm spring forces the pressure plate into contact with the friction linings on the friction disc, and simultaneously pushes the friction disc forwards on its splines, forcing it against the flywheel. The friction disc is now firmly sandwiched between the pressure plate and the flywheel, and drive is taken up.

6 The clutch is self-adjusting. As wear takes place on the friction disc over a period of time, the pressure plate automatically moves closer to the friction plate to compensate.

2.2 Disconnect the clutch fluid supply pipe

2.4 Prise out the wire clip a little

2.5 Prise off the piston rod clip

> ⚠ **Warning: Dust created by clutch wear and deposited on the clutch components may contain asbestos, which is a health hazard. DO NOT blow it out with compressed air, or inhale any of it. DO NOT use petrol (or petroleum-based solvents) to clean off the dust. Brake system cleaner or methylated spirit should be used to flush the dust into a suitable receptacle. After the clutch components are wiped clean with rags, dispose of the contaminated rags and cleaner in a sealed, marked container.**

> ⚠ **Warning: Hydraulic fluid is poisonous; wash off immediately and thoroughly in the case of skin contact, and seek immediate medical advice if any fluid is swallowed or gets into the eyes. Certain types of hydraulic fluid are inflammable, and may ignite when allowed into contact with hot components; when servicing any hydraulic system, it is safest to assume that the fluid is inflammable, and to take precautions against the risk of fire as though it is petrol that is being handled. Hydraulic fluid is also an effective paint stripper, and will attack plastics; if any is spilt, it should be washed off immediately, using copious quantities of fresh water. Finally, it is hygroscopic (it absorbs moisture from the air) – old fluid may be contaminated and unfit for further use. When topping-up or renewing the fluid, always use the recommended type, and ensure that it comes from a freshly opened, sealed container.**

2 Clutch master cylinder – removal and refitting

Note: *Refer to the precautions given in Section 1 regarding the use of hydraulic fluid.*

Removal

1 To reduce fluid loss, draw off as much fluid as possible from the appropriate chamber of the brake fluid reservoir, using a clean syringe, until the fluid level is below the level of the clutch master cylinder supply pipe.

2 With the fluid removed, disconnect the clutch fluid supply pipe from the reservoir **(see illustration)**.

3 With reference to Chapter 11 Section 37, remove the drivers side lower facia panel (above the pedals).

4 Prise out the wire clip a little, and disconnect the fluid pressure pipe from the clutch master cylinder **(see illustration)**. Be prepared for fluid spillage. Plug the openings to prevent contamination.

5 Prise off the clip securing the master cylinder piston rod to the operating bracket **(see illustration)**. Access is limited – patience and dexterity will be required.

6 Undo the 2 nuts and slide the master cylinder from the pedal bracket. Manoeuvre the cylinder from place, and pull the supply

hose through the bulkhead as the cylinder is withdrawn **(see illustration)**.

Refitting

7 Refitting is a reversal of removal. Bleed the clutch hydraulic system as described in Section 4.

3 Clutch slave cylinder – removal, inspection and refitting

Removal

Centrally mounted (internal) slave cylinder

1 Remove the transmission as described in Chapter 7A Section 6.

2 If not already disconnected, release the retaining clip from the clutch fluid hose on the transmission bellhousing, and remove the hose **(see illustration)**.

3 Undo the retaining bolts and withdraw the release bearing/slave cylinder from the transmission housing, complete with bleed screw connection **(see illustration)**.

External slave cylinder

4 Raise the vehicle and support it securely on axle stands (see *Vehicle jacking and support*). Undo the fasteners and remove the transmission undershield.

2.6 Master cylinder retaining nuts and fluid supply hose

3.2 Clutch fluid pipe retaining clip

3.3 Release bearing/slave cylinder retaining bolts

3.5 Undo the bolt securing the pipe clip to the transmission

3.6 Slave cylinder mounting bolts

3.7 Prise out the clip a little and disconnect the pipe

5 Unclip the fluid supply pipe from the side of the transmission **(see illustration)**.

6 Undo the mounting bolts and lower the slave cylinder from the transmission casing **(see illustration)**.

7 Prise out the clip a little, and disconnect the pipe from the slave cylinder **(see illustration)**. Plug the openings to prevent contamination. Renew the pipe O-ring seal.

Inspection

8 With internal cylinders, spin the release bearing, and check it for excessive roughness. If any excessive movement or roughness is evident, renew the bearing. If a new clutch has been fitted, it is wise to renew the release bearing as a matter of course.

Refitting

9 Refitting is a reversal of removal. Tighten the retaining bolts to the specified torque, and bleed the clutch hydraulic system as described in Section 4.

---

4 Clutch hydraulic system – bleeding

Note: *Refer to the precautions given in Section 1 regarding the use of hydraulic fluid.*

1 The correct operation of the hydraulic system is only possible after removing all air from the circuit, and this is achieved by bleeding the system.

2 During the bleeding procedure, add only clean, unused hydraulic fluid of the recommended type. Never re-use fluid that has already been bled from the system. Ensure that sufficient fluid is available before starting work.

3 If there is any possibility of incorrect fluid being already in the system, both the clutch and brake circuits must be flushed completely with uncontaminated, correct fluid, and new seals should be fitted to the various components.

4 If hydraulic fluid has been lost from the system, or air has entered because of a leak, ensure that the fault is cured before proceeding further.

5 Apply the parking brake, then jack up the front of the vehicle and support it on axle stands (see *Vehicle jacking and support*). Undo the fasteners and remove the transmission undershield.

6 Remove the dust cap from the slave cylinder bleed screw, and clean away any dirt.

7 Note that the brake fluid reservoir feeds both the brake and clutch hydraulic systems.

8 Mercedes-Benz recommended that pressure-bleeding equipment be used to bleed the system. Some pressure-bleeding kits are operated by the reservoir of pressurised air contained in a spare tyre; however, note that it will probably be necessary to reduce the pressure to a lower level than normal. Refer to the instructions supplied with the kit. If a pressure-bleeding kit is not available, use the normal bleeding method described for the brake hydraulic circuit in Chapter 9 Section 2.

9 By connecting a pressurised, fluid-filled container to the brake fluid reservoir, bleeding can be carried out simply by opening the bleed screw on the clutch slave cylinder, and allowing the fluid to flow out until no more air bubbles can be seen in the expelled fluid. This method has the advantage that the large reservoir of fluid provides an additional safeguard against air being drawn into the system during bleeding.

10 Collect a clean glass jar, a suitable length of plastic or rubber tubing which is a tight fit

over the bleed screw, and a ring spanner to fit the screw.

11 Fit the spanner and tube to the slave cylinder bleed screw **(see illustrations)**, place the other end of the tube in the jar, and pour in sufficient fluid to cover the end of the tube.

12 Connect the pressure-bleeding equipment to the brake/clutch fluid reservoir in accordance with its manufacturer's instructions.

13 Loosen the bleed screw half a turn using the spanner, and allow fluid to drain into the jar until no more air bubbles emerge.

14 When bleeding is complete, tighten the bleed screw, and disconnect the hose and the pressure bleeding equipment.

15 Wash off any spilt fluid, check once more that the bleed screw is tightened securely, and refit the dust cap.

16 Check the hydraulic fluid level in the reservoir, and top-up if necessary (see *Weekly checks*).

17 Discard any hydraulic fluid that has been bled from the system, as it will not be fit for re-use.

18 Check the feel of the clutch pedal. If it feels at all spongy, air must still be present in the system, and further bleeding is required. Failure to bleed satisfactorily after a reasonable repetition of the bleeding procedure may be due to worn master or slave cylinder seals.

19 On completion, refit the undershield and lower the vehicle to the ground.

4.11a Clutch internal slave cylinder bleed screw

4.11b External slave cylinder bleed screw – located on the left-hand side of the transmission

5.3 Pressure plate retaining bolts

5.4a Note the fitted position of the clutch plate/friction disc

5.4b Twin-disc clutch friction plate and drive gear

5 Clutch assembly – removal, inspection and refitting

⚠️ *Warning: Dust created by clutch wear and deposited on the clutch components may contain asbestos, which is a health hazard. DO NOT blow it out with compressed air, or inhale any of it. DO NOT use petrol or petroleum-based solvents to clean off the dust. Brake system cleaner or methylated spirit should be used to flush the dust into a suitable receptacle. After the clutch components are wiped clean with rags, dispose of the contaminated rags and cleaner in a sealed, marked container.*

Removal

1 Remove the transmission as described in Chapter 7A Section 6.

5.12a Special tool to adjust the pressure plate...

5.12c Turn the adjusting ring anti-clockwise...

2 If the original clutch is to be refitted, make alignment marks between the clutch pressure plate assembly and the flywheel, so that the clutch can be refitted in its original position.

3 Progressively unscrew the bolts securing the clutch pressure plate assembly to the flywheel, and recover the washers (where fitted) **(see illustration)**.

4 Withdraw the clutch pressure plate assembly (cover) and disc from the flywheel **(see illustrations)**. Be prepared to catch the friction disc, and note which way round the friction disc is fitted – the two sides of the disc may be marked Engine side and Transmission side, or the side with the part number on faces the flywheel. The greater projecting side of the hub faces away from the flywheel. On some models a twin-plate clutch is fitted. On these models, the friction disc hub drive gear locates in the second disc centre – it's not possible to fit this plate the wrong way around.

5.12b ...which presses down on the diaphragm spring fingers

5.12d ...and release the pressure on the diaphragm

Inspection

Note: *Due to the amount of work involved in removing the clutch assembly, it is considered to be normal practice to replace the assembly regardless of condition.*

5 Clean the cover, disc, and flywheel. Do not inhale the dust, as it may contain asbestos, which is dangerous to health.

6 Examine the fingers of the diaphragm spring for wear or scoring. If the depth of any scoring is excessive, a new cover assembly must be fitted.

7 Examine the pressure plate for scoring, cracking and discoloration. Light scoring is acceptable, but if excessive, a new assembly must be fitted.

8 Examine the friction disc linings for wear cracking, and for contamination with oil or grease. Using vernier calipers, check the thickness of the linings and compare with the details given in the Specifications. Check the disc hub and splines for wear by temporarily fitting it on the transmission input shaft. Renew the friction disc as necessary.

9 Examine the flywheel friction surface for scoring, cracking and discoloration (caused by overheating). If excessive, it may be possible to have the flywheel machined by an engineering works, otherwise it should be renewed.

10 Ensure that all parts are clean, and free of oil or grease, before reassembling. Do not apply any lubricant to the splines of the friction disc hub. Note that a new pressure plate may be coated with protective grease. It is only permissible to clean the grease away from the friction disc lining contact area. Removal of the grease from other areas will shorten the service life of the clutch.

11 Check the spigot bearing in the end of the crankshaft or in the centre of the flywheel. Make sure that it turns smoothly and quietly. If the transmission input shaft contact face on the bearing is worn or damaged, fit a new bearing.

Refitting

12 If you are re-using the pressure plate, the adjustment ring will need to be reset. Position the pressure plate in a hydraulic press (Mercedes technicians use a special tool) **(see illustrations)**, with a block of wood placed

5.16a Centralise the clutch plate...

5.16b ...and fit the assembly onto the flywheel

18 Check the release bearing in the front of the transmission for smooth operation, and if necessary renew it with reference to Section 3.

19 Refit the transmission as described in Chapter 7A Section 6.

6 Release bearing – renewal

Note: *This procedure only applies to transmissions fitted with an external slave cylinder. On other transmissions, the bearing function is incorporated into the centrally mounted slave cylinder.*

Renewal

1 Remove the transmission as described in Chapter 7A Section 6.

2 Firmly pull the release arm from the ballstud on the transmission, and slide it over the input shaft **(see illustration)**.

3 Squeeze together the clips on the back of the bearing and detach it from the release arm **(see illustration)**.

4 Press the new bearing into the arm, ensuring the clips engage securely.

5 Slide the release arm over the input shaft, and press it firmly onto the ballstud.

6 Refit the transmission as described in Chapter 7A Section 6.

---

under the central portion of the pressure plate, directly below the diaphragm spring fingers (not on the friction face). Apply pressure to the diaphragm spring fingers until the adjusting ring is loose. While still applying pressure, use a screwdriver to rotate the adjusting ring anti-clockwise **(see illustrations)**. Hold the adjustment ring in place, and then release the pressure on the diaphragm spring fingers.

13 It is important to ensure that no oil or grease gets onto the friction disc linings, or the pressure plate and flywheel faces. It is advisable to refit the clutch assembly with clean hands, and to wipe down the pressure plate and flywheel faces with a clean rag before assembly begins.

14 Offer the disc to the flywheel, with the greater projecting side of the hub facing away from the flywheel (most friction discs will have an Engine side marking which should face the flywheel, or Gearbox side (Getriebeseite) which should face the gearbox). Hold the friction disc against the flywheel while the pressure plate assembly is offered into position, or alternatively use the centralising tool described later to hold the disc on the flywheel.

15 Fit the clutch pressure plate assembly, where applicable aligning the marks with those on the flywheel. Ensure that the pressure plate assembly locates over the dowels on the flywheel. Insert the securing bolts and washers, and tighten them finger-tight, so

that the friction disc is gripped, but can still be moved. Note that new pressure plates are supplied with the adjustment ring pre-set.

16 The friction disc must now be centralised, to ensure correct alignment of the transmission input shaft with the spigot bearing in the crankshaft/flywheel **(see illustrations)**. To do this, a proprietary tool may be used, or alternatively, use a wooden mandrel made to fit inside the friction disc hub and spigot bearing. Insert the tool through the friction disc into the spigot bearing, and make sure that it is central.

17 Tighten the clutch pressure plate bolts progressively and in diagonal sequence, until the specified torque setting is achieved, and then remove the centralising tool.

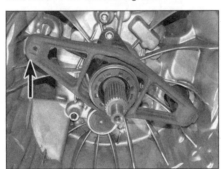

6.2 Pull the release lever from the ballstud

6.3 Squeeze together the clips and detach the bearing

Chapter 7 Part A
Manual gearbox

Contents

	Section number		Section number
Gearbox – removal and refitting	6	General information	1
Gearbox oil – draining and refilling	2	Output flange oil seal – renewal	4
Gearbox overhaul – general information	7	Reversing light switch – removal and refitting	5
Gearchange lever assembly – removal and refitting	3		

Degrees of difficulty

Easy, suitable for novice with little experience		Fairly easy, suitable for beginner with some experience		Fairly difficult, suitable for competent DIY mechanic		Difficult, suitable for experienced DIY mechanic		Very difficult, suitable for expert DIY or professional	

Specifications

General

Type	6-speed with optional sequential automated operation
Code	711.65, 711.67, 716.60 or 716.65

Lubrication

Recommended oil	See *Lubricants and fluids*
Capacity:	
711 transmissions:	
711.653/654 transmission code	1.5 litres
711.655/656 transmission code	1.2 litres
711.670 transmission code	1.8 litres
716 transmissions:	
716.60 transmission code	1.2 litres
716.65 transmission code	1.5 litres

Torque wrench settings

	Nm	lbf ft
Drain plug:		
716 transmission	30	22
711 transmission	33	24
Filler plug	35	25
Gearbox-to-engine bolts	40	30
Gearbox mounting bolts:		
M8	28	21
M10	50	37
Gearbox mounting bracket-to-floor:		
M10 x 22 mm Silver	70	52
M10 x 22 mm Black	55	41
M10 x 24 mm	50	37
Output flange retaining nut: *		
Stage 1	200	147
Stage 2	Slacken	
Stage 3	160	118
Release bearing sleeve bolt	12	9

*Do not re-use

2.2a Transmission fluid drain plug location

2.2b Transmission fluid filler/level plug location

1 General information

1 A 6-speed manual transmission is bolted to the rear of the engine. Drive is transmitted from the crankshaft via the clutch to the input shaft, which has a splined extension to accept the clutch friction disc. The transmission output shaft transmits the drive via the propeller shaft to the rear differential. The input shaft runs in line with the output shaft. The input shaft and output shaft gears are in constant mesh with the layshaft gear cluster. Selection of gears is by sliding synchromesh hubs, which lock the appropriate output shaft gears to the output shaft.

2 Gear selection is via a floor-mounted lever and selector mechanism incorporating a gearchange rod or cable. The selector mechanism causes the appropriate selector fork to move its respective synchro-sleeve along the shaft, to lock the gear pinion to the synchro-hub. Since the synchro-hubs are splined to the output shaft, this locks the pinion to the shaft, so that drive can be transmitted. To ensure that gear-changing can be made quickly and quietly, a synchromesh system is fitted to all forward gears, consisting of baulk rings and spring-loaded fingers, as well as the gear pinions and synchro-hubs. The synchromesh cones are formed on the mating faces of the baulk rings and gear pinions.

3 Some models have an optional Sequentronic six-speed manual transmission that has an electro/hydraulic-operated clutch and shifting system. The result is a transmission that is conventional in its gears and internal components; but which is operated instead in response to commands from the gear lever through the ECU, so when changing gear it operates more like an automatic transmission. Mercedes call it an 'automated manual transmission'.

2 Gearbox oil – draining and refilling

Note: *Models with sequentronic transmissions, will need to be taken to a Mercedes Dealer to check the transmission oil level, as special tools are required.*

1 Raise the vehicle and support it securely on axle stands (see *Vehicle jacking and support*). Undo the fasteners and remove the transmission undershield.

2 Place a suitable container beneath the transmission drain plug, at the bottom of the casing, then unscrew the plug. Undo the level/filler plug, located on the right-hand side of the transmission, to assist draining. A hexagonal key should be used to unscrew the plugs, but a tool can be improvised using a long nut, or a length of hexagonal bar, and a spanner **(see illustrations)**.

3 Once all the fluid has drained, refit and tighten the drain plug.

4 Fill the transmission until the fluid level is 10 mm below the filler opening. Note that the vehicle must be in a level position.

5 When the level is correct, refit the plug, and tighten to the specified torque.

3 Gearchange lever assembly – removal and refitting

Removal

Rod gearshift

1 Position the gear lever in the neutral position.

2 Carefully prise up the gear lever gaiter, and pull it up around the gear knob **(see illustration)**.

3 To remove the gear knob from the gear lever, lift the gaiter from around the lever and turn the gaiter inside out, pulling it upwards over the gear knob. Turn the locking ring, below the gear knob anti-clockwise, and then pull the gear knob upwards to remove it from the gear lever **(see illustration)**.

4 Remove the insulating material from above the gearchange lever housing.

3.2 Prise up the gaiter

3.3 Rotate the locking ring anti-clockwise

3.5 Undo the bolts at the rear

3.10a Lift the securing clip...

3.10b ...and slide it out of the transmission casing

3.11a Pull the locking clip out of the selector rod...

3.11b ...and the gear linkage rod

transmission output flange. A suitable tool can be made up using two pieces of flat bar and bolts – engage the tool with two of the bolts holes in the output flange, and use it to counterhold the flange. Note that it must be possible to gain access to the output flange nut with the tool in place.

4 Counterhold the output flange, then unscrew the flange securing nut. Discard the nut, a new one must be used on refitting **(see illustration)**.

5 Pull the output flange from the shaft, using a suitable puller if necessary.

6 Prise the oil seal from the housing using a screwdriver.

7 Thoroughly clean the oil seal seating in the rear transmission cover.

8 Tap the new seal into position, using a suitable socket or tube, until the outer face of the seal is flush with the end face of the housing.

9 Refit the output flange to the output shaft, and secure using a new nut. Tighten the nut to the specified torque.

10 Reconnect the propeller shaft to the output flange, with reference to Chapter 8 Section 7.

5 Undo the bolts at the rear of the gearchange lever **(see illustration)**.

6 Remove the reinforcing brace beneath the propeller shaft.

7 Remove the bracket for the transmission undershield.

8 Detach the front of the propeller shaft from the transmission as described in Chapter 8 Section 7.

9 Using a jack for support, lower the rear of the transmission slightly.

10 Pull out the pin securing the support bracket to the rear of the transmission **(see illustrations)**.

11 Pull out the pin securing the linkage rod to the selector shaft **(see illustrations)**.

12 Lower the gearchange lever assembly from place.

Sequentronic transmission

13 Remove the key from the ignition lock.

14 Remove the centre console as described in Chapter 11 Section 36.

15 Disconnect the wiring plug from the rear of the gearchange lever assembly.

16 Undo the 3 retaining bolts, and manoeuvre the gearchange lever assembly from place.

Refitting

17 Refitting is the reverse of the removal procedure, applying a smear of the specified grease to all linkage pivot points (see *Lubricants and fluids*). Ensure all nuts and bolts are securely tightened'.

4 Output flange oil seal – renewal

1 With reference to Chapter 8 Section 7, detach the front of the propeller shaft from the rear of the transmission.

2 Ensure that the transmission is in neutral.

3 Bolt a suitable holding tool to the

4.4 The flange securing nut will be tight

5.1 Reversing light/gear position switch location

5 Reversing light switch – removal and refitting

Removal

Note: *Some models do not have a reversing light switch fitted to the transmission, on these models the ECU controls the operation of the reversing lights.*

1 Where fitted, the reversing light circuit is controlled by a switch located at the rear/top of the transmission **(see illustration)**. If a fault develops in the circuit, first ensure that the circuit fuse has not blown.

2 For access to the switch, it will be necessary to apply the parking brake, and then jack up the front of the vehicle and support it on axle stands (see *Vehicle jacking and support*). Undo the fasteners and remove the transmission undershield.

3 To test the switch, disconnect the wiring connector, and use a multimeter (set to the

6.5 Transmission wiring plugs

6.8 Clutch fluid pipe union

6.11 Reach over the top of the transmission to unscrew the upper bolts

resistance function) or a battery-and-bulb test circuit to check that there is continuity between the switch terminals only when reverse gear is selected. If this is not the case, and there are no obvious breaks or other damage to the wires, the switch is faulty, and must be renewed.

4 To remove the switch, disconnect the wiring plug, undo the retaining bolt(s) and withdraw the switch from the transmission.

Refitting

5 Refitting is a reversal of removal.

6 Gearbox – removal and refitting

Note: *This is a difficult operation, due to the limited access to the engine-to-transmission bolts. It is suggested that the procedure is read through thoroughly before starting the operation. Suitable ratchet extensions will be required to reach some of the engine-to-transmission bolts.*

Removal

1 Disconnect the battery negative lead as described in Chapter 5A Section 4.

2 Ensure the transmission is in Neutral, then raise the vehicle and support it securely on axle stands (see *Vehicle jacking and support*). Undo the fasteners and remove the engine/transmission undershields.

3 Remove the catalytic converter and particulate filter rear mounting bracket.

4 Remove the exhaust pipe mounting bracket from the transmission.

5 Disconnect any wiring plugs from the transmission **(see illustration)**.

6 Support the transmission using a transmission jack, then remove the rear transmission mounting complete with support bracket.

7 Remove the propeller shaft as described in Chapter 8 Section 7.

8 Release the securing clip and disconnect the clutch fluid pipe from the transmission/slave cylinder, with reference to Chapter 6. Place a suitable container beneath the pipe to catch the fluid which will be released, and plug or cover the open ends of the pipe and hose.

Note: *The hydraulic fluid pipe from the clutch master cylinder loops over the transmission bellhousing, and an alternative method is to disconnect the union on the side of the transmission* **(see illustration)***, and leave the pipe in position while the transmission is being removed. If this course of action is taken, fit a hose clamp to the fluid supply hose leading from the brake fluid reservoir to the clutch master cylinder. Place a suitable container beneath the union to catch the fluid which will be released, and plug or cover the open ends of the pipe and hose.*

9 Prise off the securing clips, and disconnect the gear selector rods from the rear of the transmission.

10 Support the engine, as otherwise it will tilt rearwards and damage the brake pipes at the engine compartment bulkhead.

11 Unscrew all the engine-to-transmission bolts, leaving one bolt on either side of the transmission. Access to the upper bolts is very difficult, even with the assembly tilted, and several long socket extensions will be required. Remove the two upper, outer bolts first, removing the retaining brackets and soundproofing from the top of the transmission (where fitted) **(see illustration)**.

12 Unscrew the two remaining engine-to-transmission bolts, and then, with the help of an assistant, pull the transmission rearwards and release the transmission input shaft from the clutch. Take care not to allow the weight of the transmission to hang on the clutch and input shaft, and where applicable take care not to damage the clutch fluid pipe during this procedure. If necessary, rotate the transmission to enable the top of the bellhousing to clear the vehicle body.

13 Once the input shaft is clear of the clutch, lower the transmission to the ground and withdraw from under the vehicle.

Refitting

14 The gearbox is refitted by a reversal of the removal procedure, bearing in mind the following points:

a) *Apply a very thin smear of high-temperature grease (MB No. A 000 989 76 51) to the transmission input shaft splines. Take great care not to allow any grease*

to contact the release bearing or clutch plates.

b) *Ensure the locating dowels are correctly positioned prior to installation.*

c) *Tighten all nuts and bolts to the specified torque (where given).*

d) *On completion, refill the gearbox with the specified type and quantity of lubricant (see Lubricants and fluids 0 Section 5) then check the oil level as described in Section 2.*

7 Gearbox overhaul – general information

1 Overhauling a manual gearbox unit is a difficult and involved job for the DIY home mechanic. In addition to dismantling and reassembling many small parts, clearances must be precisely measured and, if necessary, changed by selecting shims and spacers. Internal gearbox components are also often difficult to obtain, and in many instances, extremely expensive. Because of this, if the gearbox develops a fault or becomes noisy, the best course of action is to have the unit overhauled by a specialist repairer, or to obtain an exchange reconditioned unit.

2 Nevertheless, it is not impossible for the more experienced mechanic to overhaul the gearbox, provided the special tools are available, and the job is done in a deliberate step-by-step manner, so that nothing is overlooked.

3 The tools necessary for an overhaul include internal and external circlip pliers, bearing pullers, a slide hammer, a set of pin punches, a dial test indicator, and possibly a hydraulic press. In addition, a large, sturdy workbench and a vice will be required.

4 During dismantling of the gearbox, make careful notes of how each component is fitted, to make reassembly easier and more accurate.

5 Before dismantling the gearbox, it will help if you have some idea what area is malfunctioning. Certain problems can be closely related to specific areas in the gearbox, which can make component examination and replacement easier. Refer to the *Fault finding* Section of this manual for more information.

Chapter 7 Part B
Automatic gearbox

Contents

Section number

Automatic transmission – removal and refitting 6
Automatic transmission oil renewal 5
Automatic transmission overhaul – general information 7
Electronic transmission control module (ETC) –
   removal and refitting. 9

Section number

General information 1
Ignition lock control cable – removal, refitting and adjustment 4
Selector lever assembly – removal and refitting. 2
Selector rod – removal, refitting and adjustment 3
Torque converter oil seal – renewal 8

Degrees of difficulty

Easy, suitable for novice with little experience	Fairly easy, suitable for beginner with some experience	Fairly difficult, suitable for competent DIY mechanic	Difficult, suitable for experienced DIY mechanic	Very difficult, suitable for expert DIY or professional

Specifications

Type . . . . Five forwards speeds and reverse.
Transmission code . . . . 722.640, 722.646, 722.694 or 722.699

Type . . . . Seven forwards speeds, and two reverse speeds.
Transmission code . . . . 722.908 or 722.996

Transmission fluid capacity (initial fill):
5-speed transmission. . . . . 7.5 L
7-speed transmission. . . . . 9.0 L
Installed height of torque converter: . . . .
  5-speed transmission. . . . . 7.0 mm
  7-speed transmission:
    Helical screwed connection . . . . 9.5 mm
    Axial screwed connection. . . . . 19.5 mm

Torque wrench settings	Nm	lbf ft
Gearbox housing-to-engine bolts	38	28
Oil drain plug	20	15
Rear mounting-to-transmission:		
M8	30	22
M10	50	37
Rear support bracket-to-body:		
M10 x 22 mm Silver	70	52
M10 x 22 mm Black	55	41
M10 x 24 mm	50	37
Torque converter bolts:		
Straight-threaded connection bolts (M8)	42	32
Angle-threaded connection bolts:		
Stage 1	4	2
Stage 2	30	22
Stage 3	Angle-tighten a further 90°	
Torque converter drain plug:		
M8	10	7
M10	15	11

1 General information

1 The vehicles covered in this manual are equipped with a five-speed (model 722.6) or seven-speed (model 722.9) automatic transmission. All transmissions have a torque converter clutch system that improves fuel economy. The TCC engages in drive and overdrive modes. The TCC system consists of a solenoid, controlled by the ECU, which locks the torque converter when the vehicle is cruising on level ground and the engine is fully warmed-up. A transmission oil cooler is also fitted.

2 The transmission comprises a torque converter, an epicyclic geartrain, and hydraulically-operated brakes and clutches.

3 The torque converter provides a fluid coupling between the engine and transmission, and acts as a clutch, also providing a degree of torque multiplication when accelerating.

4 The epicyclic geartrain provides the forward and reverse gear ratios, according to which of its component parts are held stationary or allowed to turn. The components of the geartrain are held or released by brakes and clutches, which are activated by a hydraulic control unit. A fluid pump within the transmission provides the necessary hydraulic pressure to operate the brakes and clutches.

5 Driver control of the transmission is by a selector lever or optional steering wheel controls, and a two-position switch. This alters the hydraulic control pressure in the transmission, according to throttle position. The 'drive' position (D) provides automatic changing throughout the range of all forward gear ratios, and is the position selected for normal driving. An automatic kickdown facility shifts the transmission down a gear if the accelerator pedal is fully depressed. The 'hold' facility is similar to the 'drive' position, but limits the number of gear ratios available – ie, when the selector lever is in the 3 position, only the first three ratios can be used; in the 2 position, only the first two can be used, and so on. The lower ratio 'hold' is useful when travelling down steep gradients, or for preventing unwanted selection of high gears on twisty roads.

6 Due to the complexity of the automatic transmission, any repair or overhaul work must be left to a Mercedes-Benz dealer or automatic transmission specialist with the necessary special equipment for fault diagnosis and repair. The contents of the following Sections are therefore confined to supplying general information, and any service information and instructions that can be used by the owner.

2 Selector lever assembly – removal and refitting

Removal

1 Ensure the selector lever is in position 'P', then disconnect the battery negative lead as described in Chapter 5A Section 4.

2 Apply the parking brake, then jack up the front of the vehicle, and support securely on axle stands (see *Vehicle jacking and support*). Undo the fasteners and remove the rear section of the engine/transmission undershield.

Early models

3 Working under the vehicle, prise off the metal retaining clip, and disconnect the selector rod from the bottom of the selector lever (see illustration).

Later models

4 Later models have a different design of clip securing the selector rod to the base of the selector lever (see illustration). This type of clip must not be removed. If it is damaged the complete mechanism must be replaced.

5 Instead of disconnecting the rod at the base of the lever, slide off the clip and disconnect the rod at the lever on the transmission (see illustration).

All models

6 Working inside the vehicle, prise up the selector lever panel (see illustration).

7 Disconnect the wiring plug, then pull selector lever panel and gaiter up around the selector lever knob.

8 Rotate the collar beneath the knob anti-clockwise, then pull the knob, gaiter and panel from the lever (see illustration). Disconnect any wiring plugs as the panel is withdrawn.

9 Starting at the front edge, carefully prise up the lever aperture surround panel (see illustration).

2.3 Prise off the selector rod retaining clip

2.4 This type of 'push-on' clip must not be removed

2.5 Prise up the tab, and slide off the clip securing the rod to the transmission lever

2.6 Carefully prise up the panel around the selector lever

2.8 Rotate the collar anti-clockwise

2.9 Pull up and remove the surround panel

2.10 Ashtray/power socket panel retaining bolts

2.11 Lever up the catch and rotate the collar 90°

2.13 Selector lever assembly retaining bolts

10 Undo the two retaining bolts and remove the ashtray/power socket panel from the front of console aperture **(see illustration)**. Disconnect the wiring plugs as the panel is withdrawn.
11 At the front of the gear lever housing, disconnect the ignition switch control cable from the housing by levering up the catch, rotating the collar 90° and pulling it from place **(see illustration)**.
12 Disconnect the wiring plugs from the selector lever assembly.
13 The selector lever assembly is retained by 1 bolt at the front, and 2 at the rear **(see illustration)**. Undo the bolts and manoeuvre the lever assembly from place.

Refitting

14 Refitting is a reversal of removal.

3 Selector rod – removal, refitting and adjustment

Removal

1 Apply the parking brake, move the selector lever to position D, then jack up the front of the vehicle and support it on axle stands (see *Vehicle jacking and support*). Undo the fasteners and remove the rear section of the engine/transmission undershield.
2 Prise the securing clip from the front end of the selector rod at the lever on the transmission **(see illustration 2.5)**.
3 Slacken the grub screw at base of the selector lever fitting, and slide the selector rod from place **(see illustration)**.
Caution: Do not prise off the clip securing the fitting to the base of the selector lever, as the mechanism will be irreparably damaged.

Refitting

4 Refitting is a reversal of removal, but check and adjust the selector rod as follows.

Adjustment

5 An assistant will be required to hold the selector lever in position D. This needs to be held in this position, throughout the complete procedure.

6 Working under the vehicle, slacken the grub screw at the bottom of the selector lever **(see illustration 3.3)**.
7 Ensure the selector lever on the transmission is in the 'D' position (fully forwards), then tighten the grub screw securely.

4 Ignition lock control cable – removal, refitting and adjustment

Removal

1 On models without the 'Keyless Go' system, turn the ignition key to position 'O'.
2 On models with the 'Keyless Go' system, press the start-stop button repeatedly until the ignition is switched off.
3 Remove the centre console as described in Chapter 11 Section 36.
4 Remove the facia mounted audio system as described in Chapter 12 Section 16.
5 At the front of the gear lever housing, disconnect the ignition switch control cable from the housing **(see illustration 2.11)**. Raise the retaining lug, and pressing against the spring pressure, rotate the collar through 90° and detach the cable.
6 Remove the ignition/starter switch as described in Chapter 12 Section 5.
7 Pull the air duct in the drivers footwell from the heater housing, and move it to one side.
8 Squeeze together the retaining lugs and disconnect the control cable from the ignition switch.
9 Note its routing, then release any retaining

3.3 Slacken the grub screw

clips and manoeuvre the control cable from the facia.

Refitting

10 Refitting is a reversal of removal.

5 Automatic transmission oil renewal

5-speed transmission

Note: *Note that the top of the fluid level dipstick tube is fitted with a tamperproof cap incorporating a plastic clip. The clip is broken when the cap is removed, and a new clip must be fitted when the cap is refitted. The dipstick is not fitted inside the tube, but must be obtained as a separate tool (number 140 589 15 21 00) from a Mercedes-Benz dealer. The alternative is to take the vehicle to a dealer for the fluid level check.*
1 With the parking brake fully applied, shift the selector lever to position 'N' and turn off the ignition.
2 Raise the vehicle and support it securely on axle stands (see *Vehicle jacking and support*). Release the fasteners and remove the transmission undershield. Note that the vehicle should be level to ensure accurate fluid level.
3 Position a container under the transmission, undo the drain plug and allow the fluid to flow in to the container **(see illustration)**. Renew the drain plug sealing ring.
4 When the fluid has stopped draining, refit the drain plug with a new washer, and tighten it to the specified torque.

5.3 5-speed automatic transmission fluid drain plug

5 Prise out the cover from the lower part of the bell housing, then using a socket on the crankshaft pulley, rotate the engine clockwise until the torque converter drain plug is accessible through the bell housing aperture **(see illustration)**.

6 Move the container under the bell housing, remove the torque converter drain plug and allow the fluid to flow out. Renew the drain plug sealing washer.

7 When the fluid has stopped draining, refit the plug with a new sealing washer and tighten it to the specified torque.

8 Break the plate of the locking pin, and remove the cap from the top of the filler tube. Note that a new cap will be required.

9 With the transmission cold (approximately 25°C) add 5 litres of new fluid through the filler tube.

10 Move the selector lever to position 'P', start the engine and allow it to idle.

11 Move the selector lever through the various positions several times, ending in position 'P'.

12 Insert the dipstick into the filler tube, remove it and examine the oil level on the dipstick. The 'MAX' and 'MIN' marks at the lower end of the dipstick are for fluid at 25°C.

13 If necessary, add fluid through the filler tube to bring the level upto the cold 'MAX' mark on the dipstick.

14 Mercedes recommend that if shifting problems occur, the fluid level should be checked with the transmission fluid temperature at 80°C. At this temperature, the upper marks on the dipstick should be used.

15 When the fluid level is correct, stop the engine, fit the new cap to the filler tube, and press it down until it latches.

16 Refit the transmission undershield and lower the vehicle to the ground.

7-speed transmission

17 Renewal of the fluid in the 7-speed transmission requires access to Mercedes STAR diagnostic equipment (or equivalent), and several special tools. In order to obtain the correct fluid level, the fluid must be accessed accurately at several different temperatures, depending on vehicle specification. Consequently, we recommend this task is entrusted to a Mercedes dealer or suitably equipped repairer.

5.5 Prise the cover from the bell housing

6 Automatic transmission –
removal and refitting

Note: *This is a difficult operation, due to the limited access to the engine-to-transmission bolts, and to the weight of the transmission assembly. It is suggested that the procedure is read through thoroughly before starting the operation. Suitable ratchet extensions will be required to reach some of the engine-to-transmission bolts.*

Removal

1 Fully apply the parking brake, then move the transmission selector lever to position 'N', then disconnect the battery negative lead as described in Chapter 5A Section 4.

2 Raise the bonnet to its fully open position. Take care to protect any brake pipes or wiring at the rear of the engine compartment.

3 Jack up the front of the vehicle and support it on axle stands (see *Vehicle jacking and support*). The vehicle must be raised sufficiently high to enable the transmission to be lowered and removed from under the vehicle. Remove the engine/transmission undershields.

4 Remove the catalytic converter/particulate filter as described in Chapter 4A.

5 Remove the plastic cover from the top of the engine.

6 Remove the air cleaner assembly as described in Chapter 4A Section 2.

7 On 5-speed transmissions, undo the bolt securing the upper end of the transmission oil filler pipe.

6.12 Disconnect the transmission earth lead

8 Drain the transmission fluid as described in Section 5.

9 Remove the undershield rear support bracket.

10 Remove the exhaust support bracket from the rear of the transmission.

11 Release the retaining clip and detach the selector rod from the transmission.

12 Disconnect the earth lead from the transmission **(see illustration)**.

13 Remove the heatshield from the right-hand side of the transmission, and disconnect any wiring plugs from the transmission **(see illustration)**.

14 Remove the cover in the lower section of the sump casing to access the torque converter bolts **(see illustration)**.

15 Unscrew and remove the torque converter retaining bolts. It will be necessary to turn the engine, using the crankshaft pulley bolt, so that each of the bolts can be unscrewed through the aperture **(see illustration)**.

Caution: Ensure the engine is turned only in the correct direction of rotation (clockwise).

16 Disconnect and remove the transmission fluid cooler pipes. Be prepared for fluid spillage. Plug the openings to prevent contamination. Renew the cooler O-ring seals.

17 On 7-speed transmissions fitted to 2143 cc engines (Type 651), remove the starter as described in Chapter 5A Section 9.

18 The engine and transmission must now be supported. Mercedes technicians use a support bar which locates in the tops of the inner wing panels – proprietary engine support bars are available from tool outlets.

19 If a support bar is not available, an engine

6.13 Heatshield retaining screw

6.14 Prise out the cover...

6.15 ...to access the torque converter bolts

hoist should be used. With an engine hoist the engine/transmission can be manoeuvred more easily and safely, balancing the engine on a jack is not recommended.

20 Undo the bolts and remove the rear crossmember, complete with rear transmission mounting.

21 Disconnect the propeller shaft flexible coupling from the transmission output shaft as described in Chapter 8, and pull the shaft rearwards a little. Support the shaft to prevent damage.

22 Make a final check to ensure all relevant wiring has been disconnected.

23 Lower the engine/transmission slightly and support it on a transmission jack.

24 Undo the bolts securing the transmission to the engine, pull it rearwards a little, and move the starter to one side with the wiring still attached. The help of an assistant will be required.

25 On 5-speed transmissions, slacken the retaining bolt and pull the oil filler pipe from the transmission. Renew the O-ring seal.

26 With the help of an assistant, withdraw the transmission squarely from the engine, making sure that the torque converter comes away with the transmission, and does not stay in contact with the driveplate. If this precaution is not taken, there is a risk of the torque converter falling out and being damaged. converter remains on the transmission input shaft.

27 Lower the transmission to the ground.

Refitting

28 Where removed, refit the torque converter as follows:

a) *Lightly grease the torque converter drive flange. Molykote grease is recommended.*

b) *Using 2 bolts, manipulate the converter into position. Move the converter back-and forth-as it is fitted to ensure that it is fully engaged with the input shaft and primary pump. The converter is fully engaged when the distance between the bellhousing face and torque converter driveplate face is as specified at the start of this Chapter.*

c) *Turn the torque converter until two of the converter-to-driveplate bolt holes are positioned at the access hole of the transmission bellhousing.*

29 With the help of an assistant, raise the transmission, and locate it on the rear of the driveplate. Ensure the transmission is correctly aligned with the locating dowels, before pushing it fully into engagement with the engine. **Note:** *The torque converter must remain in full engagement with the fluid pump at the correct installation depth throughout the fitting procedure.*

30 Working your way around the transmission casing, refit the transmission-to-engine bolts. Do not fully tighten the retaining bolts until all the bolts are in place, then tighten to the specified torque setting.

31 Tighten the torque converter retaining bolts to the specified torque. Turn the engine as required to bring each of the bolts into view. **Note:** *Insert all of the bolts before fully tightening them to the specified torque.*

32 The remainder of the refitting procedure is a reversal of the removal procedure, noting the following special points:

d) *Tighten all retaining bolts to their specified torque wrench setting (where given).*

e) *Reconnect and adjust the selector rod, as described in Section 3.*

f) *Renew the transmission fluid as described in Section 5.*

g) *If a new unit has been fitted, depending on the transmission type, it may be necessary to have the transmission ETC 'matched' to the engine management ECM electronically, to ensure correct operation – seek the advice of your Mercedes dealer or automatic transmission specialist.*

h) *Road test the car to check the transmission for correct operation.*

7 Automatic transmission overhaul – general information

1 In the event of a fault occurring on the transmission, it is first necessary to determine whether it is of an electrical, mechanical or hydraulic nature, and to achieve this, special test equipment is required. It is therefore essential to have the work carried out by a Mercedes dealer, or a suitably-equipped specialist if a transmission fault is suspected.

2 Do not remove the transmission from the vehicle for possible repair before professional fault diagnosis has been carried out, since most tests require the transmission to be in the vehicle.

8 Torque converter oil seal – renewal

1 Remove the gearbox as described in Section 6, and slide the torque converter from the gearbox input shaft.

2 Using a flat-bladed screwdriver, prise the oil seal from the input shaft housing. Note the fitted depth of the seal.

3 Ensure that the oil seal recess in the gearbox, and the torque converter spigot are clean and dry. Lubricate the new oil seal with clean gearbox fluid, and fit it to the gearbox. Use a

9.3 Remove the polystyrene impact absorber

tubular drift that bears only on the hard outer edge of the seal. Fit the seal squarely into the housing, with the inner lip facing the gearbox.

4 Position the torque converter over the input shaft, and check that it is fully located.

9 Electronic transmission control module (ETC) – removal and refitting

Removal

Note: *This procedure only applies to vehicles fitted with the 5-speed transmission upto model year 2008. On vehicles after this date, the electronic control unit is integrated into the transmission casing.*

1 Remove the ignition key.

2 Move the passengers seat to the rearmost position, and fold the footwell carpet back. The ETC is located under the passengers floor.

3 Remove the impact absorber **(see illustration)**.

4 Undo the fasteners and remove the floor plate **(see illustration)**.

5 Undo the retaining nuts, move the ETC rearwards and disconnect the wiring plugs **(see illustration)**.

Refitting

6 Refitting is a reversal of removal. Note that if a new ETC module has been fitted, it may need to be configured using Mercedes Benz diagnostic equipment. Entrust this task to a Mercedes dealer or suitably equipped specialist.

9.4 The floor plate is secured by 3 nuts

9.5 Remove the electronic transmission control module

Notes

Chapter 8
Driveshafts, propeller shaft and final drive

Contents

Section number

Driveshaft – removal and refitting. 5
Driveshaft gaiters – renewal 6
Final drive unit – draining and refilling 2
Final drive unit – removal and refitting 3
Final drive unit seals – renewal. 4

Section number

General information 1
Propeller shaft – removal and refitting 7
Propeller shaft centre bearing – check and renewal 9
Propeller shaft rubber coupling – check and renewal 8
Propeller shaft universal joint – check and renewal 10

Degrees of difficulty

Easy, suitable for novice with little experience	Fairly easy, suitable for beginner with some experience	Fairly difficult, suitable for competent DIY mechanic	Difficult, suitable for experienced DIY mechanic	Very difficult, suitable for expert DIY or professional

Specifications

Final drive
Type . . . . Rubber bush-mounted to rear suspension crossmember

Driveshaft
Type . . . . Steel shafts with ball-and-cage type constant velocity joints at each end

Propeller shaft
Type . . . . Two-piece tubular shaft with centre bearing and universal joint. Rubber coupling at front and rear joints

Constant velocity joint grease capacity
82 mm diameter joint housing 80g
95 mm diameter joint housing 100g
102 mm diameter joint housing 120g
106 mm diameter joint housing 130g
112 mm diameter joint housing 140g
116 mm diameter joint housing 150g

Torque wrench settings

	Nm	lbft
Driveshaft nut: *		
Self-locking nut.	350	258
Not self-locking nut:		
Stage 1	170	125
Stage 2	Angle-tighten a further 45°	
Final drive:		
Filler plug	50	37
Drain plug	50	37
Front mount bracket to crossmember	150	111
Front mounting bolt	65	48
Rear mounting bolts	170	125
Pinion nut:		
All except M22 nut	130	96
M22 nut.	100	74
Propeller shaft:		
Front or rear flexible coupling nuts*	68	50
Crossbrace-to-floor	20	15
Roadwheel bolts.	130	96

*Do not re-use

1 General information

1 Power is transmitted from the transmission to the rear axle by a two-piece propeller shaft, joined in front of the centre bearing by a 'slip joint': a sliding, splined coupling. The slip joint allows slight fore-and-aft movement of the propeller shaft. The propeller shaft is attached to the flanges of the transmission and final drive unit by flexible rubber couplings, a vibration damper being fitted between the front coupling and the shaft. The middle of the propeller shaft is supported by the centre bearing, which is bolted to the vehicle body. A universal joint is located at the rear of the centre bearing, to compensate for movement of the transmission and differential on their mountings, and for any flexing of the chassis.
2 The final drive assembly includes the drive pinion, the ring gear, the differential and the output flanges. The drive pinion, which drives the ring gear, is also known as the differential input shaft, and is connected to the propeller shaft via an input flange. The differential is bolted to the ring gear and drives the rear wheels through a pair of output flanges bolted to driveshafts. The differential allows the wheels to turn at different speeds when cornering, although only to a limited amount on models fitted with ASD (limited-slip differential).
3 The driveshafts deliver power from the final drive unit output flanges to the rear wheels. The driveshafts are equipped with constant velocity (CV) joints at each end. The inner CV joints are bolted to the differential flanges; the outer CV joints engage the splines of the wheel hubs, and are secured by a large nut.
4 Major repair work on the differential assembly components (drive pinion, ring-and-pinion and differential) requires many special tools and a high degree of expertise, and therefore should not be attempted by the home mechanic. If major repairs become necessary, we recommend that they be performed by a Mercedes-Benz service department or other suitably-equipped automotive engineer.

2 Final drive unit – draining and refilling

1 This operation is much quicker and more efficient if the car is first taken on a journey of sufficient length to warm the final drive unit up to normal operating temperature.
2 Park the car on level ground, switch off the ignition and apply the parking brake firmly. For improved access, jack up the rear of the car and support it securely on axle stands (see *Vehicle jacking and support*). Note that the car must be level, to ensure accuracy, when refilling and checking the oil level.

3 Wipe clean the area around the filler/level plug, which is situated on the left-hand side of the final drive unit, next to the driveshaft flange, and unscrew it **(see illustration)**.
4 Position a suitable container under the drain plug, and unscrew the plug from the right-hand side of the housing **(see illustration)**.
5 Allow the oil to drain completely into the container. If the oil is hot, take precautions against scalding. Clean both the filler/level and the drain plugs, being especially careful to wipe any metallic particles off the magnetic inserts.
6 When the oil has finished draining, clean the drain plug threads and those of the final drive casing. Apply a little thread-locking compound to the plug, then tighten it to the specified torque. If the car was raised for the draining operation, now lower it to the ground.
7 Refilling the final drive unit is an extremely awkward operation. Above all, allow plenty of time for the oil level to settle properly before checking it. Note that the car must be parked on flat level ground when checking the oil level.
8 Refill the final drive unit with the exact amount of the specified type of oil (see *Lubricants and fluids 0 Section 5*), until it begins to drip from the filler hole. Apply a little thread-locking compound to the plug, then tighten it to the specified torque. If the correct amount was poured into the final drive unit and a large amount flows out on checking the level, refit the filler/level plug and take the car on a short journey so that the new oil is distributed fully around the final drive components, then check the level again on your return.

3 Final drive unit – removal and refitting

Removal

1 Raise the rear of the vehicle and support it securely on axle stands (see *Vehicle jacking and support*). Remove both rear roadwheels.
2 Remove the rear section of the exhaust system as described in Chapter 4A Section 19.
3 Make alignment marks between the coupling and flange, then undo the three nuts and remove the bolts securing the propeller

shaft rear flexible coupling to the differential pinion flange. Lower the disconnected propeller shaft, and fasten it to one side or support it securely to prevent any damage. Do not let it hang from the rear of the transmission.
4 Remove the rear driveshafts as described in Section 5.
5 Place a jack beneath the final drive housing and just take the weight of the unit.
6 Remove the rear bolts securing the final drive unit to the suspension crossmember/subframe.
7 Undo the bolt securing the final drive to the front mounting. Note the of the compensating washer between the final drive and the mounting.
8 With the help of an assistant, carefully lower the final drive assembly from place.

Refitting

9 Refitting is a reversal of removal, noting the following points:
a) *Align the rear coupling previously made marks.*
b) *Renew all self-locking nuts.*
c) *Refit the compensating washer between the final drive and front mounting.*
d) *Tighten all fasteners to their specified torque where given.*
e) *Replenish the final drive fluid as described in Section 2.*

4 Final drive unit seals – renewal

Driveshaft oil seals

1 Chock the front wheels and loosen the rear wheel bolts. Jack up the rear of the car and support it on axle stands (see *Vehicle jacking and support*). Remove the rear wheels.
2 Remove the relevant driveshaft as described in Section 5.
3 Note the seal's fitted position in the housing, and then using a lever, carefully prise the seal out of the final drive housing.
4 Clean out the recess in the housing for the seal, and then check the new seal against the old seal to make sure it is the correct one.
5 Using a seal drift/installer or a large deep socket, install the new oil seal into the

2.3 Final drive filler/level plug

2.4 Final drive drain plug

housing, making sure it is fitted in the same location as noted on removal.

6 Lubricate the lip of the seal with clean gear oil, and then refit the driveshaft with reference to Section 5.

7 Check the oil level in the final drive unit as described in Section 2. Lower the vehicle to the ground and tighten the wheel bolts to the specified torque setting.

Pinion oil seal

8 Chock the front wheels and jack up the rear of the car and support it on axle stands (see *Vehicle jacking and support*).

9 Drain the final drive unit oil as described in Section 2.

10 Remove the rear section of the exhaust system as described in Chapter 4A Section 19.

11 Undo the three nuts and remove the bolts securing the propeller shaft rear flexible coupling to the differential pinion flange. Disconnect the propeller shaft from the flange on the differential and fasten it to the underside of the vehicle to prevent it getting damaged.

12 Using a tool/bar to prevent the flange from turning, undo the flange retaining nut **(see illustration)**.

13 Note the seal's fitted position in the housing, and then using a lever, carefully prose the seal out of the final drive housing.

14 Clean out the recess in the housing for the seal, and then check the new seal against the old seal to make sure it is the correct one.

15 Using a seal drift/installer or a large deep socket, install the new oil seal into the housing, making sure it is fitted in the same location as noted on removal.

16 Lubricate the lip of the seal with clean gear oil, and then refit the flange to the pinion shaft.

17 Fit the pinion nut and tighten it to the specified torque.

18 The remainder of refitting is a reversal of removal.

5 Driveshaft – removal and refitting

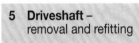

Removal

1 Slacken the 12-point driveshaft retaining nut with the car resting on its wheels. Note that this nut is extremely tight – ensure that the tools used to loosen it are of good quality, and a good fit. Do not remove the nut at this stage.

2 Chock the front wheels and slacken the rear wheel bolts. Jack up the rear of the car and support it on axle stands (see *Vehicle jacking and support*). Remove the relevant rear roadwheel.

3 Position a trolley jack under the hub carrier, and raise it until the driveshaft is approximately horizontal.

4.12 Undo the flange retaining nut

4 Disconnect the wiring plugs for the ABS wheel speed sensor, pad wear sensor and (where applicable) the rear damping valve, and unclip the wiring harnesses from the wheelarch and hub carrier. Fold the harnesses to one side.

5 Detach all the suspension control arms from the hub carrier, with the exception of the lower spring control arm, as described in Chapter 10 Section 15.

6 Lower the jack under the spring control arm, fold the hub carrier outwards and slide the outer driveshaft housing from the hub.

7 The driveshaft can now be removed from the final drive unit. Carefully lever the driveshaft out from the final drive unit, taking care not to damage the seal in the final drive unit housing or the protection ring on the shaft. Note the circlip on the driveshaft splined section to locate it in the final drive. Discard this circlip – a new one must be fitted.

6.4a Cut through the sealing cup lip...

6.4c ...to prise out the lip...

Refitting

8 Refitting is the reverse of removal, noting the following points.

a) Slide the driveshaft back into the final drive, making sure that the new circlip locates inside the differential securely.

b) Clean the threads of the driveshaft outer coupling, and fit a new driveshaft nut.

c) Tighten all fasteners to their specified torque where given.

d) Once the vehicle is resting on its wheels, tighten the driveshaft retaining nut to the specified torque. Where non-self-locking nut is fitted, stake it firmly into the driveshaft groove using a hammer and punch.

6 Driveshaft gaiters – renewal

Note: *This is a difficult procedure for the DIY'er to successfully carry out without access to a hydraulic press and suitable crimping tools. It may be prudent to simply obtain a complete replacement driveshaft.*

1 Remove the driveshaft as described in Section 5.

2 Secure the driveshaft in a vice equipped with soft jaws, and release the two outer joint gaiter retaining clips. If necessary, the retaining clips can be cut to release them.

3 Cut off the rubber gaiter and discard it, scoop out all the old dirty grease.

4 Using a hacksaw, carefully cut the sealing cup from the joint housing **(see illustrations)**.

6.4b ...then use a chisel...

6.4d ...and drive the sealing cup from the housing

6.5 Make alignment marks between the inner ring, ball retainer and joint housing

6.7 Prise the balls from the retainer

6.10 Remove the inner ring from the shaft

5 Clamp the outer constant velocity joint in a vice, and make alignment marks between the inner ring, ball retainer, and outer joint housing **(see illustration)**.

6 Align the shaft so the narrow bar of the inner ring points upwards.

7 Using a suitable thin-bladed screwdriver, prise out the upper balls from the retainer **(see illustration)**.

8 Slightly rotate the shaft and remove it, complete with the retainer and remaining balls, from the outer joint housing. Hold onto the balls to prevent them falling out.

9 Remove the remaining balls from the retainer.

10 Note its orientation, then use a hydraulic press or puller to remove the inner ring from the shaft **(see illustration)**.

11 Release the two inner joint gaiter retaining clips, and slide the gaiter from place. Do not attempt to dismantle the inner joint.

12 Using a hacksaw, carefully cut the sealing cup from the joint housing **(see illustrations 6.4a, 6.4b, 6.4c and 6.4d)**.

13 Thoroughly clean the joints, balls, etc, and examine them for wear and damage. If the either joint is worn or damaged, the complete driveshaft must be replaced.

14 Fill the inner joint with the correct quantity of grease as given in the Specifications, then renew the O-ring seal, slide the new sealing cup into place, and secure it using a hammer and a 4 mm rod to push the cup rim into the groove.

15 Slide the inner joint gaiter into place, and secure it with the new retaining clips.

16 Slide the new outer joint gaiter onto the shaft – small diameter first.

17 Slide the new sealing cup onto the shaft – small diameter first.

18 Press the outer joint inner ring onto the shaft (observing the orientation previously noted), so that the shaft protrudes 4.2 mm through the ring **(see illustration)**.

19 'Stake' the ring to the shaft at 3 points 120° apart. The stakings must be applied between the original stakings, and as close as possible to the splined profile of the shaft.

20 Fill the outer joint with the correct quantity of grease as given in the Specifications, then renew the O-ring seal, slide the new sealing cup into place, and secure it using a hammer and a 4 mm rod to push the cup ring into the groove.

21 Slide the outer joint gaiter into place, and secure it with the new retaining clips.

22 The remainder of refitting is a reversal of removal, noting the following points:

a) *Align the previously made marks between the outer joint housing, retainer and inner ring.*

b) *Fill the outer joint with the correct quantity of grease as given in Specifications.*

c) *Crimp the new retaining clips in place, with the 'open end' of the clips facing opposite to the normal direction of rotation.*

7 Propeller shaft – removal and refitting

Removal

1 Chock the front wheels. Jack up the rear of the car and support it on axle stands (see *Vehicle jacking and support*). Place the transmission in neutral, then undo the fasteners and remove the transmission undershield.

2 Remove the rear section of the exhaust system as described in Chapter 4A Section 19.

3 Undo the fasteners, remove the plastic underbody panels as necessary to allow access to the fasteners, then remove the heatshields from above the exhaust system.

4 Remove the crossbrace under the front of the propeller shaft (where fitted) **(see illustration)**.

5 Make alignment marks between the centre bearing crossbrace, then have an assistant support the propeller shaft, and undo the bolts securing the centre bearing crossbrace to the vehicle floor **(see illustration)**.

6 Make alignment marks between the flexible coupling and the transmission output flange **(see illustration)**. Repeat this process at the rear of the propeller shaft.

7 Slacken and remove the retaining nuts and bolts securing the flexible coupling to

6.18 The shaft must protrude 4.2 mm

7.4 Crossbrace retaining bolts

7.5 Centre bearing crossbrace retaining bolts

7.6 Make alignment marks between the coupling and the transmission output flange

7.7 Remove the bolts/nuts securing the flexible coupling to the transmission flange

the transmission flange **(see illustrations)**. Discard the nuts; new ones should be used on refitting.

8 Unscrew the nuts and bolts securing the coupling to the final drive unit flange and discard them; new ones must be used on refitting **(see illustration)**.

9 Slide the rear of the shaft forwards and disengage the shaft from the final drive unit. Free the front of the shaft from the transmission, and remove the shaft assembly from underneath the vehicle.

Note: *Do not separate the two halves of the shaft without first making alignment marks. If the shafts are incorrectly joined, the propeller shaft assembly may become imbalanced, leading to noise and vibration during operation. On some models, there are alignment marks already on the shaft; the raised mark on the front section must be positioned in between the two marks on the rear section universal joint.*

10 Inspect the rubber couplings, the support bearing and shaft universal joint as described later in this Chapter.

Refitting

11 Lubricate the shaft bushes with multi-purpose grease, and the shaft splines with molybdenum disulphide grease.

7.8 Undo the 3 bolts/nuts securing the coupling to the final drive flange

12 Manoeuvre the shaft into position, aligning the marks made prior to removal, and engage the shaft with the transmission and final drive unit flanges. With the marks correctly aligned, refit the centre bearing retaining bolts, tightening them lightly only at this stage.

13 Making sure the marks are correctly aligned, insert the retaining bolts securing the rear coupling to the final drive unit and fit the new retaining nuts. Tighten the retaining nuts to the specified torque setting.

14 Make sure the front coupling is correctly aligned with the transmission flange and refit the coupling bolts. Fit the new retaining nuts and tighten them to the specified torque.

15 With both the front and rear couplings correctly tightened, tighten the centre bearing retaining bolts to the specified torque setting.

16 The remainder of refitting is a reversal of removal.

8 Propeller shaft rubber coupling – check and renewal

Check

1 Raise the vehicle and support it securely on axle stands (see *Vehicle jacking and support*).

2 To improve access to the coupling, unscrew the heat shield retaining nuts and manoeuvre the heat shield out from around the exhaust system.

3 Closely examine the rubber couplings which link the propeller shaft to the transmission and final drive, looking for signs of damage such as cracking or splitting or for signs of general deterioration. If necessary, renew the coupling as follows.

Renewal

4 Remove the propeller shaft as described in Section 7.

Front coupling

5 Make alignment marks between the coupling and propeller shaft.

6 Unscrew the retaining nuts and washers, then withdraw the bolts and remove the coupling from the propeller shaft. Note carefully any additional markings or wording (which may be in German) for use when refitting. Inspect the vibration damper for signs of wear or damage, and renew if necessary.

7 Check the centring sleeve fitted to the centre of the coupling for signs of wear or damage. If necessary, the centring sleeve can be pressed out of position for renewal, having first noted its fitted depth.

8 Fit the new rubber coupling to the shaft, ensuring that (where applicable) any additional markings or wording are orientated as noted on removal. Insert the retaining bolts then fit the new retaining nuts and washers, and tighten them to the specified torque.

9 Refit the propeller shaft as described in Section 7.

Rear coupling

10 Unscrew the retaining nuts then withdraw the bolts and remove the coupling from the propeller shaft.

11 Fit the new coupling, then fit the retaining bolts and new nuts, tightening them to the specified torque.

12 Refit the propeller shaft as described in Section 7.

9 Propeller shaft centre bearing – check and renewal

Check

1 Wear in the support bearing will lead to noise and vibration when the car is driven. The bearing is best checked with the propeller shaft removed (see Section 7).

2 Rotate the bearing and check that it turns

9.5 Propeller shaft centre bearing components – typical

1 Propeller shaft   2 Propeller shaft   3 Bearing   4 Rubber gaiter   5 Centre bearing

smoothly with no sign of free play; if it's difficult to turn, or if it has a gritty feeling, renew it. Also inspect the rubber portion. If it's cracked or deteriorated, renew it.

Renewal

Note: *Bearing renewal requires the use of a puller and hydraulic press, as well as suitable spacers. If access to suitable equipment cannot be gained, entrust the task to your Mercedes-Benz dealer or suitably equipped repairer.*

3 Remove the propeller shaft as described in Section 7.

4 Make alignment marks between the front and rear sections of the propeller shaft, noting that on some models there are alignment marks already on the shaft; the raised mark on the front section must be positioned in between the two marks on the rear section universal joint.

5 Separate the two halves of the propeller shaft **(see illustration)**.

6 Remove the rubber gaiter from the front section of the shaft.

7 Using a suitable puller, draw the centre mounting assembly off the end of the shaft, noting which way around the bracket is fitted.

8 Support the mounting bracket assembly, and carefully press the bearing out of position using a tubular drift.

9 Inspect all components for signs of wear or damage and renew as necessary.

10 Support the mounting bracket securely and press the new bearing fully into position using a tubular drift which bears only on the bearing outer race.

11 Remove all traces of dirt from the propeller shaft, ensure that the mounting bracket is positioned the correct way around, and then press the assembly fully onto the shaft using

a tubular drift which bears only on the bearing inner race.

12 Lubricate the propeller shaft splines with molybdenum disulphide grease. Carefully slide the two halves of the propeller shaft together, making sure the alignment marks are correctly positioned.

13 Refit the propeller shaft as described in Section 7.

10 Propeller shaft universal joint – check and renewal

Check

1 Wear in the universal joint is characterised by vibration in the transmission, noise during acceleration, and metallic squeaking and grating sounds as the bearings disintegrate. The joint can be checked with the propeller shaft still fitted.

2 Hold the front half of the propeller shaft, and try to turn the rear half of the shaft. Free play between the propeller shaft halves indicates excessive wear. If the axial movement is excessive, renew the propeller shaft.

Renewal

3 At the time of writing, no spare parts were available to enable renewal of the universal joints to be carried out. Therefore, if any joint shows signs of damage or wear the propeller shaft assembly must be renewed. Consult your Mercedes-Benz dealer or parts supplier for latest information on parts availability.

4 If renewal of the propeller shaft is necessary, it may be worthwhile seeking the advice of an automotive engineering specialist. They may be able to repair the original shaft assembly, or supply a reconditioned shaft on an exchange basis.

Chapter 9
Braking system

Contents

Section number

Anti-lock braking system (ABS) – general information and
  sensor replacement 18
Braking system switches – removal and refitting 17
Front brake caliper – removal, overhaul and refitting 8
Front brake disc – inspection, removal and refitting 6
Front brake pads – renewal 4
General information 1
Hydraulic pipes and hoses – renewal 3
Hydraulic system – bleeding 2
Master cylinder – removal, overhaul and refitting 10

Section number

Parking brake – adjustment 13
Parking brake cables – removal and refitting 15
Parking brake pedal – removal and refitting 14
Parking brake shoes – removal and refitting 16
Rear brake caliper – removal, overhaul and refitting 9
Rear brake disc – inspection, removal and refitting 7
Rear brake pads – renewal 5
Vacuum pump – testing, removal and refitting 19
Vacuum servo unit – testing, removal and refitting 11
Vacuum servo unit check valve – removal, testing and refitting 12

Degrees of difficulty

Easy, suitable for novice with little experience	Fairly easy, suitable for beginner with some experience	Fairly difficult, suitable for competent DIY mechanic	Difficult, suitable for experienced DIY mechanic	Very difficult, suitable for expert DIY or professional

Specifications

Front brakes

Caliper type	Single piston sliding caliper
Disc:	
Type	Ventilated
Thickness:	
New	25 or 28 mm
Minimum:	
25 mm discs	22.4 mm
28 mm discs	25.4 mm
Pad friction material minimum thickness	2.0 mm

Rear brakes

Caliper type	Single piston sliding caliper
Disc:	
Thickness:	
New:	
278 mm diameter discs	9.0 mm
300 mm diameter discs	10.0 mm
Minimum thickness:	
9.0 mm discs	7.3 mm
10.0 mm discs	8.3 mm
Maximum runout	0.08 mm
Pad friction material minimum thickness	2.0 mm
Parking brake shoe friction material minimum thickness	N/A

Parking brake

Type	Cable operated brake shoes with drum machined into rear disc hub
Number of notches adjusting wheel	8

Torque wrench settings

	Nm	lbf ft
Bleed screw	18	13
Front brake caliper-to-hub carrier*	115	85
Front caliper guide pin bolts:		
M8 x 28 mm	34	25
M8 x 70 mm	29	21
Disc retaining screw	10	7
Master cylinder nuts	25	18
Rear caliper bracket-to-hub carrier bolts*	115	85
Rear caliper guide pin bolts	25	17
Roadwheel bolts	130	96
Servo retaining nuts	20	15
Vacuum pump bolts:		
2148 cc engines (Type 646)	14	10
2143 cc engines (Type 651)	9	7
Yaw rate sensor	7	5

*Do not re-use

1 General information

1 The braking system is of the servo-assisted, dual-circuit hydraulic type. The layout is such that under normal circumstances, both circuits operate in unison. Should a hydraulic failure occur in one of the circuits, full braking force will still be available in the other circuit (operating on two diagonally-opposite roadwheels), albeit with increased pedal travel.

2 All models have disc brakes at the front and rear wheels as standard. An Anti-lock Braking System (ABS) is fitted as standard to all models (refer to the appropriate section for further information on the operation of the ABS).

3 Models are equipped with various Mercedes-Benz braking assist systems, including Active braking, brake assist, hill-start assist, dry braking, etc. All of these functions are incorporated into the ABS system. All models are also equipped with the Electronic Stability Program (ESP), which uses the braking system to help steer the car in extreme circumstances. For further information on the functions of these systems, refer to your owners handbook or a Mercedes-Benz dealer.

4 The front and rear disc brakes are actuated by sliding single-piston calipers. This design of caliper ensures that equal pressure is applied to each disc pad.

5 The parking brake provides an independent, mechanical means of applying the rear brakes. A drum and shoe arrangement is fitted in the centre of each rear brake disc. The parking brake is applied by a foot pedal, and is released by a hand lever on the facia panel; both controls actuate the brake shoes via cables.

Caution: When servicing any part of the system, work carefully and methodically; also observe scrupulous cleanliness when overhauling any part of the hydraulic system. Always renew components (in axle sets, where applicable) if in doubt about their condition, and use only genuine Mercedes-Benz parts, or at least those of known good quality. Note the warnings given in Safety first! and at relevant points in this Chapter concerning the dangers of asbestos dust and hydraulic fluid.

2 Hydraulic system – bleeding

⚠️ *Warning: Hydraulic fluid is poisonous; wash off immediately and thoroughly in the case of skin contact, and seek immediate medical advice if any fluid is swallowed or gets into the eyes. Certain types of hydraulic fluid are flammable, and may ignite when allowed into contact with hot components; when servicing any hydraulic system, it is safest to assume that the fluid is flammable, and to take precautions against the risk of fire as though it is petrol that is being handled. Hydraulic fluid is also an effective paint stripper, and will attack plastics; if any is spilt, it should be washed off immediately, using copious quantities of fresh water. Finally, it is hygroscopic (it absorbs moisture from the air) – old fluid may be contaminated and unfit for further use. When topping-up or renewing the fluid, always use the recommended type, and ensure that it comes from a freshly-opened sealed container.*

General

1 The correct operation of any hydraulic system is only possible after removing all air from the components and circuit; this is achieved by bleeding the system.

2 During the bleeding procedure, add only clean, unused hydraulic fluid of the recommended type; never re-use fluid that has already been bled from the system. Ensure that sufficient fluid is available before starting work.

3 If there is any possibility of incorrect fluid being already in the system, the brake components and circuit must be flushed completely with uncontaminated, correct fluid, and new seals should be fitted to the various components.

4 If hydraulic fluid has been lost from the system, or air has entered because of a leak, ensure that the fault is cured before continuing further.

5 Park the car on level ground, switch off the engine and select first or reverse gear, then chock the wheels and release the parking brake.

6 Check that all pipes and hoses are secure, unions tight and bleed screws closed. Clean any dirt from around the bleed screws.

7 Unscrew the master cylinder reservoir cap, and top the master cylinder reservoir up to the MAX level line; refit the cap loosely, and remember to maintain the fluid level at least above the MIN level line throughout the procedure, or there is a risk of further air entering the system.

8 There are a number of one-man, do-it-yourself brake bleeding kits currently available from motor accessory shops. It is recommended that one of these kits is used whenever possible, as they greatly simplify the bleeding operation, and reduce the risk of expelled air and fluid being drawn back into the system. If such a kit is not available, the basic (two-man) method must be used, which is described in detail below.

9 If a kit is to be used, prepare the car as described previously, and follow the kit manufacturer's instructions, as the procedure may vary slightly according to the type being used; generally, they are as outlined below in the relevant sub-section.

10 Whichever method is used, the same sequence must be followed (paragraphs 11 and 12) to ensure that all air is removed from the system. On completion, test the operation of the braking system exhaustively, before bringing the car back into service on the road.

Bleeding sequence

11 If the system has been only partially disconnected, and suitable precautions were taken to minimise fluid loss, it should be necessary only to bleed that part of the system.
12 If the complete system is to be bled, then it should be done working in the following sequence:
a) *Right-hand rear brake*
b) *Left-hand rear brake*
c) *Right-hand front brake*
d) *Left-hand front brake*

Basic (two-man) method

13 Collect a clean glass jar, a suitable length of plastic or rubber tubing which is a tight fit over the bleed screw, and a ring spanner to fit the screw. The help of an assistant will also be required.
14 Remove the dust cap from the first screw in the sequence. Fit the spanner and tube to the screw, place the other end of the tube in the jar, and pour in sufficient fluid to cover the end of the tube.
15 Ensure that the master cylinder reservoir fluid level is maintained at least above the MIN level line throughout the procedure.
16 Have the assistant fully depress the brake pedal several times to build-up pressure, and then maintain it on the final downstroke.
17 While pedal pressure is maintained, unscrew the bleed screw (approximately one turn) and allow the compressed fluid and air to flow into the jar. The assistant should maintain pedal pressure, following it down to the floor if necessary, and should not release it until instructed to do so. When the flow stops, tighten the bleed screw again, have the assistant release the pedal slowly, and recheck the reservoir fluid level.
18 Repeat the steps given in paragraphs 16 and 17 until the fluid emerging from the bleed screw is free from air bubbles. If the master cylinder has been drained and refilled, and air is being bled from the first screw in the sequence, allow approximately five seconds between cycles for the master cylinder passages to refill.
19 When no more air bubbles appear, tighten the bleed screw to the specified torque, remove the tube and spanner, and refit the dust cap. Do not overtighten the bleed screw.
20 Repeat the procedure on the remaining screws in the sequence, until all air is removed from the system and the brake pedal feels firm again.

Using a one-way valve kit

21 As their name implies, these kits consist of a length of tubing with a one-way valve fitted, to prevent expelled air and fluid being drawn back into the system; some kits include a translucent container, which can be positioned so that the air bubbles can be more easily seen flowing from the end of the tube **(see illustration)**.
22 The kit is connected to the bleed screw, which is then opened. The user returns to the driver's seat, depresses the brake pedal with a smooth, steady stroke, and slowly releases it;

this is repeated until the expelled fluid is clear of air bubbles.
23 Note that these kits simplify work so much that it is easy to forget the master cylinder reservoir fluid level; ensure that this is maintained at least above the MIN level line at all times.

Using a pressure-bleeding kit

Note: *This is the method recommended by Mercedes-Benz*
24 These kits are usually operated by the reservoir of pressurised air contained in a spare tyre. However, note that it will probably be necessary to reduce the pressure to a lower level than normal; refer to the instructions supplied with the kit.
Note: *Mercedes-Benz specify that a pressure of 2 bar (29 psi) should not be exceeded.*
25 By connecting a pressurised, fluid-filled container to the master cylinder reservoir, bleeding can be carried out simply by opening each brake caliper bleed screw in turn (in the specified sequence – see paragraph 12), and allowing the fluid to flow out until no more air bubbles can be seen in the expelled fluid.
26 This method has the advantage that the large reservoir of fluid provides an additional safeguard against air being drawn into the system during bleeding.
27 Pressure-bleeding is particularly effective when bleeding 'difficult' systems, or when bleeding the complete system at the time of routine fluid renewal.

All methods

28 When bleeding is complete, and firm pedal feel is restored, wash off any spilt fluid, tighten the bleed screws to the specified torque, and refit their dust caps.
29 Check the hydraulic fluid level in the master cylinder reservoir, and top-up if necessary (see *Weekly checks*).
30 Discard any hydraulic fluid that has been bled from the system; it will not be fit for re-use.
31 Check the feel of the brake pedal. If it feels at all spongy, air must still be present in the system, and further bleeding is required. Failure to bleed satisfactorily after a reasonable repetition of the bleeding procedure may be due to worn master cylinder seals.

2.21 Brake bleeding kit

3 Hydraulic pipes and hoses – renewal

Note: *Before starting work, refer to the warnings in Section 1 and Section 2.*
1 If any pipe or hose is to be renewed, minimise fluid loss by first removing the master cylinder reservoir cap, then tightening it down onto a piece of polythene to obtain an airtight seal. Alternatively, flexible hoses can be sealed, if required, using a proprietary brake hose clamp; metal brake pipe unions can be plugged (if care is taken not to allow dirt into the system) or capped immediately they are disconnected. Place a wad of rag under any union that is to be disconnected, to catch any spilt fluid.
2 If a flexible hose is to be disconnected, unscrew the brake pipe union nut and remove the clip, which secures the hose to its mounting bracket **(see illustration)**.
3 To unscrew the union nuts, it is preferable to obtain a brake pipe spanner of the correct size; these are available from most large motor accessory shops. Failing this, a close-fitting open-ended spanner will be required, though if the nuts are tight or corroded, their flats may be rounded-off if the spanner slips. In such a case, a self-locking wrench is often the only way to unscrew a stubborn union, but it follows that the pipe and the damaged nuts must be renewed on reassembly. Always clean a union and surrounding area before disconnecting it; this helps to prevent the entry of dirt into the hydraulic system. If disconnecting a component with more than one union, make a careful note of the connections before disturbing any of them.
4 If a brake pipe is to be renewed, it can be obtained, cut to length and with the union nuts and end flares in place, from Mercedes-Benz dealers. All that is then necessary is to bend it to shape, following the line of the original, before fitting it to the car. Alternatively, most motor accessory shops can make up brake pipes from kits, but this requires very careful measurement of the original, to ensure that the new one is of the correct length. The safest answer is usually to take the original to the shop as a pattern.

3.2 Undo the union nut and remove the clip

5 On refitting, do not overtighten the union nuts. It is not necessary to exercise brute force to obtain a sound joint!

6 Ensure that the pipes and hoses are correctly routed, with no kinks, and that they are secured in the clips or brackets provided. After fitting, remove the polythene from the reservoir, and bleed the hydraulic system as described in Section 2. Wash off any spilt fluid, and check carefully for fluid leaks.

7 Finally, test the operation of the braking system exhaustively, before bringing the car back into service on the road.

4 Front brake pads – renewal

⚠️ **Warning: Renew both sets of front brake pads at the same time – never renew the pads on only one wheel, as uneven braking may result. Note that the dust created by wear of the pads may contain asbestos, which is a health hazard. Never blow it out with compressed air, and don't inhale any of it. An approved filtering mask should be worn when working on the brakes. DO NOT use petrol or petroleum-based solvents to clean brake parts; use brake cleaner or methylated spirit only.**

1 Apply the handbrake, then slacken the front roadwheel bolts. Jack up the front of the vehicle and support it on axle stands (see *Vehicle jacking and support*). Remove both front roadwheels.

2 If new pads are to be fitted, reduce the fluid level in the master cylinder reservoir to the minimum level using a syringe (or similar).

3 Follow the relevant accompanying photos **(illustrations 4.3a to 4.3u)** for the actual pad replacement procedure. Be sure to stay in order and read the caption under each illustration.

a) *New pads may have an adhesive foil on the backplates. Remove this foil prior to installation.*

b) *Mercedes-Benz insist that no lubricant/paste/grease is applied to the pads or caliper.*

c) *When pushing the caliper piston back to accommodate new pads, keep a close eye on the fluid level in the reservoir.*

4.3a Undo the bolt securing the pad wear sensor wiring harness…

4.3b …then unplug the wear sensor wiring plug

4.3c On discs with a significant wear lip, use a screwdriver to force the piston slightly back into the caliper body

4.3d Hold the guide pin stationary with an open-ended spanner…

4.3e …undo the bolts…

4.3f …and slide the caliper from place

4.3g Suspend the caliper from the suspension strut with wire/string to prevent straining the rubber hose

4.3h Remove the outer pad…

4.3i … and the inner pad

4.3j Remove the upper and lower shims from the caliper mounting bracket

4.3k Clean the caliper and bracket with aerosol cleaner and a soft brush

4.3l Measure the pad friction material thickness. If it's less than 2.0 mm, renew all four front pads

4.3m If new pads are to be fitted, push the piston fully into the caliper body using a piston retraction tool. Keep an eye on the reservoir fluid level as the piston is pushed back.

4.3n Fit the shims to the caliper mounting bracket

4.3o Insert the wear sensor into the hole in the inner pad friction material. Note that inner pads on both sides have an arrow indicating direction of rotation

4.3p Fit the inner brake pad – ensure the friction material is against the disc face!

4.3q Fit the outer brake pad

4.3r Slide the caliper back into place. Don't forget to feed the pad wear sensor wiring through the aperture on the right-hand caliper.

4.3s Apply a little thread-locking compound...

4.3t ...then refit the guide pin bolts and tighten them to the specified torque

4.3u Reconnect the wiring plug, and secure the harness

4.6 Apply a little anti-seize grease to the hub surface

4 Repeat the above procedure on the remaining caliper.

5 Depress the brake pedal repeatedly, until the pads are pressed into firm contact with the brake disc, and normal (non-assisted) pedal pressure is restored.

6 Apply a little anti-seize grease to the hub surface, then refit the roadwheels, lower the vehicle to the ground and tighten the roadwheel bolts to the specified torque **(see illustration)**.

7 Check the hydraulic fluid level as described in *Weekly checks*.

Caution: New pads will not give full braking efficiency until they have bedded-in. Be

prepared for this, and avoid hard braking as far as possible for the first hundred miles or so after pad renewal.

5 Rear brake pads – renewal

⚠ **Warning: Renew both sets of rear brake pads at the same time – never renew the pads on only one wheel, as uneven braking may result. Note that the dust created by wear of the pads may contain asbestos, which is a health hazard. Never blow it out with compressed air, and don't inhale any of it. An approved filtering mask should be worn when working on the brakes. DO NOT use petrol or petroleum-based solvents to clean brake parts; use brake cleaner or methylated spirit only.**

1 Apply the handbrake, then slacken the rear roadwheel bolts. Jack up the rear of the vehicle and support it on axle stands (see *Vehicle jacking and support*). Remove both rear roadwheels.

2 If new pads are to be fitted, reduce the fluid level in the master cylinder reservoir to the minimum level using a syringe (or similar).

3 Follow the relevant accompanying photos

(illustrations 5.3a to 5.3r) for the actual pad replacement procedure. Be sure to stay in order and read the caption under each illustration.

a) *New pads may have an adhesive foil on the backplates. Remove this foil prior to installation.*

b) *Mercedes-Benz insist that no grease/ paste/lubricant is applied to the pads or caliper.*

c) *When pushing the caliper piston back to accommodate new pads, keep a close eye on the fluid level in the reservoir.*

4 Depress the brake pedal repeatedly, until the pads are pressed into firm contact with the brake disc, and normal (non-assisted) pedal pressure is restored.

5 Repeat the above procedure on the remaining rear brake caliper.

6 Apply a little anti-seize grease to the hub surface, then refit the roadwheels, lower the vehicle to the ground and tighten the roadwheel bolts to the specified torque.

7 Check the hydraulic fluid level as described in *Weekly checks*.

Caution: New pads will not give full braking efficiency until they have bedded-in. Be prepared for this, and avoid hard braking as far as possible for the first hundred miles or so after pad renewal.

5.3a Use a screwdriver to prise the caliper spring from place

5.3b Where fitted, undo the retaining bolt...

5.3c ...and disconnect the pad wear sensor wiring plug

5.3d Prise out the cap...

5.3e ...then unscrew the upper guide pin bolt using a 7 mm Allen key/bit

5.3f If there's a wear lip on the disc, use a screwdriver to lever the caliper to the outside, forcing the piston into the caliper body a little.

5.3g Pivot the caliper downwards

5.3h Remove the outer brake pad...

5.3i ...and unclip the inner pad from the piston

5.3j Clean the caliper and mounting bracket using aerosol brake cleaner and a soft brush

5.3k If new pads are to be fitted, push the piston fully into the caliper body using a piston retraction tool. Keep an eye on the fluid level in the reservoir as the piston is pushed back

5.3l Insert the wear sensor into the hole in the inner pad friction material. Note that the sensor is only fitted to the right-hand side brake pads.

5.3m Clip the new inner pad into the caliper piston

5.3n Remove the protective foil from the outer pad backing plate (where applicable), and fit the outer pad to the bracket. Ensure the pad friction material is against the disc face!

5.3o Pivot the caliper back into place, Don't forget to feed the pad wear sensor wiring through the aperture (where applicable)

5.3p Apply a little threadlocking compound then refit the upper guide pin bolt, and tighten it to the specified torque

5.3q Refit the plastic cap

5.3r Refit the caliper retaining spring, then reconnect the pad wear sensor wiring plug, and tighten the harness retaining bolt securely (where applicable)

6.3 Use a micrometer to check the thickness of the disc

6.8 Caliper mounting bracket-to-hub carrier bolts

6.9 Undo the Torx screw and remove the disc

6 Front brake disc – inspection, removal and refitting

Note: *Before starting work, refer to the note at the beginning of Section 4 concerning the dangers of asbestos dust.*

Inspection

Note: *If either disc requires renewal, BOTH should be renewed at the same time, to ensure even and consistent braking. New brake pads should also be fitted.*

1 Apply the handbrake, then jack up the front of the car and support it on axle stands (see *Vehicle jacking and support*. Remove the appropriate front roadwheel.
2 Slowly rotate the brake disc so that the full area of both sides can be checked; remove the brake pads if better access is required to the inboard surface. Light scoring is normal in the area swept by the brake pads, but if heavy scoring or cracks are found, the disc must be renewed.
3 It is normal to find a lip of rust and brake dust around the disc's perimeter; this can be scraped off if required. If, however, a lip has formed due to excessive wear of the brake pad swept area, then the disc's thickness must be measured using a micrometer **(see illustration)**. Take measurements at several places around the disc, at the inside and outside of the pad swept area; if the disc has worn at any point to the specified minimum thickness or less, the disc must be renewed.
4 If the disc is thought to be warped, it can be

checked for run-out. Either use a dial gauge mounted on any convenient fixed point, while the disc is slowly rotated, or use feeler blades to measure (at several points all around the disc) the clearance between the disc and a fixed point, such as the caliper mounting bracket. If the measurements obtained are at the specified maximum or beyond, the disc is excessively warped, and must be renewed; however, it is worth checking first that the hub bearing is in good condition (Chapters 1 and/ or 10). If the run-out is excessive, the disc must be renewed.
5 Check the disc for cracks, especially around the wheel stud holes, and any other wear or damage, and renew if necessary.

Removal

6 Remove the front brake pads as described in Section 4.
7 Using a piece of wire or string, tie the caliper to the front suspension coil spring, to avoid placing any strain on the hydraulic brake hose.
8 Unscrew the two bolts securing the brake caliper mounting bracket to the hub carrier, then slide the bracket assembly off the disc **(see illustration)**. Discard the bolts – new ones must be fitted.
9 Use chalk or paint to mark the relationship of the disc to the hub, then remove the screw securing the brake disc to the hub, and remove the disc **(see illustration)**. If it is tight, lightly tap its rear face with a hide or plastic mallet.

Refitting

10 Refitting is the reverse of the removal procedure, noting the following points:

a) Ensure that the mating surfaces of the disc and hub are clean and flat.
b) Align (if applicable) the marks made on removal, and tighten the disc retaining screw to the specified torque.
c) If a new disc has been fitted, use a suitable solvent to wipe any preservative coating from the disc, before refitting the caliper.
d) Tighten the new caliper mounting bolts to the specified torque setting.
e) Fit the brake pads as described in Section 4.
f) Refit the roadwheel, then lower the vehicle to the ground and tighten the roadwheel nuts to the specified torque. On completion, repeatedly depress the brake pedal until normal (non-assisted) pedal pressure returns.

7 Rear brake disc – inspection, removal and refitting

Note: *Before starting work, refer to the note at the beginning of Section 5 concerning the dangers of asbestos dust.*

Inspection

Note: *If either disc requires renewal, BOTH should be renewed at the same time, to ensure even and consistent braking. New brake pads should also be fitted.*

1 Firmly chock the front wheels, then jack up the rear of the car and support it on axle stands (see *Vehicle jacking and support*). Remove the appropriate rear roadwheel. Release the handbrake.
2 Inspect the disc as described in Section 6.

Removal

3 Undo the 2 caliper mounting bracket bolts, and slide the bracket, complete with caliper and brake pads, from place **(see illustration)**. Discard the bolts – new ones must be fitted.
4 Suspend the caliper assembly from the vehicle suspension/body to prevent straining the brake hose.
5 Insert a screwdriver through a wheel bolt hole in the brake disc, and rotate the adjuster knurled wheel on the pivot to retract the shoes **(see illustration 13.4)**.
6 Slacken and remove the brake disc retaining screw **(see illustration)**.

7.3 Caliper mounting bracket bolts

7.6 Rear brake disc retaining screw

7 If the disc is to be refitted, make alignment marks between the disc and hub.

8 It should now be possible to withdraw the brake disc from the rear hub by hand. If it is tight, lightly tap its rear face with a hide or plastic mallet.

Refitting

9 If a new disc is been fitted, use a suitable solvent to wipe any preservative coating from the disc. Ensure the disc mounting surface on the hub is free from dirt and corrosion.

10 Align (if applicable) the marks made on removal, then fit the disc and tighten the retaining screw to the specified torque.

11 Refit the caliper mounting bracket, and tighten the new bolts to the specified torque.

12 Adjust the parking brake shoes and cable as described in Section 13.

13 Fit the brake pads as described in Section 5.

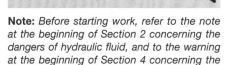

8 Front brake caliper –
removal, overhaul and refitting

Note: *Before starting work, refer to the note at the beginning of Section 2 concerning the dangers of hydraulic fluid, and to the warning at the beginning of Section 4 concerning the dangers of asbestos dust.*

Removal

1 Apply the handbrake, then jack up the front of the vehicle and support it on axle stands (see *Vehicle jacking and support*). Remove the appropriate roadwheel.

2 Make a note of the wiring harness routing, then disconnect the wiring plugs from the caliper.

3 Minimise fluid loss by using a brake hose clamp, a G-clamp or a similar tool to clamp the flexible hose.

4 Clean the area around the union, then slacken the brake hose union nut.

5 Remove the brake pads as described in Section 4.

6 Unscrew the caliper from the end of the brake hose and remove it from the vehicle.

Overhaul

7 At the time of writing, no replacement parts appear to be available for the front calipers. If

they are defective, replacement calipers must be fitted.

Refitting

8 Screw the caliper fully onto the flexible hose union.

9 Refit the brake pads as described in Section 4.

10 Securely tighten the brake pipe union nut.

11 Remove the brake hose clamp, and bleed the hydraulic system as described in Section 2. Note that, providing the precautions described were taken to minimise brake fluid loss, it should only be necessary to bleed the relevant front brake.

12 Refit the roadwheel, then lower the vehicle to the ground and tighten the roadwheel nuts to the specified torque. On completion, check the hydraulic fluid level as described in *Weekly checks*.

9 Rear brake caliper –
removal, overhaul and refitting

Note: *Before starting work, refer to the note at the beginning of Section 2 concerning the dangers of hydraulic fluid, and to the warning at the beginning of Section 5 concerning the dangers of asbestos dust.*

Removal

1 Chock the front wheels, then jack up the rear of the vehicle and support on axle stands (see *Vehicle jacking and support*). Remove the relevant rear wheel.

2 Minimise fluid loss by using a brake hose clamp, a G-clamp or a similar tool to clamp the flexible hose.

3 Clean the area around the union, then loosen the brake hose union nut.

4 Remove the brake pads as described in Section 5.

5 Unscrew the caliper from the end of the flexible hose, and remove it from the vehicle.

Overhaul

6 At the time of writing, it would appear that no replacement parts are available for the rear caliper. If defective, the complete caliper must be replaced.

Refitting

7 Screw the caliper fully onto the flexible hose union.

8 Refit the brake pads as described in Section 5.

9 Securely tighten the brake pipe union nut.

10 Remove the brake hose clamp, and bleed the hydraulic system as described in Section 2. Note that, providing the precautions described were taken to minimise brake fluid loss, it should only be necessary to bleed the relevant rear brake.

11 Refit the roadwheel, then lower the vehicle to the ground and tighten the roadwheel nuts to the specified torque. On completion, check the hydraulic fluid level as described in *Weekly checks*.

10 Master cylinder –
removal, overhaul and refitting

Note: *Before starting work, refer to the warning at the beginning of Section 2 concerning the dangers of hydraulic fluid.*

Removal

1 Disconnect the battery negative terminal (Chapter 5A Section 4) and then depress the brake pedal several times to remove the vacuum from the brake servo unit.

2 Undo the bolt, and remove the strut adjacent to the master cylinder **(see illustration)**.

3 Unscrew the reservoir cap, lift out the filter, and remove as much brake fluid as possible using a syringe (or similar).

Warning: Do not syphon the fluid by mouth, as it is poisonous; use a syringe or an old antifreeze tester.

4 Disconnect the wiring plug from the reservoir.

5 Place absorbent rags around the reservoir/master cylinder, then disconnect the clutch fluid supply hose from the reservoir **(see illustration)**. Plug the openings to prevent contamination.

6 Undo the retaining bolt and pull the reservoir upwards from the master cylinder **(see illustration)**. Renew the reservoir-to-master cylinder seals.

10.2 Undo the bolt and remove the strut

10.5 Disconnect the clutch fluid supply hose

10.6 Using a mirror to located the reservoir retaining bolt

7 Make a note of the correct fitted positions of the unions, then unscrew the union nuts and carefully withdraw the pipes. Plug or tape over the pipe ends and master cylinder orifices, to minimise the loss of brake fluid, and to prevent the entry of dirt into the system. Wash off any spilt fluid immediately with cold water.

8 Release any wiring from the master cylinder, then undo the mounting nuts and pull the master cylinder from the servo unit. Renew the master cylinder-to-servo O-ring seal.

Overhaul

9 At the time of writing, it would appear that no replacement parts are available for the master cylinder. If defective, the complete master cylinder must be replaced.

Refitting

10 Remove all traces of dirt from the master cylinder and servo unit mating surfaces, and renew the seal.

11 Fit the master cylinder to the servo unit, ensuring that the servo unit pushrod enters the master cylinder bore centrally. Fit the master cylinder retaining nuts, and tighten them to the specified torque.

12 Wipe clean the brake pipe unions, then refit them to the master cylinder/hydraulic unit ports and tighten them securely.

13 Press the new reservoir seals firmly into the master cylinder ports, then ease the reservoir into position. Refit the reservoir locking pin securely. Reconnect the fluid hose(s) to the reservoir, and reconnect the wiring connector(s).

14 The remainder of refitting is a reversal of removal, noting the following points:
e) *Tighten all fasteners to their specified torque where given.*
f) *Refill the master cylinder reservoir with new fluid, and bleed the complete hydraulic system as described in Section 2.*

11 Vacuum servo unit – testing, removal and refitting

Note: *Note that a vacuum servo unit is only fitted to models without Sensotronic Brake Control (SBC)*

Testing

1 To test the operation of the servo unit, depress the footbrake several times with the engine off, to exhaust the vacuum from the servo. Now start the engine whilst keeping the pedal firmly depressed. There should be a noticeable 'give' in the brake pedal as the engine starts and the vacuum builds-up.

2 Allow the engine to run for at least two minutes, then switch it off. If the brake pedal is now depressed it should feel normal, but further applications should result in the pedal

11.9 Unscrew the pivot pin

feeling progressively firmer, with the pedal stroke decreasing on each application.

3 If the servo does not operate as described, first inspect the servo unit check valve as described in Section 12.

4 If the servo uni still fails to operate correctly, the fault lies within the unit itself. Repairs to the unit are not possible – if faulty, the servo unit must be replaced.

Removal

5 Remove the master cylinder as described in Section 10.

6 Disconnect the vacuum pipe from the servo unit.

7 Remove the drivers side lower facia panel as described in Chapter 11 Section 35.

8 Disconnect the brake light switch wiring plug.

9 Unscrew the servo pushrod pivot pin **(see illustration)**. Note that a new pin must be fitted.

10 Undo the 2 nuts securing the servo unit to the bulkhead.

11 Working in the engine compartment, manoeuvre the servo unit from place.

Refitting

12 Refitting is a reversal of removal, noting the following points:
a) *Renew the gasket between the servo unit and the engine compartment bulkhead.*
b) *Tighten all fasteners to their specified torque where given.*
c) *Check for correct braking system operation before venturing out onto the road.*

12 Vacuum servo unit check valve – removal, testing and refitting

Removal

1 Pull the vacuum hose connection(s) from the servo unit **(see illustration)**.

2 Trace the hose back and disconnect it from the vacuum pump.

3 The valve is integral with the hose. If the

12.1 Pull the vacuum hose connection(s) from the servo

valve is faulty, the complete hose assembly must be renewed.

Testing

4 Examine the vacuum hose, check the valve for signs of damage, and renew if necessary.

5 The valve may be tested by blowing through the hose in both directions; air should glow through the valve in one direction only – when blown through the from the servo unit end of the hose. Renew the hose assembly is this not the case.

Refitting

6 Ensuring the hose is correctly routed, securely reconnect it to the pump and the servo unit.

7 On completion, start the engine and check the valve to servo unit connection for signs of air leaks. Test the operation of the braking system before venturing out onto the road.

13 Parking brake – adjustment

Note: *If the parking brake shoe clearance requires significant amount of adjustment, it is advisable to inspect the brake shoe lining thickness.*

1 The parking brake cable is self-adjusting on all models, The following procedure is intended merely to compensate for wear of the shoe friction material, which should occur at a very slow and even rate and make routine adjustment unnecessary.

2 Chock the front wheels, slacken the rear wheel bolts, raise the rear of the vehicle and support it securely on axle stands (see *Vehicle jacking and support*). Remove the rear wheels, and fully release the parking brake.

3 Turn one of the rear brake discs so that access can be gained to the parking brake shoe adjuster, situated between the parking brake shoes, at the rear.

4 Using a long slim screwdriver engaged in the teeth of the adjuster, turn the adjuster until the parking brake shoes make contact with the drum and the disc can no longer be turned (see illustration). Repeat the procedure on the other rear brake. To apply the brake shoes, the adjuster on the left-hand brake is turned from the front rearwards, whist the adjuster on the right-hand brake is turned from the rear forwards.

5 Now back both adjusters off exactly 8 teeth. It must now be possible to freely rotate both discs by hand.

6 Upon completion, refit the rear wheels, lower the vehicle to the ground and tighten the wheel bolts to the specified torque.

14 Parking brake pedal –
removal and refitting

Removal

1 Chock the front wheels and fully release the parking brake.

2 Undo the fasteners and remove the drivers side lower facia panel as described in Chapter 11 Section 35. Disconnect any wiring plugs as the panel is withdrawn.

3 Disconnect the parking brake warning switch wiring plug.

4 Unhook the return spring, and disconnect the upper release cable from the lever on the pedal assembly **(see illustration)**.

5 Press the separation point downwards, and unhook the front release cable **(see illustration)**.

6 Undo the 2 bolts securing the pedal assembly **(see illustration)**.

7 Squeeze together the clips and pull the front cable from the pedal bracket **(see illustration)**.

8 Detach the upper release cable from the bracket **(see illustration)**.

9 If necessary, release the clips and remove the switch from the pedal assembly.

Refitting

10 Refitting is a reversal of removal. Adjust the parking brake as described in Section 13.

15 Parking brake cables –
removal and refitting

Rear cables

Removal

1 Chock the front wheels, slacken the rear wheel bolts, raise the vehicle and support is securely on axle stands (see *Vehicle jacking and support*). Fully release the parking brake and remove the rear wheels.

2 Remove the parking brake shoes as described in Section 16.

3 Undo the retaining bolt and pull each cable from the hub carrier **(see illustration)**.

4 Detach the left-hand cable from the separation point on the right-hand cable, then disconnect the right-hand cable from the centre cable **(see illustration)**.

13.4 Insert a screwdriver through one of the wheel bolt holes and engage it with the teeth of the adjuster (disc removed for clarity)

14.4 Unhook the spring and detach the cable

14.5 Front separation point

14.6 Pedal retaining bolts (rear bolt under the carpet)

14.7 Squeeze together the clips each side

14.8 Slide the upper cable from the bracket

15.3 Handbrake cable retaining bolt

15.4 Left-hand cable separation point above the final drive unit

15.15 Front-to-centre cable separation point

16.2a Note the positions of the components at the front...

16.2b ...and rear of the parking brake assembly

5 Work along the cable length, and release it from any grommets/retaining brackets/clips.

Refitting

6 Refitting is a reversal of removal. Adjust the parking brake as described in Section 13.

Front cable

Removal

7 Chock the front wheels, slacken the rear wheel bolts, raise the rear of the vehicle and support it securely on axle stands (see *Vehicle jacking and support*). Fully release the parking brake, and remove the rear wheels.

8 Undo the fasteners and remove the rear section of the engine/transmission undershield.

9 Remove the drivers side lower facia panel as described in Chapter 11 Section 35.

10 Press down the front separation point, and unhook the front brake cable **(see illustration 14.5)**.

11 Unclip the front cable from the pedal bracket **(see illustration 14.7)**.

12 Peel back the carpet, release the front cable from the retaining clips on the floor, and prise out the rubber grommet in the transmission tunnel.

13 Remove the catalytic converter/particulate filter, and exhaust system as described in Chapter 4A Section 19.

14 Undo the fasteners and slide the heatshields rearwards a little above the propeller shaft centre bearing.

15 Detach the front cable from the centre cable at the separation point **(see illustration)**.

16 On models with automatic transmission, detach the selector road from the transmission as described in Chapter 7B Section 3.

17 Support the transmission, then remove the rear crossbrace.

18 Disconnect the front of the propeller shaft as described in Chapter 8 Section 7, then lower the rear of the transmission a little.

19 Release the parking brake front cable from any retaining clips and manoeuvre it from place.

Refitting

20 Refitting is a reversal of removal. Adjust the parking brake cable as described in Section 13.

---

16 Parking brake shoes – removal and refitting

Removal

1 Remove the rear brake discs as described in Section 7.

2 Make a note of the correct fitted location of all components, then clean the parking brake shoe assembly using brake cleaner **(see illustrations)**. Place rags below the brake assembly to catch any spillage. DO NOT use compressed air to blow out the brake dust.

3 Carefully unhook and remove the parking brake shoe front return spring, noting which way round the spring is fitted – it is not symmetrical **(see illustration)**.

4 Using a pair of thin-nosed pliers, compress the upper shoe retaining spring then rotate it through 90° and remove it from the backplate. Access to the spring can be gained through the hub flange holes **(see illustration)**.

5 Lift the upper shoe, disengage the rear return spring, and remove the adjuster mechanism **(see illustrations)**.

6 Using a pair of thin-nosed pliers, compress the lower shoe retaining spring then rotate it through 90° and remove it from the

16.3 Unhook the front return spring

16.4 Compress the retaining spring then rotate it 90° and remove it

16.5a Unhook the rear return spring...

16.5b ...and remove the adjuster mechanism...

16.6 Access the retaining spring through the holes in the hub flange

16.7a Press out the pin...

16.7b ...and remove the expansion lock

backplate (see illustration). Access to the spring can be gained through the hub flange holes.

7 Fold open the expansion lock, press out the pin, and detach the parking brake cable (see illustrations).

8 With the shoes removed, clean and inspect the condition of the shoe adjuster and expander mechanisms, and renew them if they show signs of wear or damage. If all is well, apply a fresh coat of brake grease (Mercedes-Benz recommend Molykote Paste U or G-Rapid) to the threads of the adjuster and sliding surfaces of the expansion lock. Do not allow the grease to contact the shoe friction material.

Refitting

9 Prior to installation, clean the backplate, and apply a thin smear of high-temperature brake grease (see paragraph 9) or anti-seize compound to all those surfaces of the backplate which bear on the shoes. Do not allow the lubricant to foul the friction material.

10 Fully retract the adjuster mechanism.

11 Reconnect the parking brake cable to the expansion lock.

12 Manoeuvre the shoes into position, engaging them with the adjuster and expansion lock, then refit the front and rear return springs.

13 Refit the shoe retaining springs.

14 Refit the discs as described in Section 7.

17 Braking system switches – removal and refitting

Parking brake warning light switch

Removal

1 Undo the fasteners and remove the drivers side lower facia panel as described in Chapter 11 Section 37. Disconnect any wiring plugs as the panel is withdrawn.

2 Disconnect the switch wiring plug (see illustration).

3 Squeeze the switch retaining lugs and detach it from the bracket.

Refitting

4 Refitting is a reversal of removal.

Stop light switch

Removal

5 Undo the fasteners and remove the drivers side lower facia panel as described in Chapter 11 Section 37. Disconnect any wiring plugs as the panel is withdrawn.

6 Disconnect the switch wiring plug.

7 Pull the switch rearwards a little, then squeeze together the clips in front of the bracket at the top and bottom edges and remove the bracket along with the switch (see illustrations).

Refitting

8 Fully depress the brake pedal and hold it in position, then insert the switch and bracket into place. Press the switch fully forwards. Slowly release the brake pedal and allow it to return to its stop. This will automatically adjust the stop-light switch.

9 Reconnect the wiring connector, and check the operation of the stop-lights. The stop-lights should illuminate after the brake pedal has travelled approximately 5 mm. If the switch is not functioning correctly, it is faulty and must be renewed; no other adjustment is possible.

10 Refit the drivers side lower facia panel.

18 Anti-lock braking system (ABS) – general information and sensor replacement

General information

1 Depending on model, specification and market, the C-Class W204 range may be equipped with Anti-lock braking system (ABS), Anti-clip regulation (ASR), Emergency Brake Assist (BAS), Active brake assist (ABA), Adaptive brake (ABR) and Electronic stability program (ESP).

2 Essentially, all of these systems use sensors to monitor the speed of each roadwheel, combined with sensors to monitor

17.2 Parking brake warning switch wiring plugs

17.7a Pull the switch rearwards...

17.7b ...squeeze together the clips, and pull the bracket from place (switch removed for clarity)

18.7 Press-down the wiring clip and pull the plug from the connector

18.9 Undo the sensor retaining bolt...

18.10 ...and pull out the sensor

the position/rate of change of the brake pedal, and vehicle yaw (lateral acceleration) rate, then control the fluid pressure to each wheel brake caliper to prevent wheel lock, and assist in vehicle directional control during emergency situations. The systems are capable on interpreting the drivers braking patterns, anticipating emergency braking, and applying the brakes accordingly.

3 The fluid pressure to each wheel is modulated by a electro/hydraulic control unit, incorporating solenoid valves and pump(s). The system is equipped with a sophisticated self-diagnosis system, and communicates with vehicles other electronic control modules via a data network. If a fault should develop, and warning light on the instrument cluster will illuminate, and one or more fault codes will be generated and stored in the control module. The system can then be interrogated using diagnostic equipment via the 16-pin connector on the lower, right-hand side of the facia.

4 The electro/hydraulic control units are extremely complex, and specialist tools are required to remove, refit and configure them. Consequently, the replacement procedures detailed in this manual are restricted to sensor removal and replacement. Any other tasks should be entrusted to a Mercedes dealer or suitably equipped specialist.

Sensor replacement

Front wheel speed sensor

5 Slacken the front roadwheel bolts, raise the

front of the vehicle and support it securely on axle stands (see *Vehicle jacking and support*). Remove the front roadwheels.

6 Undo the fasteners and remove the rear section of the wheelarch liner.

7 Trace the sensor wiring back to the connector. Press-down the retaining clip, and pull out the wiring plug **(see illustration)**.

8 Unclip the sensor wiring from any retaining clips, noting the loom routing.

9 Undo the sensor retaining bolt **(see illustration)**..

10 Pull the sensor from the hub carrier **(see illustration)**. If the sensor is to be refitted, renew the O-ring seal.

11 Refitting is a reversal of removal. Tighten the sensor retaining bolt to the specified torque.

Rear wheel speed sensor

12 Slacken the rear roadwheel bolts, chock the front wheels, raise the rear of the vehicle and support it securely on axle stands (see *Vehicle jacking and support*). Remove the rear wheels.

13 Release the fasteners and remove the rear wheel arch liner(s).

14 Trace the sensor wiring back to the connector, then using a screwdriver, release the spring retaining clip and disconnect the wiring plug.

15 Release the sensor wiring loom from any retaining clips, noting the loom routing.

16 Undo the retaining bolt, and pull the sensor from the hub carrier.

17 Refitting is a reversal of removal. Tighten

the new sensor retaining bolt to the specified torque.

Yaw rate/lateral acceleration sensor

18 Remove the passengers seat as described in Chapter 11 Section 30.

19 Pull up and remove the passengers side sill panel trim.

20 Pull the floor vent rearwards to unclip it **(see illustration)**.

21 Fold back the carpet under the seat, and disconnect the sensor wiring plug.

22 Undo the retaining nuts and remove the sensor.

Caution: Handle the sensor with extreme care. Rough handling/knocks may cause damage to the sensor.

23 Refitting is a reversal of removal. If a new sensor has been fitted, it may need to be initialized using Mercedes STAR diagnostic equipment (or after-market equivalent).

---

19 Vacuum pump – testing, removal and refitting

Testing

1 The operation of the braking system vacuum pump can be checked using a vacuum gauge.

2 Disconnect the vacuum pipe from the pump, and connect the gauge to the pump union using a suitable length of hose.

3 Start the engine and allow it to idle, and then measure the vacuum created by the pump. As a guide, a minimum of approximately 500 mm Hg should be recorded. If the vacuum registered is significantly less than this, it is likely that the pump is faulty. However, seek the advice of a Mercedes-Benz dealer or specialist before condemning the pump.

Removal

2148 cc engines

4 Remove the plastic cover from the top of the engine.

5 Squeeze together the sides, and disconnect the pipe from the vacuum pump **(see illustration)**.

18.20 Pull the vent rearwards

19.5 Disconnect the vacuum pipe

6 Detach the breather hose above the vacuum pump.

7 Undo the retaining bolts and remove the engine cover mounting bracket **(see illustration)**.

8 Undo the mounting bolts and pull the vacuum pump from place. Renew the pump seals.

2143 cc engines

9 Raise the front of the vehicle and support it securely on axle stands (see *Vehicle jacking and support*). Undo the fasteners and remove the engine undershield.

10 Remove the throttle body as described in Chapter 4A Section 14.

11 Remove the charge air temperature sensor, then remove the charge air duct downstream of the intercooler.

12 Depress the clips and disconnect the pipe from the vacuum pump **(see illustration)**.

13 Undo the 2 retaining bolts and remove the vacuum pump **(see illustrations)**. Renew the pump gasket.

Refitting

14 Refitting is a reversal of removal.

19.7 Undo the bolts and remove the mounting bracket

19.12 Depress the clip each side and disconnect the pipe

19.13a Vacuum pump retaining bolts

19.13b Renew the pump gasket

Notes

Chapter 10
Suspension and steering

Contents

Section number

Front anti-roll bar – removal and refitting 8
Front anti-roll bar link rods – removal and refitting. 9
Front hub and bearing – removal, overhaul and refitting 3
Front hub bearing – checking and adjustment. 2
Front hub carrier – removal and refitting 4
Front subframe – removal and refitting 10
Front suspension arms – removal and refitting 7
Front suspension coil spring – removal and refitting 6
Front suspension strut – removal and refitting. 5
General information 1
Power steering pump – removal and refitting 23
Power steering system – bleeding. 24
Rear anti-roll bar – removal and refitting 16

Section number

Rear anti-roll bar link rods – removal and refitting 17
Rear hub bearing – renewal 12
Rear hub carrier – removal and refitting. 11
Rear suspension coil spring – removal and refitting 14
Rear suspension control arms – removal and refitting. 15
Rear suspension shock absorber – removal, testing and refitting . . . 13
Steering column – removal, inspection and refitting 19
Steering lock control unit – removal and refitting. 20
Steering rack – removal, overhaul and refitting 21
Steering rack gaiter – renewal 22
Steering wheel – removal and refitting. 18
Track rod end – removal and refitting. 25
Wheel alignment and steering angles – general information 26

Degrees of difficulty

Easy, suitable for novice with little experience	**Fairly easy,** suitable for beginner with some experience	**Fairly difficult,** suitable for competent DIY mechanic	**Difficult,** suitable for experienced DIY mechanic	**Very difficult,** suitable for expert DIY or professional

Specifications

Front suspension
Type . . . . Independent, multi-link suspension, with MacPherson struts incorporating coil springs, telescopic shock absorbers and anti-roll bar connected to the struts by connecting drop links. Anti-roll bar fitted to all models.

Rear suspension
Type . . . . Independent, multi-link with coil springs and telescopic shock absorbers. Anti-roll bar fitted to all models. Models with the Agility Control System are fitted with self-pumping auto-levelling shock absorbers.

Steering system
Type . . . . Hydraulic power assisted, with rack and pinion.

Front wheel alignment and steering angles
Camber . . . . Permissible difference between sides 24'
Castor . . . . Permissible difference between sides 30'
Toe-in . . . . $0°10' \pm 10'$

Rear wheel alignment angles
Toe-in . . . . $0°22' \pm 7'$

Front hub bearing
Endfloat . . . . 0.01 to 0.02 mm

Front hub grease capacity
Grease cap. 15g
Hub and bearing. 70g

Tyre pressures – see end of *'Weekly checks'*

Torque wrench settings	Nm	lbf ft
Front suspension		
Anti-roll bar clamp bolts.	30	22
Anti-roll bar link rod nut*.	98	72
Front subframe/axle carrier bolts*	180	133
Hub nut clamp bolt.	11	8
Cross strut:		
To-axle carrier: *		
M14 x 115 mm:		
Stage 1	80	60
Stage 2	Angle-tighten a further 120°	
M14 x 120 mm:		
Stage 1	120	89
Stage 2	Angle-tighten a further 180°	
To-hub carrier: *		
Stage 1	50	37
Stage 2	Angle-tighten a further 60°	
Suspension strut:		
Upper mounting bolts.	33	24
To-hub carrier (upper bolt) M14:		
Stage 1	100	74
Stage 2	Angle-tighten a further 90°	
To-hub carrier (lower bolt) M12:		
Stage 1	70	52
Stage 2	Slacken	
Stage 3	100	74
Piston rod nut*	100	74
Torque strut:		
To-axle carrier: *		
Stage 1	80	60
Stage 2	Angle-tighten a further 120°	
To-hub carrier: *		
Stage 1	50	37
Stage 2	Angle-tighten a further 60°	
Rear suspension		
Anti-roll bar:		
Clamp bolts	80	59
Link rod:		
To-anti-roll bar	50	37
To-control arm:		
Stage 1	20	15
Stage 2	Angle-tighten a further 180°	
Axle/subframe bolts: *		
Stage 1	80	59
Stage 2	Slacken	
Stage 3	80	59
Stage 4	Angle-tighten a further 90°	
Camber strut: *		
To-axle carrier:		
Stage 1	50	37
Stage 2	Angle-tighten a further 90°	
To-hub carrier:		
Stage 1	50	37
Stage 2	Angle-tighten a further 90°	
Driveshaft retaining nut: *		
Self-locking nut.	350	258
Non-self-locking nut: *		
Stage 1	170	125
Stage 2	Angle-tighten a further 45°	
Shock absorber upper mounting nut:		
Stage 1	15	11
Stage 2	35	26
Shock absorber lower mounting nut: *		
Stage 1	55	41
Stage 2	Angle-tighten a further 60°	
Shock absorber piston nut.	28	21

Torque wrench settings (continued)

	Nm	lbf ft
Rear suspension (continued)		
Spring control arm: *		
To-rear subframe/axle carrier:		
Stage 1	50	37
Stage 2	Angle-tighten a further 90°	
To-hub carrier:		
Stage 1	80	59
Stage 2	Angle-tighten a further 90°	
Thrust arm: *		
Stage 1	50	37
Stage 2	Angle-tighten a further 90°	
Tie-rod: *		
To-hub carrier:		
Stage 1	50	37
Stage 2	Angle-tighten a further 90°	
To-axle carrier*	110	81
Torque strut: *		
Stage 1	50	37
Stage 2	Angle-tighten a further 90°	
Wheel bearing assembly bolts	70	52
Steering		
Column:		
Column mounting bolts	26	19
Lower pinch bolt nut*	30	22
Upper UJ pinch bolt	23	17
Power steering pump mounting bolts:		
Normal threads.	20	15
Self-tapping threads.	35	26
Steering rack-to-subframe:		
Stage 1	70	52
Stage 2	Angle-tighten a further 90°	
Steering rack retaining plate-to-subframe	110	81
Steering wheel bolt*	80	59
Track rod end nut: *		
Stage 1	50	37
Stage 2	Angle-tighten a further 90°	

Do not re-use

1 General information

1 The independent front suspension is of the MacPherson strut type, incorporating coil springs and integral telescopic shock absorbers. The lower end of the strut is attached to the hub carrier. The hub carrier, which carry the wheel bearings, brake calipers and the hub/disc assemblies, is located by the torque strut at the front, and a cross strut at the rear. These struts are attached to the hub carrier by means of balljoints, and to the front axle/sub frame/vehicle body by bolts through metal/rubber bushes. A front anti-roll bar is fitted to all models. The anti-roll bar is rubber-mounted, and is connected to both suspension struts by short drop links.

2 The independent rear suspension also incorporates coil springs and telescopic shock absorbers. The shock absorbers are located by transverse lower suspension arms, which use rubber mounting bushes. The hub assemblies are fastened to the lower arms, and are joined to the rear subframe by four control arms; two upper arms and two lower ones. Coil springs are fitted between the lower arms and vehicle body. A rear anti-roll bar is fitted to all models. The anti-roll bar is rubber-mounted and is connected to the hub carrier by connecting links **(see illustration)**.

1.2 Rear suspension link arms/struts

1 Camber strut
2 Torque strut
3 Tie rod
4 Thrust arm
5 Spring control arm

3 The steering gear is mounted onto the front subframe, and is connected by two track rods, with balljoints at their inner and outer ends, to the steering arms projecting forwards from the wheel hub carriers. The track rod ends are threaded to the track rods in order to allow adjustment of the front wheel toe setting.

4 Power-assisted steering is standard on all models. The hydraulic steering system is powered by a belt-driven pump which is driven off the crankshaft pulley.

Note: *Many of the suspension and steering components are secured in position with self-locking nuts and bolts. Whenever a self-locking nut or bolt is disturbed, it must be discarded and a new nut/bolt fitted.*

2 Front hub bearing – checking and adjustment

1 Mercedes-Benz recommend the use of a dial gauge to check the hub endfloat, as a means of checking the bearing adjustment. While this is certainly the method for assuring the maximum accuracy, a competent mechanic will be able to check and adjust the bearing by feel.

2 If the bearing is worn to the extent that the droning noise can be heard inside the car, there is no point trying to 'adjust' the bearing to reduce the noise. Fit a new bearing as described in Section 3.

Without a dial gauge

3 Chock the rear wheels and firmly apply the parking brake. Jack up the front of the car and support it on axle stands (see *Vehicle jacking and support*).

4 Grasp the wheel at the top and bottom, and shake it to assess free play **(see illustration)**. Repeat the check with the wheel held on the left and right sides. A very small amount of play may be noticed, but if the play is excessive, the bearings should be adjusted as described below.

5 If adjustment is required, the wheel must be removed. This will probably entail lowering the car temporarily to loosen the wheel bolts, then raising the car once more.

6 Refit one of the wheel bolts, in the hole

opposite the brake disc retaining screw. This is simply to prevent the disc from moving in relation to the hub.

7 Taking care not to damage the pad friction material or the disc surface, use a large flat-bladed screwdriver to push the brake pads and pistons back into the caliper, away from the disc so that the pads do not drag.

8 Tap or prise the grease cap out from the centre of the hub **(see illustration)**. If the cap is damaged on removal, it must be renewed.

9 Using an Allen key or socket, slacken the hub nut clamp bolt so that the nut is free to turn **(see illustration)**.

10 Rotate the brake disc and at the same time lightly tighten the hub nut until the disc starts to become difficult to turn **(see illustration)**. From this point, slacken the hub nut by approximately one-third of a turn, and then tap the end of the hub spindle with a soft-faced mallet to relieve the tension on the bearing.

11 Slacken the hub nut fully, then very lightly tighten it by hand only until resistance is felt. A few attempts may be required, but there should be a clear point at which, without effort, all free play is eliminated without loading the bearing. Do not tighten the hub nut using tools, or any tighter than described, as this will quickly destroy it.

12 Tighten the hub nut clamp bolt to the specified torque.

13 Pack the grease cap with fresh grease, and tap it fully back into place **(see illustration)**.

14 Refit the wheel, then lower the car to the ground and tighten the wheel bolts to the specified torque.

15 Depress the brake pedal repeatedly until normal pressure returns.

16 If a new bearing has been fitted, recheck the adjustment within approximately 500 miles.

With a dial gauge

17 Chock the rear wheels and firmly apply the parking brake. Loosen the front wheel bolts, and then jack up the front of the car and support it on axle stands (see *Vehicle jacking and support*). Remove the relevant front roadwheel.

18 Using spacers if necessary, refit two of the wheel bolts (to locate the brake disc), positioning them on opposite sides, and tightening them securely.

19 Taking care not to damage the pad friction material or the disc surface, use a large flat-bladed screwdriver to push the brake pads and pistons back into the caliper, away from the disc so that the pads do not drag.

20 Tap the grease cap out from the centre of the hub. If the cap is damaged on removal, it must be renewed.

21 Mount a dial gauge onto the front face of the hub/disc, and position the gauge probe so that it is in contact with the end of the axle shaft. Zero the gauge scale, then grasp the disc at two opposite points and pull it in and out. Note the reading obtained on the gauge, and check that the hub bearing endfloat is within the limits given in the Specifications at the start of this Chapter.

22 If all is well, remove the dial gauge. Pack the grease cap with grease, and tap the cap

2.4 Shake the wheel to assess play in the bearing

2.8 Tap the grease cap out from the centre of the hub (brake disc removed)

2.9 Unscrew the hub nut clamp bolt

2.10 Turn the hub/disc slowly whilst lightly tightening the hub nut

2.13 Tap the cap into place

into position. Remove the wheel bolts and refit the roadwheel, then lower the car to the ground and tighten the wheel bolts to the specified torque.

23 If adjustment is required, use an Allen key to slacken the hub retaining nut clamp bolt until the retaining nut is free to turn.

24 Rotate the brake disc while lightly tightening the hub nut, until the disc starts to become difficult to turn. From this point, slacken the hub nut by approximately one-third of a turn, and then tap the end of the hub spindle with a soft-faced mallet to relieve the tension on the bearing.

25 Check the hub bearing endfloat as previously described. If necessary adjust the endfloat by rotating the hub nut as required.

26 Recheck the bearing endfloat, then refit all disturbed components as described.

27 If a new bearing has been fitted, recheck the adjustment within approximately 500 miles.

3 Front hub and bearing – removal, overhaul and refitting

Note: *The hub assembly should not be removed unless the bearings are to be renewed; the hub bearing inner race is a press-fit on the hub carrier, and removal of the hub will almost certainly damage the bearings. A press will be required to dismantle and rebuild the assembly; if such a tool is not available, a large bench vice and spacers (such as large sockets) will serve as an adequate substitute. The bearing's inner races are an interference fit on the hub; if the inner race remains on the hub when it is pressed out of the hub carrier, a knife-edged bearing puller will be required to remove it.*

Removal

1 Remove the front brake disc, and ABS sensor as described in Chapter 9.

2 Tap the grease cap out from the centre of the hub **(see illustration)**. If the cap is damaged on removal, it must be renewed.

3 Slacken the hub nut clamp bolt, then slacken and remove the hub nut from the axle **(see illustration)**.

4 Take off the hub outer bearing, and place it

to one side where it can be kept clean **(see illustration)**.

5 The front hub assembly can now be withdrawn from the hub carrier. If the hub assembly is a tight fit on the axle, a puller will be required to draw it off.

6 If the inner bearing race remains on the hub carrier, a knife-edge type puller will be required to remove it. With the race removed, slide off the hub oil seal.

7 Inspect the hub carrier axle shaft for signs of damage, and renew if necessary.

Overhaul

8 With the hub mounted in a bench vice, carefully drive the inner bearing, inner race and oil seal from place **(see illustration)**. Take care to drive the bearing out gradually and squarely.

9 Drive the outer bearing races from place.

10 Clean the hub and examine the bearing

locations. If wear or damage is evident, the hub and bearing assembly must be replaced.

11 Using a bearing insertion tool, or a suitable socket, washers and a length of threaded-rod with nuts, draw the new outer bearing outer race into the hub **(see illustration)**.

12 Repeat the procedure to fit the inner bearing outer race.

13 Generously coat the inner bearing with lithium or Moly grease, then locate it in the hub and fit the new oil seal **(see illustrations)**. *Caution: Take care not to damage the outer face of the oil seal. The face of the seal incorporates small magnetic elements which are utilised by the ABS wheel speed sensor.*

Refitting

14 Apply a smear of grease to the hub rear oil seal lip, and locate the hub assembly onto the hub carrier shaft.

3.2 Tap the grease cap from the hub

3.3 Slacken and remove the hub nut

3.4 Remove the hub outer bearing

3.8 Drive the inner bearing, race and oil seal from place

3.11 Fitting the new race using a bearing insertion tool

3.13a Work the grease into the bearing

3.13b The oil seal should be flush with the edge of the hub

4.3 Disc shield retaining bolts

5.2 Undo the anti-roll bar link rod nut

5.4 Remove the strut-to-hub carrier upper bolt/nut

15 Pack the outer bearing with grease, working it well into the bearing tracks. Fit the outer bearing into position over the hub carrier shaft, and slide it fully into the hub location.
16 Screw on the hub nut. Rotate the hub assembly whilst using the hub nut to press the hub assembly onto the hub carrier shaft. Once the hub assembly is correctly seated, adjust the hub bearing endfloat as described in Section 2.
17 Pack the grease cap with grease, then tap it squarely into position.
18 Refit the brake disc shield, ABS wheel speed sensor and brake disc as described in Chapter 9.

4 Front hub carrier – removal and refitting

Removal

1 Chock the rear wheels and firmly apply the parking brake. Loosen the front wheel bolts, and then jack up the front of the car and support it on axle stands (see *Vehicle jacking and support*). Remove the relevant front roadwheel.
2 Remove the front hub assembly as described in Section 3.
3 Undo the fasteners and remove the brake disc shield **(see illustration)**.
4 Slacken and remove the nut securing the track rod balljoint to the hub carrier, and release the balljoint tapered shank using

a universal balljoint separator **(see illustration 25.3)**.
5 Undo the 2 lower bolts, and the upper bolt/nut securing the front suspension strut to the hub carrier **(see illustrations 5.4 and 5.5a)**.
6 Remove the ABS wheel speed sensor as described in Chapter 9 Section 18.
7 Similarly, release the balljoints securing the hub carrier to the two suspension lower arms, with reference to Section 7. Manoeuvre the hub carrier from place.
8 Inspect the carrier for signs of wear or damage, and renew as necessary.

Refitting

9 Refitting is a reversal of removal, noting the following points:
a) *Clean any threads by running a tap of the correct thread size and pitch down them.*
b) *Thoroughly clean the balljoint tapers and their locating holes, also clean the balljoint threads if necessary, using a wire brush.*
c) *Check all the balljoint rubbers for signs of damage or perishing. If the rubber has split, this will lead to loss of lubricant and dirt entry, which will destroy the joint. If any balljoints are suspect, take the opportunity to fit new components.*
d) *Fit a new locking nuts, where fitted.*
e) *Tighten bolts and nuts to the specified torque setting where applicable.*
f) *Refit the hub and bearing assembly as described in Section 3.*
g) *Where new parts have been fitted, it is advisable to the front wheel tow setting ('tracking') checked on completion.*

5 Front suspension strut – removal and refitting

Note: *Refer to the note at the end of Section 1 before proceeding. Shock absorbers should always be renewed in pairs on the same axle, to preserve safe handling.*

Removal

1 Chock the rear wheels, and firmly apply the parking brake. Loosen the front wheel bolts, and then jack up the front of the car and support it on axle stands (see *Vehicle jacking and support*). Remove the relevant front roadwheel.
2 Undo the nut and detach the upper end of the anti-roll bar link rod from the strut **(see illustration)**. Counterhold the rod balljoint shank with a Torx bit/key.
3 Release any wiring harnesses from the strut.
4 Undo the nut and press the upper bolt securing the strut to the hub carrier from place **(see illustration)**. Note that the bolt is inserted from the rear. Renew the self-locking nut.
5 Undo the 2 bolts securing the lower end of the strut to the hub carrier **(see illustrations)**. Support the hub carrier to prevent straining the brake hose or wiring harness, then release the cable tie, and slide the harness/hose plastic bracket from the strut.
6 Working in the engine compartment, undo the suspension strut upper mounting bolts **(see illustration)**.

5.5a Hub carrier-to- strut lower bolts

5.5b Slide the harness/hose plastic bracket from the strut

5.6 Front suspension strut upper mounting bolts

5.7 Release the cap by pressing-in the clips

6.2 Paint alignment marks between the seat, spring and strut

6.3 Compress the spring until the seats are not under tension

7 Squeeze together the sides of the cap, then with the help of an assistant, press the strut control arm downwards, and manoeuvre the suspension strut from place **(see illustration)**.

Refitting

8 Check the strut body for leaking fluid, dents, cracks and other obvious signs of damage. Also check the coil spring for any cracks and inspect the spring seat for any general deterioration. Renew any faulty components.
9 Refitting is a reversal of removal, noting the following points:
a) Renew all self-locking nuts.
b) Tighten all fasteners to their specified torque, where given.
c) Only tighten the suspension strut lower bolt/nut once the weight of the vehicle is back on its' wheels.

---

6 Front suspension coil spring – removal and refitting

Note: Refer to the note at the end of Section 1 before proceeding. Springs should always be renewed in pairs on the same axle, to preserve safe handling.

 Warning: Before attempting to dismantle the suspension strut, a suitable tool to hold the coil spring in compression must be obtained. Adjustable coil spring compressors are readily available, and are recommended for this operation. Any attempt to dismantle the strut without such a tool is likely to result in damage or personal injury.

Removal

1 With the strut removed from the car as described in Section 6, clean away all external dirt. If necessary, mount it upright in a vice during the dismantling procedure
2 Make alignment marks between the upper seat, spring and strut **(see illustration)**.
3 Fit the spring compressor, and compress the coil spring until all tension is relieved from the upper spring seat **(see illustration)**.

4 Depress the clip each side, remove the cap, then unscrew and remove the piston rod retaining nut, whilst retaining the strut piston with an Allen key/bit **(see illustrations)**.
5 Remove the upper spring retainer, spring and seat, complete with gaiter and bump stop. If required, remove the bump stop **(see illustrations)**.
6 With the strut assembly now completely dismantled, examine all the components for wear, damage or deformation, and check the bearing for smoothness of operation. Renew any of the components as necessary.
7 Examine the strut for signs of fluid leakage. Check the strut piston for signs of pitting along its entire length, and check the strut body for signs of damage.

6.4a Depress the clip each side

6.5a Remove the retainer, spring, and gaiter...

8 If any doubt exists about the condition of the coil spring, carefully remove the spring compressors, and check the spring for distortion and signs of cracking. Renew the spring if it is damaged or distorted, or if there is any doubt as to its condition.
9 Inspect all other components for signs of damage or deterioration, and renew as necessary.

Refitting

10 Refit the bump stop to the strut.
11 Fit the coil spring (together with the compressor tool, gaiter and upper seat) onto the strut, making sure its lower end is

6.4b Hold the piston stationary, then unscrew the piston nut

6.5b ...and bump stop

6.11 Ensure the lower end of the spring is against the seat stop

7.2 Cross strut-to-subframe bolt

7.4a Slacken the nut...

correctly located against the spring seat stop **(see illustration)**,

12 Fit a new piston rod nut and tighten it to the specified torque, whilst counterholding the piston rod.

13 Clip the cap into place over the piston nut.

14 Refit the strut as described in Section 5.

---

7   Front suspension arms –
    removal and refitting

Removal

Cross strut

1 Slacken the wheel bolts, raise the front of the vehicle and support it securely on axle stands (see *Vehicle jacking and support*. Undo the fasteners and remove the engine undershield.

7.4b ...then use a balljoint separator tool

7.7 Torque strut balljoint retaining nut

2 Undo the nut securing the inner end of the cross strut to the subframe **(see illustration)**. Note that the bolt must not be allowed to rotate at all as the nut is slackened, otherwise the locating lugs for the caster adjustment on the bush will be sheared off. Note the fitted position of the bolt in relation to the bush in the strut.

3 Pull the strut from the subframe.

4 Unscrew the outer balljoint nut, then detach the balljoint from the hub carrier using a balljoint separator tool **(see illustrations)**. Note that a new nut will be required.

5 Examine the inner mounting bushes and outer balljoint for wear, damage and deterioration. No overhaul of the strut is possible. Note that two different struts may be fitted – early and late. They are differentiated by the casting marks on their undersides **(see illustration)**. Only the later type is available as a replacement part. Mercedes-Benz insist

7.5 Note the locations of the lugs on the new and old type of cross struts

7.8 Torque strut inner pivot bolt

that the types must not be mixed on the same axle, consequently, if the older type of arms are fitted, and one of them requires replacement, both sides must be replaced.

Torque strut

6 With reference to Section 5, detach the suspension strut from the hub carrier.

7 Undo the retaining nut, then using a universal balljoint separator, detach the outer end of the torque strut from the hub carrier **(see illustration)**.

8 At the inner end of the torque strut, undo the retaining nut and remove the pivot bolt **(see illustration)**. Note that the bolt must not be allowed to rotate at all as the nut is slackened, otherwise the locating lugs for the caster adjustment on the bush will be sheared off. Note the fitted position of the bolt in relation to the bush in the strut.

9 Manoeuvre the torque strut from position.

10 Examine the strut and bush. If required, the bush can be renewed separately from the strut, but a press will be required. Note orientation and fitted depth of the bush before removing it. Press the new bush into the same position. Note that there are several variations of bush design. Ensure the replacement bush matches the one removed.

Refitting

11 Refitting is a reversal of removal, noting the following points:

a) *Renew all self-locking nuts.*
b) *The arms' inner pivot bolt nuts must only be tightened once the weight of the vehicle is back on its' wheels.*
c) *Tighten all fasteners to their specified torque where given.*
d) *Have the front wheel alignment checked at the earliest opportunity.*

---

8   Front anti-roll bar –
    removal and refitting

Removal

1 Slacken the front roadwheel bolts, raise the front of the vehicle and support it securely on axle stands (see *Vehicle jacking and support*). Remove the roadwheels.

2 Undo the fasteners and remove the engine undershield.

3 Undo the bolts and remove the mounting plate from beneath the steering rack **(see illustration 21.11)**.

4 Undo the nuts and detach the lower ends of the link rods from the anti-roll bar **(see illustration)**.

5 Where applicable, detach the suspension height sensor bracket from the anti-roll bar.

6 Undo the bolts securing the anti-roll bar clamps to the subframe **(see illustration)**. Note that the rubber mountings and clamps are vulcanised to the anti-roll bar. If defective/damages, the complete anti-roll bar must be renewed.

7 Manoeuvre the anti-roll bar from under the vehicle.

Refitting

8 Refitting is a reversal of removal, tightening all fasteners to their specified torque where given.

9 Front anti-roll bar link rods – removal and refitting

Removal

1 Slacken the front roadwheel bolts, raise the front of the vehicle and support it securely on axle stands (see *Vehicle jacking and support*). Remove the roadwheels.

2 Using an Torx key/bit to counterhold the balljoint, undo the retaining nut at the upper, and lower end of the anti-roll bar link rod **(see illustration 8.4)**. Discard the retaining nuts – new ones must be fitted.

3 Manoeuvre the link rod from place.

Refitting

4 Refitting is a reversal of removal. Tighten the fasteners to their specified torque where given.

10 Front subframe – removal and refitting

Removal

1 Ensure the front wheels are in the 'straight-ahead' position. During this procedure, the steering wheel must not be rotated.

2 Remove the plastic covers from the top of the engine.

3 Remove the air cleaner housing as described in Chapter 4A Section 2.

4 Use syringe or poultry baster to remove as much fluid as possible from the power steering fluid reservoir.

5 Slacken the front roadwheel bolts, raise the front of the vehicle and support it securely on

8.4 Counterhold the anti-roll bar link nut with a Torx key in the ball joint shank

axle stands (see *Vehicle jacking and support*). Remove the roadwheels.

6 Undo the fasteners and remove the engine undershield.

7 Detach the trackrod end balljoints from the hub carriers, as described in Section 25.

8 Detach the lower end of the link rods from the anti-roll bar as described in Section 8.

9 Detach the cross struts and and torque struts from the subframe/axle carrier as described in Section 7.

10 Move the steering wheel to its fully extended position.

11 Working in the engine compartment, undo the pinch bolt/nut and slide the steering column lower shaft universal joint upwards from the steering rack pinion. Discard the bolt – a new one must be fitted.

12 In order to support the engine whilst the subframe is removed, attach a suitable lifting hoist to the engine.

13 Remove the bolts securing the left-, and right-hand engine mountings to the subframe.

14 Note its fitted position, then disconnect any wiring plugs/harness from the steering rack.

15 Where applicable, thoroughly clean the area around the steering rack pinion housing/pipes, then undo the bolts, remove the retaining plate, and pull the fluid pipes from the pinion housing. Plug the openings to prevent contamination. Renew the O-ring seals.

16 Support the front subframe using workshop jack(s) and suitable pieces of wood.

17 Remove the retaining bolts each side, the lower the subframe/axle carrier from place.

11.1 Relieve the nut staking

8.6 Undo the bar clamp bolts each side

Refitting

18 Refitting is a reversal of removal, noting the following points:

a) Replace all self-locking nuts.
b) Tighten all fasteners to their specified torque where given.
c) Bleed the power steering system as described in Section 24.
d) Have the wheel alignment checked at the earliest opportunity.

11 Rear hub carrier – removal and refitting

Note: *Before proceeding, refer to the note in Section 1.*

Removal

1 Prise out the cap from the centre of the rear wheel, then using a hammer and pointed-nose chisel, carefully relieve the driveshaft retaining nut staking (where applicable) **(see illustration)**.

2 Slacken the driveshaft retaining nut with the car resting on its wheels. Note that this nut is extremely tight – ensure that the tools used to loosen it are of good quality, and a good fit. Discard the nut – a new one must be fitted.

3 Chock the front wheels, slacken the rear roadwheel bolts, raise the rear of the vehicle and support it securely on axle stands (see *Vehicle jacking and support*). Remove the rear roadwheels.

4 Remove the parking brake shoes as described in Chapter 9 Section 16, then pull the parking brake cable from the hub carrier.

5 Undo the retaining bolt and pull the wheel speed sensor from the hub carrier – see Chapter 9 Section 18.

6 Position a workshop jack under the hub carrier, then raise it until the driveshaft is approximately horizontal.

7 With reference to Section 15, detach the torque strut, camber strut, tie rod and thrust arm from the hub carrier.

8 Lower the jack supporting the hub carrier, then remove the bolt securing the spring control arm to the hub carrier.

9 Withdraw the hub assembly from the end of the driveshaft joint. If necessary, tap the joint out of the hub using a soft-faced mallet. If this fails to free it from the hub, the joint will have to be pressed out using a suitable tool which is bolted to the hub.

Note: *Support the driveshaft by hanging it from the vehicle underbody using a piece of wire. Do not allow the driveshaft to hang under its own weight, as the CV joint may be damaged.*

Refitting

10 Refitting is a reversal of removal, noting the following points:

a) *Loosely attach the torque strut, camber strut, tie-rod, thrust arm and spring control arm. Tighten the bolts fully only when the weight of the vehicle is back on its wheels.*

b) *Tighten all fasteners to their specified torque, where given.*

c) *Where a non-self-locking driveshaft nut is fitted, once fully tightened, 'stake' the nut to the shaft using a chisel or punch.*

d) *Have the rear wheel alignment checked at the earliest opportunity.*

12 Rear hub bearing – renewal

Note: *In order to fit the driveshaft flange/hub, Mercedes technicians use tool nos. 202 589 04 43 10 and 211 589 00 33 00. These tools attach to the end of the driveshaft, and pull the flange into place. If these tools are not available, it will be necessary to remove the hub carrier in order to renew the bearing.*

13.2 Protective cover retaining clips

13.6 Shock absorber lower mounting bolt/nut

With the Mercedes special tools

1 Prise out the cap from the centre of the rear wheel, then using a hammer and pointed-nose chisel, carefully relieve the driveshaft retaining nut staking (where applicable) **(see illustration 11.1)**.

2 Slacken the driveshaft retaining nut with the car resting on its wheels. Note that this nut is extremely tight – ensure that the tools used to loosen it are of good quality, and a good fit. Discard the nut – a new one must be fitted.

3 Chock the front wheels, slacken the rear roadwheel bolts, raise the rear of the vehicle and support it securely on axle stands (see *Vehicle jacking and support*). Remove the rear roadwheels.

4 Remove the parking brake shoes as described in Chapter 9 Section 16.

5 Using a slide hammer and suitable attachments, pull the driveshaft flange from the bearing assembly.

6 The wheel bearing assembly is bolted to the hub carrier. Undo the bolts and remove the bearing assembly. Press the driveshaft slightly to one side to access the bolts.

Caution: Take care not to damage any of the aluminium surfaces of the rear axle/suspension. Any scratches, cracks or notches may shorten the service life of the components.

7 The inner race of the bearing remains on the hub flange. If the flange is to be re-used, remove the bearing race with a knife-edged bearing puller.

8 Before commencing refitting, clean the water drain channel in the hub carrier.

13.5 Use a trolley jack to compress the suspension slightly

13.8 Rear shock absorber upper mounting nuts

9 Position the new bearing assembly on the hub carrier, refit the bolts and tighten them to the specified torque.

10 Use Mercedes tools Nos. 202 589 04 43 10 and 211 589 00 33 00 to draw the driveshaft flange/hub into place.

11 The remainder of refitting is a reversal of removal, noting the following points:

a) *Tighten all fasteners to their specified torque where given.*

b) *Where a non-self-locking driveshaft nut is fitted, once fully tightened, 'stake' the nut to the shaft using a chisel or punch.*

Without the Mercedes special tools

12 Remove the hub carrier as described in Section 11.

13 Undo the retaining bolts and detach the hub bearing/driveshaft flange from the hub carrier.

14 If the driveshaft flange/hub is to be re-used, press it from the bearing assembly, then use a knife-edge puller to remove the bearing inner race which will have remained on the flange.

15 Before commencing reassembly, clean the water channel in the hub carrier.

16 Press the new bearing assembly onto the driveshaft flange. Take care to only press on the inner race of the bearing assembly.

17 Position the flange/bearing assembly on the hub carrier and tighten the retaining bolts to the specified torque.

18 Refit the hub carrier as described in Section 11.

13 Rear suspension shock absorber – removal, testing and refitting

Note: *Refer to the note at the end of Section 1 before proceeding. Shock absorbers should always be renewed in pairs on the same axle, to preserve safe handling.*

Removal

1 Chock the front wheels, and loosen the rear wheel bolts. Jack up the rear of the car and support it on axle stands (see *Vehicle jacking and support*). To improve access, remove the rear roadwheel.

2 Squeeze together the retaining clip lugs and remove the protective cover from the base of the suspension lower arm **(see illustration)**.

3 On models with the Advanced Agility Package, disconnect the wiring plug from the shock absorber body.

4 Release the fasteners and remove the wheelarch liner.

5 Place a trolley jack under the hub carrier, and compress the suspension slightly **(see illustration)**.

6 Undo the shock absorber lower mounting bolt/nut **(see illustration)**.

7 Remove the luggage compartment side trim panel as described in Chapter 11 Section 35.

8 Slacken and unscrew the upper mounting nuts **(see illustration)**.

13.10a Pull/lever down the upper half of the shock absorber...

13.10b ...and withdraw it from the wheel arch

9 Lower the hub carrier slightly to release any tension on the shock absorber.

10 Pull down the upper half of the shock absorber to collapse it slightly, and then manoeuvre it out from underneath the wheel arch **(see illustrations)**.

11 If required, undo the piston nut and remove the upper mounting, followed by the bump stop and protective cap **(see illustrations)**.

Testing

12 Examine the shock absorber for signs of fluid leakage. Check the piston for signs of pitting along its entire length, and check the body for signs of damage.

13 While holding it in an upright position, test the operation of the shock absorber by moving the piston through a full stroke, and then through short strokes of 50 to 100 mm. In both cases, the resistance felt should be smooth and continuous. If the resistance is jerky, or uneven, or if there is any visible sign of wear or damage, renewal is necessary.

14 Inspect all other components for signs of damage or deterioration, and renew any that are suspect.

13.11a Undo the nut, counterholding the piston rod with a Torx bit...

Refitting

15 If a new shock absorber is being fitted, gently compress and release the unit a few times, to prime it before fitting.

16 Slide the bump stop onto the shock absorber piston, then refit the cap. Tighten the nut to the specified torque.

17 Refitting is a reversal of removal, but only tighten the shock absorber lower mounting bolt/nut once the weight of the vehicle is back on its' wheels.

13.11b ...and remove the mounting, and bump stop/protective cap

14 Rear suspension coil spring – removal and refitting

Note: *Refer to the note at the end of Section 1 before proceeding.*

Removal

1 Chock the front wheels, and loosen the rear wheel bolts. Jack up the rear of the car and support it on axle stands (see *Vehicle jacking and support*). Remove the relevant rear roadwheel.

2 Squeeze together the lugs, release the clips and remove the protective cover from the base of the spring control arm **(see illustration 13.2)**.

3 Disconnect the lower end of the anti-roll bar link and shock absorber from the control arm **(see illustration)**.

4 Insert a suitable steel bar through the hole in the control arm, then position a jack beneath the bar at inner end of the spring control arm, and raise the jack head until the arm is securely supported **(see illustration)**.

5 Slacken and remove the nut and bolt

14.3 Remove the bolts/nuts securing the anti-roll bar and shock absorber

14.4 Insert a large-diameter steel bar through the hole in the control arm

14.5 Remove the bolt securing the arm to the subframe

14.6a Lower the arm until the spring can be removed

14.6b Remove the spring seats

securing the spring control arm to the subframe **(see illustration)**.

6 Carefully lower the lower suspension arm until it is possible to remove the coil spring and spring seats **(see illustrations)**.

 Warning: Take great care during this procedure, If the control arm is lowered uncontrollably, there is a chance that the spring could escape at great speed!.

7 Inspect the coil spring for signs of wear or damage, and renew if necessary. The upper spring seat should also be renewed if it is damaged or shows signs of deterioration.

Refitting

8 Ensure that the spring control arm spring seat is clean, then fit the upper spring seat to the coil spring and manoeuvre the spring into position.

9 Locate the lower end of the spring correctly against the stop on the spring control arm seat. Align the upper spring seat with the body mounting, and carefully raise the spring control arm whilst also aligning it with the subframe.

10 Check that the spring is correctly located, and then insert the spring control arm pivot bolt. Fit a new nut to the pivot bolt, tightening it lightly only at this stage. Refit the shock absorber mounting bolt, and the anti-roll bar link rod bolt. Tighten the new retaining nuts to the specified torque.

11 Remove the jack from beneath the spring control arm.

12 Refit the roadwheel, then lower the car to the ground and tighten the wheel bolts to the specified torque.

13 With the car resting on its wheels, rock it to settle the spring and spring control arm in position.

14 Tighten the spring control arm pivot bolt nut to the specified torque setting.

15 Refit the protective cover to the spring control arm.

15 Rear suspension control arms – removal and refitting

Note: *Refer to the note at the end of Section 1 before proceeding.*

Removal

1 Chock the front wheels, slacken the rear wheel bolts, raise the rear of the vehicle and support it securely on axle stands (see *Vehicle jacking and support*). Remove the rear wheels.

Camber strut

Note: *This is an involved procedure requiring the rear axle/subframe assembly to be lowered. Ensure you have enough working space/lifting equipment before starting.*

2 Lower the rear axle/subframe as described in the description for 'Torque strut – removal and refitting' later in this Section.

3 Position a workshop jack under the hub carrier, and raise the jack until the rear driveshaft is approximately horizontal.

4 On models with the Advanced Agility Package, detach the height level sensor arm from the bracket on the camber strut.

5 Undo the nuts, and withdraw the bolts at the inner, and outer ends of the camber strut **(see illustrations)**. Note the locations of any washers/shims.

6 Manoeuvre the camber strut from position.

Torque strut

Note: *This is an involved procedure requiring the rear axle/subframe assembly to be lowered. Ensure you have enough working space/lifting equipment before starting.*

Note: *Lowering the rear axle/subframe requires the fuel filler pipe to be disconnected from the tank. Consequently, this procedure is best done when the tank is almost empty.*

7 Remove the complete exhaust system as described in Chapter 4A Section 19.

8 Undo the fasteners and remove the rear underfloor panelling.

9 With reference to Chapter 8 Section 7, detach the propeller shaft rear flexible coupling from the final drive flange.

10 Remove the rear brake pads as described in Chapter 9 Section 5.

11 Working along their lengths, unclip the left- and right-hand wheel speed sensor/brake pad contact sensor wiring harnesses from their retaining clips.

12 Undo the nuts, and withdraw the bolts securing the base of both shock absorbers to the control arms.

13 Position a workshop jack under each hub carrier, then raise the jack until the driveshafts are approximately horizontal.

14 Remove the bolt securing the outer end of the torque strut to the hub carrier **(see illustration)**.

15.5a Remove the bolt/nut securing the camber strut to the axle/subframe...

15.5b ...and to the hub carrier

15.14 Torque strut-to-hub carrier bolt

15.18 Torque strut-to-axle/subframe bolt

15.22 Spring control arm-to-hub carrier bolt

15.26 The large diameter bolt must be renewed

15.28 Thrust arm rear mounting bolt

15.31 Inner mounting bolt eccentric washer

15.32 Detach the tie-rod from the hub carrier

15 Release the clamp and disconnect the fuel filler hose from the tank.

16 Position workshop jacks under the rear axle/subframe, undo the bolts and lower the assembly a little. The help of an assistant will make the task easier. Ensure no strain is placed on any wiring or hoses as the assembly is lowered. Note that new bolts must be fitted.

17 Use a marker pen to make alignment marks between the inner end of the torque strut and the axle/subframe. If a new strut is to be fitted, the marks can be transferred to the new strut.

18 Remove the bolt securing the inner end of the torque strut to the axle/subframe, and manoeuvre it from place **(see illustration)**.

Spring control arm

19 Remove the steel coil spring as described in Section 14.

20 Position a workshop jack under the hub carrier, and raise the jack until the driveshaft is approximately horizontal.

21 Detach the tie-rod from the hub carrier **(see illustration 15.32)**.

22 Remove the bolt securing the control arm to the hub carrier **(see illustration)**. Note that a new bolt and nut will be required.

23 Manoeuvre the spring control arm from place.

24 Check the arm for signs of wear or damage. If necessary, the rubber bush can be replaced using a suitable press. Note the fitted orientation of the bush prior to removal.

Thrust arm

25 Undo the fasteners and remove the rear section of the underbody panelling.

26 Undo the 3 bolts and remove the stop plate from the front of the subframe **(see**

illustration)**. Note that the larger diameter bolt must be renewed.

27 Place a workshop jack under the hub carrier, then raise the jack until the driveshaft is approximately horizontal.

28 Undo the nuts, and withdraw the bolts securing the inner and outer ends of the thrust arm **(see illustration)**. Manoeuvre the arm from place.

29 Examine the rubber bush. If it is damaged/worn, the complete thrust arm must be replaced.

Tie-rod

30 Place a workshop jack under the hub carrier, then raise the jack until the driveshaft is approximately horizontal.

31 Make alignment marks between the tie-rod inner mounting bolt eccentric washer and the subframe, to aid refitting **(see illustration)**.

32 Undo the nuts, and withdraw the bolts securing the inner and outer ends of the rod to the hub carrier and axle carrier/subframe **(see illustration)**.

33 Examine the rubber bushes for wear or damage. If the bushes are defective, the complete tie-rod must be replaced.

Refitting

34 Refitting is a reversal of removal, noting the following points:
a) *Install the arms/rod/strut mounting bolts, but only tighten them once the weight of the vehicle is back on its' wheels.*
b) *Tighten all fasteners to their specified torque where given.*
c) *Renew all self-locking nuts.*
d) *Have the rear wheel alignment checked at the earliest opportunity.*

16 Rear anti-roll bar – removal and refitting

Note: *Refer to the note at the end of Section 1.*

Removal

1 As described in Section 15 (Torque strut removal), lower the rear axle carrier/subframe a little to gain access to the anti-roll bar mounting clamps.

2 Undo the nuts and detach the outer ends of the anti-roll bar from the link rods **(see illustration 17.3)**.

3 Undo the bolts securing the anti-roll bar clamps to the rear axle carrier/subframe **(see illustration)**. Manoeuvre the anti-roll bar from place.

Refitting

4 Refitting is a reversal of removal. Tighten all fasteners to their specified torque.

16.3 Undo the bolt securing the anti-roll bar clamp to the subframe

17 Rear anti-roll bar link rods – removal and refitting

1 Refer to the note at the end of Section 1.

Removal

2 Chock the front wheels, and then jack up the rear of the car and support it on axle stands (see *Vehicle jacking and support*). If required, to make access easier remove the relevant rear roadwheel.

3 Slacken and remove the nut securing the connecting link to the anti-roll bar **(see illustration)**.

4 Unscrew the bolt securing the lower part of the connecting link to the lower arm and remove it from the car **(see illustration)**.

5 Inspect the connecting link mounting bush for signs of damage or deterioration. Also check that the balljoint is free to move easily, and that its gaiter is undamaged. Renew the connecting link if necessary.

Refitting

6 Manoeuvre the link rod into position, and fit lower retaining bolt to the spring control arm. Tighten the bolt to the specified torque.

7 Engage the upper end of the link rod with the anti-roll bar, and tighten the nut to the specified torque.

8 Where applicable, refit the roadwheel, and lower the vehicle to the ground.

18.3 Undo the bolt from the centre of the steering wheel

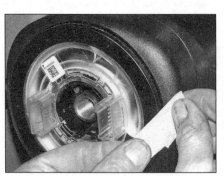

18.5 Apply tape to prevent the contact unit from rotating

17.3 Detach the upper end of the link from the anti-roll bar

18 Steering wheel – removal and refitting

Removal

1 Set the front wheels in the straight-ahead position, and remove the ignition key. Pull the steering wheel out to its fully-extended position.

2 Remove the drivers airbag as described in Chapter 12 Section 20.

3 Slacken and remove the steering wheel retaining bolt **(see illustration)**. Hold the steering wheel firmly to prevent rotation. Note that a new bolt will be required.

4 Although the wheel has a 'master spline' to locate in on the column shaft, mark the

18.4 The wheel has a 'master spline' to locate it on the shaft

19.4 Unclip the wiring harness guide

17.4 Detach the lower end of the link from the spring control arm

steering wheel and steering column shaft in relation to each other, then lift the steering wheel off the column splines. If it is tight, tap it up near the centre, using the palm of your hand, or twist it from side-to-side, whilst pulling upwards to release it from the shaft splines **(see illustration)**. Disconnect the steering wheel wiring plugs as they become accessible.

5 Apply a strip of self-adhesive tape to the unit to prevent the rotary contact clockspring from being rotated **(see illustration)**.

Caution: Do not turn the column shaft or airbag contact unit whilst the steering wheel is removed.

Refitting

6 Refitting is a reversal of removal, noting the following points:

a) *Ensure that the steering wheel locates correctly with the contact unit as the steering wheel is refitted.*

b) *Reconnect the wiring plugs.*

c) *Engage the wheel with the column splines, aligning the marks made on removal, and tighten the steering wheel retaining bolt to the specified torque setting.*

d) *Refit the airbag as described in Chapter 12 Section 20.*

19 Steering column – removal, inspection and refitting

Note: *Refer to the note at the end of Section before proceeding.*

Removal

1 Fully extend the steering column, and ensure the front wheels are in the 'straight-ahead' position.

2 Raise the front of the vehicle and support it securely on axle stands (see *Vehicle jacking and support*). Release the fasteners and remove the engine undershield.

3 Remove the steering column combination switch as described in Chapter 12 Section 5.

4 Unclip the wiring harness guide **(see illustration)**.

5 On models with the electrically adjustable steering column, remove the instrument

19.6 Unclip the panel from the facia

19.10 Universal joint pinch bolt

19.12a Undo the 2 bolts above the column...

19.12b ...and the 2 bolts below

20.3a Undo the nut...

20.3b ...and depress the stud

cluster as described in Chapter 12 Section 10.
6 Unclip the steering column gaiter from the facia **(see illustration)**.
7 Remove the drivers side lower facia panel as described in Chapter 11 Section 35.
8 Note their fitted position, then disconnect any wiring plugs from the steering column.
9 Where fitted, unclip the air vent from the column.
10 Remove the bolt securing the steering column upper universal joint **(see illustration)**. Note that a new bolt will be required.
11 Pull the steering column upper universal joint from the column.
12 Remove the mounting bolts, and manoeuvre the steering column from place **(see illustrations)**.

Inspection

13 The steering column incorporates a telescopic safety feature. In the event of a front-end crash, the lower section of the shaft collapses and prevents the steering wheel injuring the driver. Before refitting the steering column, examine the column and mountings for signs of damage and deformation, and renew as necessary.
14 Check the steering shaft for signs of free play in the column bushes. If any damage or wear is found on the steering column bushes, the column should be overhauled. Overhaul of the column is a complex task requiring several special tools, and should be entrusted to a Mercedes-Benz dealer.

Refitting

15 Refitting is a reversal of removal, but tighten the column retaining bolts in the following order:
a) *Right-hand rear*
b) *Right-hand front*
c) *Left-hand rear*
d) *Left-hand front*

20 Steering lock control unit – removal and refitting

Removal

1 Remove the steering column as described in Section 19.
2 Disconnect the control unit wiring plug.
3 Undo the retaining nut, depress the stud and detach the lock control unit from the column **(see illustrations)**.

Refitting

4 Refitting is a reversal of removal.

21 Steering rack – removal, overhaul and refitting

Removal

1 Ensure the front wheels are in the 'straight-ahead' position, then fully extend the steering column. It's essential that the steering wheel is not rotated during the following procedures.

2 Slacken the front wheel bolts, raise the front of the vehicle and support it securely on axle stands (see *Vehicle jacking and support*). Remove the front roadwheels.
3 Disconnect the battery negative lead as described in Chapter 5A Section 4.
4 Release the fasteners and remove the engine undershield.
5 Remove the plastic cover from the top of the engine.
6 On 2148 cc engines, using a syringe or poultry baster, remove as much fluid as possible from the power steering fluid reservoir.
7 Detach the track rods ends from the hub carriers as described in Section 25.
8 Undo the fasteners and remove the heat shield (where fitted) from the subframe.
9 Undo the bolt, slide the column shaft from the pinion **(see illustration)**. Renew the nut.

21.9 Steering column shaft pinch bolt/nut (viewed from beneath)

21.11 Undo the bolts and remove the mounting plate

21.12 Disconnect any wiring plugs from the rack

21.13 Steering rack mounting bolts

10 On 2148 cc engines, undo the bolt, remove the clamping plate, and pull the fluid pipes from the steering rack pinion housing. Plug the openings to prevent contamination. Be prepared for fluid spillage. Renew the pipe O-ring seals.

11 Undo the bolts and remove the mounting plate from beneath the rack **(see illustration)**.

12 Disconnect any wiring plugs from the steering rack assembly **(see illustration)**.

13 Place a workshop jack under the steering rack, undo the mounting bolts and lower the assembly from place **(see illustration)**. The help of an assistant during this procedure will be helpful – the assembly is heavy!

Overhaul

14 Examine the steering rack assembly for signs of wear, leakage or damage. If overhaul of the steering rack assembly is necessary, the task must be entrusted to a Mercedes-Benz dealer or specialist.

Refitting

15 Manoeuvre the steering rack into position. Ensure the marks made on removal are correctly aligned.

16 Fit the steering rack mounting bolts and tighten them to the specified torque.

17 The remainder of refitting is a reversal of removal, noting the following points:
a) *Renew the fluid pipes' O-ring seals.*
b) *Tighten all fasteners to their specified torque where given.*
c) *Bleed the power steering system as described in Section 24.*
d) *Have the front wheel alignment checked at the earliest opportunity.*

22 Steering rack gaiter –
renewal

Renewal

1 Raise the front of the vehicle and support it securely on axle stands (see *Vehicle jacking and support*). Undo the fasteners and remove the engine undershield.

2 Remove the track rod end as described in Section 25.

3 Release the inner and outer clamp, then slide

22.3 Steering rack gaiter inner, and outer clamps

the gaiter from the steering rack **(see illustration)**. Renew the O-ring seal on the steering rack.

4 With the new O-ring in place, slide the gaiter over the track rod, and into position on the steering rack. Note that some gaiters incorporate a diaphragm valve. This valve must point rearwards.

5 Position the new inner, and outer clamp, then tighten them.

6 Refit the track rod end with reference to Section 25.

23 Power steering pump –
removal and refitting

Removal

2148 cc engines only

1 Undo the fasteners and remove the plastic cover from the top of the engine.

2 Using a syringe or poultry baster, remove as much fluid as possible from the power steering fluid reservoir.

3 Remove the auxiliary drivebelt as described in Chapter 1 Section 6.

4 Release the clamp and disconnect the fluid supply hose from the pump **(see illustration)**. Be prepared for fluid spillage.

5 Undo the union and pull the fluid pressure pipe from the pump. Renew the union O-ring seal. Be prepared for fluid spillage.

6 Undo the 3 retaining bolts and manoeuvre the power steering plump from place. Plug the openings to prevent contamination.

23.4 Disconnect the fluid hose and pressure pipe

Refitting

7 If the power steering pump is faulty, seek the advice of your Mercedes-Benz dealer as to the availability of spare parts. If spares are available, it may be possible to have the pump overhauled by a suitable specialist or alternately obtain an exchange unit. If not, the pump must be renewed.

8 Refitting is a reversal of removal, noting the following points:
a) *Tighten all fasteners to their specified torque where given.*
b) *Bleed the power steering system as described in Section 24.*

24 Power steering system –
bleeding

1 Raise the front of the vehicle and support it securely on axle stands (see *Vehicle jacking and support*).

2 Release the fasteners and remove the plastic cover from the top of the engine.

3 With the engine stopped, fill the fluid reservoir to within 10 mm of the top of the reservoir. Use only the specified type of fluid (see Lubricants and fluids 0 Section 5).

4 With the engine stopped, slowly move the steering from lock-to-lock several times to purge out the trapped air, then top-up the level in the fluid reservoir. Repeat this procedure until the fluid level in the reservoir does not drop any further.

5 Have an assistant start the engine, whilst

25.2a Slacken the locknut...

25.2b ...and mark the position on the threads

25.3 Use a balljoint separator

you keep watch on the fluid level. Be prepared to add more fluid as the engine starts, as the fluid level is likely to drop quickly. The fluid level must not be allowed to drop too far, or more air will be drawn into the system. Don't turn the steering wheel during this process.

6 With the engine running at idle speed, turn the steering wheel slowly two or three times approximately 45° to the left and right of the centre, then turn the wheel twice from lock-to-lock. Do not hold the wheel on either lock, as this imposes strain on the hydraulic system. Repeat this procedure until bubbles cease to appear in fluid reservoir.

7 If, when turning the steering, an abnormal noise is heard from the fluid lines, it indicates that there is still air in the system. Check this by turning the wheels to the straight-ahead position and switching off the engine. If the fluid level in the reservoir rises, then air is present in the system and further bleeding is necessary.

8 Once all traces of air have been removed from the power steering hydraulic system, turn the engine off and allow the system to cool. Once cool, check that fluid level is up to the maximum mark, topping-up if necessary.

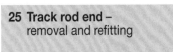

25 Track rod end –
removal and refitting

Note: *Refer to the note at the end of Section 1 before proceeding.*

Removal

1 Chock the rear wheels, and loosen the front wheel bolts. Jack up the front of the car and support it on axle stands (see *Vehicle jacking and support*). Remove the relevant front roadwheel.

2 Clean the end of the track rod and slacken the locknut **(see illustrations)**. Make a mark on the track rod arm threads to aid refitting. It will be needed to ensure that the wheel alignment remains correctly set when the balljoint is installed.

3 Slacken and remove the balljoint nut, and free the balljoint from the hub carrier. If necessary, free the balljoint tapered shank using a universal balljoint separator **(see illustration)**.

4 Counting the exact number of turns necessary to do so, unscrew the balljoint from the track rod.

5 Carefully clean the balljoint and the threads – the balljoint taper must not have any lubricant on it, otherwise it will not lock into position. Renew the balljoint if its movement is sloppy or too stiff, is excessively worn, or is damaged in any way; carefully check the stud taper and threads.

Refitting

6 Screw the balljoint back onto the track rod by the number of turns noted on removal, and tighten the locknut. This should position the balljoint at the relevant marks made on removal.

7 Refit the balljoint shank to the hub carrier, then fit a new retaining nut and tighten it to the specified torque.

8 Refit the roadwheel, then lower the car to the ground and tighten the roadwheel bolts to the specified torque.

9 Have the front wheel alignment checked at the earliest opportunity.

26 Wheel alignment and
steering angles –
general information

Definitions

1 A car's steering and suspension geometry is defined in four basic settings – all angles are expressed in degrees; the steering axis is defined as an imaginary line drawn through the axis of the suspension strut, extended where necessary to contact the ground **(see illustration)**.

2 Camber is the angle between each roadwheel and a vertical line drawn through its centre and tyre contact patch, when viewed from the front or rear of the car. Positive camber is when the roadwheels are tilted outwards from the vertical at the top; negative camber is when they are tilted inwards.

3 The front camber angle is adjusted by removing the nut, withdrawing the spring control arm inner bolt, and reinserting it into one of two positions. The angle should be measured using a camber angle gauge. The rear wheel camber is not adjustable.

4 Castor is the angle between the steering axis and a vertical line drawn through each roadwheel's centre and tyre contact patch, when viewed from the side of the car. Positive castor is when the steering axis is tilted so that it contacts the ground ahead of the vertical;

26.1 Wheel alignment details

negative castor is when it contacts the ground behind the vertical.

5 The front castor angle is adjusted by removing the nut, withdrawing the torque strut inner bolt, and re-inserting in one of two positions. The setting must measured using a castor angle gauge. The rear wheel castor is not adjustable.

6 Toe is the difference, viewed from above, between lines drawn through the roadwheel centres and the car's centre-line. 'Toe-in' is when the roadwheels point inwards, towards each other at the front, while 'toe-out' is when they splay outwards from each other at the front.

7 The front wheel toe setting is adjusted by screwing the track rod in or out of its balljoints, to alter the effective length of the track rod assembly.

8 Rear wheel toe setting is also adjustable. The toe setting is adjusted by slackening the tie-rod inner mounting bracket bolts, rotating the adjusting nut to achieve the desired setting, then tightening the bolts again.

Checking and adjustment

9 Due to the special measuring equipment necessary to check the wheel alignment and steering angles, and the skill required to use it properly, the checking and adjustment of these settings is best left to a Mercedes-Benz dealer or similar expert. Note that most tyre-fitting shops now possess sophisticated checking equipment.

Chapter 11
Bodywork and fittings

Contents

Section number

Body exterior fittings – removal and refitting 34
Bonnet – removal, refitting and adjustment 6
Bonnet emblem – removal and refitting 10
Bonnet release cables – removal and refitting 8
Bonnet support strut – removal and refitting 7
Boot lid (Saloon) – removal and refitting 11
Boot lid lock components (Saloon) – removal and refitting 12
Bumpers – removal and refitting 16
Central locking system components – removal and refitting 25
Centre console – removal and refitting. 36
Door – removal and refitting. 26
Door mirror – removal and refitting. 28
Door module and control unit – removal and refitting 18
Door trim panel – removal and refitting 17
Facia panel assembly – removal and refitting 37
Front door exterior handle – removal and refitting. 21
Front door lock assembly – removal and refitting 22
Front door window glass and electric motor – removal and refitting 19
Front seats – removal and refitting. 30

Section number

General information 1
Interior mirror – removal and refitting. 29
Interior trim – removal and refitting 35
Maintenance – bodywork and underframe. 2
Maintenance – upholstery and carpets 3
Major body damage – repair 5
Minor body damage – repair 4
Radiator grille – removal and refitting. 9
Rear door exterior handle – removal and refitting 23
Rear door lock assembly – removal and refitting. 24
Rear door window glass and electric motor – removal and refitting . 20
Rear seats – removal and refitting 31
Seat belts – removal and refitting. 32
Sunroof – general information 33
Tailgate (Estate) – removal and refitting 13
Tailgate automatic opening/closing – component renewal 15
Tailgate lock and release handle (Estate) – removal and refitting. . . 14
Windscreen and fixed window glass – general information 27

Degrees of difficulty

Easy, suitable for novice with little experience	Fairly easy, suitable for beginner with some experience	Fairly difficult, suitable for competent DIY mechanic	Difficult, suitable for experienced DIY mechanic	Very difficult, suitable for expert DIY or professional

Specifications

Torque wrench settings	Nm	lbf ft
Seat belt anchorage	32	24
Seat belt inertia reel	32	24
Seat belt rear inertia reel bracket-to-pillar	8	6
Seat bolts	50	37

1 General information

1 The body is of unitary high-strength-steel construction with extruded aluminium sections, and incorporates computer-calculated impact crumple zones at the front and rear, with a central safety cell passenger compartment. During manufacture the body is dip-primed, fully sealed and undercoated, then painted with multi-layered base and top-coats.

2 The bodyshell on all models covered by this manual is of four-door Saloon or five-door Estate configuration.

3 A number of structural components and body panels are made of galvanised steel to provide a high level of protection against corrosion. Extensive use is also made of plastic materials, mainly in the interior, but also in exterior components. The front and rear bumpers are moulded from a synthetic material that is very strong and yet light. Plastic components such as wheel arch liners are fitted to the underside of the vehicle to further improve corrosion resistance.

2 Maintenance – bodywork and underframe

1 The general condition of a vehicle's bodywork is the one thing that significantly affects its value. Maintenance is easy but needs to be regular. Neglect, particularly after minor damage, can lead quickly to further deterioration and costly repair bills. It is important also to keep watch on those parts of the vehicle not immediately visible, for instance the underside, inside all the wheel arches and the lower pan of the engine compartment.

2 The basic maintenance routine for the bodywork is washing – preferably with a lot of water, from a hose. This will remove all the loose solids, which may have stuck to the vehicle. It is important to flush these off in such a way as to prevent grit from scratching the finish. The wheel arches and underframe need washing in the same way to remove any accumulated mud, which will retain moisture and tend to encourage rust. Paradoxically, the best time to clean the underframe and wheel arches is in wet weather when the mud is thoroughly wet and soft. In very wet weather the underframe is usually cleaned of large accumulations automatically and this is a good time for inspection.

3 Periodically, except on vehicles with a wax-based underbody protective coating, it is a good idea to have the whole of the underframe of the vehicle steam cleaned, engine compartment included, so that a thorough inspection can be carried out to see what minor repairs and renovations are necessary. Steam cleaning is available at many garages and is necessary for removal of the accumulation of oily grime, which sometimes is allowed to become thick in certain areas. If steam-cleaning facilities are not available, there are some excellent grease solvents available which can be brush applied. The dirt can then be simply hosed off. Note that these methods should not be used on vehicles with wax-based underbody protective coating or the coating will be removed. Such vehicles should be inspected annually, preferably just prior to winter, when the underbody should be washed down and any damage to the wax coating repaired. Ideally, a completely fresh coat should be applied. It would also be worth considering the use of such wax-based protection for injection into door panels, sills, box sections, etc, as an additional safeguard against rust damage where such protection is not provided by the vehicle manufacturer.

4 After washing paintwork, wipe off with a chamois leather to give an unspotted clear finish. A coat of clear protective wax polish will give added protection against chemical pollutants in the air. If the paintwork sheen has dulled or oxidised, use a cleaner/polisher combination to restore the brilliance of the shine. This requires a little effort, but such dulling is usually caused because regular washing has been neglected. Care needs to be taken with metallic paintwork, as special non-abrasive cleaner/polisher is required to avoid damage to the finish. Always check that the door and ventilator opening drain holes and pipes are completely clear so that water can be drained out. Bright work should be treated in the same way as paintwork. Windscreens and windows can be kept clear of the smeary film that often appears by the use of a proprietary glass cleaner. Never use any form of wax or other body or chromium polish on glass.

3 Maintenance – upholstery and carpets

1 Mats and carpets should be brushed or vacuum cleaned regularly to keep them free of grit. If they are badly stained remove them from the vehicle for scrubbing or sponging and make quite sure they are dry before refitting. Seats and interior trim panels can be kept clean by wiping with a damp cloth. If they do become stained (which can be more apparent on light coloured upholstery) use a little liquid detergent and a soft nail brush to scour the grime out of the grain of the material. Do not forget to keep the headlining clean in the same way as the upholstery. When using liquid cleaners inside the vehicle do not over-wet the surfaces being cleaned. Excessive damp could get into the seams and padded interior causing stains, offensive odours or even rot. If the inside of the vehicle gets wet accidentally it is worthwhile taking some trouble to dry it out properly, particularly where carpets are involved. Do not leave oil or electric heaters inside the vehicle for this purpose.

4 Minor body damage – repair

Minor scratches

1 If the scratch is very superficial, and does not penetrate to the metal of the bodywork, repair is very simple. Lightly rub the area of the scratch with a paintwork renovator, or a very fine cutting paste, to remove loose paint from the scratch and to clear the surrounding bodywork of wax polish. Rinse the area with clean water.

2 In the case of metallic paint, the most commonly found scratches are not in the paint, but in the lacquer top coat, and appear white. If care is taken, these can sometimes be rendered less obvious by very careful use of paintwork renovator (which would otherwise not be used on metallic paintwork); otherwise, repair of these scratches can be achieved by applying lacquer with a fine brush.

3 Apply touch-up paint to the scratch using a fine paintbrush; continue to apply fine layers of paint until the surface of the paint in the scratch is level with the surrounding paintwork. Allow the new paint at least two weeks to harden, and then blend it into the surrounding paintwork by rubbing the scratch area with a paintwork renovator or a very fine cutting paste. Finally, apply wax polish.

4 Where the scratch has penetrated right through to the metal of the bodywork, causing the metal to rust, a different repair technique is required. Remove any loose rust from the bottom of the scratch with a penknife, and then apply rust-inhibiting paint to prevent the formation of rust in the future. Using a rubber or nylon applicator, fill the scratch with bodystopper paste. If required, this paste can be mixed with cellulose thinners to provide a very thin paste, which is ideal for filling narrow scratches. Before the stopper-paste in the scratch hardens, wrap a piece of smooth cotton rag around the top of a finger. Dip the finger in cellulose thinners, and then quickly sweep it across the surface of the stopper-paste in the scratch; this will ensure that the surface of the stopper-paste is slightly hollowed. The scratch can now be painted over as described earlier in this Section.

Dents

5 When deep denting of the vehicle's bodywork has taken place, the first task is to pull the dent out, until the affected bodywork almost attains its original shape. There is little point in trying to restore the original shape completely, as the metal in the damaged area will have stretched on impact and cannot be reshaped fully to its original contour. It is better to bring the level of the dent up to a point which is about 3 mm below the level of the surrounding bodywork. In cases where the dent is very shallow anyway, it is not worth trying to pull it out at all. If the underside of the dent is accessible, it can be hammered out gently from behind, using a mallet with a wooden or plastic head. Whilst doing this, hold a suitable block of wood firmly against the outside of the panel to absorb the impact from the hammer blows and thus prevent a large area of the bodywork from being 'belled-out'.

6 Should the dent be in a section of the bodywork, which has a double skin or some other factor making it inaccessible from behind, a different technique is called for. Drill several small holes through the metal inside the area – particularly in the deeper section. Then screw long self-tapping screws into the holes just sufficiently for them to gain a good purchase in the metal. Now the dent can be pulled out by pulling on the protruding heads of the screws with a pair of pliers.

7 The next stage of the repair is the removal of the paint from the damaged area, and from an inch or so of the surrounding 'sound' bodywork. This is accomplished most easily by using a wire brush or abrasive pad on a power drill, although it can be done just as effectively by hand using sheets of abrasive paper. To complete the preparation for filling, score the surface of the bare metal with a screwdriver or the tang of a file, or alternatively, drill small holes in the affected area. This will provide a really good 'key' for the filler paste.

8 To complete the repair see the Section on filling and re-spraying.

Rust holes or gashes

9 Remove all paint from the affected area and from an inch or so of the surrounding 'sound' bodywork, using an abrasive pad or a wire brush on a power drill. If these are not available a few sheets of abrasive paper will do the job just as effectively. With the paint removed you will be able to gauge the severity of the corrosion and therefore decide whether to renew the whole panel (if this is possible) or to repair the affected area. New body panels are not as expensive as most people think and it is often quicker and more satisfactory to fit a new panel than to attempt to repair large areas of corrosion.

10 Remove all fittings from the affected area except those, which will act as a guide to the original shape of the damaged bodywork. Then, using tin snips or a hacksaw blade, remove all loose metal and any other metal badly affected by corrosion. Hammer the edges of the hole inwards in order to create a slight depression for the filler paste.

11 Wire-brush the affected area to remove the powdery rust from the surface of the remaining metal. Paint the affected area with rust -inhibiting paint – if the back of the rusted area is accessible, treat this also.

12 Before filling can take place it will be necessary to block the hole in some way. This can be achieved by the use of aluminium or plastic mesh, or aluminium tape.

13 Aluminium or plastic mesh is probably the best material to use for a large hole. Cut a piece to the approximate size and shape of the hole to be filled, then position it in the hole so that its edges are below the level of the surrounding bodywork. It can be retained in position by several blobs of filler paste around its periphery.

14 Aluminium tape should be used for small or very narrow holes. Pull a piece off the roll and trim it to the approximate size and shape required, then pull off the backing paper (if used) and stick the tape over the hole; it can be overlapped if the thickness of one piece is insufficient. Burnish down the edges of the tape with the handle of a screwdriver or similar, to ensure that the tape is securely attached to the metal underneath.

Filling and re-spraying

15 Before using this Section, see the Sections on dent, deep scratch, rust holes and gash repairs.

16 Many types of bodyfiller are available, but generally speaking those proprietary kits which contain a tin of filler paste and a tube of resin

hardener are best for this type of repair. A wide, flexible plastic or nylon applicator will be found invaluable for imparting a smooth and well-contoured finish to the surface of the filler.

17 Mix up a little filler on a clean piece of card or board – measure the hardener carefully (follow the maker's instructions on the pack) otherwise the filler will set too rapidly or too slowly. Using the applicator, apply the filler paste to the prepared area; draw the applicator across the surface of the filler to achieve the correct contour and to level the filler surface. As soon as a contour that approximates to the correct one is achieved, stop working the paste – if you carry on too long, the paste will become sticky and begin to 'pick up' on the applicator. Continue to add thin layers of filler paste at twenty-minute intervals until the level of the filler is just proud of the surrounding bodywork.

18 Once the filler has hardened, excess can be removed using a metal plane or file. From then on, progressively finer grades of abrasive paper should be used, starting with a 40-grade production paper and finishing with 400-grade (or higher) wet-and-dry paper. Always wrap the abrasive paper around a flat rubber, cork, or wooden block – otherwise the surface of the filler will not be completely flat. During the smoothing of the filler surface, the wet-and-dry paper should be periodically rinsed in water. This will ensure that a very smooth finish is imparted to the filler at the final stage.

19 At this stage the 'dent' should be surrounded by a ring of bare metal, which in turn should be encircled by the finely 'feathered' edge of the good paintwork. Rinse the repair area with clean water, until all of the dust produced by the rubbing-down operation has gone.

20 Spray the whole repair area with a light coat of primer – this will show up any imperfections in the surface of the filler. Repair these imperfections with fresh filler paste or bodystopper, and once more smooth the surface with abrasive paper. If bodystopper is used, it can be mixed with cellulose thinners to form a really thin paste, which is ideal for filling small holes. Repeat this spray-and-repair procedure until you are satisfied that the surface of the filler, and the feathered edge of the paintwork are perfect. Clean the repair area with clean water, and allow to dry fully.

21 The repair area is now ready for final spraying. Paint spraying must be carried out in a warm, dry, windless and dust-free atmosphere. This condition can be created artificially if you have access to a large indoor working area, but if you are forced to work in the open, you will have to pick your day very carefully. If you are working indoors, dousing the floor in the work area with water will help to settle the dust that would otherwise be in the atmosphere. If the repair area is confined to one body panel, mask off the surrounding panels; this will help to minimise the effects of a slight mis-match in paint colours. Bodywork fittings (e.g. rubbing strips, door handles, etc)

will also need to be masked off. Use genuine masking tape and several thicknesses of newspaper for the masking operations.

22 Before commencing to spray, agitate the aerosol can thoroughly, and then spray a test area (an old tin, or similar) until the technique is mastered. Cover the repair area with a thick coat of primer; the thickness should be built up using several thin layers of paint rather than one thick one. Using 400-grade (or higher) wet-and-dry paper, rub down the surface of the primer until it is really smooth. While doing this, the work area should be thoroughly doused with water, and the wet-and-dry paper periodically rinsed in water. Allow to dry before spraying on more paint.

23 Spray on the top coat, again building up the thickness by using several thin layers of paint. Start spraying at the top of the repair area and then, using a side-to-side motion, work downwards until the whole repair area and about 2 inches of the surrounding original paintwork is covered. Remove all masking material 10 to 15 minutes after spraying on the final coat of paint.

24 Allow the new paint at least two weeks to harden, then, using a paintwork renovator or a very fine cutting paste, blend the edges of the paint into the existing paintwork. Finally, apply wax polish.

Plastic components

25 With the use of more and more plastic body components by the vehicle manufacturers (e.g. bumpers, spoilers, and in some cases major body panels), rectification of more serious damage to such items has become a matter of either entrusting repair work to a specialist in this field, or renewing complete components. Repair of such damage by the DIY owner is not really feasible, owing to the cost of the equipment and materials required for effecting such repairs. The basic technique involves making a groove along the line of the crack in the plastic using a rotary burr in a power drill. The damaged part is then welded back together by using a hot-air gun to heat up and fuse a plastic filler rod into the groove. Any excess plastic is then removed and the area rubbed down to a smooth finish. It is important that a filler rod of the correct plastic is used, as body components can be made of a variety of different types (e.g. polycarbonate, ABS, polypropylene).

26 Damage of a less serious nature (abrasions, minor cracks etc) can be repaired by the DIY owner using a two-part epoxy filler repair material. Once mixed in equal proportions, this is used in similar fashion to the bodywork filler used on metal panels. The filler is usually cured in twenty to thirty minutes, ready for sanding and painting.

27 If the owner is renewing a complete component himself, or if he has repaired it with epoxy filler, he will be left with the problem of finding a suitable paint for finishing which is compatible with the type of plastic used. At one time the use of a universal paint

6.2 Prise out the strut clip a little

was not possible, owing to the complex range of plastics encountered in body component applications. Standard paints, generally speaking, will not bond to plastic or rubber satisfactorily. However, it is now possible to obtain a plastic body parts finishing kit, which consists of a pre-primer treatment, a primer and coloured top coat. Full instructions are normally supplied with a kit, but basically the method of use is to first apply the pre-primer to the component concerned and allow it to dry for up to 30 minutes. Then the primer is applied and left to dry for about an hour before finally applying the special coloured top coat. The result is a correctly coloured component where the paint will flex with the plastic or rubber, a property that standard paint does not normally possess.

5 Major body damage – repair

1 Where serious damage has occurred, or large areas need renewal due to neglect, it means that complete new panels will need welding in, and this is best left to professionals. If the damage is due to impact, it will also be necessary to completely check the alignment of the bodyshell, and this can only be carried out accurately by a Mercedes-Benz dealer using special jigs. If the body is left misaligned, it is primarily dangerous as the car will not handle properly, and secondly, uneven stresses will be

imposed on the steering, suspension and possibly transmission, causing abnormal wear, or complete failure, particularly to such items as the tyres.

6 Bonnet – removal, refitting and adjustment

Removal

1 Raise the bonnet to the vertical position.
2 With the aid of an assistant to support the bonnet, extract the strut upper retaining clip, then unhook and remove the strut from the bonnet on both sides **(see illustration)**.
3 Mark the position of the hinge bolts on both sides, so that the bonnet can be refitted in its original position.
4 With the help of an assistant, loosen and withdraw the hinge bolts, and carefully lift off the bonnet. Store the bonnet in a safe place to prevent any damage.

Refitting and adjustment

5 With the bonnet closed, check the gap between the bonnet and front wings on both sides (transverse adjustment), the alignment of the front edge of the bonnet with the front edge of the wing when looking down (longitudinal adjustment), and the height of the bonnet front edge and top edge in relation to the wing (height adjustment). The help of an assistant would be useful when adjusting the bonnet.
6 Open the bonnet and slacken the two bolts securing the lock striker plate to the bonnet. There are two striker plates fitted to the bonnet, one on the left and one on the right.
7 By trial and error, move the striker plate until an equal gap exists between the bonnet and the front wings on each side.
8 From within the engine compartment, slacken the locknut and screw down the bonnet rubber buffer.
9 Slacken the hinge retaining bolts.
10 By trial and error, move the bonnet as necessary, tightening the hinge bolts each time until the bonnet upper edge and front wing edge are aligned.
11 Now raise the rubber buffer a few turns at

a time until the front edge of the bonnet and the edge of the wing, when viewed from the front, are aligned. Tighten the buffer locknut when adjustment is correct.

7 Bonnet support strut – removal and refitting

Removal

1 Raise the bonnet to the vertical position and have an assistant support the bonnet.
2 Extract the strut retaining clip, then unhook and remove the strut from the bonnet **(see illustration 6.2)**.
3 Working at the lower end of the strut, extract the retaining clip, then unhook and remove the strut from the inner wing panel.

Refitting

4 Refitting is a reversal of removal.

8 Bonnet release cables – removal and refitting

Removal

1 Open the bonnet. If the bonnet release cable has broken, it is probably best to seek the advice of a Mercedes dealer or specialist, as to the best course of action.
2 Remove the drivers side lower facia panel as described in Section 37, then disconnect the cable **(see illustration)**.
3 Tie string to the release cable so that, as the cable is pulled through the bulkhead, it will pull the string with it.
4 Remove the cover from the engine compartment fuse/relay box, and release the cable.
5 Remove the cable junction box, prise it open with a screwdriver, and disconnect the rear cable **(see illustration)**.
6 Pull the rear cable from the bulkhead, leaving the string in place to aid refitting.
7 If required, undo the bolts and remove the right-, and left hand bonnet catches, then disconnect the cables **(see illustration)**. Release the cables from any retaining clips.

8.2 Pull the outer cable from the bracket, and detach the inner cable end fitting

8.5 Open the junction box and disconnect the cable

8.7 Bonnet catch retaining bolts

9.1 Gently push the lower edge of the grille rearwards

9.2 Carefully spread apart the clip each side

10.1 Rotate the emblem retaining clip anti-clockwise

Refitting

8 Refitting is the reverse sequence to removal – use the string to draw the new cable through the bulkhead into the car. With the help of an assistant, make sure that the lock is working satisfactorily before closing the bonnet.

9 Radiator grille – removal and refitting

Removal

1 Open the bonnet, gently push the radiator grille rearwards to release it **(see illustration)**.
2 Release the 2 clips on the rear of the grille, and carefully lift it from place **(see illustration)**.

Refitting

3 Refitting is a reversal of removal.

10 Bonnet emblem – removal and refitting

Removal

1 From the underside of the bonnet, turn the emblem retaining clip 90° anti-clockwise – the clip has raised sides to make it easier to grip with pliers **(see illustration)**.
2 Pull the emblem upwards out of the bonnet to remove.

Refitting

3 Refitting is a reversal of removal.

11 Boot lid (Saloon) – removal and refitting

Removal

1 Remove the boot trim panel as described in Section 35.
2 Disconnect the wiring plugs from the boot lid lock and number plate lights, then release the wiring harness from the retaining clips.
3 Mark the outline of the bolts on the hinge using a pencil.

4 Place some rags beneath the lower corners of the boot lid and, with the help of an assistant, undo the hinge retaining bolts. Remove the boot lid upwards out of the restraining hooks, and out from the car.

Refitting

5 Refitting is the reverse sequence to removal, but align the hinges with the outline marks made prior to removal before tightening the bolts. Adjust the lock striker plate as necessary to achieve satisfactory opening and closing of the boot lid.

12 Boot lid lock components (Saloon) – removal and refitting

Removal

1 Open the boot lid, then disconnect the

12.3 Remove the 2 screws above the number plate

12.5 Prise down the panel

battery negative lead as described in Chapter 5A Section 4.
2 Remove the boot lid inner trim panel as described in Section 35.

Boot lid release handle

3 Undo the 2 retaining screws securing the panel above the number plate location **(see illustration)**.
4 Undo the 2 retaining screws on the inside of the boot, adjacent to the boot release handle **(see illustration)**.
5 Carefully prise the panel down from the boot lid **(see illustration)**.
6 Disconnect the wiring plug, then release the clips and detach the handle from the boot lid.

Boot lid lock and cylinder

7 Disconnect the wiring plug from the lock, then undo the 2 screws securing the lock to the boot lid **(see illustration)**.

12.4 Undo the 2 screws each side of the release handle

12.7 Boot lid lock retaining screws

12.8 Remove the plastic cover

12.9a Undo the screw whilst rotating the lock cylinder clockwise...

12.9b ...then manoeuvre the lock and cylinder from the boot lid

12.10 Detach the cable from the lock cylinder

8 Prise away the plastic cover from the lock **(see illustration)**.

9 Undo the retaining screw whilst applying a clockwise rotational force to the lock cylinder, then manoeuvre the lock and cylinder from the boot lid **(see illustrations)**.

10 Slide the outer cable fitting from the lock cylinder, then detach the inner cable fitting **(see illustration)**.

13.4 Detach the harness guide tubes

13.5 Make alignment marks between the hinges and the tailgate

13.6 Prise out the clips a little and disconnect the struts

14.2 Paint alignment marks around the retaining screws

14.3 Note any shims between the lock and tailgate

Refitting

11 Refitting is a reversal of removal. Adjust the lock striker plate as necessary to achieve satisfactory opening and closing of the boot lid.

13 Tailgate (Estate) – removal and refitting

Removal

1 Open the tailgate, then disconnect the battery as described in Chapter 5A Section 4.
2 Remove the tailgate trim panels as described in Section 35.
3 Disconnect the wiring connectors and washer hose from their connections in the tailgate.
4 Release the harness guide tubes **(see illustration)**, and pull the harnesses/hoses from each side.
5 Mark the fitted positions of the hinges on the tailgate, so that the tailgate can be accurately aligned when refitting **(see illustration)**.
6 Have an assistant support the tailgate, then slide out the strut retaining clips a little, then unhook and remove the struts from the tailgate **(see illustration)**.
7 Have an assistant support the tailgate, then undo the bolts and remove the tailgate.

14 Tailgate lock and release handle (Estate) – removal and refitting

Removal

1 Remove the tailgate trim panel as described in Section 35.

Lock

2 Make alignment marks between the lock retaining screws and the tailgate **(see illustration)**.
3 Disconnect the lock wiring plug, then undo the lock retaining screws. Recover any shims fitted between the lock and the tailgate **(see illustration)**.

14.4 Disconnect the release cable from the lock

14.6a Disconnect the wiring plug...

14.6b ...and manoeuvre the release motor from the tailgate

4 Manoeuvre the lock from the tailgate, and disconnect the release cable (where applicable) **(see illustration)**.

Lock release motor

5 Remove the tailgate lock as previously described in this Section.
6 Disconnect the wiring plug, and manoeuvre the lock release motor from the tailgate recess **(see illustrations)**.
7 Open the foam jacket to expose the motor **(see illustration)**. No further dismantling is recommended.

Release handle

8 Undo the 3 bolts securing the wiper motor **(see illustration)**. This is necessary so the motor can be moved a little to access the release handle panel screws.
9 Remove the 2 screws on the inside of the release handle panel, and the 2 on the outside **(see illustrations)**.
10 Using a blunt, flat-bladed tool, carefully prise the release handle panel down from the tailgate **(see illustration)**. Disconnect any wiring plugs as the panel is withdrawn.
11 Release the clips and detach the tailgate release handle **(see illustration)**. Disconnect the wiring plug as it becomes accessible.

Refitting

12 Refitting is a reversal of removal. If necessary, adjust the position of the striker to achieve satisfactory opening and closing.

15 Tailgate automatic opening/ closing – component renewal

Tailgate drive unit

1 Removal of the tailgate opener drive unit requires removal of the headlining. Consequently, we recommend that this task is entrusted to a Mercedes dealer or suitably experienced repairer.

Control module

2 Removal of the tailgate opener drive unit control module requires removal of the headlining. Consequently, we recommend that this task is entrusted to a Mercedes dealer or suitably experienced repairer.

14.7 Open the foam jacket

14.8 Undo the wiper motor retaining bolts

14.9a Undo the 2 screws on the inside of the panel...

14.9b ...and the 2 screws on the outside

14.10 Prise the panel from the tailgate

14.11 Reach inside, and squeeze together the clips

16.2 Lift the flap each side at the top edge of the bumper

16.4 Undo the bolt each side

16.6 Undo the bolts securing the bumper to the wing bracket

16.7 Disconnect the front sensors wiring plug, and the fog light plug each side

16.8 Unscrew the bolt each side beneath the foglights

16.9 Pull out the rear edges of the bumper

16 Bumpers – removal and refitting

Front bumper

1 Chock the rear wheels and firmly apply the parking brake, then jack up the front of the car and support it on axle stands (see *Vehicle jacking and support*).
2 Prise up the rubber flap each side from the top edge of the bumper **(see illustration)**.
3 Remove the radiator grille as described in Section 9,
4 Undo and remove the bolt each side of the radiator grille aperture **(see illustration)**.

5 Undo the fasteners and remove the front section of the wheel arch liner each side, for access to the bumper side mounting bolts. Where applicable, unclip the height sensor wiring harness.
6 Undo the 2 bolts each side securing the bumper to the wing bracket **(see illustration)**.
7 Note their fitted positions, then disconnect any wiring plugs from the front bumper assembly **(see illustration)**.
8 Working in the wheelarch aperture, remove the bolt each side beneath the foglight location **(see illustration)**.
9 With the help of an assistant, pull out the rear edge a little and manoeuvre the bumper assembly forwards **(see illustration)**.
10 Refitting is a reversal of removal.

Rear bumper

11 Raise the rear of the vehicle and support it securely on axle stands (see *Vehicle jacking and support*).
12 Open the boot lid/tailgate, then disconnect the battery negative lead as described in Chapter 5A Section 4.

Saloon models

13 Slacken the 2 plastic nuts, and prise the slide the boot lid sill trim panel upwards from place **(see illustration)**.
14 Undo the 2 nuts securing the bumper to the boot sill panel **(see illustration)**. The nuts are deeply recessed. Use a very deep socket, or crow's foot spanner on a extension rod.

16.13 Slacken the plastic nut each side

16.14 Using a crow's foot spanner to undo the recessed nuts

16.16a Prise up the covers...

16.16b ...and remove the stowage anchor bolts

16.17a Undo the central bolt...

16.17b ...and slacken the nut each side

16.18 Using a crow's foot adapter to unscrew the deeply-recessed nuts

16.20a Undo the screws in the centre...

16.20b ...and the scrivets at the lower edge of the bumper

16.22 Unclip the hose

16.23 Remove the bolt each side in the wheelarch aperture

Estate models

15 Lift out them luggage compartment floor panel.

16 Prise up the covers, undo the bolts and remove the stowage anchor each side **(see illustrations)**.

17 Undo the nuts/bolt and prise up the tailgate sill inner trim panel **(see illustrations)**.

18 Undo the 2 nuts securing the bumper to the sill panel **(see illustration)**. The nuts are deeply recessed. Use a extremely deep socket or crow's foot spanner on an extension rod.

All models

19 On models with Parktronic system, disconnect the wiring plug and feed the wiring harness through the opening in the boot sill panel.

20 Remove the screws/scrivets along the underside of the bumper **(see illustrations)**.

21 Release the fasteners and pull forwards the rear section of the wheelarch liner each side.

22 Where applicable, unclip the hose from the right-hand side of the bumper **(see illustration)**.

17.2 Prise the window frame trim away

23 Undo the bolt each side securing the bumper to the rear wing **(see illustration)**.

24 Pull out the front edges, then with the help of an assistant, manoeuvre the bumper rearwards.

25 Refitting is a reversal of removal.

17 Door trim panel – removal and refitting

Removal

Front door

1 Fully lower the window.

2 Using a blunt, flat-bladed tool, carefully prise the window frame trim away at the rear of the door **(see illustration)**.

17.3 Push-in the pin and prise out the rivet

17.4 Remove the screws under the pull handle

17.5 Working around the front, rear and lower edges, prise the panel from the door

3 Push-in the centre pin and remove the plastic expansion rivet from the rear edge of the trim panel **(see illustration)**.

4 Remove the 2 screws on the underside of the door pull handle **(see illustration)**.
5 Using a wide-bladed or wedge tool,

carefully prise away the door trim panel, working progressively around the edge of the panel until all the clips have been released **(see illustration)**. Do not use excessive force; otherwise the clips will be broken.
6 Manoeuvre the door trim panel upwards, guiding the lock button from the panel as it's withdrawn. Disconnect the operating handle cable, and the door trim panel wiring plugs as they become accessible **(see illustrations)**.

Rear door

7 Undo the 2 screws on the underside of the pull handle **(see illustration)**.
8 Using a wide-bladed or wedge tool, carefully prise off the door trim panel, working progressively around the edge of the panel until all the clips have been released **(see illustration 17.5)**. Do not use excessive force; otherwise the clips will be broken.
9 Manoeuvre the door trim panel to the side. Disconnect the operating handle cable, and the door trim panel wiring plugs as they become accessible **(see illustrations)**.
10 Squeeze together the clips and detach the lock button fitting from the underside of the panel **(see illustration)**.

17.6a Lift the panel over the lock button

17.6b Disconnect the operating handle cable…

Refitting

11 Refitting is a reversal of removal. Renew any broken clips.

17.6c …and disconnect the wiring plugs from the control unit

17.7 Remove the Torx screws under the handle

17.9a Disconnect the operating handle cable…

17.9b …and the wiring plugs from the control unit

17.10 Disconnect the lock button fitting

18.2 Prise out the rubber grommets

18.3 Window clamp bolts

18.6 Prise the mirror trim from the door

18 Door module and control unit – removal and refitting

Door module

Removal

Front door

1 Remove the front door inner trim panel as described in Section 17.

2 Prise out the 2 rubber grommets from the module (see illustration).

3 Temporarily reconnect the wiring plug to the door control unit, then raise the window until the window clamp bolts are accessible through the grommet apertures (see illustration). Once the window has been raised, disconnect the control unit wiring plug again.

4 Slacken the clamp bolts and slide the window glass upwards and secure it to the door frame with self-adhesive tape.

5 Disconnect the battery negative lead as described in Chapter 5A Section 4.

6 Carefully prise the triangular door mirror trim from the frame, and disconnect the wiring plug (see illustration).

7 Remove the insulation material from the door mirror triangular trim aperture, and release the wiring harness from the clip (see illustration).

8 Remove the exterior handle as described in Section 21.

9 Peel away the rubber gaskets, then undo the 2 bolts, and slide the door exterior handle bracket towards the front and unhook it (see illustration).

10 Disconnect the wiring plugs from the door control unit (see illustration).

11 Undo the 3 bolts securing the lock at the rear edge of the door (see illustration).

12 Drill out the 10 rivets securing the module to the door frame (see illustration).

18.7 Remove the insulation material

18.9 Exterior handle bracket retaining bolts

18.10 Door control unit wiring plugs

18.11 Undo the door lock bolts

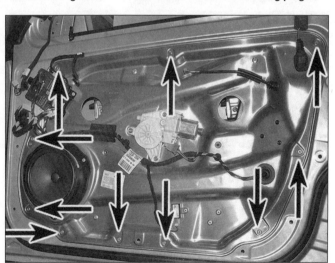

18.12 The door module is secured by 10 rivets

18.13 Carefully remove the door module

18.16 Remove the rubber grommet

18.17 Raise the window until the clamp
bolt is visible

13 Carefully manoeuvre the module from the door **(see illustration)**. Take great care not to bend the module.
14 Before refitting the module, remove all rivet debris from the door frame.

Rear door

15 Remove the door inner trim panel as described in Section 17.
16 Prise the rubber grommet from the module to access the window clamp bolt **(see illustration)**.
17 Temporarily reconnect the door control unit wiring plug, then raise the window until the clamp bolt is accessible though the grommet

aperture **(see illustration)**. Disconnect the control unit wiring plug again.
18 Slacken the clamp bolt and slide the window fully upwards. Secure it to the door frame with self-adhesive tape.
19 Disconnect the battery negative lead as described in Chapter 5A Section 4.
20 Remove the exterior door handle as described in Section 23.
21 Peel away the rubber gaskets, then undo the 2 bolts, and slide the door exterior handle bracket towards the front and unhook it **(see illustrations)**.
22 Disconnect the door harness wiring

plug at the pillar, then prise out the rubber grommet and pull the harness from the door frame.
23 Undo the 3 bolts securing the lock at the rear edge of the door **(see illustration)**.
24 Drill out the 9 rivets securing the module to the door frame **(see illustration)**.
25 Carefully manoeuvre the module from the door **(see illustration)**. Take great care not to bend the module.

Refitting

26 Remove any rivets/drilling swarf from the door frame.

18.21a Peel away the rubber gaskets

18.21b Undo the Torx bolts

18.23 Remove the door lock bolts

18.24 Drill out the door module rivets

18.25 Manoeuvre the module from the door

27 Manoeuvre the module into position, then secure it with new rivets.

28 The remainder of refitting is a reversal of removal.

Door control unit

Removal

Note: *When renewing the front or rear door control unit, prior to removal, the basic data from the old control unit should be transferred to the Mercedes-Benz STAR diagnostic tool, then transferred to the new control unit once fitted.*

29 Open the door, then remove the ignition key and place it at least 2 m away from the vehicle.

Front door

30 Using a blunt, flat-bladed tool, starting at the front edge, carefully prise the control unit cover from the front section of the door trim panel **(see illustration)**.

31 Press the clip at the front edge, and slide the control unit forwards a little **(see illustration)**.

32 Note their fitted positions, and disconnect the wiring plugs, and unclip the harness from the unit **(see illustration)**.

Rear door

33 Remove the door inner trim panel as described in Section 17.

34 Undo the 2 retaining bolts, disconnect the wiring plugs and remove the door control unit **(see illustration)**.

Refitting

35 Refitting is a reversal of removal.

18.30 Starting at the front edge, remove the cover

18.32 Disconnect the wiring plugs from the control unit

18.31 Release the clip at the front edge (panel removed for clarity)

18.34 Rear door control unit retaining bolts

> **19 Front door window glass and electric motor** – removal and refitting

Removal

1 Remove the door inner trim panel as described in Section 17.

Window

2 Prise out the 2 rubber grommets from the module **(see illustration 18.2)**.

3 Temporarily reconnect the wiring plug to

the door control unit, then raise the window until the window clamp bolts are accessible through the grommet apertures **(see illustration 18.3)**. Once the window has been raised, disconnect the control unit wiring plug again.

4 Starting at the rear, unclip the window inner weatherstrip from the door **(see illustration)**.

5 Slacken the window glass clamp bolts, lift up the rear of the glass and manoeuvre it from the door **(see illustration)**.

Electric motor

6 Undo the 3 retaining bolts and remove the electric window motor **(see illustration)**. Disconnect the wiring plug as the motor is withdrawn.

Refitting

7 Refitting is the reverse sequence to removal. Lubricate the regulator sliding channels when reassembling.

> **20 Rear door window glass and electric motor** – removal and refitting

Removal

1 Remove the door inner trim panel as described in Section 17.

Window glass

2 Fully lower the window.

3 Carefully prise up the inner rubber sealing

19.4 Pull up the inner weatherstrip

19.5 Lift the rear of the window and manoeuvre it from the door

19.6 Electric window motor retaining bolts

20.3 Prise up the inner sealing strip

20.4a Prise out the rear rubber strip...

20.4b ...and the front rubber strip

20.5a Undo the Torx screws...

20.5b ...and remove the exterior cover

6 Prise out the rubber grommet from the door module to access the window clamp bolt **(see illustration 18.16)**.
7 Temporarily reconnect the door control unit wiring plugs, then raise/lower the window until the clamp bolt is accessible though the grommet aperture **(see illustration 18.17)**. Disconnect the control unit wiring plugs again.
8 Slacken the window clamp bolt.
9 Manoeuvre the window glass from the door **(see illustration)**.

Electric motor

10 Disconnect the wiring plug, undo the 3 bolts and pull the electric motor from place **(see illustration)**.

Refitting

11 Refitting is the reverse sequence to removal. Lubricate the regulator sliding channels when reassembling.

20.9 Slide the glass upwards and outwards

20.10 Window motor retaining bolts

21 Front door exterior handle – removal and refitting

Removal

1 Prise out the grommet from the rear edge of the door **(see illustration)**.
2 Using a T20 Torx screwdriver, slacken the screw until the rear handle cover is released **(see illustration)**.
3 Operate the handle and remove the rear cover **(see illustration)**.

strip from the upper edge of the door **(see illustration)**.
4 Carefully pull out the outer rear rubber strip from the rear edge of the door front frame,

followed the front edge **(see illustrations)**.
5 Undo the 3 Torx screws and remove the exterior cover from the front of the door frame **(see illustrations)**.

21.1 Prise the grommet from the door

21.2 Slacken the screw until the handle cover is released

21.3 Remove the rear cover

21.4 Disconnect the wiring plug from the cylinder

4 On the drivers side, operate the handle again, and withdraw the lock cylinder assembly **(see illustration)**. Disconnect any wiring plug as the assembly is withdrawn.

22.2 Lift the clip and slide the bearing bracket from place

22.4 Slide the fitting from the bracket and disconnect the cable

22.7 Drill out the rivet, and press-out the plastic 'bolts'

21.5 Pull the handle rearwards

5 Pull the exterior handle rearwards and away from the door **(see illustration)**. Disconnect any wiring plugs as they become accessible.

22.3 Disengage the rod from the lever

22.6 Lift the clip and remove the cover

23.1 Remove the rubber grommet

Refitting

6 Refitting is the reverse sequence to removal. Check the lock operation before closing the door.

22 Front door lock assembly – removal and refitting

Removal

1 Remove the door module as described in Section 18.
2 Unclip the bearing bracket from the cover **(see illustration)**.
3 Unhook the release rod from the lock **(see illustration)**.
4 Unhook the release cable from the bearing bracket **(see illustration)**.
5 Unclip the wiring harness from the bearing bracket.
6 Release the clip and remove the cover from the lock **(see illustration)**.
7 Drill out the rivet at the front of the lock, and press-out the 3 plastic 'bolts' with a suitable punch **(see illustration)**. Take care not to bend the door module.
8 Unclip the wiring harness from the door lock.
9 Using a suitable tool, prise the door lock from the module in the area of the bracket.
10 Unclip the rubber grommets, then remove the lock, feeding the release cables through the module as it's withdrawn.

Refitting

11 Refitting is a reversal of removal.

23 Rear door exterior handle – removal and refitting

Removal

1 Prise out the rubber grommet at the rear edge of the door **(see illustration)**.
2 Slacken the T20 Torx retaining bolt just enough until the door handle cover is loose **(see illustration)**.

23.2 Slacken the Torx screw until the handle cover is loose

23.3 Operate the handle and pull out the cover

23.4 Slide/pull the handle from the door

3 Pull the exterior handle, and remove the door handle cover **(see illustration)**.
4 Pull the exterior handle rearwards and away from the door **(see illustration)**. Disconnect any wiring plugs as they become accessible.

Refitting

5 Refitting is a reversal of removal, ensuring the handle gaskets/seals are in place.

24 Rear door lock assembly – removal and refitting

Removal

1 Remove the door module as described in Section 18.
2 Release the catch and detach the bearing bracket **(see illustrations)**.

3 Unhook the release cable from the bracket **(see illustration)**.
4 Drill out the two rivets at the front of the door lock **(see illustration)**.
5 Move the cover aside, then knock out the 3 plastic plugs with a suitable punch **(see illustration)**. Take care not to bend the door module.
6 Carefully prise the door lock from the module.
7 Unclip the wiring harness, and disconnect the wiring plug from the lock.
8 Unclip the rubber grommets, then manoeuvre the lock from place, feeding the cables through the door module apertures as it's withdrawn.

Refitting

9 Refitting is a reversal of removal.

25 Central locking system components – removal and refitting

Lock switches and actuators

1 The switches and actuators are all part of the door lock assemblies. Remove the lock assemblies as described in the relevant Section. See your local Mercedes dealer for availability of components for the lock assembly.

Infra-red receivers

2 The receivers are only fitted to those locks which are equipped with lock switches, ie, the front doors.
3 The receivers for the front doors are incorporated into the exterior handles. Removal of the handles are described in Section 21.

Control units

4 The door control units are located behind the door inner trim panels. Removal and refitting of the units is described in Section 18.

'Keyless Go' control module

5 Remove the access panel in the right-hand side luggage compartment trim panel.
6 Where applicable, remove the first aid kit.
7 Slacken the 2 retaining bolts then withdraw the control module and bracket. Disconnect the wiring plugs as the module is withdrawn.

26 Door – removal and refitting

Removal

Front door

1 Fully lower the door window, then prise the cover from the front edge of the door inner trim panel **(see illustration 18.30)**.
2 Disconnect the battery negative lead as described in Chapter 5A Section 4.
3 Disconnect the door wiring harness plugs from the door control unit.
4 Unclip the wiring harness gaiter from the door, and pull the wiring harness through.

24.2a Lift the catch...

24.2b ...and detach the bearing bracket

24.3 Detach the release cable

24.4 Drill out the two rivets

24.5 Punch out the plastic plugs

5 Prise off the caps and remove the hinge bolts **(see illustration)**.
6 With the help of an assistant, lift the door from the hinge, and manoeuvre it from the vehicle.

Rear door

7 Fully lower the window, then remove the ignition key and place it at least 2 m away from the vehicle.
8 Disconnect the battery negative lead as described in Chapter 5A Section 4.
9 Release the catch and disconnect the door wiring harness plug at the B-pillar.
10 Prise off the caps, and remove the hinge bolts **(see illustration 26.5)**.
11 With the help of an assistant, lift the door from the hinge, and manoeuvre it from the vehicle.

Refitting

12 Refitting is a reversal of removal.

27 Windscreen and fixed window glass – general information

1 Due to the methods of attachment, and the special equipment required to complete the task successfully, removal and refitting of the windscreen, rear/tailgate window (and rear side windows on Estate models) should be entrusted to a dealer or an automotive glass specialist.

28 Door mirror – removal and refitting

Complete mirror assembly

1 Unclip the mirror inner cover from the inside of the door **(see illustration)**, then remove the sound insulation material.
2 Prise the cover from the front of the door **(see illustration 18.30)**.
3 Disconnect the mirror wiring plugs from the door control unit, and unclip the mirror wiring harness **(see illustration)**.
4 Undo the 3 retaining bolts, and remove the mirror **(see illustration)**. Take care not to drop the bolts.

26.5 Prise off the caps

28.3 Disconnect the mirror wiring plugs

5 Manoeuvre the mirror along with wiring, from the door.
6 Refitting is a reversal of removal.

Mirror glass

7 Pull the lower edge of the mirror glass rearwards, then using a plastic wedge (or similar) lever the mirror rearwards to release the retaining clips **(see illustrations)**. Disconnect any wiring plugs as the mirror is withdrawn.
8 Clip the glass back into place from the bottom upwards.

Mirror cover

Early models

9 Remove the mirror glass as described earlier in this Section.
10 Undo the 3 bolts and remove the mirror frame.
11 Fold the mirror rearwards.
12 Depress the retaining clips and remove the mirror cover.

28.1 Prise the cover from place

28.4 Door mirror retaining bolts

13 Refitting is a reversal of removal.

Later models

14 Remove the mirror glass as described earlier in this Section.
15 Release the catch and slide the mirror upper trim upwards **(see illustrations)**.

28.7a Carefully prise the lower edge rearwards to release the clips

28.7b Disconnect the mirror wiring plugs

28.15a Prise the catch rearwards a little...

28.15b ...and slide the mirror trim upwards

28.16 Lower trim retaining bolts

29.2 Gently prise down the rain/light sensor cover

29.3 Unclip the mirror base cover

16 Undo the 2 retaining bolts, release the 3 clips and slide the mirror lower trim downwards **(see illustration)**.
17 If required, unclip the ambient light unit from the lower trim.
18 Refitting is a reversal of removal.

29 Interior mirror – removal and refitting

Removal

1 Switch off the ignition and remove the key from the EIS. On models with 'Keyless Go' place the transmitter key out of range of the vehicle.

2 Using a blunt, flat-bladed tool, carefully prise the rain/light sensor cover downwards and remove it **(see illustration)**.
3 Unclip the mirror base cover from the overhead console **(see illustration)**.
4 Using a blunt, flat-bladed tool, press-in the clip at the rear and lower the overhead control panel **(see illustrations)**.
5 Disconnect the mirror wiring plugs from the overhead console.
6 Gently pull down the front edge and release the mirror from it's base **(see illustration)**.

Refitting

7 Squeeze together the retaining pins with pliers until the clip engages, and retains the pins **(see illustration)**.
8 Press the mirror up into position. As the clip

contacts the mounting, the retaining pins will be released, securing the mirror.
9 The remainder of refitting is a reversal of removal.

30 Front seats – removal and refitting

Removal

1 Lower the head restraint, move the front seat fully upright, fully forward, and as high as possible.
2 Unclip the seat belt anchor trim from the seat outer panel **(see illustration)**.
3 Undo the bolt and detach the seat belt from the seat cushion **(see illustration)**.

29.4a Use a flat tool...

29.4b ..to press-in the clip

29.6 Pull down the front edge and release the mirror

29.7 Squeeze until the clip engages

30.2 Starting at the lower edge, unclip the trim

30.3 Undo the seat belt bolt

30.4 Seat rail rear bolts

30.5 Note the brackets under the bolt heads

30.8 Disconnect the wiring plugs from the underside of the front seat

4 Undo the 2 bolts at the rear of the seat rails **(see illustration)**.

5 Move the seat fully rearwards, then undo the bolts at the front of the seat rails **(see illustration)**.

6 Disconnect the battery negative lead as described in Chapter 5A Section 4.

7 Wait at least 10 minutes for any residual electric energy to dissipate.

8 Lift up the front of the seat, note their fitted positions, and disconnect the various wiring plugs **(see illustration)**. Unclip the wiring harness from the seat underside.

9 Where applicable, disconnect the air pipe from the seat underside.

10 With the help of an assistant, carefully manoeuvre the seat from the passenger cabin. *Caution: The seats are extremely heavy!*

Refitting

11 Refitting is a reversal of removal, noting the following points:
a) *Renew the seat mounting bolts.*
b) *Tighten all fasteners to their specified torque where given.*
c) *Reconnect the battery negative lead as described in Chapter 5A Section 4.*

31 Rear seats – removal and refitting

Seat cushion

1 Pull up the front edge of the cushion to

release it from the guide sleeves each side **(see illustration)**.

2 Push the cushion rearwards and disengage the retaining brackets at the rear from the guides.

3 Disconnect any wiring plugs and remove the seat cushion from the vehicle.

Seat backrest

Non-through loading – Saloon

4 Remove the seat cushion as previously described in this Section.

5 Undo the retaining bolts and nuts each side at the lower, front edge.

6 Working in the luggage compartment, release the catch each side and push the backrest forwards **(see illustration)**.

7 Lift the backrest a little, pull out the seat belts, and manoeuvre the backrest from place.

Through-loading – Saloon and Estate

8 Remove the rear seat cushion as described previously in this Section.

9 Undo the screw at the lower edge, then pull the side bolster each side forwards to release the retaining clip **(see illustrations)**.

10 Lift the upholstery strip at the base of the backrest, and unclip the wire hook from the bracket, then remove the strip **(see illustration)**.

11 Undo the centre seat belt lower anchorage

31.1 Firmly pull up the front edge of the seat cushion

31.6 Working through the holes, move the release catch to the left

31.9a Undo the screw...

31.9b ...pull the bolster forwards to release the centre clip, then downwards to release the loop

31.10 Unclip the wire hook from the bracket

31.11 Centre seat belt lower anchorage bolt

31.12a Undo the screw...

31.12b ...and pivot up the cover

31.14 Undo the pivot bracket bolts each side

bolt, and disconnect the wiring plug **(see illustration)**.

12 Undo the centre bracket screw, and pivot upwards the bracket cover **(see illustrations)**.

13 Release the catches and fold the backrest forwards.

14 Undo the 2 bolts each side at the pivot brackets **(see illustration)**.

15 Manoeuvre the backrest(s) from place. Disconnect any wiring plugs as the backrest(s) are withdrawn.

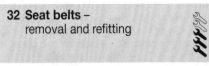

32 Seat belts –
removal and refitting

Warning: All models are equipped with spring-loaded automatic tensioning devices fitted to the

front seat belt inertia reel assemblies. The belt tensioners are triggered by the airbag system in the event of an accident. For safety reasons, no attempt should be made to dismantle the front seat belt inertia reels, and no electrical testing should be performed on any of the wiring associated with the airbag or belt tensioner system – work of this nature must be entrusted to a Mercedes-Benz dealer.

Caution: Although no specific precautions are given by the manufacturer, it seems prudent to treat the seat belt tensioner with as much care as an airbag unit (see Chapter 12). Therefore, do not drop or strike the tensioner, nor subject it to extremes of heat. If there is any doubt about the condition of the seat belt or tensioner, refer to a Mercedes-Benz dealer – DO NOT attempt to dismantle the belt

reel or tensioner, as this could be highly dangerous. If any noise has been noted from the seat belt mechanism, do not attempt to cure this by applying lubricants of any kind. A noise from the tensioner may indicate an internal fault, or it may be that the unit has 'fired', and is therefore no longer operative.

Front belts

Inertia reel

1 Prise up the cover, undo the bolt and disconnect the seat belt anchorage from the seat **(see illustration 30.2 and 30.3)**.

2 Disconnect the battery negative lead as described in Chapter 5A Section 4.

3 Remove the B-pillar trim panel as described in Section 35.

4 Undo the nut and remove the seat belt upper anchorage **(see illustration)**.

5 Undo seat belt guide bolt from the B-pillar.

6 Undo the retaining bolts and remove the reel **(see illustration)**. Disconnect the wiring plugs as the inertia reel is withdrawn.

7 Refitting is a reversal of removal, tightening the retaining bolts to their specified torque where given.

Note: *On models with the 'Pre-Safe' option, if a new inertia reel is fitted, it must be initialised using Mercedes-Benz Start diagnostic equipment (or equivalent).*

Buckle

8 Remove the relevant front seat as described in Section 30.

9 Undo the seat belt buckle retaining nut.

10 Unclip the seat belt buckle wiring plug, and release the wiring harness from any clips.

Rear belts

Inertia reel – side belts

11 Disconnect the battery negative lead as described in Chapter 5A Section 4.

Saloon

12 Remove the C-pillar trim panels as described in Section 35.

13 Move the insulation material to one side, undo the retaining bolt and manoeuvre the seat belt inertia reel from place **(see illustration)**. Disconnect the wiring plugs as the inertia reel is withdrawn.

32.4 Seat belt upper anchorage bolt

32.6 Inertia reel retaining bolts

32.13 Rear side seat belt inertia reel retaining bolt

14 Refitting is a reversal of removal, tightening the retaining bolts to their specified torque where given.

Estate

15 Remove the rear seat cushion as described in Section 31.

16 Undo the seat belt lower anchorage bolt **(see illustration)**.

17 Remove the luggage compartment side trim panel and C-pillar trim panel as described in Section 35.

18 Undo the bolt at the lower edge, pull the centre of the side bolster from the clip, then lower it to release the upper clip **(see illustrations 31.9a and 31.9b)**.

19 Undo the retaining bolt and remove the cover over the inertia reel **(see illustration 35.69)**.

20 Undo the 4 bolts/2 nuts and remove the reel along with the bracket **(see illustration)**. Disconnect the wiring plug as the reel is withdrawn.

21 If required, undo the bolt and detach the inertia reel from the bracket.

22 Refitting is a reversal of removal, tightening the retaining bolts to their specified torque where given.

Inertia reel – centre belt

Estate, and Saloon models with through-loading

23 Where fitted, the centre seat belt is incorporated into the seat itself, and can only be removed by dismantling the seat, which includes removing the seat covering. This job is considered beyond the scope of this manual, and is best entrusted to a Mercedes-Benz dealer.

Saloon – without through-loading

24 Remove the rear parcel shelf as described in Section 35.

25 Undo the seat belt lower anchorage bolt.

26 Undo the retaining bolt and manoeuvre the seat belt inertia reel from place.

27 Refitting is a reversal of removal. Tighten the fasteners to their specified torque where given.

Buckle

28 Remove the rear seat cushion as described in Section 31.

29 Undo the bolt and remove the relevant seat belt stalk.

30 Refitting is a reversal of removal, tightening the retaining bolts to their specified torque where given.

33 Sunroof – general information

1 A sliding sunroof, either mechanically- or electrically-operated, is available as a factory-fitted option. Adjustment or repair of the sunroof or its component parts should be left to the dealer or specialist, as the complexity of the unit and the need for special tools and equipment renders these operations beyond the scope of this manual.

34 Body exterior fittings – removal and refitting

Wheelarch liners and body under-panels

1 The various plastic covers fitted to the underside of the vehicle are secured in position by a mixture of screws, nuts and retaining clips, and removal will be fairly obvious on inspection **(see illustration)**. Work methodically around, removing its retaining screws and releasing its retaining clips until the panel is free and can be removed from the underside of the vehicle. Most clips used on the vehicle are simply prised out of position. Other clips can be released by unscrewing/

32.16 Seat belt lower anchorage bolt

prising out the centre pins and then removing the clip.

2 On refitting, renew any retaining clips that may have been broken on removal, and ensure that the panel is securely retained by all the relevant clips and screws.

Body trim strips and badges

3 The various body trim strips and badges are held in position with a special adhesive tape. Removal requires the trim/badge to be heated, to soften the adhesive, and then cut away from the surface. Due to the high risk of damage to the vehicle's paintwork during this operation, it is recommended that this task should be entrusted to a Mercedes dealer or suitably-equipped specialist.

35 Interior trim – removal and refitting

Interior trim panels – general

1 The interior trim panels are secured using either screws or various types of trim fasteners, usually studs or clips.

2 Check that there are no other panels overlapping the one to be removed; usually

32.20 Seat belt real bracket retaining nuts/bolts

34.1 Wheelarch liner fasteners – there are more along the outer edges

35.8 Pull the top edge from the pillar...

35.9 ...and slide the panel upwards

35.13 Pull up the front and rear door sill trim panels

there is a sequence that has to be followed that will become obvious on close inspection.
3 Remove all obvious fasteners, such as screws. If the panel will not come free, it is held by hidden clips or fasteners. These are usually situated around the edge of the panel and can be prised up to release them; note, however that they can break quite easily so new ones should be available. The best way of releasing such clips, without the correct type of tool, is to use a large flat-bladed screwdriver. Note that some panels are secured by plastic expanding rivets, where the centre pin must be prised up before the rivet can be removed. Note in many cases that the adjacent sealing strip must be prised back to release a panel.
4 When removing a panel, never use excessive force or the panel may be damaged; always check carefully that all fasteners have been removed or released before attempting to withdraw a panel.

5 Refitting is the reverse of the removal procedure; secure the fasteners by pressing them firmly into place and ensure that all disturbed components are correctly secured to prevent rattles.

A-pillar trim panel

6 Due to the proximity of the headlining airbag, disconnect the battery negative lead as described in Chapter 5A Section 4, then wait at least 10 minutes for any residual electrical energy to dissipate.
7 Pull the rubber weatherstrip away adjacent to the A-pillar.
8 Using a blunt-, flat-bladed tool, carefully prise the upper edge of the A-pillar trim panel from place (see illustration).
9 Slide the A-pillar trim panel upwards from the retaining clip guides (see illustration).
10 Refitting is a reversal of removal; secure the fasteners by pressing them firmly into place

and ensure that all disturbed components are correctly secured to prevent rattles.

B-pillar trim panel

11 Move the front seat fully forwards and upwards, the prise the cover from the seat base, and remove the seat belt anchorage bolt (see illustration 30.2 and 30.3).
12 Pull the rubber weatherstrip from each side of the B-pillar.
13 Starting at the rear edges, pull up and remove the front, and rear door sill trim panels (see illustration).
14 Using a blunt, flat-bladed tool, carefully prise the upper and lower B-pillar panel retaining clips from the metal pillar. Feed the seat belt through the upper trim panel as it's withdrawn (see illustrations).
15 Refitting is a reversal of removal; secure the fasteners by pressing them firmly into place and ensure that all disturbed components are correctly secured to prevent rattles.

C-pillar trim panel

Saloon

16 Remove the rear seat cushion as described in Section 31.
17 Pull away the rubber weatherstrip adjacent to the C-pillar.
18 Undo the rear side seatbelt lower anchorage bolt(s).
19 Pull the pillar trim panel inwards at the front top edge to release the retaining clip, then rotate the panel forwards and manoeuvre it from place (see illustrations). Note how the panel engages with the parcel shelf.

35.14a Prise the pillar panel clip from the pillar

35.14b Note the lugs at the top of the upper trim panel

35.19a Pull the top of the C-pillar trim panel inwards...

35.19b ...then rotate it forwards to release the clip...

35.19c ...and disengage it from the parcel shelf

35.23a Release the C-pillar trim panel retaining clips

35.23b Note the lug at the top of the panel

35.24 Press the metal clips onto the pillar edge

20 Refitting is a reversal of removal; fit the rear upper retaining clip to the panel prior to refitting.

Estate

21 Fold the seat backrest fully forwards.
22 Pull away the rubber weatherstrip adjacent to the C-pillar.
23 Pull the front edge of the C-pillar trim panel forwards a little to release the clips, then pull the rear edge rearwards to release the clips, Lower the panel from place noting the lug at the upper edge (**see illustrations**).
24 Refitting is a reversal of removal. Detach the rear metal clips from the trim panel and

fit them to the pillar edge prior to refitting the panel (**see illustration**).

D-pillar trim panel

25 Due to the proximity of the headlining airbag on some models, disconnect the battery negative lead as described in Chapter 5A Section 4, then wait at least 10 minutes for any residual electrical energy to dissipate.
26 On models equipped with a speaker in the D-pillar trim panel, using a blunt, flat-bladed tool, carefully prise the rear edge of the speaker grille from the panel, and remove it. Disconnect any wiring plugs as it's withdrawn.
27 On models without a speaker in the

D-pillar trim panel, prise out the light unit and disconnect the wiring plug (**see illustration**).
28 Pull the D-pillar trim panel inwards to release the retaining clips (**see illustrations**).
29 Refitting is a reversal of removal.

Door trim panels

30 See Section 17.

Tailgate trim panels

31 Using a blunt, flat-bladed tool, carefully prise the pull-down handle trims and remove the 2 screws exposed (**see illustrations**).
32 Pull the lower trim panel from the tailgate (**see illustration**). Disconnect the wiring plugs as they become accessible.

35.27 Prise out the light unit

35.28a Pull the D-pillar trim panel inwards...

35.28b ...to release the clips

35.31a Prise the pull-down hand trim from place...

35.31b ...and undo the Torx screws

35.32 Prise the lower trim panel from the tailgate

35.33 Pull the trim panel away to release the clips

35.34 Prise the rear window surround trim from place

33 Using a suitable tool, carefully prise the main trim panel away from the tailgate, and remove the clip in the centre **(see illustration)**.
34 Using a blunt, flat-bladed tool, carefully unclip the rear window left-hand trim surround **(see illustration)**.
35 Then unclip the right-hand trim surround.

Boot lid trim panel

36 Undo the 4 screws at the rear edge, prise out the 3 retaining clips and remove the plastic panel from the rear of the boot lid **(see illustrations)**. Disconnect any wiring plugs as the panel is withdrawn.
37 Prise out the clip securing the hinge cover each side **(see illustration)**.
38 Remove the warning triangle, then release the 4 retaining clips and remove the mounting bracket **(see illustration)**.
39 The boot lid trim panel is now secured by

numerous push-on plastic clips, Prise out the clips and remove the panel **(see illustration)**.
40 Refitting is a reversal of removal.

Parcel shelf

41 On models without through-loading, remove the rear seat backrests and cushion as described in Section 31. On models with through-loading, fold the seat backrests fully forwards.
42 Remove the C-pillar trim panels as described earlier in this Section. Note there is no need to detach the lower seat belt anchorages.

Models with an electric rear window roller blind

43 Remove the left, and right-hand rear seat belt inertia reels as described in Section 32.
44 Disconnect the roller blind wiring plug.
45 Working in the luggage compartment,

undo the nut and bolt each side on the underside of the parcel shelf.

All models

46 Prise up the centre pins, lever out the plastic expansion rivets at the front edge of the parcel shelf **(see illustration)**.
47 Lift the front edge of the parcel shelf, and manoeuvre it from place.
48 Refitting is a reversal of removal.

Headlining

49 The rigid headlining is clipped to the roof, and can only be withdrawn once all fittings such as the grab handles, sunvisors, interior light, and related trim panels have been removed, and the door, tailgate and sunroof aperture sealing strips have been prised clear.
50 As with carpet removal, taking out the headlining is not especially difficult, just time-consuming.

Footwell kick panels

51 Pull away the rubber weatherstrip adjacent to the A-pillar.
52 Pull the door sill trim panel upwards at the front edge.
53 Pull the kickpanel rearwards to release the retaining clips.
54 Refitting is a reversal of removal.

Luggage compartment side trim panel

Saloon

55 Where applicable, fold the rear seat backrests forwards, or remove the backrest as described in Section 31.

35.36a Undo the screws (right-hand screws arrowed)...

35.36b ...and prise out the clips

35.37 Prise out the clip and remove the hinge cover

35.38 Release the clips and remove the mounting bracket

35.39 Prise out the clips and remove the panel

35.46 Prise up the centre pins, and lever out the plastic expansion rivets

35.56 Prise out the clips and remove the floor panel

35.58 Boot rear panel trim retaining nuts

35.59 Prise up the covers and undo the stowage anchor bolts

35.60a Prise out the clips at the rear...

35.60b ...and the clip at the front

35.60c Prise out the upper part first, then remove the bag hook

35.61a Remove the front stowage anchors...

35.61b ...and slide the carrier plate cover rearwards

bag hook securing the luggage compartment side panels **(see illustrations)**. Note that the upper part of the hook must be prised out.
61 On models with through-loading, undo the remove the front stowage anchors, slide the carrier plate cover rearwards from behind the rear seats **(see illustrations)**.
62 Prise out the luggage compartment light, and disconnect the wiring plug (right-hand side panel only).
63 Manoeuvre the side panel from the vehicle.
64 Refitting is a reversal of removal.

Estate

65 Remove the C-pillar trim panel as described earlier in this Section.
66 Working in the luggage compartment, open the access panel, remove the 2 plastic expansion rivets, undo the 4 screws and lift the side cover guide rail upwards from the clips **(see illustrations)**.

56 Prise out the clips and lift out the luggage compartment floor panel **(see illustration)**.
57 Where applicable, lift out the spare wheel well.
58 Slacken the 2 plastic nuts, and prise the

boot rear panel trim upwards from place **(see illustration)**.
59 Undo the bolts and remove the stowage anchors **(see illustration)**.
60 Prise out the plastic clips, and the shopping

35.66a Undo the 4 screws...

35.66b ...prise out the centre pins, and remove the plastic rivets

35.66c Lift up the side cover guide rail

35.67a Undo the stowage anchor bolt

35.67b Undo the bolt, prise up the centre pin and remove the plastic rivet

35.67c Slide the side bracket reawards and remove it

35.68 Lift out the floor panel

35.69 Undo the bolt and remove the cover

67 Remove the rear stowage anchors, prise out the centre pin, undo the bolt and slide out the side bracket each side **(see illustrations)**.
68 Remove the front stowage anchors, and lift the front section of the floor panel from place **(see illustration)**.
69 Undo the bolt and remove the cover above the rear seat belt inertia reels **(see illustration)**.
70 Prise off the trim surrounding the backrest securing bracket **(see illustration)**.
71 Prise up the centre pin, and lever out the plastic expansion rivet from the front lower edge of the side panel trim **(see illustration)**.
72 Rotate the roller buffer surround clockwise and remove it **(see illustration)**.
73 Carefully lift the side panel trim from place, disconnecting any wiring plugs as they become accessible **(see illustration)**.

Glovebox

74 Move the front passengers seat fully rearward.
75 Remove passengers side lower facia panel as described in Section 37.
76 Using a blunt, flat-bladed tool, carefully prise the panel from the end of the facia **(see illustration)**. Disconnect any wiring plugs as the panel is withdrawn.
77 Where applicable, disconnect the AUX

35.70 Prise off the bracket trim

35.71 Remove the plastic expansion rivet

35.72 Rotate the buffer surround clockwise

35.73 Lift the panel trim and disconnect any wiring plugs

35.76 Prise the panel from the end of the facia

35.77a Prise out the collar a little...

35.77b ...and pull the AUX socket from the side of the glovebox

35.78a Remove the screw at the outer edge of the glovebox...

socket wiring plug at the end of the facia **(see illustrations)**.

78 Undo the screw each side at the lower edge of the glovebox **(see illustrations)**.

79 The glovebox is now secured by 5 bolts **(see illustration)**. Undo the bolts and manoeuvre the glovebox from the vehicle. Disconnect any wiring plugs as the glovebox is withdrawn.

80 Refitting is a reversal of removal.

Glovebox lock cylinder

81 Insert the emergency key into the glovebox lock cylinder, then rotate it 45° clockwise and pull the lock cylinder from the housing **(see illustration)**.

82 Refitting is a reversal of removal. The lock cylinder should emit an audible 'click' when refitted correctly.

Sunvisors

83 Prise away the mounting cover, then carefully pull down the front edge of the mounting, and unhook the rear edge **(see illustrations)**.

84 Refitting is a reversal of removal.

Grab handles

85 Prise the covers from the mountings, then insert a small screwdriver in the smaller of the two slots, release the clips and pull the grab handles from the headlining **(see illustrations)**.

86 Refitting is a reversal of removal.

35.78b ...and the screw at the inner edge

35.79 Undo the bolts and remove the glovebox

35.81 Rotate the key 45° and pull out the lock cylinder

35.83a Prise down the cover...

35.83b ...and pull down the front edge of the mounting

35.85a Prise open the cover...

35.85b ...then use a screwdriver to push-in the clip

36.2 Prise up the lever gaiter

36.3 Prise the control panel trim from place

36.5 Pull up the front edge of the panel

36.7 Ashtray/storage unit retaining screws

36.8 Remove the screw each side, and the nut in the centre

36.9 Unclip the panel at the rear

Carpet

87 The passenger compartment floor carpet is in one piece (with a separate piece used in the luggage area), and is secured at its edges by screws or clips, usually the same fasteners used to secure the various adjoining trim panels.

88 Carpet removal and refitting is reasonably straightforward, but very time-consuming, due to the fact that all adjoining trim panels must be removed first, as must components such as the seats, the centre console and seat belt lower anchorages.

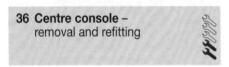

36 Centre console –
removal and refitting

Removal

1 Fully apply the parking brake, then move the selector lever to position 'N' (where applicable). Switch off the ignition and place the key at least 2 m away from the vehicle.

2 Carefully prise up the gear/selector lever gaiter **(see illustration)**.

3 On vehicles upto 2012 model year, prise the heater/AC control panel surround trim from place **(see illustration)**.

4 On vehicles from 2012 model year, remove the heating/AC control unit as described in Chapter 3 Section 8.

5 Open the ashtray/storage box at the front of the console, and starting at the front edge, pull up the gearchange/selector lever surround panel **(see illustration)**. Disconnect any wiring plugs as the panel is lifted.

6 Lift out the foam insulation (where fitted), then disconnect the wiring plug each side in the gear/selector lever aperture.

7 On vehicles from 2012 model year, undo the 2 screws and lift out the ashtray/storage unit **(see illustration)**. Disconnect any wiring plugs.

8 Undo the screw each side beneath the control panel location, and the nut at the centre-front of the gear/selector lever aperture **(see illustration)**.

9 At the rear of the console, unclip the lower panel or remove the ashtray as applicable **(see illustration)**. Disconnect any wiring plug as the cover/ashtray is withdrawn.

10 Undo the two nuts at the rear of the console **(see illustration)**.

11 Disconnect the console wiring plugs, and release the plug brackets as necessary.

12 Where applicable, unclip the media interface connector from the storage box, and feed it back through the opening **(see illustration)**.

13 Lift the lug at the front of the console, then with the help of an assistant, manoeuvre the console from place **(see illustration)**.

36.10 Undo the nuts at the rear

36.12 Feed the interface connector back through the opening

36.13 Lift the lug at the front

Refitting

14 Refitting is a reversal of removal. Ensure all wiring is securely reconnected, and the harness correctly routed.

37 Facia panel assembly –
removal and refitting

Lower facia panels

1 Pull the door sill trim panel upwards to release its' retaining clips **(see illustration)**.
2 Pull away the rubber weatherstrip from the A-pillar adjacent to the kick panel.
3 Pull the footwell kick panel rearwards to release the clips **(see illustration)**.
4 Undo the 3 retaining screws, and lower the facia panel **(see illustration)**.
5 Disconnect any wiring plugs as they become accessible and remove the panel.

Complete facia

6 Set the air distribution controls to the footwells.
7 Unlock the car, remove the ignition key and place it at least 2 m away from the vehicle.
8 Disconnect the battery negative lead as described in Chapter 5A Section 4.
9 Remove the glovebox as described in Section 35.
10 Unclip and remove the air duct from the passenger side of the facia **(see illustration)**.
11 Remove both A-pillar trim panels as described in Section 35.

37.1 Starting at the front, pull the sill trim panel upwards

Vehicles upto 2012 model year

12 Open the storage cover in the centre of the facia, or fold up the display screen as applicable.
13 Prise out the rubber buffers, then insert a suitable tool, and release the upper catches securing the central air vent **(see illustrations)**.
14 Pull the central air vent from the facia. Disconnect any wiring plugs as the vent is withdrawn.

All vehicles

15 Remove the radio/audio unit as described in Chapter 12 Section 16.
16 Remove the facia speaker as described in Chapter 12 Section 17.
17 Remove the centre console as described in Section 36.
18 If not already done so, remove the heating/AC control panel as described in Chapter 3 Section 8.

37.3 Pull the kick panel rearwards

19 On models with KEYLESS GO, disconnect the interior antenna wiring plug.
20 Remove both lower facia panels as described previously in this Section.
21 Prise the trim panel from each end of the facia **(see illustration)**. Disconnect any wiring plugs as the panels are withdrawn.
22 Reach up behind the facia and unclip the parking brake cable from the release lever **(see illustration)**.
23 Reach behind the facia and disconnect the lighting switch wiring plug.
24 Working under the facia, disconnect the wiring plug from the temperature sensor in each end air vent duct, and release the wiring harnesses from the clips.
25 Remove the steering column combination switch assembly, as described in Chapter 12 Section 5.
26 Remove the instrument cluster as described in Chapter 12 Section 10.

37.4 Lower facia panel retaining screws

37.10 Prise out the clip and remove the air duct

37.13a Insert the rods through the holes...

37.13b ...then depress the clips and pull the centre air vent rearwards

37.21 Prise the panel from each end of the facia

37.22 Disconnect the brake cable from the lever

37.28 Unclip the panel from the facia

37.29 Use a pair of pliers to unscrew the switch trim ring

37.31 Prise up the panel in the centre of the facia

27 Remove the facia COMAND display unit as described in Chapter 12 Section 16.

28 Unclip the harness bracket from the steering column gaiter, then unclip the gaiter and surround panel from the facia **(see illustration)**.

29 On vehicles before 28/02/11, unscrew the ignition switch trim ring, and press the switch into the facia **(see illustration)**.

30 On vehicles after this date, disconnect the wiring plug from the ignition switch.

31 Prise up the panel and disconnect the wiring plugs from the sensor/warning light in the centre of the facia **(see illustration)**.

32 Disconnect the wiring plug from the drivers knee airbag (where fitted), and undo the nuts at each end of the underside of the air bag **(see illustration)**.

33 Disconnect the wiring plug from each end of the passengers airbag.

34 The upper facia panel is secured by 7 screws **(see illustrations)**. Undo the screws, and with the help of an assistant, manoeuvre the facia panel from place. Note their fitted positions, then disconnect any wiring plugs, and release the wiring harnesses as necessary.

Caution: Take care not to damage the headlining airbag wiring plugs as the upper

section of the facia is manoeuvred from place.

Refitting

35 Refitting is a reversal of removal, noting the following points:

a) *Ensure that all wiring is correctly routed, and is not trapped as the facia panels are refitted.*

b) *Reconnect the battery negative lead as described in Chapter 5A Section 4. Ensure no-one is in the car.*

c) *Upon completion, check that all the electrical components and switches function correctly.*

37.32 Undo the nut and disconnect the wiring plug at each end

37.34a The upper facia panel is secured by 2 screws at the drivers end...

37.34b ...2 screws in the centre, lower area...

37.34c ...a screw beneath the passengers airbag...

37.34d ...a screw at the passengers end...

37.34e ...and one in the aperture top, centre

Chapter 12
Body electrical systems

Contents

Section number

Airbag system – general information and precautions. 19
Airbag system components – removal and refitting. 20
Anti-theft alarm – general information 18
Bulbs (exterior lights) – renewal 6
Cameras – removal and refitting 22
Electrical connectors – general information. 4
Electrical fault finding – general information 2
Exterior light units – removal and refitting 8
Fuses, relays and SAM control units – general information. 3
General information and precautions. 1
Headlight beam adjustment – general information 9
Horns – removal and refitting. 12

Section number

Infotainment units – removal and refitting 16
Instrument panel – removal and refitting 10
Interior lights – general information, removal and refitting. 7
Parktronic (PTS) system – general information and component
    renewal 21
Rain/light sensor – removal and refitting 11
Speakers and amplifiers – removal and refitting 17
Switches – removal and refitting 5
Windscreen wiper motor and linkage – removal and refitting 14
Windscreen/tailgate washer system components – removal and
    refitting 15
Wiper arm – removal and refitting 13

Degrees of difficulty

Easy, suitable for novice with little experience	**Fairly easy,** suitable for beginner with some experience	**Fairly difficult,** suitable for competent DIY mechanic	**Difficult,** suitable for experienced DIY mechanic	**Very difficult,** suitable for expert DIY or professional

Specifications

System type.	12 volt negative earth
Fuses	See inside fusebox lid

Bulbs — Wattage

Exterior lights:
Front direction indicator	
Up to 2012 model year.	21 PY
From 2012 model year	24 PY
Directional indicator – Rear	21 PY or LED
Direction indicator side repeater	5W5
Front foglight	55 H11
Front sidelight.	5 capless or LED
Headlight:	
Main beam	55 H7
Dipped beam:	
Halogen.	55 H7
Bi-Xenon	35 DS2
High level stop light	LED
Number plate light	5 festoon
Rear fog light	P21
Reverse.	P21
Stoplight	P21
Tail light.	P21

Interior lights:
Door puddle lights	5 capless
Glovebox light.	5 capless
Interior lights.	5 capless
Luggage compartment lights	5 capless
Overhead console lights.	5 capless
Tailgate lights.	5 capless
Vanity lights	5 capless
Footwell lights.	5 capless

Torque wrench settings

	Nm	lbf ft
Airbag control unit bolts	10	7
Impact sensor bolts	8	6
Passengers airbag nuts	5	4
Steering wheel airbag screws	7	5
Suspension strut to body	33	24

1 General information and precautions

Warning: Before carrying out any work on the electrical system, read through the precautions given in Safety first! at the beginning of this manual and in Chapter 5A Section 1.

1 The electrical system is of the 12 volt negative-earth type. Power for the lights and all electrical accessories is supplied by a lead-acid or AGM (Absorbent Glass Matt) type battery, which is located in the luggage compartment, and is charged by the alternator.

2 This Chapter covers repair and service procedures for the various electrical components not associated with the engine. Information on the battery, alternator and starter motor can be found in Chapter 5A.

3 It should be noted that prior to working on any component in the electrical system, the battery negative terminal should first be disconnected to prevent the possibility of electrical short-circuits and/or fires.

2 Electrical fault finding – general information

Note: Refer to the precautions given in Safety first! and in Chapter 5A Section 1 before starting work. The following tests relate to testing of the main electrical circuits, and should not be used to test delicate electronic circuits (such as anti-lock braking systems), particularly where an electronic control unit/ module (ECU/ECM) is used.

General

1 A typical electrical circuit consists of an electrical component; any switches, relays, motors, fuses, fusible links or circuit breakers related to that component, and the wiring and connectors which link the component to both the battery and the chassis. To help to pin-point a problem in an electrical circuit, wiring diagrams are included at the end of this Chapter.

2 Before attempting to diagnose an electrical fault, first study the appropriate wiring diagram to obtain a complete understanding of the components included in the particular circuit concerned. The possible sources of a fault can be narrowed down by noting if other components related to the circuit are operating properly. If several components or circuits fail at one time, the problem is likely to be related to a shared fuse or earth connection.

3 Electrical problems usually stem from simple causes, such as loose or corroded connections, a faulty earth connection, a blown fuse, a melted fusible link, or a faulty relay (refer to Section 3 for details of testing relays). Visually inspect the condition of all fuses, wires and connections in a problem circuit before testing the components. Use the wiring diagrams to determine which terminal connections will need to be checked in order to pin-point the trouble spot.

4 The basic tools required for electrical fault finding include a circuit tester or voltmeter (a 12 volt bulb with a set of test leads can also be used for certain tests); a self-powered test light (sometimes known as a continuity tester); an ohmmeter (to measure resistance); a battery and set of test leads; and a jumper wire, preferably with a circuit breaker or fuse incorporated, which can be used to bypass suspect wires or electrical components. Before attempting to locate a problem with test instruments, use the wiring diagram to determine where to make the connections.

Warning: Under no circumstances may live measuring instruments such as ohmmeters, voltmeters or a bulb and test leads be used to test any of the airbag circuitry. Any testing of these components must be left to a Mercedes dealer or specialist, as there is a danger of activating the system if the correct procedures are not followed.

5 To find the source of an intermittent wiring fault (usually due to a poor or dirty connection, or damaged wiring insulation), a 'wiggle' test can be performed on the wiring. This involves wiggling the wiring by hand to see if the fault occurs as the wiring is moved. It should be possible to narrow down the source of the fault to a particular section of wiring. This method of testing can be used in conjunction with any of the tests described in the following sub-Sections.

6 Apart from problems due to poor connections, two basic types of fault can occur in an electrical circuit – open-circuit, or short-circuit.

7 Open-circuit faults are caused by a break somewhere in the circuit, which prevents current from flowing. An open-circuit fault will prevent a component from working, but will not cause the relevant circuit fuse to blow.

8 Short-circuit faults are caused by a 'short' somewhere in the circuit, which allows the current flowing in the circuit to 'escape' along an alternative route, usually to earth. Short-circuit faults are normally caused by a breakdown in wiring insulation, which allows a feed wire to touch either another wire, or an earthed component such as the bodyshell. A short-circuit fault will normally cause the relevant circuit fuse to blow.

Caution: The C-Class electrical system is extremely complex. Many of the ECMs are connected via a 'Databus' system, where they are able to share information from the various sensors, and communicate with each other. For instance, as the automatic gearbox approaches a gear ratio shift point, it signals the engine management ECM via the Databus. As the gearchange is made by the transmission ECM, the engine management ECM retards the injection timing, momentarily reducing engine output, to ensure a smoother transition from one gear ratio to the next. Due to the design of the Databus system, it is not advisable to backprobe the ECMs with a multimeter, in the traditional manner. Instead, the electrical systems are equipped with a sophisticated self-diagnosis system, which can interrogate the various ECMs to reveal stored fault codes, and help pin-point faults. In order to access the self-diagnosis system, specialist test equipment (Mercedes STAR – or equivalent) is required.

Finding an open-circuit

9 To check for an open-circuit, connect one lead of a circuit tester or voltmeter to either the negative battery terminal or a known good earth.

10 Connect the other lead to a connector in the circuit being tested, preferably nearest to the battery or fuse.

11 Switch on the circuit, bearing in mind that some circuits are live only when the ignition switch is moved to a particular position.

12 If voltage is present (indicated either by the tester bulb lighting or a voltmeter reading, as applicable), this means that the section of the circuit between the relevant connector and the battery is problem-free.

13 Continue to check the remainder of the circuit in the same fashion.

14 When a point is reached at which no voltage is present, the problem must lie between that point and the previous test point with voltage. Most problems can be traced to a broken, corroded or loose connection.

Finding a short-circuit

15 To check for a short-circuit, first disconnect the load(s) from the circuit (loads are the components which draw current from a circuit, such as bulbs, motors, heating elements, etc).

16 Remove the relevant fuse from the circuit, and connect a circuit tester or voltmeter to the fuse connections.

17 Switch on the circuit, bearing in mind that some circuits are live only when the ignition switch is moved to a particular position.

18 If voltage is present (indicated either by the tester bulb lighting or a voltmeter reading, as applicable), this means that there is a short-circuit.

19 If no voltage is present, but the fuse still blows with the load(s) connected, this indicates an internal fault in the load(s).

Finding an earth fault

20 The battery negative terminal is connected to 'earth' – the metal of the engine/transmission and the car body – and most systems are wired so that they only receive a positive feed, the current returning through the metal of the car body **(see illustrations)**. This means that the component mounting and the body form part of that circuit. Loose

2.20a Earth connections are located in various places, including the transmission/body...

2.20b ...lower A-pillars...

2.20c ...right-hand side of the luggage compartment...

2.20d ...upper section of the tailgate...

2.20e ...front section of the rear wheelarches...

2.20f ...passengers side of the transmission tunnel...

2.20g ...chassis member under the driver's seat...

2.20h ...front suspension turret...

2.20i ...and the front section of the inner wing each side

or corroded mountings can therefore cause a range of electrical faults, ranging from total failure of a circuit, to a puzzling partial fault. In particular, lights may shine dimly (especially when another circuit sharing the same earth point is in operation), motors (eg, wiper motors or the heater fan motor) may run slowly, and the operation of one circuit may have an apparently unrelated effect on another.

21 Note that on many vehicles, earth straps are used between certain components, such as the engine/transmission and the body, usually where there is no metal-to-metal contact between components due to flexible rubber mountings, etc.

22 To check whether a component is properly earthed, disconnect the battery and connect one lead of an ohmmeter to a known good earth point. Connect the other lead to the wire or earth connection being tested. The resistance reading should be zero; if not, check the connection as follows.

23 If an earth connection is thought to be faulty, dismantle the connection and clean back to bare metal both the bodyshell and the wire terminal or the component earth connection mating surface. Be careful to remove all traces of dirt and corrosion, and then use a knife to trim away any paint, so that a clean metal-to-metal joint is made.

24 On reassembly, tighten the joint fasteners securely; if a wire terminal is being refitted, use serrated washers between the terminal and the bodyshell to ensure a clean and secure connection. When the connection is remade, prevent the onset of corrosion in the future by applying a coat of petroleum jelly or silicone-based grease or by spraying on (at regular intervals) a proprietary ignition sealer or a water-dispersant lubricant.

3 Fuses, relays and SAM control units – general information

Main fuses

1 Most of the fuses are situated in the main fusebox, located at in the right-hand rear corner of the engine compartment; there is also another fusebox in the luggage compartment (see illustrations). Note that the fuse allocation chart is located with the vehicle toolkit in the luggage compartment.

2 To access the engine compartment fusebox, unclip the cover in the right-hand rear corner. To access the luggage compartment fuses, unclip the right-hand access panel from luggage compartment (see illustrations).

3 A list of the circuits each fuse protects is given on a diagram sheet inside the toolkit under the luggage compartment floor panel.

3.1a Luggage compartment fuse box

3.1b Engine compartment fusebox

3.2a Release the engine compartment fusebox cover clips

3.2b Unclip the panel to access the luggage compartment fusebox

4 To remove a fuse, first switch off the circuit concerned (or the ignition), and then pull the fuse out of its terminals. The wire within the fuse should be visible; if the fuse is blown it will be broken or melted **(see illustrations)**.

5 Always renew a fuse with one of an identical rating; never use a fuse with a different rating from the original or substitute anything else. Never renew a fuse more than once without tracing the source of the trouble. The fuse rating is stamped on top of the fuse; note that the fuses are also colour-coded for easy recognition.

6 If a new fuse blows immediately, find the cause before renewing it again; a short to earth as a result of faulty insulation is most likely. Where a fuse protects more than one circuit, try to isolate the defect by switching on each circuit in turn (if possible) until the fuse blows again. Always carry a supply of spare fuses of each relevant rating on the vehicle; a spare of each rating should be clipped into the base of the fusebox.

Relays

7 The majority of the relays are located in the engine compartment fuse/relay box.

8 In order to access the relays, release the clips, and remove the cover from the box located in the right-hand rear corner of the engine compartment **(see illustration 3.2a)**. On models equipped with 'Stop-Start' system, an additional relay is located under the luggage compartment floor panel **(see illustration)**.

9 If a circuit or system controlled by a relay develops a fault and the relay is suspect, operate the system; if the relay is functioning it should be possible to hear it click as it is energised. If this is the case the fault lies with the components or wiring of the system. If the relay is not being energised then either the relay is not receiving a main supply or a switching voltage or the relay itself is faulty. Testing is by the substitution of a known good unit but be careful; while some relays are identical in appearance and in operation,

3.4a The fuses simply pull from place

others look similar but perform different functions.

10 To renew a relay, first ensure that the ignition switch is off. The relay can then simply be pulled out from the socket and the new relay pressed in.

SAM control units

11 A SAM (Signal Acquisition and Actuation Module) functions much as a network router does on a computer or communications network. It monitors input from various switches, controls, monitoring devices, and warning systems. When a switch is activated, the signal goes through a SAM before the device you are controlling responds. If there is a fault with the device you are attempting to operate, there will probable be an error message delivered through the SAM to the CAN (Controller Area Network) databus. The CAN bus will send the error message to the "error screen" on the instrument cluster.

12 SAM units are integrated into the fuse/ relay boxes, and are therefore located in the luggage compartment and the engine compartment.

13 No repair or overhaul of the SAM units is possible. If a fault is suspected, have the self-diagnosis system interrogated using Mercedes STAR (or equivalent) diagnostic equipment,

3.4b If the fuse is 'blown', the wire will be melted

using the 16-pin socket located under the drivers side of the facia **(see illustration)**.

4 Electrical connectors – general information

1 Most electrical connections on these vehicles are made with multiwire plastic connectors. The mating halves of many connectors are secured with locking clips molded into the plastic connector shells. The mating halves of some large connectors, such as some of those under the instrument panel, are held together by a bolt through the center of the connector.

2 To separate a connector with locking clips, use a small screwdriver to pry the clips apart carefully, then separate the connector halves. Pull only on the shell, never pull on the wiring harness, as you may damage the individual wires and terminals inside the connectors. Look at the connector closely before trying to separate the halves. Often the locking clips are engaged in a way that is not immediately clear. Additionally, many connectors have more than one set of clips.

3 Each pair of connector terminals has a male half and a female half. When you look

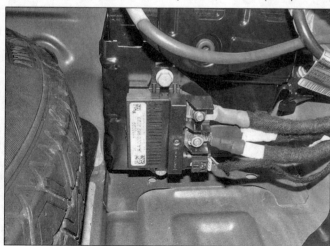

3.8 The Stop-Start relay is located adjacent to the additional relay in under the luggage compartment floor panel

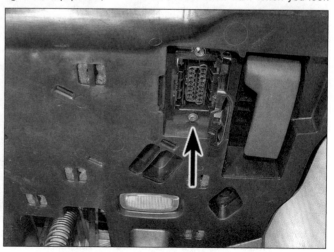

3.13 Unclip the cover to access the diagnostic socket

at the end view of a connector in a diagram, be sure to understand whether the view shows the harness side or the component side of the connector. Connector halves are mirror images of each other, and a terminal shown on the right side end-view of one half will be on the left side end-view of the other half.

4 It is often necessary to take circuit voltage measurements with a connector connected. Whenever possible, carefully insert a small straight pin (not your meter probe) into the rear of the connector shell to contact the terminal inside, then clip your meter lead to the pin. This kind of connection is called "backprobing." When inserting a test probe into a terminal, be careful not to distort the terminal opening. Doing so can lead to a poor connection and corrosion at that terminal later. Using the small straight pin instead of a meter probe results in less chance of deforming the terminal connector. "T" pins are a good choice as temporary meter connections. They allow for a larger surface area to attach the meter leads too.

Electrical connectors

5 Typical electrical connectors:

Electronic ignition switch control unit

Note: *If a new ignition switch unit (EZS) is to be fitted, connect Mercedes STAR diagnostic equipment and transfer the basic data from the EZS to the STAR. Upon completion reverse the process.*

4.5a Most electrical connectors have a single release tab that you depress to release the connector

4.5b Some electrical connectors have a retaining tab which must be pried up to free the connector

4.5c Some connectors have two release tabs that you must squeeze to release the connector

4.5d Some connectors use wire retainers that you squeeze to release the connector

4.5e Critical connectors often employ a sliding lock (1) that you must pull out before you can depress the release tab (2)

4.5f Here's another sliding-lock style connector, with the lock (1) and the release tab (2) on the side of the connector

4.5g On some connectors the lock (1) must be pulled out to the side and removed before you can lift the release tab (2)

4.5h Some critical connectors, like the multi-pin connectors at the Electronic Control Module employ pivoting locks that must be flipped open

5.3a Using a thin-nosed pair of pliers...

5.3b ...unscrew and remove the collar

1 Disconnect the battery negative lead as described in Chapter 5A Section 4.
2 Remove the steering column combination switch assembly as described later in this Section.
3 Using a pair of pliers (or similar) unscrew the collar from around the EZS unit on the facia **(see illustrations)**.
4 On models from 28/02/11, carefully prise the decorative panel around the central air vent from place **(see illustration 10.5)**.
5 Carefully prise the instrument panel surround trim from place, starting at the top as described in Section 10.
6 Release the wiring harness, then unclip and remove the gaiter between the steering column and instrument panel **(see illustration 5.14)**.
7 Reach through the aperture and unclip ignition switch/unit **(see illustration)**. If necessary, unclip the air duct behind the unit.
8 Disconnect the wiring plugs from the unit as they become accessible.
9 On models with automatic transmission, unclip the selector lever release cable from the EZS unit **(see illustration)**.
10 Manoeuvre the EZS unit from place.
11 Refitting is a reversal of removal.

Steering column combination switch/module

Note: *If a new steering column switch/module is to be fitted, connect Mercedes STAR diagnostic equipment and transfer the basic data from the switch/module to the STAR. Upon completion reverse the process.*
12 The steering column combination switch/module, contains the horns and air bag spring clock contacts, steering angle sensor, control unit and switches. If defective, the complete assembly must be renewed.
13 Remove the steering wheel as described in Chapter 10 Section 18.

5.7 Reach through the aperture to release the clips

14 Working around the circumference, use a blunt, flat-balded tool to release the clips and remove the steering column tube cover **(see illustration)**.
15 Slide the steering column switch module from place **(see illustrations)**. Disconnect the wiring plugs as the module is withdrawn.
16 To refit the switch/module, slide it over the end of the column and down into place. Note that the switch/module is fully fitted once the red indicator is flush with the underside of the cover **(see illustration)**.
17 The remainder of refitting is a reversal of removal.

5.9 Squeeze together the tabs and disconnect the release cable

5.14 Unclip the cover between the column shroud and the instrument panel trim

5.15a Pull the steering column switch module over the end of the shaft...

5.15b ...and disconnect the wiring plug

5.16 The switch/module is fully fitted when the red indicator is flush with the cover

5.18 Select parking lights, and pull out the knob

5.19 Rotate the knob to '0' and remove the surround

Lighting control switch

Models up to 05/01/10

18 Rotate the light switch to select the parking lights, then pull the switch knob outwards one click (see illustration).
19 Now rotate the knob to position '0', and remove the knob surround (see illustration).
20 Squeeze together the 3 clips and pull the switch from the facia (see illustrations). Disconnect the wiring plugs as the switch is withdrawn.
21 Refitting is a reversal of removal.

Models from 06/01/10

22 Turn the ignition switch to select the parking lights, then push-in the switch knob, then turn it back to the side light position.
23 Carefully pull the switch assembly from the facia, and disconnect the wiring plugs.
24 Refitting is a reversal of removal.

Upper control panel (ESP/heated seats/electric roller blind/etc.)

Vehicles upto 2012 model year

25 Open the central storage tray or fold open the display screen as applicable.
26 Remove the rubber buffers at the base of the storage tray/display aperture.

27 Where applicable, remove the rubber map from the base of the tray.
28 Insert a suitable rod into the holes exposed by removing the buffers, depress the clips and pull the centre air vent from place (see illustrations). Disconnect the wiring plugs as the vent is withdrawn.

Vehicles from 2012 model year

29 Using a blunt, flat-bladed tool, carefully prise the decorative panel around the centre air vent from place (see illustration 10.5). Disconnect the wiring plug(s) as the panel/vent assembly is withdrawn.

All models

30 Remove the radio/facia audio unit as described in Section 16.
31 Undo the screws, release the clips and detach the control panel from the radio/facia audio unit (see illustration).
32 Refitting is a reversal of removal.

Heating/air conditioning switches

33 The heating/air conditioning switches are integral with the control panel. Removal of the control panel is described in Chapter 3 Section 8.

Audio/COMAND selector

34 Remove the centre console as described in Chapter 11 Section 36.

5.20a Squeeze together the 3 clips...

5.20b ...and remove the switch

5.28a Insert rods into the holes...

5.28b ...depress the clips and pull the centre vent from place

5.31 Undo the screws on the underside of the unit

5.35a Pull up the tray and undo the screw

5.35b Prise up the surround panel

5.36a Undo the remaining screw...

5.36b ...and remove the switch

5.40 Steering wheel switch retaining screws

5.45a Panel switch retaining screw

5.45b Drivers side switch retaining screws

5.48 Unclip the mirror base cover

5.49 Press the clips forwards to release the console

35 Pull up the oddment tray, then undo the screw and prise up the switch surround panel **(see illustrations)**.

36 Disconnect the wiring plug, unclip the wiring harness, then undo the remaining screw and lift the switch **(see illustrations)**.

37 Refitting is a reversal of removal.

Stop light switch

38 Removal of the stop light switch is described in Chapter 9 Section 17.

Steering wheel switches

39 Remove the drivers airbag as described in Section 20.

40 Disconnect the wiring plug, then undo the retaining screws and remove the switch from the steering wheel **(see illustration)**.

41 Refitting is a reversal of removal.

Parking brake-on warning switch

42 Removal of the switch is described in Chapter 9 Section 17.

Oil pressure warning switch

43 Removal of the switch is described in Chapter 2A Section 18, or as applicable.

Door panel switches

44 Remove the door inner trim panel as described in Chapter 11 Section 17.

45 Disconnect the wiring plug, undo the retaining screw(s) and detach the relevant switch assembly from the trim panel **(see illustrations)**.

46 Refitting is a reversal of removal.

Overhead console panel

Note: *If a new overhead console panel/control unit is being fitted, connect Mercedes STAR*

diagnostic equipment and transfer the basic data from the switch/module to the STAR. Upon completion reverse the process.

47 Switch off the ignition, and move the key to at least 2 m away from the vehicle.

48 Unclip the mirror base cover **(see illustration)**.

49 Insert a credit card/trim removal tool between the rear of the console and the headlining, depress the clips and lower the console from place **(see illustration)**.

50 Disconnect the wiring plugs as the console is withdrawn.

51 Refitting is a reversal of removal. On models with a tilt/slide sunroof, normalise the system by full closing the roof, continue to hold the switch in the 'close' position for 1 second, then move the switch to the tilt position. Once the end position is reached, continue to hold the switch in this position for 1 second.

6.2 Rotate the cover anti-clockwise to remove it

6.3a Push the wiring plug downwards...

6.3b ...and withdraw the bulb

6 Bulbs (exterior lights) – renewal

General

1 Whenever a bulb is renewed, note the following points:

a) *Disconnect the battery negative lead as described in Chapter 5A Section 4 before starting work.*

b) *Remember that if the light has just been in use, the bulb may be extremely hot.*

c) *Always check the bulb contacts and holder, ensuring that there is clean metal-to metal contact between the bulb and the socket contacts. Clean off any corrosion or dirt before fitting a new bulb.*

d) *Wherever bayonet-type bulbs are fitted, ensure that the live contact(s) bear firmly against the bulb contact.*

e) *Always ensure that the new bulb is of the correct rating and that it is completely clean before fitting it; this applies particularly to headlight/foglight bulbs (see below).*

f) *With quartz halogen bulbs (headlights and similar applications), use a tissue or clean cloth when handling the bulb; do not touch the bulb glass with the fingers. Even small quantities of grease from the fingers will cause blackening and premature failure. If a bulb is accidentally touched, clean it with methylated spirit and a clean rag.*

6.5 Align the lower edge with the reflector, and the upper lug with the slot

Headlight

Main beam

2 Rotate the inner cover anti-clockwise and remove it **(see illustration)**.

Vehicles upto 2012 model year

3 Push the bulb wiring plug downwards to release it, and withdraw the bulb from the reflector **(see illustrations)**.

4 Pull the bulb from wiring plug. Take care not to touch the glass with your fingers.

5 Press the wiring plug onto the new bulb, then align the lower edge of the bulb with the socket in the reflector, and push the wiring plug upwards until it engages **(see illustration)**.

6 Refit the cover, then rotate it clockwise to secure.

Vehicles from 2012 model year

7 Rotate the bulbholder anti-clockwise and withdraw it from the reflector **(see illustration)**.

6.7 Rotate the bulbholder anti-clockwise and withdraw it

8 Pull the bulb from the holder **(see illustration)**. Take care not to touch the bulb glass with bare skin.

9 Press the new bulb into the holder, then insert it into the reflector socket, and rotate it clockwise until it engages.

10 Refit the cover, then rotate it clockwise to secure.

Dipped beam

Halogen bulb

11 Rotate the cover on the rear of the headlight anti-clockwise and remove it **(see illustration)**.

Vehicles upto 2012 model year

12 Pull the wiring plug from the bulb **(see illustration)**.

13 Fold the retaining clip downwards, and withdraw the bulb from the reflector **(see**

6.8 Pull the bulb from the holder

6.11 Rotate the outer cover anti-clockwise

6.12 Disconnect the wiring plug

6.13 Push the clip to one side, and fold it downwards

6.14 Align the lug on the bulb flange with the slot in the reflector socket

6.16 Rotate the bulbholder anti-clockwise and withdraw it

illustration).Take care not to touch the glass with your fingers.

14 Manoeuvre the new bulb into the reflector socket, and secure it with the retaining clip (see illustration). Note that the bulb will only fit correctly in one position.

15 Press the wiring plug onto the bulb contacts, then refit the cover.

Vehicles from 2012 model year

16 Rotate the bulbholder anti-clockwise and withdraw the bulb from the reflector (see illustration).

17 Pull the bulb from the holder (see illustration 6.8).

18 Press the new bulb into the holder, then manoeuvre the bulb and holder into the reflector socket, and rotate it clockwise until it engages.

19 Refit the cover, then rotate it clockwise to secure it.

Bi-Xenon High-intensity discharge bulb

Caution: Bi-Xenon bulbs are pressurised to approximately 22 bar. Take extreme care when handling these bulbs – wear safety glasses and gloves.

20 Due to the high-voltages required to produce the electric arc between the bulbs electrodes, disconnect the battery as described in Chapter 5A Section 4, then wait at least 10 minutes for any residual electrical energy to dissipate.

21 Rotate the cover behind the dipped beam location anti-clockwise and remove it.

22 Squeeze together the ends of the retaining clip, and fold it upwards.

23 Carefully withdraw the ignition unit/bulb from the reflector. Take care not to touch the bulb with bare fingers.

24 Disconnect the wiring plug from the ignition unit.

25 Refitting is a reversal of removal. If a new unit/bulb has been fitted, the systems operating counter must be reset to zero using Mercedes STAR diagnostic equipment (or equivalent). Entrust this task to a Mercedes dealer or suitably equipped specialist.

Front side lights

26 On vehicles upto 2012 model year, rotate the cover at the rear of the headlamp anti-

clockwise and remove it (see illustration). On vehicles after this date, remove the cover behind the main beam location (see illustration 6.2).

27 Pull the bulbholder from the reflector (see illustration).

28 Pull the capless bulb from the holder.

29 Refitting is a reversal of removal.

Front directional indicator

Vehicles upto 2012 model year

30 The bulbholder is integral with the plastic cover.

31 Rotate the bulbholder anti-clockwise and pull it from the rear of the headlight (see illustration).

32 Press the bulb into the holder slightly,

rotate it anti-clockwise and pull it from the holder (see illustration).

33 Refitting is a reversal of removal. Note that the bulb bayonet pins are offset – the bulb will only fit correctly in one position.

Vehicles from 2012 model year

Caution: These vehicles are fitted with high-pressure indicator bulbs, designed to last the lifetime of the vehicle. Always wear eye protection and gloves when handling these bulbs.

34 Remove the headlight as described in Section 8.

35 Undo the 2 screws and remove the cover from the underside of the headlight.

36 Squeeze together the clip each side and pull the bulb/holder from place (see

6.26 Rotate the covers anti-clockwise to access the side lights

6.27 Withdraw the bulbholder and bulb

6.31 Reach behind the headlight and twist the directional indicator bulbholder anti-clockwise

6.32 Press-in the bulb and rotate it anti-clockwise

6.36a Squeeze together the clips and withdraw the bulb/holder

6.36b The indicator bulb is integral with the holder

6.41 Rotate the bulb/holder anti-clockwise and withdraw it

6.44 Release the catch and remove the access panel

6.45a Squeeze together the clips – Estate models...

6.45b ...and Saloon models

illustrations). Note the bulb is integral with the holder.

37 Refitting is a reversal of removal.

Side repeater

38 On all models, the side repeaters are LEDs, designed to last the lifetime of the vehicle. Should the unit fail, replace the side repeater as described in Chapter 11 Section 28.

Front foglight

39 Raise the front of the vehicle and support it securely on axle stands (see *Vehicle jacking and support*).

40 Release the fasteners and pull the front section of the wheelarch liner rearwards a little.

41 Disconnect the wiring plug, rotate the

6.46 Press-in and rotate the bulb anti-clockwise (bayonet bulbs)

bulb/holder anti-clockwise and remove it from the rear of the fog light **(see illustration)**.

42 Note that the bulb is integral with the holder.

43 Refitting is a reversal of removal.

Rear light assembly

Note: *On some models, the traditional rear turn signal and reversing light bulbs have been replaced by LED units, which are designed to last the lifetime of the vehicle. If the light should fail, the complete bulbholder or light unit may need to be replaced. Consult a Mercedes dealer or parts specialist.*

44 Open the access panel in the luggage compartment side trim panel **(see illustration)**.

45 Squeeze together the retaining clips pull the bulbholder assembly from the rear light **(see illustrations)**.

6.50 Rotate the bulbholder anti-clockwise

46 The bulbs are removed from the bulbholder by pressing them in slightly, then rotating anti-clockwise (bayonet fitting bulbs), or simply pulling from place (wedge, capless bulbs) **(see illustration)**.

47 Refitting is a reversal of removal.

High level stop light

48 The high-level stop light is illuminated by LEDs. If faulty, the complete assembly must be renewed as described in Section 8.

Number plate light

49 Remove the tailgate main trim panel or boot lid trim panel (as applicable) as described in Chapter 11 Section 35.

50 Rotate the bulbholder anti-clockwise and withdraw it from the light unit **(see illustration)**.

51 Pull the capless bulb from the holder.

52 Refitting is a reversal of removal.

---

7 Interior lights – general information, removal and refitting

General information

1 Illumination of some of the interior lights is provided by LED's. Consequently, should a fault develop the complete assembly may need to be renewed. Consult a Mercedes dealer or parts specialist.

7.2 Prise down the mirror base cover

7.3a Using a flat tool...

7.3b ...press forward the retaining clip

7.4 Pull the bulb from the holder

7.6a Prise each corner from the headlining

7.6b Rotate the bulholder anti-clockwise and withdraw it

Front overhead console lights

2 Carefully prise the mirror base cover from place **(see illustration)**.

3 Insert a blunt, flat-bladed tool between the console and headlining, and press-forwards the retaining clip. Lower the console from place, noting how the hooks at the front edge engage **(see illustrations)**.

4 Rotate the bulbholder anti-clockwise and remove it **(see illustration)**. Pull the capless bulb from the holder.

5 Refitting is a reversal of removal.

Rear overhead light console

6 Using a blunt, flat-bladed tool, carefully prise each corner of the rear overhead light console from the headlining, the rotate the bulbholder(s) anti-clockwise, remove the bulbholder, and pull the capless bulb from the holder **(see illustrations)**.

Vanity lights

7 Carefully prise the vanity light unit from the headlining, then pull the capless bulb from the contacts **(see illustration)**.

Luggage compartment light

8 Carefully prise the light unit from the trim panel **(see illustration)**. Disconnect the wiring plug as the light unit is withdrawn, then remove the festoon bulb.

9 Refitting is a reversal of removal.

Tailgate mounted lights

10 Remove the lower section of the tailgate trim panel as described in Chapter 11 Section 35.

7.7 Prise the vanity light unit from the headlining

7.8 Prise the luggage compartment light from the trim panel

7.11 Rotate the bulbholder clockwise

7.14 Compress the clip and prise out the light unit

7.15 Rotate the bulbholder clockwise and withdraw it

7.17 Prise the inner end of the lens from place

7.21 Rotate the bulbholder and withdraw it

Door panel lights

20 Remove the relevant door panel as described in Chapter 11 Section 17.
21 Rotate the bulbholder and withdraw it from the panel **(see illustration)**.
22 Pull the capless bulb from the holder.
23 Refitting is a reversal of removal.

---

8 Exterior light units – removal and refitting

Headlight

1 Prise up the centre pins, lever out the plastic expansion rivets, and remove the plastic cover over the headlight **(see illustrations)**.
2 Remove the front bumper as described in Chapter 11 Section 16.
3 On models with headlight washers, undo the bolt securing the washer jets to the base of the headlight, release the catch then slide it rearwards.
4 Pull the wheelarch liner to one side, and remove the rearmost headlight retaining screw **(see illustration)**.

11 Rotate the bulbholder clockwise and withdraw it from the light lens **(see illustration)**.
12 Pull the capless bulb from the holder.
13 Refitting is a reversal of removal.

D-pillar lights

14 Insert a blunt, flat-bladed tool between the rear edge of the light unit and the pillar trim, compress the clip and prise the light from the trim **(see illustration)**. Disconnect the wiring plug as the light is withdrawn.

15 If required, rotate the bulbholder clockwise, withdraw it from the light unit, then pull the capless bulb from the holder **(see illustration)**.
16 Refitting is a reversal of removal.

Glovebox light

17 Open the glovebox, and carefully prise the inner end of the lens from place **(see illustration)**.
18 Pull the capless bulb from the holder.
19 Refitting is a reversal of removal.

8.1a Prise up the centre pins, lever out the plastic rivets...

8.1b ...and remove the plastic cover

8.4 Remove the rear headlight retaining screw

8.5a Holding the nut, unscrew the rear, upper retaining bolt...

8.5b ...and the inner retaining bolt

5 Remove the rear, upper headlight retaining bolt, then push the air intake duct to one side, and remove the inner retaining bolt **(see illustrations)**.
6 Manoeuvre the headlight forwards from position. Disconnect the wiring plugs as the headlight is withdrawn **(see illustration)**.
7 Refitting is a reversal of removal. If necessary, have the headlight alignment checked at the earliest opportunity.

Side repeater light

8 Remove the exterior mirror cover as described in Chapter 11 Section 28.
9 Undo the retaining screws/release the clips and detach the side repeater from the cover.
10 Refitting is a reversal of removal.

Tail light

Saloon

11 Remove the luggage side trim panel as described in Chapter 11 Section 35.
12 Disconnect the wiring plug, undo the 4 retaining nuts and carefully pull the light unit rearwards **(see illustration)**.
13 Where applicable, move the dynamic seat control pneumatic pump and bracket to one side.

8.6 Disconnect the wiring plug from the rear of the headlight

14 Refitting is a reversal of removal.

Estate

15 Release the catch and remove the access cover from the luggage compartment side trim panel **(see illustration)**.
16 If removing the right-hand tail light, remove the first aid kit.
17 Disconnect the wiring plug, undo the retaining nuts and withdraw the light unit rearwards **(see illustration)**.
18 Refitting is a reversal of removal. Ensure

8.12 Tail light retaining nuts

the tail light seal is positioned beneath the tailgate seal.

High-level brake light

Saloon

19 Remove the parcel shelf as described in Chapter 11 Section 35.
20 Lift the insulating foam from the parcel shelf location.
21 Trace the light unit wiring back to the wiring plug and disconnect it.

8.15 Release the catch and open the access cover

8.17 Tail light retaining nuts

8.22a Unscrew the centre pins...

8.22b ...pull out the 5 'scrivets'...

8.22c ...and remove the high-level brake light assembly

8.23 Depress the clip and slide out the centre bracket

8.24a Remove the metal clips...

8.24b ...spread the moulding and remove the light unit

22 Unscrew and remove the 5 plastic 'scrivets' and manoeuvre the light unit from place **(see illustrations)**.

8.28 Depress the 6 clips (3 left-hand clips arrowed), and gently ease the high-level brake light from place

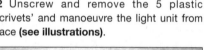

23 Release the clip and slide out the centre bracket from the light fitting **(see illustration)**.
24 Prise off the metal clips, then gently spread the plastic moulding, and lift the high-level light from place **(see illustrations)**.
25 Refitting is a reversal of removal.

Estate

26 Remove the tailgate upper trim panel as described in Chapter 11 Section 35.
27 Unclip the high-level brake light wiring harness from the tailgate.
28 Work along the length of the brake light, releasing the 6 retaining clips **(see illustration)**. Gently pull the brake light from the tailgate as the clips are released. Take care as the light unit is fragile.
29 Rotate the collar, disconnect the washer hose, then disconnect the wiring plug **(see illustration)**.

30 Refitting is a reversal of removal.

Front fog light

Note: *Some models are equipped with LED fog lights. On these models, no bulb replacement procedure is applicable, and no provision is made for adjustment.*
31 Raise the front of the vehicle and support it securely on axle stands (see *Vehicle jacking and support*). Undo the fasteners and remove the front section of the engine undershield.
32 Release the fasteners and pull back the front section of the wheelarch liner.
33 Disconnect the wiring plug from the rear of the fog light.
34 Undo the screws or release the clips, and manoeuvre the fog light from place **(see illustrations)**.
35 Refitting is a reversal of removal. Note that if required, the fog light aim can be adjusted

8.29 Rotate the collar and disconnect the hose

8.34a Front fog light retaining screws

8.34b Front fog light retaining clips

8.35 Fog light aim adjusting screw

9.2 Headlight beam adjustment screws

Inner screw – horizontal adjustment   Outer screw – vertical adjustment

by rotating the screw at the front. Note that the actual location of the adjusting screw, varies from model to model **(see illustration)**.

Bi-Xenon HID lights control unit

36 The control units are located on the underside of the headlights. Remove the headlight as previously described in this Section, then undo the 3 retaining screws, lift the unit and disconnect the wiring plug.
37 Refitting is a reversal of removal. Note that if a new control unit has been fitted, the initial start-up of the unit must be carried out using Mercedes-Benz STAR diagnostic equipment (or equivalent).

9 Headlight beam adjustment – general information

1 Accurate adjustment of the headlight beam is only possible using optical beam setting equipment and this work should therefore be carried out by a Mercedes dealer or suitably-equipped workshop.
2 For reference, the headlights can be adjusted by rotating the adjuster screws on the top of the headlight unit **(see illustration)**.
3 All models have an electrically-operated headlight beam adjustment system which is controlled through the switch in the facia. On these models ensure that the switch is set to the off position before adjusting the headlight aim.

10 Instrument panel – removal and refitting

Removal

Note: *If a new instrument panel/cluster is to be fitted, the stored data must be transferred*

to Mercedes STAR diagnostic equipment (or equivalent), then reloaded to the new panel/cluster upon completion.
1 Move the steering wheel fully rearwards, and to its lowest position.
2 Disconnect the battery negative lead as described in Chapter 5A Section 4.

Vehicles upto 28.02.11

3 Starting at the top edge, gently prise the instrument panel surround trim rearwards to release the retaining clips **(see**

illustrations)**. Take care as the clips are easily damaged.
4 Pull the trip reset knob from place **(see illustration)**.

Vehicles from 28.02.11

5 Using a blunt, flat-bladed tool, carefully prise the decorative trim around the centre air vent rearwards to release the retaining clips **(see illustration)**.
6 Carefully prise the instrument cluster lower trim panel from place, followed by the

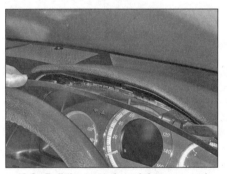

10.3a Pull the top edge of the surround trim rearwards...

10.3b ...and manoeuvre it from place

10.4 Pull the reset knob from the panel

10.5 Prise the decorative trim rearwards

10.6a Unclip the lower trim panel...

10.6b ...followed by the upper trim panel...

10.6c ...and centre trim panel

10.7a Undo the 2 screws each side...

10.7b ...and manoeuvre the instrument panel/cluster from the facia

upper trim panel, and centre trim panel **(see illustrations)**.

All models

7 Undo the 4 Torx screws, and manoeuvre the instrument panel/cluster rearwards until the wiring plugs are accessible **(see illustrations)**. Disconnect the wiring plugs, and remove the panel/cluster. Note that the retaining bolts are captive with the cluster/panel.
8 Refitting is a reversal of removal.

Refitting

9 Refitting is a reversal of removal. If the panel has been renewed, it will need to be configured using Mercedes diagnostic equipment (or equivalent).

11 Rain/light sensor – removal and refitting

Removal

1 Carefully unclip the cover from in front of the interior mirror base **(see illustration)**.
2 Carefully unclip the rain/light sensor **(see illustration)**. Take care as the clips are easily damaged. Do not touch the lens of the sensor.
3 Disconnect the sensor wiring plug.

Refitting

4 Refitting is a reversal of removal. If a new sensor has been fitted, it must be configured using Mercedes STAR diagnostic equipment or equivalent.

12 Horns – removal and refitting

Removal

1 The horns are located each side behind the front bumper. Raise the front of the vehicle and support it securely on axle stands (see *Vehicle jacking and support*). Release the fasteners and remove the front section of the engine undershield.
2 If removing the left-hand horn, release the washer fluid reservoir from its mountings, and move it to one side with reference to Section 15. There's no need to disconnect the hoses/wiring.
3 If removing the right-hand horn, release the fasteners and pull back the front section of the wheelarch liner.
4 Undo the retaining bolt and remove the horn **(see illustration)**. Disconnect the wiring plug(s) as the horn is withdrawn.

Refitting

5 Refitting is a reversal of removal.

13 Wiper arm – removal and refitting

Removal

Front wiper arms

1 With the wipers in the 'at rest' position,

11.1 Unclip the sensor cover

11.2 Release the sensor retaining clips

12.4 Undo the bolt and remove the horn

13.4 Lift up the spindle cover and undo the nut

13.5 Prise out the caps

13.7 Lift up the cover and undo the spindle nut

switch off the ignition switch, and remove the key. On models with 'Keyless Go' system move the transmitter out of range of the vehicle.

2 Open the bonnet.

3 Mark the position of the wipers arm on the windscreen using a strip of insulating tape.

4 Lift up the cover, then undo the drivers side spindle nut and pull the arm from the spindle **(see illustration)**.

5 Prise out the caps, undo the passengers side wiper arm linkage nuts, then pull the arms from the spindles **(see illustration)**.

Tailgate wiper arm

6 Use tape to mark the position of the wiper blade on the rear screen.

7 Prise open the spindle cover and undo the arm retaining nut **(see illustration)**.

8 Pull the wiper arm from the spindle. If necessary use a suitable puller to release the wiper arm **(see illustration)**.

Refitting

9 Refit the wiper arms to the spindles, aligning the blades to the marks/tape on the windscreen.

---

14 Windscreen wiper motor and linkage – removal and refitting

---

Removal

Front wiper motor

1 Remove the front wiper arms as described in Section 13.

2 Remove the bulkhead seal centre piece **(see illustration)**.

3 Undo the centre pins, pull out the 4 scrivets, then pull the scuttle trim panel upwards from the base of the windscreen **(see illustrations)**. Disconnect the washer jet hose as the panel is withdrawn.

4 Undo the bolt and remove the strut **(see illustration)**.

5 Undo the retaining nuts/bolt, and manoeuvre the wiper linkage/motor from

13.8 If necessary, use a puller to release the wiper arm

14.2 Pull up the rubber seal

14.3a Remove the scrivet each side of the strut...

14.3b ...the 2 on the passengers side...

14.3c ...and pull the scuttle trim upwards from the windscreen

14.4 Strut retaining bolt

14.5 Wiper motor linkage retaining nuts/bolt

14.9 Rear wiper motor retaining bolts

15.3 Reservoir bracket securing bolt

place **(see illustration)**. Disconnect the wiring plug as the assembly is withdrawn

Note: *Take care not to alter the position of the front mounting bolt bracket, as this would alter the contact pressure of the wiper arms.*

Rear wiper motor

6 Remove the rear wiper arm as described in Section 13.

7 Remove the tailgate lower trim panel as described in Chapter 11 Section 35.

8 Disconnect the wiper motor wiring plug.

9 Undo the 3 bolts and remove the rear wiper motor **(see illustration)**.

Refitting

10 Refitting is a reversal of removal.

15.4 Undo the bolt at the base of the filler neck

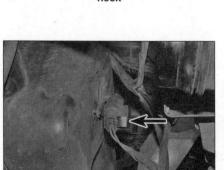

15.8b Prise out the locking tab, and disconnect the level sensor wiring plug from the front of the reservoir

15 Windscreen/tailgate washer system components – removal and refitting

Washer reservoir

Removal

1 Slacken the left-hand front roadwheel bolts, raise the front of the vehicle and support it securely on axle stands (see *Vehicle jacking and support*). Remove the left-hand front roadwheel.

2 Prise up the centre pins, lever out the 2 plastic expansion rivets, then remove the cover over the left-hand headlight **(see illustration 8.1a and 8.1b)**.

15.8a Reservoir lower retaining bolt

15.11 Pump hose and wiring plug

3 Undo the bolt securing the bracket to the bonnet slam panel, and unclip it from the reservoir **(see illustrations)**.

4 Remove the bolt securing the reservoir filler neck **(see illustration)**.

5 Release the fasteners and remove the front section of the left-hand front wheelarch liner.

6 Unclip the hose and pull the washer pump from the reservoir grommet. Be prepared for fluid spillage.

7 On models with a headlamp cleaning system, disconnect the washer hose at the coupling on the headlamp washer pump, and disconnect the pump wiring plug.

8 Undo the lower retaining bolt, then lower the reservoir from position **(see illustrations)**. Disconnect any wiring plugs as the reservoir is withdrawn. On models with the washer fluid heater system, unclip the heat exchanger from the reservoir.

Refitting

9 Refitting is a reversal of removal.

Windscreen and headlight washer pumps – removal and refitting

Removal

10 One pump provides fluid to the front and rear windscreens, and another pump supplies fluid to the headlight washers (where fitted). Begin by removing the left-hand front roadwheel and wheelarch liner as described earlier in this Section.

11 Note their fitted positions, then disconnect the wiring plug and hoses from the relevant pump **(see illustration)**. The innermost pump is for the headlight washers, and the outermost for the windscreens.

12 Pull the relevant pump from the fluid reservoir. Be prepared for fluid spillage. Examine the rubber sealing grommet, and renew if necessary.

Refitting

13 Refitting is a reversal of removal.

Jets

Windscreen jets

14 Remove the wiper arms as described in Section 13.

15 Pull up the centre section of the bulkhead seal **(see illustration 14.2)**.

16 Undo the centre pins, pull out the 4 scrivets, then pull the scuttle trim panel upwards from the base of the windscreen **(see illustrations 14.3a, 14.3b and 14.3c)**. Disconnect the washer jet hose as the panel is withdrawn **(see illustration)**.

17 Disconnect any wiring plug, then unclip the jet from the panel.

18 Refitting is a reversal of removal.

Tailgate screen jet

19 Remove the high-level brake light as described in Section 8.

20 Carefully unclip the jet from the light unit **(see illustration)**.

Note: *The jet retaining clips are fragile.*

21 Refitting is a reversal of removal.

---

16 Infotainment units –
removal and refitting

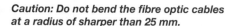

Caution: Do not bend the fibre optic cables at a radius of sharper than 25 mm.

Audio/COMAND display

Note: *If a new display unit is being fitted, use Mercedes-Benz STAR diagnostic equipment (or equivalent) to store the unit's basic data.*

Vehicles up to 2012 model year

1 Remove the rubber buffers from the lower edge, then insert suitable rods to release the clips, and pull the centre air vent from the facia **(see illustrations)**. Disconnect any wiring plugs as the unit is withdrawn.

2 Undo the 2 bolts on the underside of the display unit **(see illustration)**.

3 Manoeuvre the display unit diagonally upwards from the facia. Disconnect the wiring plugs as the unit is withdrawn.

Vehicles from 2012 model year

4 Carefully prise the decorative trim and

15.16 Disconnect the hoses from the base of the jets

16.1a Insert a rod into each hole...

centre vent rearwards from the facia **(see illustration 10.5)**.

5 Remove the instrument panel lower, upper and central trim panels as described in Section 10.

6 Undo the 2 retaining bolts and manoeuvre the unit from the facia **(see illustration)**. Disconnect the wiring plugs as the unit is withdrawn.

All vehicles

7 Refitting is a reversal of removal. Where applicable, transfer the basic data to the new control unit using STAR diagnostic equipment (or equivalent).

15.20 Release the jet retaining clip each side

16.1b ...then depress the clips and pull the centre air vent rearwards

DAB radio control unit
Estate models

Note: *If a new control unit is being fitted, use Mercedes-Benz STAR diagnostic equipment (or equivalent) to store the unit's basic data.*

8 Remove the front section of the luggage compartment floor panel.

9 Disconnect the wiring plug, and fibre optic cable connections from the control unit.

10 Undo the screws and remove the control unit along with the mounting bracket.

11 If required, detach the control unit from the bracket.

16.2 Remove the screws at the lower edge of the unit

16.6 Display unit retaining bolts

16.14a Release the clip on the underside of the unit (facia removed for clarity)

16.14b Disconnect the wiring plug and the fibre optic lead from the control unit (facia removed for clarity)

12 Refitting is a reversal of removal. Where applicable, transfer the basic data to the new control unit using STAR diagnostic equipment (or equivalent).

Media interface control unit

13 Remove the passengers glovebox as described in Chapter 11 Section 35.
14 Unclip the media interface control unit from the facia bracket, then disconnect the wiring plugs and fibre optic connector(s) as it's withdrawn (see illustrations).

16.17a Undo the screw each side...

16.18 Undo the locking screws to the 'stop'

15 Refitting is a reversal of removal. If a new control unit has been fitted, the initial start-up of the unit must be carried out using Mercedes-Benz STAR diagnostic equipment (or equivalent).

Facia radio/audio unit

Note: *If a new radio/audio unit is to be fitted, the basic data must be transferred to Mercedes STAR diagnostic equipment (or equivalent), then loaded into the new radio/audio unit upon completion.*

16 Remove the centre air vent as described

16.17b ...and fully slide up the locking catches

16.19 Manoeuvre the unit rearwards, and disconnect the cables as they become accessible

earlier in this Section for 'Audio/COMAND display'.

Vehicles up to 2012 model year

17 Working in the centre vent aperture, undo the screw each side, and fully slide up the locking catch in the lower corners (see illustrations).

Vehicles from 2012 model year

18 Undo the locking screw each side to the 'stop', then press then fully down (see illustration).

All vehicles

19 Manoeuvre the radio/audio/display unit rearwards from the facia, and disconnect the various wiring plugs/fibre optic cables as they become accessible (see illustration).
20 Refitting is a reversal of removal.

Antenna amplifier module

21 Removal and refitting of the antenna amplifier module requires the removal of the rear section of the headlining. This is best entrusted to a Mercedes-Benz dealer or upholstery specialist.

Antennas/aerials

22 All antennas/aerials are integrated into the rear screen, and cannot be renewed separately.

17 Speakers and amplifiers – removal and refitting

Note: *The following procedure descriptions apply to various vehicle specification levels. Therefore, the actual fitment of components will vary greatly.*
Caution: *Do not bend the fibre optic cables at a radius of sharper than 25 mm.*

17.7 Drill out the rivets

Speaker amplifier control unit

1 Remove the left-hand side luggage compartment trim panel as described in Chapter 11 Section 35.
2 Fold back the insulation material to access the control unit.
3 Release the locking clamp, disconnect the wiring plug, followed by the fibre optic cable.
4 Undo the 4 retaining nuts and remove the control unit.
5 Refitting is a reversal of removal.

Door speakers

Main speakers

6 Remove the door module as described in Chapter 11 Section 18.
7 Drill out the rivets, and remove the speaker **(see illustration)**.

Tweeters

8 Carefully prise the mirror mounting triangular trim from the front door. Disconnect the wiring plug as the trim panel is withdrawn.
9 Detach the tweeter from the trim **(see illustration)**.

Facia speaker

10 Starting at the rear edges, carefully prise the speaker grille from the facia using a blunt, flat-bladed tool **(see illustration)**.
11 Undo the 2 retaining screws, and lift the speaker from the facia. Disconnect the wiring plug as it becomes accessible.
12 Refitting is a reversal of removal.

17.9 Release the clips and detach the tweeter

Parcel shelf speaker

13 Remove the parcel shelf as described in Chapter 11 Section 35.
14 Disconnect the wiring plugs, rotate the speaker housing anti-clockwise and remove it.
15 Refitting is a reversal of removal.

D-pillar speaker (Estate models)

16 Starting at the rear edge, carefully prise the speaker trim from the pillar.
17 Disconnect the wiring plug, and detach the speaker from the trim.
18 Refitting is a reversal of removal.

18 Anti-theft alarm – general information

Note: *This information is applicable only to the anti-theft alarm system fitted by Mercedes-Benz as standard equipment.*
1 All models are fitted with an anti-theft alarm system as standard equipment. The alarm has switches on all the doors (including the boot lid), the bonnet, the audio unit and the ignition switch, and also a tilt switch, which is sensitive to shocks. If the boot lid, bonnet or either of the doors are opened, the ignition switch or audio unit are switched on whilst the alarm is set, or if the tilt switch senses the vehicle is being tampered with, the alarm horn will sound and the hazard warning lights will flash. The alarm also has an immobiliser function, which makes the ignition/starter (as applicable) system inoperable whilst the alarm is triggered.
2 On later models, the scope of alarm functions is increased, with switchable interior motion sensors and anti-jacking/tilt sensor.
3 The alarm is set using the key in the front door lock or boot/tailgate lock; on later models, the alarm is also set when the doors are locked using the remote central locking device. The LED on the centre console will flash to indicate that the alarm system is operational.
4 Models are equipped with the Mercedes-Benz Driver Authorisation System (DAS). This advanced security system does away with a conventional key for locking

17.10 Prise the speaker grille from the facia

and unlocking the doors and, instead, a sophisticated electronic remote-control handset/electronic key is provided. Without this handset, the engine cannot be started.
5 Should the alarm system become faulty, the vehicle should be taken to a Mercedes-Benz dealer for examination. They will have access to a special diagnostic tester, which will quickly trace any fault present in the system.

19 Airbag system – general information and precautions

1 A driver's airbag(s), passenger airbag, front side airbags (incorporated into the seats), rear side airbags and window air bags are fitted as standard to all models.
2 Airbag units have the word AIRBAG or SRS-AIRBAG stamped on them. The airbag system comprises of the airbag unit(s) (each with a gas generator), the control unit (with an integral roll-over sensor), front and side impact sensors, and a warning light in the instrument panel. The airbag control unit features 'intelligent' software, and also operates the front seat belt tensioner mechanisms at the same time as the airbag (see Chapter 11).
3 The driver's and passenger's front airbags will only be triggered in the event of a heavy frontal impact above a predetermined force; depending on the point of impact (rear impacts will not usually trigger the airbag system). The side airbags will only be triggered if the car is hit from the side, and only on the side from which the car has been hit. The passenger airbags and seat belt tensioner will only be triggered if the passenger seat is occupied – a sensor built into the seat cushion informs the control unit of this. Light impacts, such as those which might be sustained when parking, will not trigger the system.
4 The airbag is inflated within milliseconds, and forms a safety cushion between the driver, steering wheel and door, or between the passenger, facia and door, depending on the severity of the accident. This prevents contact between the upper body and wheel/facia/door, and therefore greatly reduces the risk of injury. The airbag then deflates almost immediately.
5 Every time the ignition is switched on, the airbag control unit performs a self-test. The self-test takes approximately 4 seconds and during this time the airbag warning light in the instrument panel is illuminated. After the self-test has been completed the warning light should go out. If the warning light fails to come on, remains illuminated after the initial period or comes on at any time when the vehicle is being driven, there is a fault in the airbag system. The vehicle should be taken to a Mercedes-Benz dealer for examination at the earliest possible opportunity.

 Warning: Before carrying out any operations on the airbag system, disconnect the battery negative

terminal, and wait for at least 2 minutes. This will allow any residual electrical energy to dissipate. When operations are complete, make sure no one is inside the vehicle when the battery is reconnected.

● Note that the airbag(s) must not be subjected to temperatures in excess of 90°C (194°F). When the airbag is removed, ensure that it is stored the correct way up to prevent possible inflation (padded surface uppermost).
● The airbags, impact sensors and control unit are both sensitive to impact. If either is dropped or damaged they should be renewed.
● Disconnect the airbag control unit wiring plug prior to using arc-welding equipment on the vehicle.
● Do not allow any solvents or cleaning agents to contact the airbag assemblies. They must be cleaned using only a damp cloth.

20 Airbag system components – removal and refitting

Caution: Refer to the warnings in the previous Section before carrying out the following operations.

Steering wheel airbag

1 Fully extend the steering column.
2 Disconnect the battery negative lead as described in Chapter 5A Section 4.

20.3 Use a T30 Torx bit to undo the airbag retaining screw each side

Vehicles up to 2012 model year

3 Insert a T30 Torx bit into the the front face of the steering wheel boss, and unscrew the airbag retaining screw each side (see illustration).
4 Lift the airbag unit from the steering wheel, release the locking tabs and disconnect the wiring plugs (see illustration). Note that the airbag must not be knocked or dropped, and should be stored the correct way up (padded surface uppermost).
5 Refitting is a reversal of removal. Tighten the airbag unit retaining screws to the specified torque.

Vehicles from 2012 model year

6 With the steering wheel in the straight-ahead position, insert a T20 Torx screwdriver (or similar) into the holes each side of the steering wheel boss. Note that if the airbag has not previously been removed, it will

20.4 Release the locking tabs and disconnect the wiring plugs

be necessary to pierce the material at the positions indicated by depressions in the steering wheel boss (see illustrations).
7 Depress the spring clip each side and lift the airbag from the steering wheel a little, then disconnect the wiring plugs (see illustration).
8 Refitting is a reversal of removal.

Drivers knee airbag

9 Disconnect the battery negative lead as described in Chapter 5A Section 4.
10 Carefully prise the end panel from the drivers end of the facia (see illustration).
11 Remove the right-hand A-pillar trim panel as described in Chapter 11 Section 35.
12 Remove the instrument cluster as described in Section 10.
13 Remove the steering column combination switch/module as described in Section 5.
14 Unclip and remove the steering column gaiter (see illustration).

20.6a Pierce the material at the depression each side...

20.6b ...then insert a screwdriver/rod...

20.6c ...and press-in the end of the spring each side (airbag removed for clarity)

20.7 Release the clips and disconnect the wiring plug

20.10 Prise the panel from the facia

20.14 Unclip the gaiter

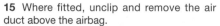

20.17 Disconnect the wiring plug and remove the nut at each end

20.20 Passengers airbag retaining nuts

20.28 Side airbag retaining nuts

15 Where fitted, unclip and remove the air duct above the airbag.
16 Remove the drivers side lower facia panel as described in Chapter 11 Section 35.
17 Undo the nuts/bolts, then lower the knee airbag until the wiring plugs can be disconnected **(see illustration)**. Manoeuvre the airbag from place.
18 Refitting is a reversal of removal.

Passengers airbag
19 Remove the facia as described in Chapter 11 Section 37.
20 Undo the 4 retaining nuts and detach the airbag from the facia **(see illustration)**.
21 Refitting is a reversal of removal. Tighten the airbag unit retaining nuts to the specified torque.

Front seat airbags
22 Removal of the seat airbags requires the seat upholstery to be removed. This is a complex task, requiring patience and experience. Consequently, we recommend this is entrusted to a Mercedes dealer or specialist.

Rear side airbags
23 Remove the rear seat backrest as described in Chapter 11 Section 31.
24 Starting at the front edge, pull the door sill trim panel upwards to release the retaining clips, then slide it forwards.
25 Pull the rubber weatherstrip from the door aperture adjacent to the side bolster.
26 Release the clips and pull the side trim panel from place.

27 Disconnect the wiring plug from the airbag unit.
28 Undo the 2 nuts, and remove the airbag unit **(see illustration)**.
29 Refitting is a reversal of removal.

Headlining airbags
30 On each side of the passenger cabin, a window airbag is fitted. The airbag runs from the lower part of the windscreen pillar to the C/D-pillar. To remove the airbag, the entire headlining must be removed. This task is outside the scope of the DIY'er, and therefore we recommend that the task be entrusted to a Mercedes dealer or specialist.

Airbag/tensioner control unit
31 Remove the centre console as described in Chapter 11 Section 36.
32 Detach the air ducts from the air distribution housing, and swivel them to one side.
33 Pivot the release levers, and disconnect the wiring plugs from the control unit **(see illustration)**.
34 Remove the insulation above the unit, then undo the 4 retaining bolts, and manoeuvre the control unit from place **(see illustration)**. Note the earth connection under the rear-left bolt.
35 Refitting is a reversal of removal. If a new control unit has been fitted, it must be configured using Mercedes STAR diagnostic equipment or equivalent. Tighten the control unit retaining bolts to the specified torque.

Impact sensors
Front sensors
36 Raise the front of the vehicle and support

it securely on axle stands (see 'Vehicle jacking and support'). Release the fasteners and remove the front section of the engine undershield.
37 Disconnect the battery negative lead as described in Chapter 5A Section 4.
Left-hand sensor
38 Remove the windscreen washer fluid reservoir as described in Section 15. Note that it's not necessary to disconnect the hoses – place the reservoir to one side.
39 Disconnect the sensor wiring plug, then undo the retaining bolt and manoeuvre the sensor from place.
40 Refitting is a reversal of removal.
Right-hand sensor
41 Release the fasteners and remove the front section of the right-hand front wheelarch liner.
42 Disconnect the wiring plug, then undo the retaining bolt and remove the sensor **(see illustration)**.
43 Refitting is a reversal of removal.

Side impact sensors
44 Remove the lower part of the B-pillar trim panel as described in Chapter 11 Section 35.
45 Pull the carpet away from the base of the B-pillar.
46 Lift the locking catches, and open the cable ducting.

20.33 Depress the buttons, and pivot over the levers

20.34 Note the earth lead

20.42 Right-hand front impact sensor retaining bolt

20.47 Side impact sensor

20.50 Side deployment pressure sensor

47 Undo the bolt and remove the side impact sensor **(see illustration)**. Disconnect the wiring plug as the sensor is withdrawn.
48 Refitting is a reversal of removal, tightening the sensor retaining bolts to the specified torque.

Side deployment pressure sensors

49 Remove the door module as described in Chapter 11 Section 18.
50 Disconnect the sensor wiring plug, then drill out the rivets securing the sensor to the door module **(see illustration)**.
51 Refitting is a reversal of removal.

Rotary contact unit (clockspring)

52 The rotary contact unit (clockspring) is integral with the steering column combination switch/module. Removal of the switch/module is described in Section 5.

21 Parktronic (PTS) system
– general information and component renewal

General information

1 Available as an option, the Parktronic system is an ultrasonic parking aid. The system uses sensors in the front and rear bumpers to transmit a signal which then bounces off any objects in range in front of or behind the car. The sensors receive the reflected signal, and the control unit can then calculate the distance of the object from the car. The system works at speeds up to 9 mph. The resulting distance information is conveyed to the driver by visual display and audio signal.
2 There are six sensors in the front bumper, and four at the rear. The control unit is located under front passengers floor. The audio/visual warning units are located on the top of the facia, and above the rear screen in the headlining.
3 When the ignition is switched on, the system performs a self-test. If the system develops a fault, this will be indicated by just the red sections of the visual warning units staying on. In the event of a fault, first check the connections at the bumper-mounted sensors, as these may be subject to dirt and water entry. After checking this, and the wiring as far as possible, it is advisable to take the car to a Mercedes-Benz dealer for testing using diagnostic equipment.

Electronic control module

Note: *If a new PTS control unit is to be fitted,* *the existing basic data must be transferred to Mercedes STAR diagnostic equipment (or equivalent), then transferred to the new control unit upon completion.*

4 Disconnect the battery negative lead as described in Chapter 5A Section 4.
5 Reach under the passengers side of the facia, then fold back the carpet and insulation material.
6 Undo the fasteners and fold back the foot rest **(see illustration)**.
7 Undo the 2 retaining bolts, detach the control unit from the footrest, and disconnect the wiring plugs **(see illustration)**.
8 Refitting is a reversal of removal.

Ultrasonic sensors

Front sensors

9 Remove the front bumper as described in Chapter 11 Section 16.
10 Detach the impact absorber from the bumper until the relevant sensor is accessible.
11 Disconnect the wiring plug from the relevant sensor.
12 Release the clips and detach the sensor from the bumper.

Rear sensors

13 Remove the rear bumper as described in Chapter 11 Section 16.

21.6 Undo the nuts and pull back the foot rest

21.7 PTS control unit retaining bolts

21.14 Spread apart the clips and withdraw the sensor

14 Disconnect the wiring plug, then unclip the relevant sensor from the bumper **(see illustration)**.

All sensors

15 Refitting is a reversal of removal.

22 Cameras – removal and refitting

Multifunction camera

Note: *If a new camera is to be fitted, before use it must be calibrated using Mercedes-Benz STAR diagnostic equipment (or equivalent).*

1 Switch off the ignition, and position the key at least 2 m from the vehicle.
2 Unclip the cover from beneath the camera at the top of the windscreen **(see illustration 11.1)**.
3 Release the clips at the front of the camera, slide it from the rear lugs, and remove it. Disconnect the wiring plugs as the camera is withdrawn. Take care not to touch the camera lens.
4 Refitting is a reversal of removal.

Reversing camera

Note: *If a new camera is fitted, prior to use it must be calibrated using Mercedes-Benz STAR diagnostic equipment (or equivalent).*

Saloon models

5 Remove the boot lid release handle as described in Chapter 11 Section 12. Note that there is no need to detach the handle from the panel.
6 Disconnect the wiring plug, then release the catch and remove the camera **(see illustration)**.

22.6 Depress the catch and remove the camera

22.9b ...and the ones on the outside...

Estate models

7 Remove the tailgate lower trim panel as described in Chapter 11 Section 35.
8 Undo the tailgate wiper motor retaining bolts.
9 Undo the bolts and unclip the tailgate handle strip **(see illustrations)**.
10 Disconnect the wiring plug, then release

22.9a Undo the bolts on the inside...

22.9c ...then prise the strip from place

the catches and detach the camera from the handle strip.

All models

11 Check the condition of the seal between the camera and the boot lid/tailgate panel, and renew if necessary.
12 The remainder of refitting is a reversal of removal.

FRONT ELECTRICAL PREFUSE BOX (UP TO MAY 2009)

FUSE/RELAY	VALUE	DESCRIPTION
F88	400 A	Alternator
F89	125 A	Front SAM control unit with fuse and relay module
F90	40 A	Rear SAM control unit with fuse and fuse and relay module
F91	80 A	Combustion engine fan motor and air conditioning with integrated control
F100	40 A	Air conditioner housing
F101	-	Not used
F103	150 A	PTC heater booster
F104	70 A	Interior fuse box
F105	100	Front SAM control unit with fuse and relay module (N10/1)

FRONT ELECTRICAL PREFUSE BOX (FROM JUNE 2009) WITHOUT START/STOP

Fuses and relays

FUSE/RELAY	VALUE	DESCRIPTION
F151	100 A	Internal combustion engine and air conditioning fan motor with integrated 100 control
F152	150 A	Front SAM control unit with fuse and relay module (N10/1)
F153	-	Not used
F154	60 A	Front SAM control module with fuse and relay module (N10/1)
F155	-	Not used
F156	150 A	PTC heater booster
F157	-	Not used
F158	50 A	Blower regulator
F159	-	Not used
F160	60 A	Interior compartment fuse box
F161	100 A	Front SAM control module with fuse and relay module (N10/1)
F162	-	Not used
F163	150 A	Rear SAM control unit with fuse and relay module (N10/2)
F164	80 A	Rear SAM control unit with fuse and relay module (N10/2)

FRONT ELECTRICAL PREFUSE BOX (FROM JUNE 2009) WITH START/STOP

FUSE/RELAY	VALUE	DESCRIPTION
F151	100 A	Internal combustion engine and air conditioning fan motor with integrated 100 control
F152	150 A	Front SAM control unit with fuse and relay module (N10/1)
F153	60 A	Front SAM control module with fuse and relay module (N10/1)
F154	150 A	PTC heater booster
F155	-	Not used
F156	100 A	Front SAM control module with fuse and relay module (N10/1)
F157	-	Not used
F158	150 A	Rear SAM control unit with fuse and relay module (N10/2)
F159	200 A	Additional battery relay
F160	50 A	Blower regulator
F161	-	Not used
F162	60 A	Interior compartment fuse box

Fuses and relays (continued)

FUSE AND RELAY BOX IN ENGINE COMPARTMENT

FUSE/RELAY	VALUE	DESCRIPTION
F1	25 A	Electronic Stability Program control unit
F2	30 A	Left front door control unit
F3	30 A	Right front door control unit
F4	-	Not used
F5	7.5 A	Rear SAM control unit with fuse and relay module (N10/2)
F6	10 A	CDI control unit
F7	20 A	Starter
F8	7.5 A	Supplemental restraint system control unit
F9	15 A	Glove compartment socket
F10	30 A	Wiper motor
F11	7.5 A	Audio/COMAND display or control panel
F12	7.5 A	Upper control panel control unit
F13	7.5 A	Steering column module control unit
F14	7.5 A	Electronic Stability Program control unit
F15	7.5 A	Supplemental restraint system control unit
F16	5 A	Diagnostic connector
F17	30 A	Panoramic sliding roof control module or Overhead control panel control unit
F18	7.5 A	Exterior lights switch
F19	20 A	Electronic ignition lock control unit
F20	40 A	Electronic Stability Program control unit
F21	7.5 A	Stop lamp switch, Glove compartment lamp switch
F22	15 A	Combustion engine fan motor and air conditioning with integrated control, CDI control unit
F23	20 A	Rear SAM control unit with fuse and relay module (N10/2), CDI control unit, Terminal 87 connector sleeve
F24	15 A	CDI control unit
F25	15 A	Oxygen sensor upstream of catalytic converter
F26	20 A	Radio / Radio with auto pilot system / COMAND controller unit
F27	7.5 A	Electric steering lock control unit, Electronic ignition lock control unit, CDI control unit
F28	7.5 A	Instrument cluster
F29	10 A	Right front lamp unit

Fuses and relays (continued)

F30	10 A	Left front lamp unit
F31	15 A	Left fanfare horn, Right fanfare horn
F32	-	Not used
F33	10 A	Electronic transmission control control unit, Fully integrated transmission control controller unit
F34	-	Not used
F35	-	Not used
F36	7.5 A	DISTRONIC electric controller unit or not used
R1	-	Terminal 15 relay
R2	-	Terminal 15R relay
R3	-	Backup relay
R4	-	Circuit 50 starter relay
R5	-	Engine circuit 87 relay
R6	-	Fanfare horn relay
R7	-	Not used
R8	-	Backup relay
R9	-	Chassis circuit 87 relay

FUSE AND RELAY BOX IN LUGGAGE COMPARTMENT (UP TO MAY 2009)

FUSE/RELAY	VALUE	DESCRIPTION
F1	5 A	Multimedia control unit
F2	5 A	Telephone TV tuner
F3	7.5 A	Vehicle emergency control unit or not used
F4	7.5 A	Satellite digital audio receiver control unit Audio system Camera control unit or not used
F5	-	Not used
F6	-	Not used
F7	7.5 A	Vehicle emergency control unit or not used
F8	50 A	Seat belt pretensioner, front left
F9	50 A	Seat belt pretensioner, front right
F10	5 A	Video control computer
F11	-	Not used
F12	7.5 A	Seat ventilation
F13	7.5 A	Weight sensing system (WSS) control unit
F14	15 A	12V socket
F15	20 A	Additional heater system

Fuses and relays (continued)

F16	15 A	Keyless entry control unit or not used
F17	7.5 A	Diagnostic connector, Transmission control unit
F18	15 A	Power connector or not used
F19	15 A	Front cigarette lighter Ashtray illumination or not used
F20	5 A	Tyre pressure monitoring system control unit or not used
F21	-	Not used
F22	-	Not used
F23	30 A	Sound system or not used
F24	7.5 A	Transmission oil pump relay
F25	40 A	Heated rear windscreen
F26	-	Not used
F27	-	Not used
F28	7.5 A	Antenna amplifier Alarm horn Radio antenna Interior protection control unit or not used
F29	-	Not used
F30	-	Not used
F31	5 A	Rear blower motor
F32	20 A	Fuel pump
F33	-	Not used
F34	15 A	Rear wiper motor Or Not used
F35	30 A	Control unit, rear right door
F36	30 A	Rear left door control unit or not used
F37	5 A	Front head restraints
F38	15 A	Adaptive damping control unit Or Not used
F39	25 A	DC-AC converter
F40	30 A	Passenger's seat control unit
F41	30 A	Driver's seat control unit
F42	40 A	Tailgate control unit or not used
F43	7.5 A	Multicontour seat pneumatic pump
F44	5 A	Parktronic system Distronic sensor
F45	30 A	Trailer recognition control unit or not used
F46	20 A	Trailer recognition control unit or not used
F47	15 A	Trailer connector socket or not used (5A also used)
F48	5 A	AdBlue control unit or not used
F49	7.5 A	Trailer recognition control unit
F50	15 A	Trailer recognition control unit or not used
F51	-	Not used
F52	20 A	Trailer recognition control unit Oil cooling fan motor relay
F53	-	Not used
F54	40 A	AdBlue relay
F55	-	Not used
F56	-	Not used
R1	-	Rear window heater relay
R2	-	Terminal 15 relay
R3	-	Terminal 15R relay 2
R4	-	Seat adjustment relay
R5	-	Fuel pump relay
R6	-	Terminal 15R relay 1
R7	-	Liftgate windshield wiper relay (estate version)

Fuses and relays (continued)

FUSE AND RELAY BOX IN LUGGAGE COMPARTMENT (FROM JUNE 2009)

FUSE/RELAY	VALUE	DESCRIPTION
F1	7.5 A	Media interface control unit
F2	-	Not used
F3	7.5 A	Emergency call system control unit or not used
F4	7.5 A	Satellite digital audio radio (SDAR) control unit, Digital Audio Broadcasting control unit, Backup camera control unit
F5	-	Not used
F6	-	Not used
F7	7.5 A	Emergency call system control unit
F8	50 A	Left front reversible emergency tensioning retractor
F9	50 A	Right front reversible emergency tensioning retractor
F10	-	Not used
F11	7.5 A	Radar sensors control unit or not used
F12	-	Not used
F13	-	Not used
F14	15 A	Vehicle interior power outlet
F15	-	Not used
F16	15 A	Keyless Go control unit
F17	-	Not used
F18	15 A	Cargo area connector box
F19	15 A	Front cigarette lighter with ashtray illumination or not used
F20	5 A	Tire pressure monitor control unit
F21	-	Not used
F22	-	Not used
F23	40 A	Sound system amplifier control unit
F24	-	Not used
F25	40 A	Rear window heater
F26	-	Not used
F27	-	Not used
F28	7.5 A	Antenna amplifier for rear window FM antenna, Rear window antenna amplifier 1, Alarm siren, Interior protection and tow-away protection control unit, DAB, TV 2 antenna amplifier and KEYLESS GO
F29	-	Not used
F30	-	Not used
F31	-	Not used

Fuses and relays (continued)

F32	20 A	Fused via fuel pump relay
F33	-	Not used
F34	15 A	Fused via tailgate wiper relay (estate version)
F35	30 A	Right rear door control unit
F36	30 A	Left rear door control unit
F37	7.5 A	Driver seat NECK-PRO head restraint solenoid, Front passenger seat NECK-PRO head restraint solenoid
F38	-	Not used
F39	-	Not used
F40	-	Not used
F41	-	Not used
F42	40 A	Tailgate control control unit (estate version)
F43	-	Not used
F44	7.5 A	PARKTRONIC control unit, Radar sensors control unit
F45	30 A	Trailer recognition control unit
F46	20 A	Trailer recognition control unit
F47	15 A	Trailer recognition control unit
F48	-	Not used
F49	7.5 A	Trailer recognition control unit
F50	30 A	Trailer recognition control unit
F51	-	Not used
R1	-	Heated rear window relay
R2	-	Terminal 15 relay
R3	-	Terminal 15R relay 2
R4	-	Seat adjustment relay
R5	-	Fuel pump relay
R6	-	Terminal 15R relay 1
R7	-	Tailgate windshield wiper relay (estate version)

FUSE BOX IN PASSENGER COMPARTMENT

FUSE/RELAY	VALUE	DESCRIPTION
F1	-	Not used
F2	-	Not used
F3	-	Not used
F4	-	Not used
F5	-	Not used
F6	-	Not used

Fuses and relays (continued)

F7	-	Not used
F8	-	Not used
F9	-	Not used
F10	30 A	Front passenger seat control unit
F11	-	Not used
F12	-	Not used
F13	-	Not used
F14	-	Not used
F15	-	Not used
F16	-	Not used
F17	7.5 A	Rear blower motor
F18	-	Not used
F19	15 A	Adaptive damping system control unit
F20	30 A	Driver seat control unit

FUSE BOX IN LUGGAGE COMPARTMENT

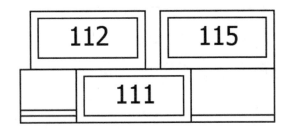

FUSE/RELAY	VALUE	DESCRIPTION
F111	60 A	Front SAM control module with fuse and relay module (N10/1)
F112	-	Not used
F115	-	Not used

Fuses and relays (continued)

Starting and Charging

*1 Engine code: 651
*2 Engine code: 646
*3 Up to May 2009
*4 From June 2009
*5 Up to May 2010
*6 From June 2010
*7 Without start stop
*8 With start stop
*9 Up to 2009
*10 From 2010

Seat heating

Advanced climate control 1 of 2

*1 LHD models
*2 RHD models
*3 From 2010
*4 Up to May 2010
*5 From June 2010
*6 Up to 2009
*7 With start stop
*8 Without start stop

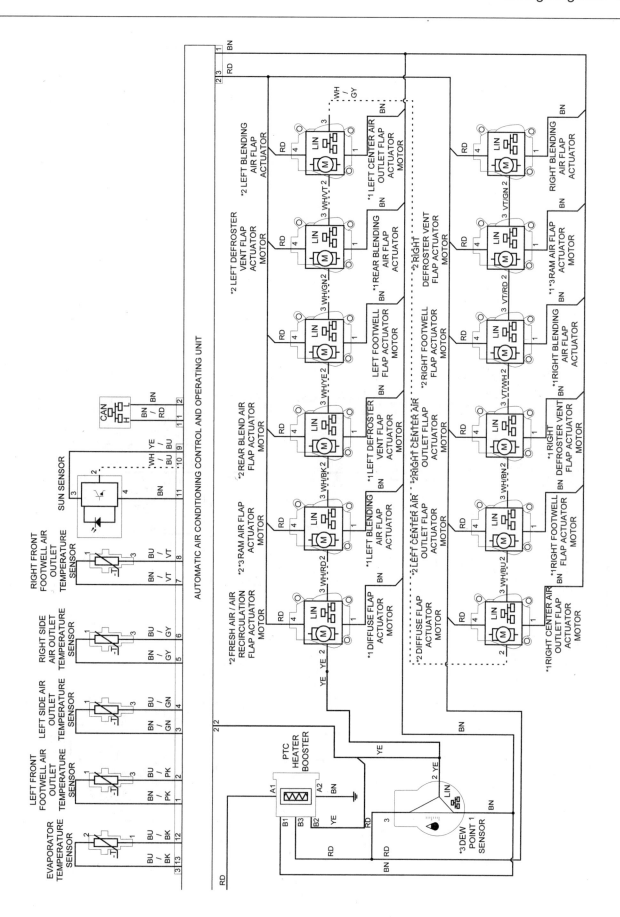

Advanced climate control 2 of 2

Standard climate control

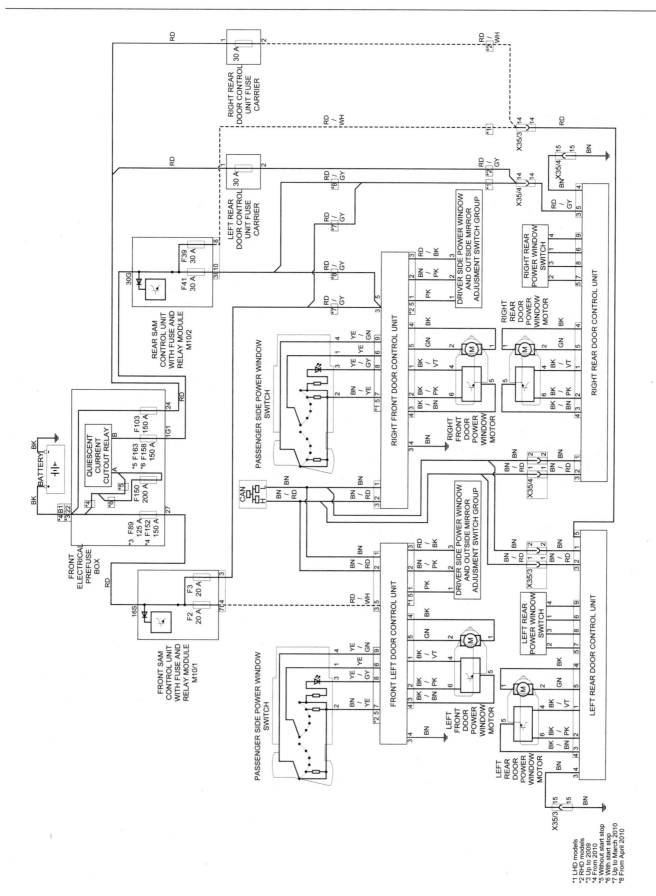

Power Windows

*1 LHD models
*2 RHD models
*3 Up to 2009
*4 From 2010
*5 Without start stop
*6 With start stop
*7 Up to March 2010
*8 From April 2010

Power door locks

*1 LHD models
*2 RHD models
*3 Up to 2009
*4 From 2010
*5 Without start stop
*6 With start stop
*7 Up to March 2010
*8 From April 2010
*9 For all models without keyless go
*10 For trunk lid control
*11 For tailgate control

Power door locks - Keyless

*1 From November 2009
*2 For saloon
*3 For estate
*4 Up to 2009
*5 From 2010
*6 Without start stop
*7 With start stop

Wiper and washers

*1 For saloon
*2 For estate
*3 LHD models
*4 RHD models
*5 Up to 2009
*6 From 2010
*7 Without start stop
*8 With start stop
*9 With CAN
*10 Without CAN

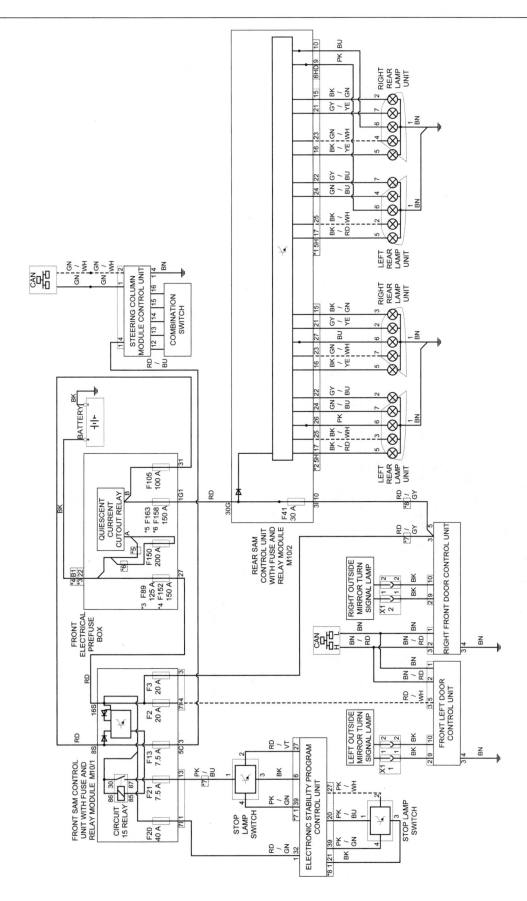

Exterior lights – rear

*1 For saloon
*2 For estate
*3 Up to 2009
*4 From 2010
*5 Without start stop
*6 With start stop
*7 Up to February 2011
*8 From May 2011

Exterior lights – with Xenon

*1 Up to 2009
*2 From 2010
*3 Up to November 2009
*4 From December 2009

Exterior lights – without Xenon

*1 Up to 2012
*2 From 2012
*3 Up to November 2009
*4 From December 2009
*5 Up to 2009
*6 From 2010

Interior lights

*1 Equipment: Classic
*2 Equipment: Avantgarde and Elegance
*3 With CAN
*4 Without CAN
*5 Up to 2009
*6 From 2010

Sound system

*1 Digital audio broadcasting
*2 Central operating unit
*3 Display
*4 For estate
*5 Up to 2009
*6 From 2010
*7 Without start stop
*8 With start stop
*9 TV tuner
*10 Radio
*11 COMAND control unit
*12 Sound system amplifier control unit
*13 Up to May 2010
*14 From June 2010
*15 Up to February 2011
*16 From March 2011
*17 For saloon

Sound system - speakers with amplifier

*1 For saloon
*2 For estate
*3 Without start stop
*4 With start stop
*5 Up to 2009
*6 From 2010
*7 TELEAID emergency call system

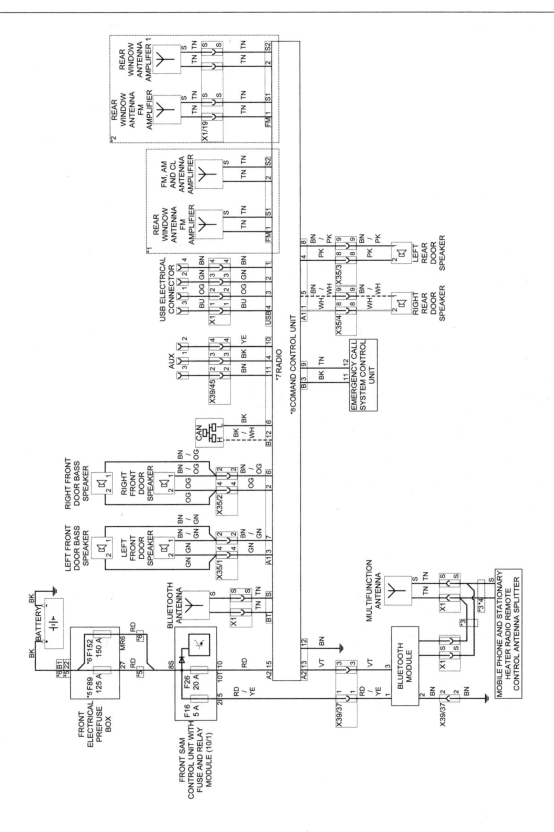

Sound system - speakers without amplifier

*1 For saloon
*2 For estate
*3 For mobile phone
*4 For stationary heater
*5 Up to 2009
*6 From 2010
*7 Radio
*8 COMAND control unit

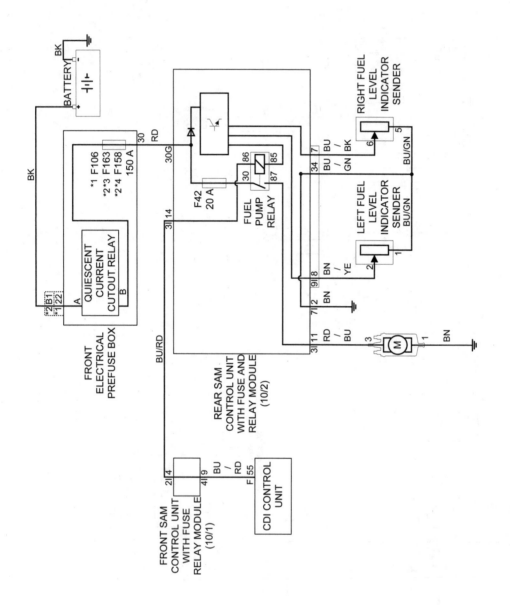

Fuel pump

*1 Up to 2009
*2 From 2010
*3 Without start stop
*4 With start stop

Dimensions and weights . . . . **REF•1**
Fuel economy. . . . . **REF•2**
Conversion factors . . . . **REF•6**
Buying spare parts . . . . **REF•7**
Vehicle identification numbers . . . . **REF•7**
General repair procedures . . . . **REF•8**
Jacking and vehicle support . . . . **REF•9**
Tools and working facilities . . . . **REF•10**
MOT test checks . . . . **REF•12**
Fault finding . . . . **REF•16**
Glossary of technical terms . . . . **REF•24**
Index. . . . . **REF•29**

Dimensions and weights

Note: *All figures are approximate, and may vary according to mode. Refer to the manufacturers data for exact figures.*

Dimensions

Overall length:
    Saloon . . . . 4591 mm
    Estate . . . . 4606 mm
Overall width (including mirrors). . . . . 2012 mm
Overall height:
    Saloon . . . . 1447 mm
    Estate . . . . 1459 mm
Wheelbase . . . . 2760 mm

Weights

Unladen . . . . 1560 to 1695 kg
Gross vehicle weight . . . . 2140 to 2460 kg
Maximum roof rack load . . . . 100 kg

Fuel economy

Although depreciation is still the biggest part of the cost of motoring for most car owners, the cost of fuel is more immediately noticeable. These pages give some tips on how to get the best fuel economy.

Working it out

Manufacturer's figures

Car manufacturers are required by law to provide fuel consumption information on all new vehicles sold. These 'official' figures are obtained by simulating various driving conditions on a rolling road or a test track. Real life conditions are different, so the fuel consumption actually achieved may not bear much resemblance to the quoted figures.

How to calculate it

Many cars now have trip computers which will

display fuel consumption, both instantaneous and average. Refer to the owner's handbook for details of how to use these.

To calculate consumption yourself (and maybe to check that the trip computer is accurate), proceed as follows.

1. Fill up with fuel and note the mileage, or zero the trip recorder.
2. Drive as usual until you need to fill up again.
3. Note the amount of fuel required to refill the tank, and the mileage covered since the previous fill-up.
4. Divide the mileage by the amount of fuel used to obtain the consumption figure.

For example:

Mileage at first fill-up (a) = 27,903
Mileage at second fill-up (b) = 28,346
Mileage covered (b - a) = 443
Fuel required at second fill-up = 48.6 litres

The half-completed changeover to metric units in the UK means that we buy our fuel in litres, measure distances in miles and talk about fuel consumption in miles per gallon. There are two ways round this: the first is to convert the litres to gallons before doing the calculation (by dividing by 4.546, or see Table 1). So in the example:

48.6 litres ÷ 4.546 = 10.69 gallons
443 miles ÷ 10.69 gallons = 41.4 mpg

The second way is to calculate the consumption in miles per litre, then multiply that figure by 4.546 (or see Table 2).

So in the example, fuel consumption is:

443 miles ÷ 48.6 litres = 9.1 mpl
9.1 mpl x 4.546 = 41.4 mpg

The rest of Europe expresses fuel consumption in litres of fuel required to travel 100 km (l/100 km). For interest, the conversions are given in Table 3. In practice it doesn't matter what units you use, provided you know what your normal consumption is and can spot if it's getting better or worse.

Table 1: conversion of litres to Imperial gallons

litres	1	2	3	4	5	10	20	30	40	50	60	70
gallons	0.22	0.44	0.66	0.88	1.10	2.24	4.49	6.73	8.98	11.22	13.47	15.71

Table 2: conversion of miles per litre to miles per gallon

miles per litre	5	6	7	8	9	10	11	12	13	14
miles per gallon	23	27	32	36	41	46	50	55	59	64

Table 3: conversion of litres per 100 km to miles per gallon

litres per 100 km	4	4.5	5	5.5	6	6.5	7	8	9	10
miles per gallon	71	63	56	51	47	43	40	35	31	28

Maintenance

A well-maintained car uses less fuel and creates less pollution. In particular:

Filters

Change air and fuel filters at the specified intervals.

Oil

Use a good quality oil of the lowest viscosity specified by the vehicle manufacturer (see *Lubricants and fluids*). Check the level often and be careful not to overfill.

Spark plugs

When applicable, renew at the specified intervals.

Tyres

Check tyre pressures regularly. Under-inflated tyres have an increased rolling resistance. It is generally safe to use the higher pressures specified for full load conditions even when not fully laden, but keep an eye on the centre band of tread for signs of wear due to over-inflation.

When buying new tyres, consider the 'fuel saving' models which most manufacturers include in their ranges.

Driving style

Acceleration

Acceleration uses more fuel than driving at a steady speed. The best technique with modern cars is to accelerate reasonably briskly to the desired speed, changing up through the gears as soon as possible without making the engine labour.

Air conditioning

Air conditioning absorbs quite a bit of energy from the engine – typically 3 kW (4 hp) or so. The effect on fuel consumption is at its worst in slow traffic. Switch it off when not required.

Anticipation

Drive smoothly and try to read the traffic flow so as to avoid unnecessary acceleration and braking.

Automatic transmission

When accelerating in an automatic, avoid depressing the throttle so far as to make the transmission hold onto lower gears at higher speeds. Don't use the 'Sport' setting, if applicable.

When stationary with the engine running, select 'N' or 'P'. When moving, keep your left foot away from the brake.

Braking

Braking converts the car's energy of motion into heat – essentially, it is wasted. Obviously some braking is always going to be necessary, but with good anticipation it is surprising how much can be avoided, especially on routes that you know well.

Carshare

Consider sharing lifts to work or to the shops. Even once a week will make a difference.

Electrical loads

Electricity is 'fuel' too; the alternator which charges the battery does so by converting some of the engine's energy of motion into electrical energy. The more electrical accessories are in use, the greater the load on the alternator. Switch off big consumers like the heated rear window when not required.

Freewheeling

Freewheeling (coasting) in neutral with the engine switched off is dangerous. The effort required to operate power-assisted brakes and steering increases when the engine is not running, with a potential lack of control in emergency situations.

In any case, modern fuel injection systems automatically cut off the engine's fuel supply on the overrun (moving and in gear, but with the accelerator pedal released).

Gadgets

Bolt-on devices claiming to save fuel have been around for nearly as long as the motor car itself. Those which worked were rapidly adopted as standard equipment by the vehicle manufacturers. Others worked only in certain situations, or saved fuel only at the expense of unacceptable effects on performance, driveability or the life of engine components.

The most effective fuel saving gadget is the driver's right foot.

Journey planning

Combine (eg) a trip to the supermarket with a visit to the recycling centre and the DIY store, rather than making separate journeys.

When possible choose a travelling time outside rush hours.

Load

The more heavily a car is laden, the greater the energy required to accelerate it to a given speed. Remove heavy items which you don't need to carry.

One load which is often overlooked is the contents of the fuel tank. A tankful of fuel (55 litres / 12 gallons) weighs 45 kg (100 lb) or so. Just half filling it may be worthwhile.

Lost?

At the risk of stating the obvious, if you're going somewhere new, have details of the route to hand. There's not much point in achieving record mpg if you also go miles out of your way.

Parking

If possible, carry out any reversing or turning manoeuvres when you arrive at a parking space so that you can drive straight out when you leave. Manoeuvering when the engine is cold uses a lot more fuel.

Driving around looking for free on-street parking may cost more in fuel than buying a car park ticket.

Premium fuel

Most major oil companies (and some supermarkets) have premium grades of fuel which are several pence a litre dearer than the standard grades. Reports vary, but the consensus seems to be that if these fuels improve economy at all, they do not do so by enough to justify their extra cost.

Roof rack

When loading a roof rack, try to produce a wedge shape with the narrow end at the front. Any cover should be securely fastened – if it flaps it's creating turbulence and absorbing energy.

Remove roof racks and boxes when not in use – they increase air resistance and can create a surprising amount of noise.

Short journeys

The engine is at its least efficient, and wear is highest, during the first few miles after a cold start. Consider walking, cycling or using public transport.

Speed

The engine is at its most efficient when running at a steady speed and load at the rpm where it develops maximum torque. (You can find this figure in the car's handbook.) For most cars this corresponds to between 55 and 65 mph in top gear.

Above the optimum cruising speed, fuel consumption starts to rise quite sharply. A car travelling at 80 mph will typically be using 30% more fuel than at 60 mph.

Supermarket fuel

It may be cheap but is it any good? In the UK all supermarket fuel must meet the relevant British Standard. The major oil companies will say that their branded fuels have better additive packages which may stop carbon and other deposits building up. A reasonable compromise might be to use one tank of branded fuel to three or four from the supermarket.

Switch off when stationary

Switch off the engine if you look like being stationary for more than 30 seconds or so. This is good for the environment as well as for your pocket. Be aware though that frequent restarts are hard on the battery and the starter motor.

Windows

Driving with the windows open increases air turbulence around the vehicle. Closing the windows promotes smooth airflow and

reduced resistance. The faster you go, the more significant this is.

And finally . . .

Driving techniques associated with good fuel economy tend to involve moderate acceleration and low top speeds. Be considerate to the needs of other road users who may need to make brisker progress; even if you do not agree with them this is not an excuse to be obstructive.

Safety must always take precedence over economy, whether it is a question of accelerating hard to complete an overtaking manoeuvre, killing your speed when confronted with a potential hazard or switching the lights on when it starts to get dark.

Conversion factors

Length (distance)

Inches (in)	x 25.4	= Millimetres (mm)	x 0.0394	= Inches (in)
Feet (ft)	x 0.305	= Metres (m)	x 3.281	= Feet (ft)
Miles	x 1.609	= Kilometres (km)	x 0.621	= Miles

Volume (capacity)

Cubic inches (cu in; in³)	x 16.387	= Cubic centimetres (cc; cm³)	x 0.061	= Cubic inches (cu in; in³)
Imperial pints (Imp pt)	x 0.568	= Litres (l)	x 1.76	= Imperial pints (Imp pt)
Imperial quarts (Imp qt)	x 1.137	= Litres (l)	x 0.88	= Imperial quarts (Imp qt)
Imperial quarts (Imp qt)	x 1.201	= US quarts (US qt)	x 0.833	= Imperial quarts (Imp qt)
US quarts (US qt)	x 0.946	= Litres (l)	x 1.057	= US quarts (US qt)
Imperial gallons (Imp gal)	x 4.546	= Litres (l)	x 0.22	= Imperial gallons (Imp gal)
Imperial gallons (Imp gal)	x 1.201	= US gallons (US gal)	x 0.833	= Imperial gallons (Imp gal)
US gallons (US gal)	x 3.785	= Litres (l)	x 0.264	= US gallons (US gal)

Mass (weight)

Ounces (oz)	x 28.35	= Grams (g)	x 0.035	= Ounces (oz)
Pounds (lb)	x 0.454	= Kilograms (kg)	x 2.205	= Pounds (lb)

Force

Ounces-force (ozf; oz)	x 0.278	= Newtons (N)	x 3.6	= Ounces-force (ozf; oz)
Pounds-force (lbf; lb)	x 4.448	= Newtons (N)	x 0.225	= Pounds-force (lbf; lb)
Newtons (N)	x 0.1	= Kilograms-force (kgf; kg)	x 9.81	= Newtons (N)

Pressure

Pounds-force per square inch (psi; lbf/in²; lb/in²)	x 0.070	= Kilograms-force per square centimetre (kgf/cm²; kg/cm²)	x 14.223	= Pounds-force per square inch (psi; lbf/in²; lb/in²)
Pounds-force per square inch (psi; lbf/in²; lb/in²)	x 0.068	= Atmospheres (atm)	x 14.696	= Pounds-force per square inch (psi; lbf/in²; lb/in²)
Pounds-force per square inch (psi; lbf/in²; lb/in²)	x 0.069	= Bars	x 14.5	= Pounds-force per square inch (psi; lbf/in²; lb/in²)
Pounds-force per square inch (psi; lbf/in²; lb/in²)	x 6.895	= Kilopascals (kPa)	x 0.145	= Pounds-force per square inch (psi; lbf/in²; lb/in²)
Kilopascals (kPa)	x 0.01	= Kilograms-force per square centimetre (kgf/cm²; kg/cm²)	x 98.1	= Kilopascals (kPa)
Millibar (mbar)	x 100	= Pascals (Pa)	x 0.01	= Millibar (mbar)
Millibar (mbar)	x 0.0145	= Pounds-force per square inch (psi; lbf/in²; lb/in²)	x 68.947	= Millibar (mbar)
Millibar (mbar)	x 0.75	= Millimetres of mercury (mmHg)	x 1.333	= Millibar (mbar)
Millibar (mbar)	x 0.401	= Inches of water (inH₂O)	x 2.491	= Millibar (mbar)
Millimetres of mercury (mmHg)	x 0.535	= Inches of water (inH₂O)	x 1.868	= Millimetres of mercury (mmHg)
Inches of water (inH₂O)	x 0.036	= Pounds-force per square inch (psi; lbf/in²; lb/in²)	x 27.68	= Inches of water (inH₂O)

(Note: subscript in "inH₂O" represents inH_2O)

Torque (moment of force)

Pounds-force inches (lbf in; lb in)	x 1.152	= Kilograms-force centimetre (kgf cm; kg cm)	x 0.868	= Pounds-force inches (lbf in; lb in)
Pounds-force inches (lbf in; lb in)	x 0.113	= Newton metres (Nm)	x 8.85	= Pounds-force inches (lbf in; lb in)
Pounds-force inches (lbf in; lb in)	x 0.083	= Pounds-force feet (lbf ft; lb ft)	x 12	= Pounds-force inches (lbf in; lb in)
Pounds-force feet (lbf ft; lb ft)	x 0.138	= Kilograms-force metres (kgf m; kg m)	x 7.233	= Pounds-force feet (lbf ft; lb ft)
Pounds-force feet (lbf ft; lb ft)	x 1.356	= Newton metres (Nm)	x 0.738	= Pounds-force feet (lbf ft; lb ft)
Newton metres (Nm)	x 0.102	= Kilograms-force metres (kgf m; kg m)	x 9.804	= Newton metres (Nm)

Power

Horsepower (hp)	x 745.7	= Watts (W)	x 0.0013	= Horsepower (hp)

Velocity (speed)

Miles per hour (miles/hr; mph)	x 1.609	= Kilometres per hour (km/hr; kph)	x 0.621	= Miles per hour (miles/hr; mph)

Fuel consumption*

Miles per gallon, Imperial (mpg)	x 0.354	= Kilometres per litre (km/l)	x 2.825	= Miles per gallon, Imperial (mpg)
Miles per gallon, US (mpg)	x 0.425	= Kilometres per litre (km/l)	x 2.352	= Miles per gallon, US (mpg)

Temperature

Degrees Fahrenheit = (°C x 1.8) + 32

Degrees Celsius (Degrees Centigrade; °C) = (°F - 32) x 0.56

It is common practice to convert from miles per gallon (mpg) to litres/100 kilometres (l/100km), where mpg x l/100 km = 282

Spare parts are available from many sources, including maker's appointed garages, accessory shops, and motor factors. To be sure of obtaining the correct parts, it will sometimes be necessary to quote the vehicle identification number. If possible, it can also be useful to take the old parts along for positive identification. Items such as starter motors and alternators may be available under a service exchange scheme – any parts returned should be clean.

Our advice regarding spare parts is as follows.

Officially appointed garages

This is the best source of parts which are peculiar to your car, and which are not otherwise generally available (eg, badges, interior trim, certain body panels, etc). It is also the only place at which you should buy parts if the vehicle is still under warranty.

Accessory shops

These are very good places to buy materials and components needed for the maintenance of your car (oil, air and fuel filters, light bulbs, drivebelts, greases, brake pads, tough-up paint, etc). Components of this nature sold by a reputable shop are of the same standard as those used by the car manufacturer.

5 Besides components, these shops also sell tools and general accessories, usually have convenient opening hours, charge lower prices, and can often be found close to home. Some accessory shops have parts counters where components needed for almost any repair job can be purchased or ordered.

Motor factors

Good factors will stock all the more important components which wear out comparatively quickly, and can sometimes supply individual components needed for the overhaul of a larger assembly (eg, brake seals and hydraulic parts, bearing shells, pistons, valves). They may also handle work such as cylinder block reboring, crankshaft regrinding, etc.

Tyre and exhaust specialists

These outlets may be independent, or members of a local or national chain. They frequently offer competitive prices when compared with a main dealer or local garage, but it will pay to obtain several quotes before making a decision. When researching prices, also ask what 'extras' may be added – for instance fitting a new valve and balancing the wheel are both commonly charged on top of the price of a new tyre.

Other sources

Beware of parts or materials obtained from market stalls, car boot sales, internet auction sites or similar outlets. Such items are not invariably sub-standard, but there is little chance of compensation if they do prove unsatisfactory. In the case of safety-critical components such as brake pads, there is the risk not only of financial loss, but also of an accident causing injury or death

Second-hand components or assemblies obtained from a car breaker can be a good buy in some circumstances, but this sort of purchase is best made by the experienced DIY mechanic.

Vehicle identification numbers

Modifications are a continuing and unpublicised process in vehicle manufacture, quite apart from major model changes. Spare parts manuals and lists are compiled upon a numerical basis, the individual vehicle identification numbers being essential to correct identification of the component concerned.

When ordering spare parts, always give as much information as possible. Quote the car model, year of manufacture, body and engine numbers as appropriate.

The vehicle identification plate is situated at the bottom of the drivers side door B-pillar **(see illustration)**. It gives the VIN (vehicle identification number), vehicle weight information and paint and trim colour codes. The vehicle identification number also stamped into the vehicle body beneath the drivers seat.

The engine number is stamped on the left-hand side of the cylinder block. On 2148 cc (type 646) engines, the number is above the left-hand engine mounting bracket, and on 2143 cc (type 651) engines, the number is below the vacuum pump.

The VIN is located on a plate at the base of the drivers door B-pillar

Whenever servicing, repair or overhaul work is carried out on the car or its components, observe the following procedures and instructions. This will assist in carrying out the operation efficiently and to a professional standard of workmanship.

Joint mating faces and gaskets

When separating components at their mating faces, never insert screwdrivers or similar implements into the joint between the faces in order to prise them apart. This can cause severe damage which results in oil leaks, coolant leaks, etc upon reassembly. Separation is usually achieved by tapping along the joint with a soft-faced hammer in order to break the seal. However, note that this method may not be suitable where dowels are used for component location.

Where a gasket is used between the mating faces of two components, a new one must be fitted on reassembly; fit it dry unless otherwise stated in the repair procedure. Make sure that the mating faces are clean and dry, with all traces of old gasket removed. When cleaning a joint face, use a tool which is unlikely to score or damage the face, and remove any burrs or nicks with an oilstone or fine file.

Make sure that tapped holes are cleaned with a pipe cleaner, and keep them free of jointing compound, if this is being used, unless specifically instructed otherwise.

Ensure that all orifices, channels or pipes are clear, and blow through them, preferably using compressed air.

Oil seals

Oil seals can be removed by levering them out with a wide flat-bladed screwdriver or similar implement. Alternatively, a number of self-tapping screws may be screwed into the seal, and these used as a purchase for pliers or some similar device in order to pull the seal free.

Whenever an oil seal is removed from its working location, either individually or as part of an assembly, it should be renewed.

The very fine sealing lip of the seal is easily damaged, and will not seal if the surface it contacts is not completely clean and free from scratches, nicks or grooves. If the original sealing surface of the component cannot be restored, and the manufacturer has not made provision for slight relocation of the seal relative to the sealing surface, the component should be renewed.

Protect the lips of the seal from any surface which may damage them in the course of fitting. Use tape or a conical sleeve where possible. Where indicated, lubricate the seal lips with oil before fitting and, on dual-lipped seals, fill the space between the lips with grease.

Unless otherwise stated, oil seals must be fitted with their sealing lips toward the lubricant to be sealed.

Use a tubular drift or block of wood of the appropriate size to install the seal and, if the seal housing is shouldered, drive the seal down to the shoulder. If the seal housing is unshouldered, the seal should be fitted with its face flush with the housing top face (unless otherwise instructed).

Screw threads and fastenings

Seized nuts, bolts and screws are quite a common occurrence where corrosion has set in, and the use of penetrating oil or releasing fluid will often overcome this problem if the offending item is soaked for a while before attempting to release it. The use of an impact driver may also provide a means of releasing such stubborn fastening devices, when used in conjunction with the appropriate screwdriver bit or socket. If none of these methods works, it may be necessary to resort to the careful application of heat, or the use of a hacksaw or nut splitter device. Before resorting to extreme methods, check that you are not dealing with a left-hand thread!

Studs are usually removed by locking two nuts together on the threaded part, and then using a spanner on the lower nut to unscrew the stud. Studs or bolts which have broken off below the surface of the component in which they are mounted can sometimes be removed using a stud extractor.

Always ensure that a blind tapped hole is completely free from oil, grease, water or other fluid before installing the bolt or stud. Failure to do this could cause the housing to crack due to the hydraulic action of the bolt or stud as it is screwed in.

For some screw fastenings, notably cylinder head bolts or nuts, torque wrench settings are no longer specified for the latter stages of tightening, "angle-tightening" being called up instead. Typically, a fairly low torque wrench setting will be applied to the bolts/nuts in the correct sequence, followed by one or more stages of tightening through specified angles.

When checking or retightening a nut or bolt to a specified torque setting, slacken the nut or bolt by a quarter of a turn, and then retighten to the specified setting. However, this should not be attempted where angular tightening has been used.

Locknuts, locktabs and washers

Any fastening which will rotate against a component or housing during tightening should always have a washer between it and the relevant component or housing.

Spring or split washers should always be renewed when they are used to lock a critical component such as a big-end bearing retaining bolt or nut. Locktabs which are folded over to retain a nut or bolt should always be renewed.

Self-locking nuts can be re-used in non-critical areas, providing resistance can be felt when the locking portion passes over the bolt or stud thread. However, it should be noted that self-locking stiffnuts tend to lose their effectiveness after long periods of use, and should then be renewed as a matter of course.

Split pins must always be replaced with new ones of the correct size for the hole.

When thread-locking compound is found on the threads of a fastener which is to be re-used, it should be cleaned off with a wire brush and solvent, and fresh compound applied on reassembly.

Special tools

Some repair procedures in this manual entail the use of special tools such as a press, two or three-legged pullers, spring compressors, etc. Wherever possible, suitable readily-available alternatives to the manufacturer's special tools are described, and are shown in use. In some instances, where no alternative is possible, it has been necessary to resort to the use of a manufacturer's tool, and this has been done for reasons of safety as well as the efficient completion of the repair operation. Unless you are highly-skilled and have a thorough understanding of the procedures described, never attempt to bypass the use of any special tool when the procedure described specifies its use. Not only is there a very great risk of personal injury, but expensive damage could be caused to the components involved.

Environmental considerations

When disposing of used engine oil, brake fluid, antifreeze, etc, give due consideration to any detrimental environmental effects. Do not, for instance, pour any of the above liquids down drains into the general sewage system, or onto the ground to soak away, as this is likely to pollute your local environment. Many local council refuse tips provide a facility for waste oil disposal, as do some garages. You can find your nearest disposal point by calling the Environment Agency on 03708 506 506 or by visiting www.oilbankline.org.uk.

Note: It is illegal and anti-social to dump oil down the drain. To find the location of your local oil recycling bank, call 03708 506 506 or visit www.oilbankline.org.uk.

The jack supplied with the vehicle tool kit should only be used for changing the roadwheels – see *Wheel changing* at the front of this manual. When carrying out any other kind of work, raise the vehicle using a hydraulic trolley jack, and always supplement the jack with axle stands positioned under the vehicle jacking points.

When using a trolley jack or axle stands, always position the jack head or axle stand head under, or adjacent to one of the relevant wheel changing jacking points under the sills. Use a block of wood between the jack or axle stand and the sill. It is permissible to raise the front with a trolley jack head under the front body crossmember, providing axle stands are placed under the sill jacking points **(see illustration)**.

3 Do not attempt to jack the vehicle under the sump, final drive unit, or any of the suspension components.

 Warning: Never work under, around, or near a raised vehicle, unless it is adequately supported in at least two places.

A rubber pad is provided under the front subframe for lifting with a workshop jack

6389 Fig.REF-Jack02 HAYNES

Position axle stands under the rubber pads in the sill

Introduction

A selection of good tools is a fundamental requirement for anyone contemplating the maintenance and repair of a motor vehicle. For the owner who does not possess any, their purchase will prove a considerable expense, offsetting some of the savings made by doing-it-yourself. However, provided that the tools purchased meet the relevant national safety standards and are of good quality, they will last for many years and prove an extremely worthwhile investment.

To help the average owner to decide which tools are needed to carry out the various tasks detailed in this manual, we have compiled three lists of tools under the following headings: *Maintenance and minor repair, Repair and overhaul*, and *Special*. Newcomers to practical mechanics should start off with the *Maintenance and minor repair* tool kit, and confine themselves to the simpler jobs around the vehicle. Then, as confidence and experience grow, more difficult tasks can be undertaken, with extra tools being purchased as, and when, they are needed. In this way, a *Maintenance and minor repair* tool kit can be built up into a *Repair and overhaul* tool kit over a considerable period of time, without any major cash outlays. The experienced do-it-yourselfer will have a tool kit good enough for most repair and overhaul procedures, and will add tools from the *Special* category when it is felt that the expense is justified by the amount of use to which these tools will be put.

Maintenance and minor repair tool kit

The tools given in this list should be considered as a minimum requirement if routine maintenance, servicing and minor repair operations are to be undertaken. We recommend the purchase of combination spanners (ring one end, open-ended the other); although more expensive than open-ended ones, they do give the advantages of both types of spanner.

☐ *Combination spanners:*
  Metric - 8 to 19 mm inclusive
☐ *Adjustable spanner - 35 mm jaw (approx.)*
☐ *Spark plug spanner (with rubber insert) - petrol models*
☐ *Spark plug gap adjustment tool - petrol models*
☐ *Set of feeler gauges*
☐ *Brake bleed nipple spanner*
☐ *Screwdrivers:*
  Flat blade - 100 mm long x 6 mm dia
  Cross blade - 100 mm long x 6 mm dia
  Torx - various sizes (not all vehicles)
☐ *Combination pliers*
☐ *Hacksaw (junior)*
☐ *Tyre pump*
☐ *Tyre pressure gauge*
☐ *Oil can*
☐ *Oil filter removal tool (if applicable)*
☐ *Fine emery cloth*
☐ *Wire brush (small)*
☐ *Funnel (medium size)*
☐ *Sump drain plug key (not all vehicles)*

Repair and overhaul tool kit

These tools are virtually essential for anyone undertaking any major repairs to a motor vehicle, and are additional to those given in the *Maintenance and minor repair* list. Included in this list is a comprehensive set of sockets. Although these are expensive, they will be found invaluable as they are so versatile - particularly if various drives are included in the set. We recommend the half-inch square-drive type, as this can be used with most proprietary torque wrenches.

The tools in this list will sometimes need to be supplemented by tools from the *Special* list:

☐ *Sockets to cover range in previous list (including Torx sockets)*
☐ *Reversible ratchet drive (for use with sockets)*
☐ *Extension piece, 250 mm (for use with sockets)*
☐ *Universal joint (for use with sockets)*
☐ *Flexible handle or sliding T "breaker bar" (for use with sockets)*
☐ *Torque wrench (for use with sockets)*
☐ *Self-locking grips*
☐ *Ball pein hammer*
☐ *Soft-faced mallet (plastic or rubber)*
☐ *Screwdrivers:*
  Flat blade - long & sturdy, short (chubby), and narrow (electrician's) types
  Cross blade – long & sturdy, and short (chubby) types
☐ *Pliers:*
  Long-nosed
  Side cutters (electrician's)
  Circlip (internal and external)
☐ *Cold chisel - 25 mm*
☐ *Scriber*
☐ *Scraper*
☐ *Centre-punch*
☐ *Pin punch*
☐ *Hacksaw*
☐ *Brake hose clamp*
☐ *Brake/clutch bleeding kit*
☐ *Selection of twist drills*
☐ *Steel rule/straight-edge*
☐ *Allen keys (inc. splined/Torx type)*
☐ *Selection of files*
☐ *Wire brush*
☐ *Axle stands*
☐ *Jack (strong trolley or hydraulic type)*
☐ *Light with extension lead*
☐ *Universal electrical multi-meter*

Sockets and reversible ratchet drive

Brake bleeding kit

Torx key, socket and bit

Hose clamp

Angular-tightening gauge

Special tools

The tools in this list are those which are not used regularly, are expensive to buy, or which need to be used in accordance with their manufacturers' instructions. Unless relatively difficult mechanical jobs are undertaken frequently, it will not be economic to buy many of these tools. Where this is the case, you could consider clubbing together with friends (or joining a motorists' club) to make a joint purchase, or borrowing the tools against a deposit from a local garage or tool hire specialist.

The following list contains only those tools and instruments freely available to the public, and not those special tools produced by the vehicle manufacturer specifically for its dealer network. You will find occasional references to these manufacturers' special tools in the text of this manual. Generally, an alternative method of doing the job without the vehicle manufacturers' special tool is given. However, sometimes there is no alternative to using them. Where this is the case and the relevant tool cannot be bought or borrowed, you will have to entrust the work to a dealer.

☐ Angular-tightening gauge
☐ Valve spring compressor
☐ Valve grinding tool
☐ Piston ring compressor
☐ Piston ring removal/installation tool
☐ Cylinder bore hone
☐ Balljoint separator
☐ Coil spring compressors (where applicable)
☐ Two/three-legged hub and bearing puller
☐ Impact screwdriver
☐ Micrometer and/or vernier calipers
☐ Dial gauge
☐ Tachometer
☐ Fault code reader
☐ Cylinder compression gauge
☐ Hand-operated vacuum pump and gauge
☐ Clutch plate alignment set
☐ Brake shoe steady spring cup removal tool
☐ Bush and bearing removal/installation set
☐ Stud extractors
☐ Tap and die set
☐ Lifting tackle

Buying tools

Reputable motor accessory shops and superstores often offer excellent quality tools at discount prices, so it pays to shop around.

Remember, you don't have to buy the most expensive items on the shelf, but it is always advisable to steer clear of the very cheap tools. Beware of 'bargains' offered on market stalls, on-line or at car boot sales. There are plenty of good tools around at reasonable prices, but always aim to purchase items which meet the relevant national safety standards. If in doubt, ask the proprietor or manager of the shop for advice before making a purchase.

Care and maintenance of tools

Having purchased a reasonable tool kit, it is necessary to keep the tools in a clean and serviceable condition. After use, always wipe off any dirt, grease and metal particles using a clean, dry cloth, before putting the tools away. Never leave them lying around after they have been used. A simple tool rack on the garage or workshop wall for items such as screwdrivers and pliers is a good idea. Store all normal spanners and sockets in a metal box. Any measuring instruments, gauges, meters, etc, must be carefully stored where they cannot be damaged or become rusty.

Take a little care when tools are used. Hammer heads inevitably become marked, and screwdrivers lose the keen edge on their blades from time to time. A little timely attention with emery cloth or a file will soon restore items like this to a good finish.

Working facilities

Not to be forgotten when discussing tools is the workshop itself. If anything more than routine maintenance is to be carried out, a suitable working area becomes essential.

It is appreciated that many an owner-mechanic is forced by circumstances to remove an engine or similar item without the benefit of a garage or workshop. Having done this, any repairs should always be done under the cover of a roof.

Wherever possible, any dismantling should be done on a clean, flat workbench or table at a suitable working height.

Any workbench needs a vice; one with a jaw opening of 100 mm is suitable for most jobs. As mentioned previously, some clean dry storage space is also required for tools, as well as for any lubricants, cleaning fluids, touch-up paints etc, which become necessary.

Another item which may be required, and which has a much more general usage, is an electric drill with a chuck capacity of at least 8 mm. This, together with a good range of twist drills, is virtually essential for fitting accessories.

Last, but not least, always keep a supply of old newspapers and clean, lint-free rags available, and try to keep any working area as clean as possible.

Micrometers

Dial test indicator ("dial gauge")

Oil filter removal tool (strap wrench type)

Compression tester

Bearing puller

This is a guide to getting your vehicle through the MOT test. Obviously it will not be possible to examine the vehicle to the same standard as the professional MOT tester. However, working through the following checks will enable you to identify any problem areas before submitting the vehicle for the test.

It has only been possible to summarise the test requirements here, based on the regulations in force at the time of printing. Test standards are becoming increasingly stringent, although there are some exemptions for older vehicles.

An assistant will be needed to help carry out some of these checks.

The checks have been sub-divided into four categories, as follows:

1 Checks carried out **FROM THE DRIVER'S SEAT**

2 Checks carried out **WITH THE VEHICLE ON THE GROUND**

3 Checks carried out **WITH THE VEHICLE RAISED AND THE WHEELS FREE TO TURN**

4 Checks carried out on **YOUR VEHICLE'S EXHAUST EMISSION SYSTEM**

---

1 Checks carried out **FROM THE DRIVER'S SEAT**

Handbrake (parking brake)

☐ Test the operation of the handbrake. Excessive travel (too many clicks) indicates incorrect brake or cable adjustment.
☐ Check that the handbrake cannot be released by tapping the lever sideways. Check the security of the lever mountings.

☐ If the parking brake is foot-operated, check that the pedal is secure and without excessive travel, and that the release mechanism operates correctly.
☐ Where applicable, test the operation of the electronic handbrake. The brake should engage and disengage without excessive delay. If the warning light does not extinguish when the brake is disengaged, this could indicate a fault which will need further investigation.

Footbrake

☐ Depress the brake pedal and check that it does not creep down to the floor, indicating a master cylinder fault. Release the pedal,

wait a few seconds, then depress it again. If the pedal travels nearly to the floor before firm resistance is felt, brake adjustment or repair is necessary. If the pedal feels spongy, there is air in the hydraulic system which must be removed by bleeding.

☐ Check that the brake pedal is secure and in good condition. Check also for signs of fluid leaks on the pedal, floor or carpets, which would indicate failed seals in the brake master cylinder.
☐ Check the servo unit (when applicable) by operating the brake pedal several times, then keeping the pedal depressed and starting the engine. As the engine starts, the pedal will move down slightly. If not, the vacuum hose or the servo itself may be faulty.

Steering wheel and column

☐ Examine the steering wheel for fractures or looseness of the hub, spokes or rim.
☐ Move the steering wheel from side to side and then up and down. Check that the steering wheel is not loose on the column, indicating wear or a loose retaining nut. Continue moving the steering wheel as before, but also turn it slightly from left to right.

☐ Check that the steering wheel is not loose on the column, and that there is no abnormal movement of the steering wheel, indicating wear in the column support bearings or couplings.
☐ Check that the ignition lock (where fitted) engages and disengages correctly.
☐ Steering column adjustment mechanisms (where fitted) must be able to lock the column securely in place with no play evident.

Windscreen, mirrors and sunvisor

☐ The windscreen must be free of cracks or other significant damage within the driver's field of view. (Small stone chips are acceptable.) Rear view mirrors must be secure, intact, and capable of being adjusted.

☐ The driver's sunvisor must be capable of being stored in the "up" position.

Seat belts and seats

Note: *The following checks are applicable to all seat belts, front and rear.*

☐ Examine the webbing of all the belts (including rear belts if fitted) for cuts, serious fraying or deterioration. Fasten and unfasten each belt to check the buckles. If applicable, check the retracting mechanism. Check the security of all seat belt mountings accessible from inside the vehicle, ensuring any height adjustable mountings lock securely in place.

☐ Seat belts with pre-tensioners, once activated, have a "flag" or similar showing on the seat belt stalk. This, in itself, is not a reason for test failure.

☐ The front seats themselves must be securely attached and the backrests must lock in the upright position.

Doors

☐ Both front doors must be able to be opened and closed from outside and inside, and must latch securely when closed.

Bonnet and boot/tailgate

☐ The bonnet and boot/tailgate must latch securely when closed.

2 Checks carried out WITH THE VEHICLE ON THE GROUND

Vehicle identification

☐ Number plates must be in good condition, secure and legible, with letters and numbers correctly spaced – spacing at (A) should be 33 mm and at (B) 11 mm. At the front, digits must be black on a white background and at the rear black on a yellow background. Other background designs (such as honeycomb) are not permitted.

☐ The VIN plate and/or homologation plate must be permanently displayed and legible.

Electrical equipment

☐ Switch on the ignition and check the operation of the horn.

☐ Check the windscreen washers and wipers, examining the wiper blades; renew damaged or perished blades. Also check the operation of the stop-lights.

☐ Check the operation of the sidelights and number plate lights. The lenses and reflectors must be secure, clean and undamaged.

☐ Check the operation and alignment of the headlights. The headlight reflectors must not be tarnished and the lenses must be undamaged.

☐ Switch on the ignition and check the operation of the direction indicators (including the instrument panel tell-tale) and the hazard warning lights. Operation of the sidelights and stop-lights must not affect the indicators - if it does, the cause is usually a bad earth at the rear light cluster. Indicators should flash at a rate of between 60 and 120 times per minute – faster or slower than this could indicate a fault with the flasher unit or a bad earth at one of the light units.

☐ Check the operation of the rear foglight(s), including the warning light on the instrument panel or in the switch.

☐ The warning lights must illuminate in accordance with the manufacturer's design. For most vehicles, the ABS and other warning lights should illuminate when the ignition is switched on, and (if the system is operating properly) extinguish after a few seconds. Refer to the owner's handbook.

Footbrake

☐ Examine the master cylinder, brake pipes and servo unit for leaks, loose mountings, corrosion or other damage. If ABS is fitted, this unit should also be examined for signs of leaks or corrosion.

☐ The fluid reservoir must be secure and the fluid level must be between the upper (A) and lower (B) markings.

☐ Inspect both front brake flexible hoses for cracks or deterioration of the rubber. Turn the steering from lock to lock, and ensure that the hoses do not contact the wheel, tyre, or any part of the steering or suspension mechanism. With the brake pedal firmly depressed, check the hoses for bulges or leaks under pressure.

Steering and suspension

☐ Have your assistant turn the steering wheel from side to side slightly, up to the point where the steering gear just begins to transmit this movement to the roadwheels. Check for excessive free play between the steering wheel and the steering gear, indicating wear or insecurity of the steering column joints, the column-to-steering gear coupling, or the steering gear itself.

☐ Have your assistant turn the steering wheel more vigorously in each direction, so that the roadwheels just begin to turn. As this is done, examine all the steering joints, linkages, fittings and attachments. Renew any component that shows signs of wear or damage. On vehicles with power steering, check the security and condition of the steering pump, drivebelt and hoses.

☐ Check that the vehicle is standing level, and at approximately the correct ride height.

Shock absorbers

☐ Depress each corner of the vehicle in turn, then release it. The vehicle should rise and then settle in its normal position. If the vehicle continues to rise and fall, the shock absorber is defective. A shock absorber which has seized will also cause the vehicle to fail.

Exhaust system

☐ Start the engine. With your assistant holding a rag over the tailpipe, check the entire system for leaks. Repair or renew leaking sections.

3 Checks carried out **WITH THE VEHICLE RAISED AND THE WHEELS FREE TO TURN**

Jack up the front and rear of the vehicle, and securely support it on axle stands. Position the stands clear of the suspension assemblies. Ensure that the wheels are clear of the ground and that the steering can be turned from lock to lock.

Steering mechanism

☐ Have your assistant turn the steering from lock to lock. Check that the steering turns smoothly, and that no part of the steering mechanism, including a wheel or tyre, fouls any brake hose or pipe or any part of the body structure.
☐ Examine the steering rack rubber gaiters for damage or insecurity of the retaining clips. If power steering is fitted, check for signs of damage or leakage of the fluid hoses, pipes or connections. Also check for excessive stiffness or binding of the steering, a missing split pin or locking device, or severe corrosion of the body structure within 30 cm of any steering component attachment point.

Front and rear suspension and wheel bearings

☐ Starting at the front right-hand side, grasp the roadwheel at the 3 o'clock and 9 o'clock positions and rock gently but firmly. Check for free play or insecurity at the wheel bearings, suspension balljoints, or suspension mount-ings, pivots and attachments.
☐ Now grasp the wheel at the 12 o'clock and 6 o'clock positions and repeat the previous inspection. Spin the wheel, and check for roughness or tightness of the front wheel bearing.

☐ If excess free play is suspected at a component pivot point, this can be confirmed by using a large screwdriver or similar tool and levering between the mounting and the component attachment. This will confirm whether the wear is in the pivot bush, its retaining bolt, or in the mounting itself (the bolt holes can often become elongated).

☐ Carry out all the above checks at the other front wheel, and then at both rear wheels.

Springs and shock absorbers

☐ Examine the suspension struts (when applicable) for serious fluid leakage, corrosion, or damage to the casing. Also check the security of the mounting points.
☐ If coil springs are fitted, check that the spring ends locate in their seats, and that the spring is not corroded, cracked or broken.
☐ If leaf springs are fitted, check that all leaves are intact, that the axle is securely attached to each spring, and that there is no deterioration of the spring eye mountings, bushes, and shackles.

☐ The same general checks apply to vehicles fitted with other suspension types, such as torsion bars, hydraulic displacer units, etc. Ensure that all mountings and attachments are secure, that there are no signs of excessive wear, corrosion or damage, and (on hydraulic types) that there are no fluid leaks or damaged pipes.
☐ Inspect the shock absorbers for signs of serious fluid leakage. Check for wear of the mounting bushes or attachments, or damage to the body of the unit.

Driveshafts (fwd vehicles only)

☐ Rotate each front wheel in turn and inspect the constant velocity joint gaiters for splits or damage. Also check that each driveshaft is straight and undamaged.

Braking system

☐ If possible without dismantling, check brake pad wear and disc condition. Ensure that the friction lining material has not worn excessively, (A) and that the discs are not fractured, pitted, scored or badly worn (B).

☐ Examine all the rigid brake pipes underneath the vehicle, and the flexible hose(s) at the rear. Look for corrosion, chafing or insecurity of the pipes, and for signs of bulging under pressure, chafing, splits or deterioration of the flexible hoses.
☐ Look for signs of fluid leaks at the brake calipers or on the brake backplates. Repair or renew leaking components.
☐ Slowly spin each wheel, while your assistant depresses and releases the footbrake. Ensure that each brake is operating and does not bind when the pedal is released.

☐ Examine the handbrake mechanism, checking for frayed or broken cables, excessive corrosion, or wear or insecurity of the linkage. Check that the mechanism works on each relevant wheel, and releases fully, without binding.

☐ It is not possible to test brake efficiency without special equipment, but a road test can be carried out later to check that the vehicle pulls up in a straight line.

Fuel and exhaust systems

☐ Inspect the fuel tank (including the filler cap), fuel pipes, hoses and unions. All components must be secure and free from leaks. Locking fuel caps must lock securely and the key must be provided for the MOT test.

☐ Examine the exhaust system over its entire length, checking for any damaged, broken or missing mountings, security of the retaining clamps and rust or corrosion.

Wheels and tyres

☐ Examine the sidewalls and tread area of each tyre in turn. Check for cuts, tears, lumps, bulges, separation of the tread, and exposure of the ply or cord due to wear or damage. Check that the tyre bead is correctly seated on the wheel rim, that the valve is sound and properly seated, and that the wheel is not distorted or damaged.

☐ Check that the tyres are of the correct size for the vehicle, that they are of the same size and type on each axle, and that the pressures are correct.

☐ Check the tyre tread depth. The legal minimum at the time of writing is 1.6 mm over the central three-quarters of the tread width. Abnormal tread wear may indicate incorrect front wheel alignment or wear in steering or suspension components.

☐ If the spare wheel is fitted externally or in a separate carrier beneath the vehicle, check that mountings are secure and free of excessive corrosion.

Body corrosion

☐ Check the condition of the entire vehicle structure for signs of corrosion in load-bearing areas. (These include chassis box sections, side sills, cross-members, pillars, and all suspension, steering, braking system and seat belt mountings and anchorages.) Any corrosion which has seriously reduced the thickness of a load-bearing area (or is within 30 cm of safety-related components such as steering or suspension) is likely to cause the vehicle to fail. In this case professional repairs are likely to be needed.

☐ Damage or corrosion which causes sharp or otherwise dangerous edges to be exposed will also cause the vehicle to fail.

Towbars

☐ Check the condition of mounting points (both beneath the vehicle and within boot/hatchback areas) for signs of corrosion, ensuring that all fixings are secure and not worn or damaged. There must be no excessive play in detachable tow ball arms or quick-release mechanisms.

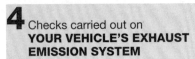

4 Checks carried out on **YOUR VEHICLE'S EXHAUST EMISSION SYSTEM**

Petrol models

☐ The engine should be warmed up, and running well (ignition system in good order, air filter element clean, etc).

☐ Before testing, run the engine at around 2500 rpm for 20 seconds. Let the engine drop to idle, and watch for smoke from the exhaust. If the idle speed is too high, or if dense blue or black smoke emerges for more than 5 seconds, the vehicle will fail. Typically, blue smoke signifies oil burning (engine wear);

black smoke means unburnt fuel (dirty air cleaner element, or other fuel system fault).

☐ An exhaust gas analyser for measuring carbon monoxide (CO) and hydrocarbons (HC) is now needed. If one cannot be hired or borrowed, have a local garage perform the check.

CO emissions (mixture)

☐ The MOT tester has access to the CO limits for all vehicles. The CO level is measured at idle speed, and at 'fast idle' (2500 to 3000 rpm). The following limits are given as a general guide:

At idle speed – Less than 0.5% CO
At 'fast idle' – Less than 0.3% CO
Lambda reading – 0.97 to 1.03

☐ If the CO level is too high, this may point to poor maintenance, a fuel injection system problem, faulty lambda (oxygen) sensor or catalytic converter. Try an injector cleaning treatment, and check the vehicle's ECU for fault codes.

HC emissions

☐ The MOT tester has access to HC limits for all vehicles. The HC level is measured at 'fast idle' (2500 to 3000 rpm). The following limits are given as a general guide:

At 'fast idle' – Less then 200 ppm

☐ Excessive HC emissions are typically caused by oil being burnt (worn engine), or by a blocked crankcase ventilation system ('breather'). If the engine oil is old and thin, an oil change may help. If the engine is running badly, check the vehicle's ECU for fault codes.

Diesel models

☐ The only emission test for diesel engines is measuring exhaust smoke density, using a calibrated smoke meter. The test involves accelerating the engine at least 3 times to its maximum unloaded speed.

Note: *On engines with a timing belt, it is VITAL that the belt is in good condition before the test is carried out.*

☐ With the engine warmed up, it is first purged by running at around 2500 rpm for 20 seconds. A governor check is then carried out, by slowly accelerating the engine to its maximum speed. After this, the smoke meter is connected, and the engine is accelerated quickly to maximum speed three times. If the smoke density is less than the limits given below, the vehicle will pass:

Non-turbo vehicles: 2.5m-1
Turbocharged vehicles: 3.0m-1

☐ If excess smoke is produced, try fitting a new air cleaner element, or using an injector cleaning treatment. If the engine is running badly, where applicable, check the vehicle's ECU for fault codes. Also check the vehicle's EGR system, where applicable. At high mileages, the injectors may require professional attention.

Engine

- [ ] Engine fails to rotate when attempting to start
- [ ] Engine rotates, but will not start
- [ ] Engine difficult to start when cold
- [ ] Engine difficult to start when hot
- [ ] Starter motor noisy or excessively rough in engagement
- [ ] Engine starts, but stops immediately
- [ ] Engine idles erratically
- [ ] Engine misfires at idle speed
- [ ] Engine misfires throughout the driving speed range
- [ ] Engine lacks power
- [ ] Engine backfires
- [ ] Oil pressure warning light illuminated with engine running
- [ ] Engine runs-on after switching off
- [ ] Whistling or wheezing noises
- [ ] Tapping or rattling noises
- [ ] Knocking or thumping noises

Cooling system

- [ ] Overheating
- [ ] Overcooling
- [ ] External coolant leakage
- [ ] Internal coolant leakage
- [ ] Corrosion

Fuel and exhaust systems

- [ ] Excessive fuel consumption
- [ ] Fuel leakage and/or fuel odour
- [ ] Excessive noise or fumes from the exhaust system

Clutch

- [ ] Pedal travels to the floor – no pressure or very little resistance
- [ ] Clutch fails to disengage (unable to select gears)
- [ ] Clutch slips (engine speed increases, with no increase in vehicle speed)
- [ ] Judder as clutch is engaged
- [ ] Noise when depressing or releasing clutch pedal

Manual transmission

- [ ] Noisy in neutral with the engine running
- [ ] Noisy in one particular gear
- [ ] Difficulty in engaging gears
- [ ] Jumps out of gear
- [ ] Vibration
- [ ] Lubricant leaks

Automatic transmission

- [ ] Fluid leakage
- [ ] Engine will not start in any gear, or starts in gears other than Park or Neutral
- [ ] Transmission slips, shifts roughly, is noisy, or has no drive in forward or reverse gears

Final drive

- [ ] Fluid leakage
- [ ] Noisy operation

Driveshafts/Propeller shaft

- [ ] Vibration when accelerating or decelerating
- [ ] Knock or clunk when taking up drive
- [ ] Metallic grating sound, consistent with vehicle speed
- [ ] Vibration consistent with vehicle speed

Braking system

- [ ] Vehicle pull to one side under braking
- [ ] Noise (grinding or high-pitched squeal) when brakes applied
- [ ] Excessive brake pedal travel
- [ ] Brake pedal feels spongy when depressed
- [ ] Excessive brake pedal effort required to stop vehicle
- [ ] Judder felt through brake pedal or steering wheel when braking
- [ ] Pedal pulsates when braking hard
- [ ] Brakes binding

Steering and suspension

- [ ] Vehicle pulls to one side
- [ ] Wheel wobble and vibration
- [ ] Excessive pitching and/or rolling around corners, or during braking
- [ ] Wandering or general instablity
- [ ] Excessively stiff steering
- [ ] Excessive play in steering
- [ ] Lack of power assistance
- [ ] Tyre wear excessive

Electrical system

- [ ] Battery will not hold charge for more than a few days
- [ ] Ignition/no-charge warning light remains illuminated with the engine running
- [ ] Lights inoperative
- [ ] Fuel or temperature gauge inaccurate
- [ ] Horn operates continuously
- [ ] Horn inoperative
- [ ] Wipers fail to operate, or operate very slowly
- [ ] Wiper blades sweep over too large, or too small an area of glass
- [ ] Wiper blades fail to clean the glass effectively
- [ ] Screen or headlight washers inoperative, or unsatisfactory in operation
- [ ] Window glass moves only in one direction
- [ ] Window glass slow to move
- [ ] Window glass fails to move
- [ ] Central locking system inoperative, or unsatisfactory in operation.

Introduction

The vehicle owner who does his or her own maintenance according to the recommended service schedules should not have to use this section of the manual very often. Modern component reliability is such that, provided those items subject to wear or deterioration are inspected or renewed at the specified intervals, sudden failure is comparatively rare. Faults do not usually just happen as a result of sudden failure, but develop over a period of time. Major mechanical failures in particular are usually preceded by characteristic symptoms over hundreds or even thousands of miles. Those components which do occasionally fail without warning are often small and easily carried in the vehicle.

With any fault-finding, the first step is to decide where to begin investigations. Sometimes this is obvious, but on other occasions, a little detective work will be necessary. The owner who makes half a dozen haphazard adjustments or replacements may be successful in curing a fault (or its symptoms), but will be none the wiser if the fault recurs, and ultimately may have spent more time and money than was necessary.

A calm and logical approach will be found to be more satisfactory in the long run. Always take into account any warning signs or abnormalities that may have been noticed in the period preceding the fault – power loss, high or low gauge readings, unusual smells, etc – and remember that failure of components such as fuses or spark plugs may only be pointers to some underlying fault

The pages which follow provide an easy-reference guide to the more common problems which may occur during the operation of the vehicle. These problems and their possible causes are grouped under headings denoting various components or systems, such as Engine, Cooling system, etc. The Chapter and/or Section which deals with the problem is also shown in brackets. Whatever the fault, certain basic principles apply. These are as follows:

Verify the fault. This is simply a matter of being sure that you know what the symptoms are before starting work. This is particularly important if you are investigating a fault for someone else, who may not have described it very accurately.

Don't overlook the obvious. For example, if the vehicle won't start, is there fuel in the tank? (Don't take anyone else's word on this particular point, and don't trust the fuel gauge either!) If an electrical fault is indicated, look for loose or broken wires before digging out the test gear.

Cure the disease, not the symptom. Substituting a flat battery with a fully-charged one will get you off the hard shoulder, but if the underlying cause is not attended to, the new battery will go the same way. Similarly, changing oil-fouled spark plugs for a new set will get you moving again, but remember that the reason for the fouling (if it wasn't simply an incorrect grade of plug) will have to be established and corrected.

Don't take anything for granted. Particularly, don't forget that a 'new' component may itself be defective (especially if it's been rattling around in the boot for months), and don't leave components out of a fault diagnosis sequence just because they are new or recently-fitted. When you do finally diagnose a difficult fault, you'll probably realise that all the evidence was there from the start.

Engine

Engine fails to rotate when attempting to start

- ☐ Battery terminal connections loose or corroded (Chapter 5A Section 4).
- ☐ Battery discharged or faulty (Chapter 5A Section 3).
- ☐ Broken, loose or disconnected wiring in the starting circuit (Chapter 12 Section 2).
- ☐ Defective starter solenoid or switch (Chapter 5A Section 2).
- ☐ Defective starter motor (Chapter 5A Section 9).
- ☐ Starter pinion or flywheel ring gear teeth loose or broken (Chapter 5A Section 10, Chapter 2A Section 14 and Chapter 2B Section 13).
- ☐ Engine earth strap broken or disconnected (Chapter 12 Section 2).
- ☐

Engine rotates, but will not start

- ☐ Fuel tank empty.
- ☐ Battery discharged (engine rotates slowly) (Chapter 5A Section 3).
- ☐ Battery terminals loose or corroded (*Weekly checks*).
- ☐ Pre-heating system faulty (Chapter 5B Section 2).
- ☐ Fuel injection system faulty (Chapter 4A Section 9).
- ☐ Air in the fuel system (Chapter 4A Section 7).
- ☐ Major mechanical failure (Chapter 2A or Chapter 2B).

Engine difficult to start when cold

- ☐ Battery discharged (Chapter 5A Section 3).
- ☐ Battery terminal connections loose or corroded (*Weekly checks*).
- ☐ Pre-heating system faulty (Chapter 5B Section 2).
- ☐ Fuel injection system faulty (Chapter 4A Section 9).
- ☐ Low cylinder compressions (Chapter 2A Section 2 or Chapter 2B Section 2).

Engine difficult to start when hot

- ☐ Air filter element dirty or clogged (Chapter 1 Section 24).
- ☐ Fuel injection system faulty (Chapter 4A Section 9).
- ☐ Low cylinder compressions (Chapter 2A Section 2 or Chapter 2B Section 2).

Starter motor noisy or excessively rough in engagement

- ☐ Starter pinion or flywheel ring gear teeth loose or broken (Chapter 5A Section 8 or Chapter 2A Section 14 and Chapter 2B Section 13).
- ☐ Starter motor mounting bolts loose or missing (Chapter 5A Section 9).
- ☐ Starter motor internal components worn or damaged (Chapter 5A Section 10).

Engine starts, but stops immediately

- ☐ Blocked injector/fuel injection system fault (Chapter 4A).
- ☐ Air in the fuel system (Chapter 4A Section 7).
- ☐ Immobiliser fault – refer to a Mercedes dealer or specialist.

Engine idles erratically

- ☐ Air filter element clogged (Chapter 1 Section 24).
- ☐ Uneven or low compressions (Chapter 2A Section 2 or Chapter 2B Section 2).
- ☐ Camshaft lobes worn (Chapter 2A Section 9 or Chapter 2B Section 9).
- ☐ Blocked injector/fuel injection system fault (Chapter 4A).

Engine misfires at idle speed

- ☐ Faulty injectors/fuel injection system fault (Chapter 4A).
- ☐ Uneven or low compressions (Chapter 2A Section 2 or Chapter 2B Section 2).

Engine (continued)

Engine misfires throughout the driving speed range
- [ ] Fuel filter choked (Chapter 1 Section 25).
- [ ] Fuel tank vent blocked, or fuel pipes restricted (Chapter 4A Section 3).
- [ ] Fault injector/fuel injection system fault (Chapter 4A).
- [ ] Uneven or low compressions (Chapter 2A Section 2 or Chapter 2B Section 2).

Engine lacks power
- [ ] Timing chain incorrectly fitted (Chapter 2A Section 7 or Chapter 2B Section 7).
- [ ] Fuel filter choked (Chapter 1 Section 25).
- [ ] Air filter blocked (Chapter 1 Section 24).
- [ ] Uneven or low compressions (Chapter 2A Section 2 or Chapter 2B Section 2).
- [ ] Faulty injectors/injection system fault (Chapter 4A).
- [ ] Brakes binding (Chapter 9).
- [ ] Clutch slipping (Chapter 6).
- [ ] Turbocharger fault (Chapter 4A Section 16)
- [ ] Turbocharger air ducts leaking.

Engine backfires
- [ ] Timing chain incorrectly fitted or tensioned (Chapter 2A Section 7 or Chapter 2B Section 7).
- [ ] Blocked injector/fuel injection system fault (Chapter 4A).

Oil pressure warning light illuminated with engine running
- [ ] Low oil level, or incorrect oil grade (Weekly checks).
- [ ] Faulty oil pressure sensor (Chapter 2A Section 18 or Chapter 2B Section 16).
- [ ] Worn engine bearings and/or oil pump (Chapter 2C).
- [ ] High engine operating temperature (Chapter 3).
- [ ] Oil pressure relief valve defective (Chapter 2A Section 12 or Chapter 2B Section 12).
- [ ] Oil pick up strainer clogged (Chapter 2A Section 12 or Chapter 2B Section 11).

Engine runs-on after switching off
- [ ] Excessive carbon build-up in engine (Chapter 2C).
- [ ] High engine operating temperature (Chapter 3).
- [ ] Fuel injection system fault (Chapter 4A).
- [ ] Incorrect oil level (Weekly checks).

Whistling or wheezing noises
- [ ] Leaking exhaust manifold or turbocharger gaskets (Chapter 4A).
- [ ] Leaking vacuum hose (Chapter 4A).
- [ ] Leaking air intake hose//intercooler ducts (Chapter 4A).

Tapping or rattling noises
- [ ] Worn valve gear or camshaft (Chapter 2C).
- [ ] Ancillary component fault (coolant pump, alternator etc.) (Chapter 3 and Chapter 5A).

Knocking or thumping noises
- [ ] Worn big-end bearings (regular heavy knocking, perhaps more under load) (Chapter 2C).
- [ ] Worn main bearings (rumbling and knocking, perhaps less under load) (Chapter 2C).
- [ ] Piston slap (most noticeable when cold) (Chapter 2C).
- [ ] Ancillary component fault (coolant pump, alternator, etc.) (Chapter 3 and Chapter 5A).

Cooling system

Overheating
- [ ] Insufficient coolant in the system (Weekly checks).
- [ ] Thermostat faulty (Chapter 3 Section 4).
- [ ] Radiator core blocked, or grille restricted (Chapter 3 Section 3).
- [ ] Electric cooling fan faulty (Chapter 3 Section 6).
- [ ] Air lock in cooling system (Chapter 1 Section 30).
- [ ] Expansion tank pressure cap faulty (Chapter 1 Section 30).
- [ ] Engine coolant temperature sensor faulty (Chapter 3 Section 7).

Overcooling
- [ ] Thermostat faulty (Chapter 3 Section 4).
- [ ] Engine coolant temperature sensor faulty (Chapter 3 Section 7).

External coolant leakage
- [ ] Deteriorated or damaged hoses or hose clips (Chapter 3 Section 2).
- [ ] Radiator core or heater matrix leaking (Chapter 3 Section 8).
- [ ] Pressure cap faulty (Chapter 1 Section 30).
- [ ] Coolant pump leaking (Chapter 3 Section 5).
- [ ] Boiling due to overheating.
- [ ] Core plug leaking (Chapter 2C Section 14).

Internal coolant leakage
- [ ] Leaking cylinder head gasket (Chapter 2A Section 10 or Chapter 2B Section 10).
- [ ] Cracked cylinder head or cylinder block (Chapter 2C).

Corrosion
- [ ] Infrequent draining and flushing (Chapter 1 Section 30).
- [ ] Incorrect coolant mixture or inappropriate coolant type (Chapter 1 Section 30).

Fuel and exhaust systems

Excessive fuel consumption

- [ ] Air filter dirty or clogged (Chapter 1 Section 24).
- [ ] Faulty injector/fuel injection system fault (Chapter 4A).
- [ ] Brakes binding (Chapter 9).
- [ ] Tyres under-inflated (*Weekly checks*).

Fuel leakage and/or fuel odour

- [ ] Damaged or corroded fuel tank, pipes or connections (Chapter 4A).

Excessive noise or fumes from the exhaust system

- [ ] Leaking exhaust system or manifold leaks (Chapter 4A).
- [ ] Leaking or corroded silencers or pipe (Chapter 4A Section 19).
- [ ] Broken mountings causing body or suspension contact (Chapter 4A Section 19).

Clutch

Pedal travels to the floor – no pressure or very little resistance

- [ ] Faulty master or slave cylinder (Chapter 6 Section 2 or Chapter 6 Section 3).
- [ ] Faulty hydraulic release system (Chapter 6).
- [ ] Broken clutch release bearing (Chapter 6 Section 5).
- [ ] Broken diaphragm spring in clutch pressure plate (Chapter 6 Section 5).

Clutch fails to disengage (unable to select gears)

- [ ] Faulty master or slave cylinder (Chapter 6 Section 2 or Chapter 6 Section 3).
- [ ] Faulty hydraulic hose.
- [ ] Clutch disc sticking on the gearbox input shaft splines (Chapter 6 Section 5).
- [ ] Clutch disc sticking on the flywheel or pressure plate (Chapter 6 Section 5).
- [ ] Faulty pressure plate assembly (Chapter 6 Section 5).
- [ ] Air in hydraulic system (Chapter 6 Section 4).

Clutch slips (engine speed increases, with no increase in vehicle speed)

- [ ] Faulty hydraulic release system (Chapter 6).

- [ ] Clutch disc linings excessively worn (Chapter 6 Section 5).
- [ ] Clutch disc lining contaminated with oil or grease (Chapter 6 Section 5).
- [ ] Faulty pressure plate or weak diaphragm spring (Chapter 6 Section 5).

Judder as clutch is engaged

- [ ] Clutch disc linings contaminated with oil or grease (Chapter 6 Section 5).
- [ ] Clutch disc linings excessively worn (Chapter 6 Section 5).
- [ ] Faulty or distorted pressure plate or diaphragm spring (Chapter 6 Section 5).
- [ ] Worn or loose engine or gearbox mountings (Chapter 2A Section 17 or Chapter 2B Section 15).
- [ ] Clutch disc or gearbox input shaft splines worn (Chapter 6 Section 5).

Noise when depressing or releasing clutch pedal

- [ ] Worn clutch release bearing (Chapter 6 Section 5).
- [ ] Worn or dry clutch pedal pivot.
- [ ] Faulty pressure plate assembly (Chapter 6 Section 5).
- [ ] Pressure plate diaphragm spring broken (Chapter 6 Section 5).

Manual transmission

Noisy in neutral with the engine running

- [ ] Input shaft bearings worn (noise apparent with clutch pedal released, but not when depressed) (Chapter 7A Section 7).*
- [ ] Clutch release bearings worn (noise apparent with clutch pedal depressed, possibly less when released (Chapter 6 Section 3).

Noisy in one particular gear

- [ ] Worn, damaged or chipped gear teeth (Chapter 7A Section 7).*

Difficulty in engaging gears

- [ ] Clutch faulty (Chapter 6).
- [ ] Clutch hydraulic hose faulty.
- [ ] Worn synchroniser units (Chapter 7A Section 7).*

Jumps out of gear

- [ ] Worn synchroniser units (Chapter 7A Section 7).*
- [ ] Worn selector forks (Chapter 7A Section 7).*

Vibration

- [ ] Lack of oil (Chapter 7A Section 2).
- [ ] Worn bearings (Chapter 7A Section 7).*

Lubricant leaks

- [ ] Leaking oil seal (Chapter 7A Section 4).
- [ ] Leaking housing joint (Chapter 7A Section 7).*
- [ ] Leaking input shaft oil seal (Chapter 7A).

Note: *Although the corrective action necessary to remedy the symptoms described in beyond the scope of the home mechanic, then above information should be helpful in isolating the cause of the condition, so that the owner can communicate clearly with a professional mechanic.*

Automatic transmission

Fluid leakage

- [ ] Automatic transmission fluid is usually dark in colour. Fluid leaks should not be confused with engine oil, which can easily be blown onto the transmission by airflow.
- [ ] To determine the source of a leak, first remove all built-up dirt and grime from the transmission housing and surrounding areas using a degreasing agent, or by steam-cleaning. Drive the vehicle at low speed, so airflow will not blow the leak far from its source. Raise and support the vehicle, and determine where the leak is coming from.

Engine will not start in any gear, or starts in gears other than Park or Neutral

- [ ] Selector lever/housing problem (Chapter 7B Section 2).
- [ ] Transmission control module problem (Chapter 7B Section 9).

Transmission slips, shifts roughly, is noisy, or has no drive in forward or reverse gears

- [ ] There are many probable causes for the above problems, but unless there is a very obvious reason (such as a loose or corroded wiring plug connection on or near the transmission), the car should be taken to a franchise dealer or specialist for the fault to be diagnosed. The transmission control module incorporates a self-diagnosis facility, and any fault codes can quickly be read and interpreted by a dealer or specialist with the proper diagnostic equipment.

Note: *Due to the complexity of the automatic transmission, it is difficult for the home mechanic to properly diagnose and service this unit. For problems other then the following, the vehicle should be taken to a dealer service department or automatic transmission specialist. Do not be too hasty in removing the transmission if a fault is suspected, as most of the testing is carried out with the unit still fitted.*

Final drive

Fluid leakage

☐ Oil seal leaking (Chapter 8 Section 4).

Noisy operation

☐ Low oil level (Chapter 8 Section 2).
☐ Worn bearings/differential gears (Chapter 8 Section 3).

Driveshafts/Propeller shaft

Vibration when accelerating or decelerating

☐ Worn constant velocity joint (Chapter 8 Section 5).
☐ Bent or distorted driveshaft (Chapter 8 Section 5).

Knock or clunk when taking up drive

☐ Worn propeller shaft universal joint bearings (Chapter 8 Section 10).
☐ Loose propeller shaft flange bolts (Chapter 8 Section 7).

Metallic grating sound, consistent with vehicle speed

☐ Severe wear in the propeller shaft universal joint bearings (Chapter 8 Section 10).
☐ Worn propeller shaft centre support bearing (Chapter 8 Section 9).

Vibration consistent with vehicle speed

☐ Propeller shaft out of balance (Chapter 8 Section 7).
☐ Wheels out of balance.Propeller shaft or driveshaft joints worn (Chapter 8).

Braking system

Vehicle pull to one side under braking

☐ Worn, defective, damaged or contaminated brake pads on one side (Chapter 9 Section 4 or Chapter 9 Section 5).
☐ Seized or partially seized front or rear brake caliper (Chapter 9 Section 8 or Chapter 9 Section 9).
☐ A mixture of brake pad lining materials fitted between sides (Chapter 9 Section 4 or Chapter 9 Section 5).
☐ Brake caliper mounting bolts loose (Chapter 9 Section 8 or Chapter 9 Section 9).
☐ Worn or damaged steering or suspension components (Chapter 10).

Noise (grinding or high-pitched squeal) when brakes applied

☐ Brake pad friction material worn down to metal backing (Chapter 9 Section 4 or Chapter 9 Section 5).
☐ Excessive corrosion of brake disc – may be apparent after the vehicle has been standing for some time (Chapter 9 Section 6).
☐ Foreign object (stone chipping, etc.) trapped between the brake disc and shield.

Excessive brake pedal travel

☐ Faulty master cylinder (Chapter 9 Section 10).
☐ Air in hydraulic system (Chapter 9 Section 2).
☐ Faulty vacuum servo unit (Chapter 9 Section 11).
☐ Faulty vacuum pump (Chapter 9 Section 19).

Brake pedal feels spongy when depressed

☐ Air in hydraulic system (Chapter 9 Section 2).
☐ Deteriorated flexible rubber brake hoses (Chapter 9 Section 3).
☐ Master cylinder mountings loose (Chapter 9 Section 10).
☐ Faulty master cylinder (Chapter 9 Section 10).

Excessive brake pedal effort required to stop vehicle

☐ Faulty vacuum servo unit (Chapter 9 Section 11).
☐ Faulty servo unit check valve (Chapter 9 Section 11).
☐ Disconnected, damaged or insecure brake servo vacuum hose (Chapter 9 Section 12).
☐ Faulty vacuum pump (Chapter 9 Section 19).
☐ Faulty brake pipe or hose (Chapter 9 Section 3).
☐ Seized brake caliper (Chapter 9 Section 8 or Chapter 9 Section 9).
☐ Brake pads incorrectly fitted (Chapter 9 Section 4, 5).
☐ Incorrect grade of brake pads fitted (Chapter 9 Section 4, 5).
☐ Brake pads contaminated (Chapter 9 Section 4, 5).

Judder felt through brake pedal or steering wheel when braking

☐ Excessive run-out or distortion of brake disc (Chapter 9 Section 6, 7).
☐ Brake pad linings worn (Chapter 9 Section 4, 5).
☐ Brake caliper mountings loose (Chapter 9 Section 8, 9).
☐ Wear in suspension or steering components or mountings (Chapter 10).

Pedal pulsates when braking hard

☐ Normal feature of ABS – no fault.

Brakes binding

☐ Seized brake caliper (Chapter 9 Section 8, 9).
☐ Incorrectly adjusted parking brake (Chapter 9 Section 13).
☐ Faulty master cylinder (Chapter 9 Section 10).

Note: *Before assuming that a brake problem exists, make sure that the tyres are in good condition and correctly inflated, that the front wheel alignment is correct, and that the vehicle is not loaded with weight in an unequal manner. Apart from checking the condition of all pipe and hose connections, any faults occurring on the anti-lock braking system should be referred to a Mercedes dealer or specialist for diagnosis.*

Steering and suspension

Vehicle pulls to one side

- [ ] Defective tyre (*Weekly checks*).
- [ ] Excessive wear in suspension or steering components (Chapter 1 Section 13).
- [ ] Incorrect front wheel alignment (Chapter 10 Section 26).
- [ ] Accident damage to steering or suspension components.

Wheel wobble and vibration

- [ ] Front roadwheels out of balance (vibration felt mainly through the steering wheel).
- [ ] Rear roadwheels out of balance (vibration felt mainly throughout the vehicle).
- [ ] Roadwheels damaged or distorted (Chapter 1 Section 13).
- [ ] Faulty or damaged tyre (*Weekly checks*).
- [ ] Worn steering or suspension joints, bushes or components (Chapter 1 Section 13).
- [ ] Wheel bolts loose (Chapter 1 Section 13).

Excessive pitching and/or rolling around corners, or during braking

- [ ] Defective shock absorbers (Chapter 10 Section 5, 13).
- [ ] Broken or weak coil spring and/or suspension components (Chapter 10).
- [ ] Worn or damaged anti-roll bar or mountings (Chapter 10 Section 8, 9, 16, 17).

Wandering or general instablity

- [ ] Incorrect wheel alignment (Chapter 10 Section 26).
- [ ] Worn steering or suspension components (Chapter 1 Section 13).
- [ ] Roadwheels out of balance.
- [ ] Faulty or damaged tyre (*Weekly checks*).
- [ ] Wheel bolts loose.Defective shock absorbers (Chapter 10 Section 5, 13).

Excessively stiff steering

- [ ] Seized track rod end balljoint or suspension balljoint (Chapter 10).
- [ ] Broken or incorrectly adjusted auxiliary drivebelt (Chapter 1 Section 6).
- [ ] Incorrect front wheel alignment (Chapter 10 Section 26).
- [ ] Steering gear damaged (Chapter 10 Section 21).

Excessive play in steering

- [ ] Worn steering column universal joints (Chapter 10 Section 19).
- [ ] Worn steering track rod end balljoints (Chapter 10 Section 25).
- [ ] Worn steering gear (Chapter 10 Section 21).
- [ ] Worn steering or suspension joints, bushes or components (Chapter 10).

Lack of power assistance

- [ ] Broken or incorrectly adjusted auxiliary drivebelt (Chapter 1 Section 6).
- [ ] Incorrect power steering fluid level (*Weekly checks*).
- [ ] Restriction in power steering hoses.
- [ ] Faulty power steering pump (Chapter 10 Section 23).
- [ ] Faulty steering gear (Chapter 10 Section 21).
- [ ] Air in hydraulic system (Chapter 10 Section 24)

Tyre wear excessive

- [ ] Tyres under inflated (wear on both edges) (*Weekly checks*).
- [ ] Incorrect camber or castor angles (wear on one edge) (Chapter 10 Section 26).
- [ ] Worn steering or suspension joints, bushes or components (Chapter 1 Section 13).
- [ ] Accident damage.Incorrect wheel alignment (feathered edges) (Chapter 10 Section 26).
- [ ] Tyres over-inflated (worn in centre of tread) (*Weekly checks*).
- [ ] Worn shock absorbers (Chapter 10 Section 5, 13).
- [ ] Tyres/wheel out of balance (tyres worn unevenly).
- [ ] Tyre/wheel damage (*Weekly checks*).

Electrical system

Battery will not hold charge for more than a few days

- ☐ Battery defective internally (Chapter 5A Section 3).
- ☐ Battery terminal connections loose or corroded (*Weekly checks*).
- ☐ Auxiliary drivebelt worn or incorrectly tensioned (Chapter 1 Section 6).
- ☐ Alternator not charging at correct output (Chapter 5A Section 5, 7).
- ☐ Short circuit causing continual current drain (Chapter 12 Section 2).

Ignition/no-charge warning light remains illuminated with the engine running

- ☐ Auxiliary drivebelt broken, worn, or incorrectly adjusted (Chapter 1 Section 6).
- ☐ Internal fault in alternator or voltage regulator (Chapter 5A Section 7).
- ☐ Broken, disconnected, or loose wiring in charging circuit (Chapter 12 Section 2).

Lights inoperative

- ☐ Blown bulb (Chapter 12 Section 6).
- ☐ Corrosion of bulbholder contacts (Chapter 12 Section 6).
- ☐ Blown fuse (Chapter 12 Section 3).
- ☐ Faulty relay (Chapter 12 Section 3).
- ☐ Broken, loose or disconnected wiring (Chapter 12 Section 2).
- ☐ Faulty switch (Chapter 12 Section 5).

Fuel or temperature gauge inaccurate

- ☐ Faulty fuel level sensor(s) (Chapter 4A Section 4).
- ☐ Faulty engine coolant temperature sensor (Chapter 3 Section 7).
- ☐ Faulty instrument cluster (Chapter 12 Section 10).

Horn operates continuously

- ☐ Horn contacts faulty (Chapter 12 Section 5).

Horn inoperative

- ☐ Horn switch contact faulty (Chapter 12 Section 5).
- ☐ Horn faulty (Chapter 12 Section 12).
- ☐ Fuse blown (Chapter 12 Section 3).

Wipers fail to operate, or operate very slowly

- ☐ Wiper blades stuck to screen, or seized linkage (Chapter 12 Section 14).
- ☐ Blown fuse (Chapter 12 Section 3).
- ☐ Faulty relay (Chapter 12 Section 3).
- ☐ Faulty wiper motor (Chapter 12 Section 14).

Wiper blades sweep over too large, or too small an area of glass

- ☐ Wiper arms incorrectly positioned on spindles (Chapter 12 Section 13).
- ☐ Excessive wear of wiper linkage (Chapter 12 Section 14).
- ☐ Wiper motor or linkage mountings loose (Chapter 12 Section 14).

Wiper blades fail to clean the glass effectively

- ☐ Wiper blade rubbers worn or perished (*Weekly checks*).
- ☐ Wiper arms defective (Chapter 12 Section 13).
- ☐ Insufficient windscreen washer additive to adequately remove road film (*Weekly checks*).

Screen or headlight washers inoperative, or unsatisfactory in operation

- ☐ Blocked washer jet (Chapter 12 Section 15).
- ☐ Disconnected, kinked or restricted fluid hose.
- ☐ Insufficient fluid in washer reservoir (*Weekly checks*).
- ☐ Blown fuse (Chapter 12 Section 3).
- ☐ Faulty washer pump (Chapter 12 Section 15).
- ☐ Faulty switch (Chapter 12 Section 5).

Window glass moves only in one direction

- ☐ Faulty switch (Chapter 12 Section 5).

Window glass slow to move

- ☐ Regulator seized or damaged, or in need of lubrication (Chapter 11 Section 19, 20).
- ☐ Door internal components or trim fouling regulator (Chapter 11 Section 17).
- ☐ Window guide rubber dirty or in need of lubrication (Silicone spray).
- ☐ Faulty motor (Chapter 11 Section 19, 20).

Window glass fails to move

- ☐ Blown fuse (Chapter 12 Section 3).
- ☐ Faulty door control unit (Chapter 11 Section 18).
- ☐ Broken or disconnected wiring or connections (Chapter 12 Section 2).
- ☐ Faulty motor (Chapter 11 Section 19, 20).

Central locking system inoperative, or unsatisfactory in operation.

- ☐ Blown fuse (Chapter 12 Section 2).
- ☐ Faulty SAM (Chapter 12 Section 3).
- ☐ Broken or disconnected wiring or connectors (Chapter 12 Section 2).
- ☐ Faulty door/boot/tailgate lock (Chapter 11 Section 12, 14, 22, 24).
- ☐ Faulty relay (Chapter 12 Section 3).

A

ABS (Anti-lock brake system) A system, usually electronically controlled, that senses incipient wheel lockup during braking and relieves hydraulic pressure at wheels that are about to skid.

Air bag An inflatable bag hidden in the steering wheel (driver's side) or the dash or glovebox (passenger side). In a head-on collision, the bags inflate, preventing the driver and front passenger from being thrown forward into the steering wheel or windscreen.

Air cleaner A metal or plastic housing, containing a filter element, which removes dust and dirt from the air being drawn into the engine.

Air filter element The actual filter in an air cleaner system, usually manufactured from pleated paper and requiring renewal at regular intervals.

Air filter

Allen key A hexagonal wrench which fits into a recessed hexagonal hole.

Alligator clip A long-nosed spring-loaded metal clip with meshing teeth. Used to make temporary electrical connections.

Alternator A component in the electrical system which converts mechanical energy from a drivebelt into electrical energy to charge the battery and to operate the starting system, ignition system and electrical accessories.

Alternator (exploded view)

Ampere (amp) A unit of measurement for the flow of electric current. One amp is the amount of current produced by one volt acting through a resistance of one ohm.

Anaerobic sealer A substance used to prevent bolts and screws from loosening. Anaerobic means that it does not require oxygen for activation. The Loctite brand is widely used.

Antifreeze A substance (usually ethylene glycol) mixed with water, and added to a vehicle's cooling system, to prevent freezing of the coolant in winter. Antifreeze also contains chemicals to inhibit corrosion and the formation of rust and other deposits that would tend to clog the radiator and coolant passages and reduce cooling efficiency.

Anti-seize compound A coating that reduces the risk of seizing on fasteners that are subjected to high temperatures, such as exhaust manifold bolts and nuts.

Anti-seize compound

Asbestos A natural fibrous mineral with great heat resistance, commonly used in the composition of brake friction materials. Asbestos is a health hazard and the dust created by brake systems should never be inhaled or ingested.

Axle A shaft on which a wheel revolves, or which revolves with a wheel. Also, a solid beam that connects the two wheels at one end of the vehicle. An axle which also transmits power to the wheels is known as a live axle.

Axle assembly

Axleshaft A single rotating shaft, on either side of the differential, which delivers power from the final drive assembly to the drive wheels. Also called a driveshaft or a halfshaft.

B

Ball bearing An anti-friction bearing consisting of a hardened inner and outer race with hardened steel balls between two races.

Bearing

Bearing The curved surface on a shaft or in a bore, or the part assembled into either, that permits relative motion between them with minimum wear and friction.

Big-end bearing The bearing in the end of the connecting rod that's attached to the crankshaft.

Bleed nipple A valve on a brake wheel cylinder, caliper or other hydraulic component that is opened to purge the hydraulic system of air. Also called a bleed screw.

Brake bleeding

Brake bleeding Procedure for removing air from lines of a hydraulic brake system.

Brake disc The component of a disc brake that rotates with the wheels.

Brake drum The component of a drum brake that rotates with the wheels.

Brake linings The friction material which contacts the brake disc or drum to retard the vehicle's speed. The linings are bonded or riveted to the brake pads or shoes.

Brake pads The replaceable friction pads that pinch the brake disc when the brakes are applied. Brake pads consist of a friction material bonded or riveted to a rigid backing plate.

Brake shoe The crescent-shaped carrier to which the brake linings are mounted and which forces the lining against the rotating drum during braking.

Braking systems For more information on braking systems, consult the *Haynes Automotive Brake Manual*.

Breaker bar A long socket wrench handle providing greater leverage.

Bulkhead The insulated partition between the engine and the passenger compartment.

C

Caliper The non-rotating part of a disc-brake assembly that straddles the disc and carries the brake pads. The caliper also contains the hydraulic components that cause the pads to pinch the disc when the brakes are applied. A caliper is also a measuring tool that can be set to measure inside or outside dimensions of an object.

Camshaft A rotating shaft on which a series of cam lobes operate the valve mechanisms. The camshaft may be driven by gears, by sprockets and chain or by sprockets and a belt.

Canister A container in an evaporative emission control system; contains activated charcoal granules to trap vapours from the fuel system.

Canister

Carburettor A device which mixes fuel with air in the proper proportions to provide a desired power output from a spark ignition internal combustion engine.

Carburettor

Castellated Resembling the parapets along the top of a castle wall. For example, a castellated balljoint stud nut.

Castellated nut

Castor In wheel alignment, the backward or forward tilt of the steering axis. Castor is positive when the steering axis is inclined rearward at the top.

Catalytic converter A silencer-like device in the exhaust system which converts certain pollutants in the exhaust gases into less harmful substances.

Catalytic converter

Circlip A ring-shaped clip used to prevent endwise movement of cylindrical parts and shafts. An internal circlip is installed in a groove in a housing; an external circlip fits into a groove on the outside of a cylindrical piece such as a shaft.

Clearance The amount of space between two parts. For example, between a piston and a cylinder, between a bearing and a journal, etc.

Coil spring A spiral of elastic steel found in various sizes throughout a vehicle, for example as a springing medium in the suspension and in the valve train.

Compression Reduction in volume, and increase in pressure and temperature, of a gas, caused by squeezing it into a smaller space.

Compression ratio The relationship between cylinder volume when the piston is at top dead centre and cylinder volume when the piston is at bottom dead centre.

Constant velocity (CV) joint A type of universal joint that cancels out vibrations caused by driving power being transmitted through an angle.

Core plug A disc or cup-shaped metal device inserted in a hole in a casting through which core was removed when the casting was formed. Also known as a freeze plug or expansion plug.

Crankcase The lower part of the engine block in which the crankshaft rotates.

Crankshaft The main rotating member, or shaft, running the length of the crankcase, with offset "throws" to which the connecting rods are attached.

Crankshaft assembly

Crocodile clip See Alligator clip

D

Diagnostic code Code numbers obtained by accessing the diagnostic mode of an engine management computer. This code can be used to determine the area in the system where a malfunction may be located.

Disc brake A brake design incorporating a rotating disc onto which brake pads are squeezed. The resulting friction converts the energy of a moving vehicle into heat.

Double-overhead cam (DOHC) An engine that uses two overhead camshafts, usually one for the intake valves and one for the exhaust valves.

Drivebelt(s) The belt(s) used to drive accessories such as the alternator, water pump, power steering pump, air conditioning compressor, etc. off the crankshaft pulley.

Accessory drivebelts

Driveshaft Any shaft used to transmit motion. Commonly used when referring to the axleshafts on a front wheel drive vehicle.

Driveshaft

Drum brake A type of brake using a drum-shaped metal cylinder attached to the inner surface of the wheel. When the brake pedal is pressed, curved brake shoes with friction linings press against the inside of the drum to slow or stop the vehicle.

Drum brake assembly

E

EGR valve A valve used to introduce exhaust gases into the intake air stream.

EGR valve

Electronic control unit (ECU) A computer which controls (for instance) ignition and fuel injection systems, or an anti-lock braking system. For more information refer to the *Haynes Automotive Electrical and Electronic Systems Manual*.

Electronic Fuel Injection (EFI) A computer controlled fuel system that distributes fuel through an injector located in each intake port of the engine.

Emergency brake A braking system, independent of the main hydraulic system, that can be used to slow or stop the vehicle if the primary brakes fail, or to hold the vehicle stationary even though the brake pedal isn't depressed. It usually consists of a hand lever that actuates either front or rear brakes mechanically through a series of cables and linkages. Also known as a handbrake or parking brake.

Endfloat The amount of lengthwise movement between two parts. As applied to a crankshaft, the distance that the crankshaft can move forward and back in the cylinder block.

Engine management system (EMS) A computer controlled system which manages the fuel injection and the ignition systems in an integrated fashion.

Exhaust manifold A part with several passages through which exhaust gases leave the engine combustion chambers and enter the exhaust pipe.

Exhaust manifold

F

Fan clutch A viscous (fluid) drive coupling device which permits variable engine fan speeds in relation to engine speeds.

Feeler blade A thin strip or blade of hardened steel, ground to an exact thickness, used to check or measure clearances between parts.

Feeler blade

Firing order The order in which the engine cylinders fire, or deliver their power strokes, beginning with the number one cylinder.

Flywheel A heavy spinning wheel in which energy is absorbed and stored by means of momentum. On cars, the flywheel is attached to the crankshaft to smooth out firing impulses.

Free play The amount of travel before any action takes place. The "looseness" in a linkage, or an assembly of parts, between the initial application of force and actual movement. For example, the distance the brake pedal moves before the pistons in the master cylinder are actuated.

Fuse An electrical device which protects a circuit against accidental overload. The typical fuse contains a soft piece of metal which is calibrated to melt at a predetermined current flow (expressed as amps) and break the circuit.

Fusible link A circuit protection device consisting of a conductor surrounded by heat-resistant insulation. The conductor is smaller than the wire it protects, so it acts as the weakest link in the circuit. Unlike a blown fuse, a failed fusible link must frequently be cut from the wire for replacement.

G

Gap The distance the spark must travel in jumping from the centre electrode to the side

Adjusting spark plug gap

electrode in a spark plug. Also refers to the spacing between the points in a contact breaker assembly in a conventional points-type ignition, or to the distance between the reluctor or rotor and the pickup coil in an electronic ignition.

Gasket Any thin, soft material - usually cork, cardboard, asbestos or soft metal - installed between two metal surfaces to ensure a good seal. For instance, the cylinder head gasket seals the joint between the block and the cylinder head.

Gasket

Gauge An instrument panel display used to monitor engine conditions. A gauge with a movable pointer on a dial or a fixed scale is an analogue gauge. A gauge with a numerical readout is called a digital gauge.

H

Halfshaft A rotating shaft that transmits power from the final drive unit to a drive wheel, usually when referring to a live rear axle.

Harmonic balancer A device designed to reduce torsion or twisting vibration in the crankshaft. May be incorporated in the crankshaft pulley. Also known as a vibration damper.

Hone An abrasive tool for correcting small irregularities or differences in diameter in an engine cylinder, brake cylinder, etc.

Hydraulic tappet A tappet that utilises hydraulic pressure from the engine's lubrication system to maintain zero clearance (constant contact with both camshaft and valve stem). Automatically adjusts to variation in valve stem length. Hydraulic tappets also reduce valve noise.

I

Ignition timing The moment at which the spark plug fires, usually expressed in the number of crankshaft degrees before the piston reaches the top of its stroke.

Inlet manifold A tube or housing with passages through which flows the air-fuel mixture (carburettor vehicles and vehicles with throttle body injection) or air only (port fuel-injected vehicles) to the port openings in the cylinder head.

J

Jump start Starting the engine of a vehicle with a discharged or weak battery by attaching jump leads from the weak battery to a charged or helper battery.

L

Load Sensing Proportioning Valve (LSPV) A brake hydraulic system control valve that works like a proportioning valve, but also takes into consideration the amount of weight carried by the rear axle.

Locknut A nut used to lock an adjustment nut, or other threaded component, in place. For example, a locknut is employed to keep the adjusting nut on the rocker arm in position.

Lockwasher A form of washer designed to prevent an attaching nut from working loose.

M

MacPherson strut A type of front suspension system devised by Earle MacPherson at Ford of England. In its original form, a simple lateral link with the anti-roll bar creates the lower control arm. A long strut - an integral coil spring and shock absorber - is mounted between the body and the steering knuckle. Many modern so-called MacPherson strut systems use a conventional lower A-arm and don't rely on the anti-roll bar for location.

Multimeter An electrical test instrument with the capability to measure voltage, current and resistance.

N

NOx Oxides of Nitrogen. A common toxic pollutant emitted by petrol and diesel engines at higher temperatures.

O

Ohm The unit of electrical resistance. One volt applied to a resistance of one ohm will produce a current of one amp.

Ohmmeter An instrument for measuring electrical resistance.

O-ring A type of sealing ring made of a special rubber-like material; in use, the O-ring is compressed into a groove to provide the sealing action.

O-ring

Overhead cam (ohc) engine An engine with the camshaft(s) located on top of the cylinder head(s).

Overhead valve (ohv) engine An engine with the valves located in the cylinder head, but with the camshaft located in the engine block.

Oxygen sensor A device installed in the engine exhaust manifold, which senses the oxygen content in the exhaust and converts this information into an electric current. Also called a Lambda sensor.

P

Phillips screw A type of screw head having a cross instead of a slot for a corresponding type of screwdriver.

Plastigage A thin strip of plastic thread, available in different sizes, used for measuring clearances. For example, a strip of Plastigage is laid across a bearing journal. The parts are assembled and dismantled; the width of the crushed strip indicates the clearance between journal and bearing.

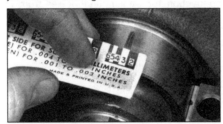
Plastigage

Propeller shaft The long hollow tube with universal joints at both ends that carries power from the transmission to the differential on front-engined rear wheel drive vehicles.

Proportioning valve A hydraulic control valve which limits the amount of pressure to the rear brakes during panic stops to prevent wheel lock-up.

R

Rack-and-pinion steering A steering system with a pinion gear on the end of the steering shaft that mates with a rack (think of a geared wheel opened up and laid flat). When the steering wheel is turned, the pinion turns, moving the rack to the left or right. This movement is transmitted through the track rods to the steering arms at the wheels.

Radiator A liquid-to-air heat transfer device designed to reduce the temperature of the coolant in an internal combustion engine cooling system.

Refrigerant Any substance used as a heat transfer agent in an air-conditioning system. R-12 has been the principle refrigerant for many years; recently, however, manufacturers have begun using R-134a, a non-CFC substance that is considered less harmful to the ozone in the upper atmosphere.

Rocker arm A lever arm that rocks on a shaft or pivots on a stud. In an overhead valve engine, the rocker arm converts the upward movement of the pushrod into a downward movement to open a valve.

Rotor In a distributor, the rotating device inside the cap that connects the centre electrode and the outer terminals as it turns, distributing the high voltage from the coil secondary winding to the proper spark plug. Also, that part of an alternator which rotates inside the stator. Also, the rotating assembly of a turbocharger, including the compressor wheel, shaft and turbine wheel.

Runout The amount of wobble (in-and-out movement) of a gear or wheel as it's rotated. The amount a shaft rotates "out-of-true." The out-of-round condition of a rotating part.

S

Sealant A liquid or paste used to prevent leakage at a joint. Sometimes used in conjunction with a gasket.

Sealed beam lamp An older headlight design which integrates the reflector, lens and filaments into a hermetically-sealed one-piece unit. When a filament burns out or the lens cracks, the entire unit is simply replaced.

Serpentine drivebelt A single, long, wide accessory drivebelt that's used on some newer vehicles to drive all the accessories, instead of a series of smaller, shorter belts. Serpentine drivebelts are usually tensioned by an automatic tensioner.

Serpentine drivebelt

Shim Thin spacer, commonly used to adjust the clearance or relative positions between two parts. For example, shims inserted into or under bucket tappets control valve clearances. Clearance is adjusted by changing the thickness of the shim.

Slide hammer A special puller that screws into or hooks onto a component such as a shaft or bearing; a heavy sliding handle on the shaft bottoms against the end of the shaft to knock the component free.

Sprocket A tooth or projection on the periphery of a wheel, shaped to engage with a chain or drivebelt. Commonly used to refer to the sprocket wheel itself.

Starter inhibitor switch On vehicles with an automatic transmission, a switch that prevents starting if the vehicle is not in Neutral or Park.

Strut See MacPherson strut.

T

Tappet A cylindrical component which transmits motion from the cam to the valve stem, either directly or via a pushrod and rocker arm. Also called a cam follower.

Thermostat A heat-controlled valve that regulates the flow of coolant between the cylinder block and the radiator, so maintaining optimum engine operating temperature. A thermostat is also used in some air cleaners in which the temperature is regulated.

Thrust bearing The bearing in the clutch assembly that is moved in to the release levers by clutch pedal action to disengage the clutch. Also referred to as a release bearing.

Timing belt A toothed belt which drives the camshaft. Serious engine damage may result if it breaks in service.

Timing chain A chain which drives the camshaft.

Toe-in The amount the front wheels are closer together at the front than at the rear. On rear wheel drive vehicles, a slight amount of toe-in is usually specified to keep the front wheels running parallel on the road by offsetting other forces that tend to spread the wheels apart.

Toe-out The amount the front wheels are closer together at the rear than at the front. On front wheel drive vehicles, a slight amount of toe-out is usually specified.

Tools For full information on choosing and using tools, refer to the *Haynes Automotive Tools Manual*.

Tracer A stripe of a second colour applied to a wire insulator to distinguish that wire from another one with the same colour insulator.

Tune-up A process of accurate and careful adjustments and parts replacement to obtain the best possible engine performance.

Turbocharger A centrifugal device, driven by exhaust gases, that pressurises the intake air. Normally used to increase the power output from a given engine displacement, but can also be used primarily to reduce exhaust emissions (as on VW's "Umwelt" Diesel engine).

U

Universal joint or U-joint A double-pivoted connection for transmitting power from a driving to a driven shaft through an angle. A U-joint consists of two Y-shaped yokes and a cross-shaped member called the spider.

V

Valve A device through which the flow of liquid, gas, vacuum, or loose material in bulk may be started, stopped, or regulated by a movable part that opens, shuts, or partially obstructs one or more ports or passageways. A valve is also the movable part of such a device.

Valve clearance The clearance between the valve tip (the end of the valve stem) and the rocker arm or tappet. The valve clearance is measured when the valve is closed.

Vernier caliper A precision measuring instrument that measures inside and outside dimensions. Not quite as accurate as a micrometer, but more convenient.

Viscosity The thickness of a liquid or its resistance to flow.

Volt A unit for expressing electrical "pressure" in a circuit. One volt that will produce a current of one ampere through a resistance of one ohm.

W

Welding Various processes used to join metal items by heating the areas to be joined to a molten state and fusing them together. For more information refer to the *Haynes Automotive Welding Manual*.

Wiring diagram A drawing portraying the components and wires in a vehicle's electrical system, using standardised symbols. For more information refer to the *Haynes Automotive Electrical and Electronic Systems Manual*.

Note: *References throughout this index are in the form* "**Chapter number**" • "**Page number**". *So, for example, 2C•15 refers to page 15 of Chapter 2C.*

A

Air bag system – 12•23 *et seq*
Air cleaner filter – 1•14
Air cleaner assembly – 4A•3
Air conditioning system – 3•13 *et seq*
Alternator – 5A•4
Antifreeze check – 1•11
Anti-lock braking system (ABS) – 9•13
Anti-roll bar (front) – 10•8, 10•9
Anti-roll bar (rear) – 10•13, 10•14
Anti-theft alarm – 12•23
Automatic transmission – 7B•1 *et seq*
   electronic transmission module – 7B•5
   removal and refitting – 7B•4
   selector lever – 7B•2
   selector rod – 7B•3
Automatic transmission oil renewal – 1•16
Auxiliary drivebelt – 1•8

B

Battery – 0•13, 5A•2
Big end bearings – 2C•12
Body electrical systems – 12•1 *et seq*
   airbag system – 12•23 *et seq*
   anti-theft alarm – 12•23
   bulbs (exterior lights) – 12•10 *et seq*
   bulbs (interior) – 12•12 *et seq*
   exterior light units – 12•14
   fuses and relays – 12•4
   headlight beam alignment – 12•17
   horn – 12•18
   instrument panel – 12•17
   Parktronic system – 12•26
   radio/infotainment unit – 12•21
   rain/light sensor – 12•18
   speakers and amplifiers – 12•22
   switches – 12•6
   windscreen/tailgate washer system – 12•20 *et seq*
   wiper arm, motor and linkage – 12•18
Bodywork and fittings – 11•1 *et seq*
   bonnet – 11•4
   bonnet release cable – 11•4
   boot lid – 11•5
   boot lid lock components – 11•5
   central locking components – 11•16
   centre console – 11•28
   door inner trim panel – 11•9
   door handle – 11•14, 11•15
   door lock components – 11•15, 11•16
   door removal, refitting and adjustment – 11•16
   door window glass and electric motor – 11•19, 11•13
   exterior mirror – 11•17
   facia panel – 11•29
   front bumper – 11•8
   interior mirror – 11•18
   interior trim – 11•21
   maintenance – 11•2
   minor body damage repair – 11•2
   rear bumper – 11•8
   seat belts – 11•20
   tailgate – 11•6, 11•7
Bonnet – 11•4
Bonnet release cables – 11•4
Boot lid and support struts – 11•5
Boot lid lock components – 11•5
Brake calipers – 9•9, 9•9
Brake disc – 9•8, 9•7
Brake fluid renewal – 1•16
Brake pads – 1•12, 9•4, 9•6
Brake pedal – 9•11
Braking system – 9•1 *et seq*
   anti-lock braking system (ABS) components – 9•13
   brake disc – 9•8
   brake light switch – 9•13
   brake pedal – 9•11
   fluid renewal – 1•16
   front brake caliper – 9•9
   front brake pads renewal – 9•4
   handbrake cables/pedal/shoes – 9•11, 9•12
   hydraulic pipes and hoses – 9•3
   hydraulic system bleeding – 9•2
   master cylinder – 9•9
   rear brake calipers – 9•9
   rear brake pads renewal – 9•6
   servo – 9•10
   servo non-return valve – 9•10
   stop light switch – 9•13
   vacuum pump – 9•14
Brake discs – 9•8
Brake fluid – 0•11,
Brake pads – 1•12, 9•4, 9•6
Bulbs
   exterior – 12•10
   interior – 12•12
Bumpers – 11•8
Buying spare parts – REF•7

C

Cameras – 12•27
Camshafts – 2A•8
Catalytic converter – 4B•3
Central locking components – 11•16
Clutch – 6•1 *et seq*
   friction disc and pressure plate – 6•4
   hydraulic system bleeding – 6•3
   master cylinder – 6•2
   release bearing and lever – 6•5
   slave cylinder – 6•2
   removal, inspection and refitting – 6•4
Compression test – 2A•3
Conversion factors – REF•6
Coolant – 0•12, 1•16
Coolant pump – 3•5
Coolant temperature sensor – 3•7
Cooling, heating and air conditioning systems – 3•1 *et seq*
   electric cooling fan – 3•6
   hoses – 3•2
   sensors and switches – 3•7
Crankshaft
   inspection – 2C•12
   oil seals – 2A•14
   pulley – 2A•5
   refitting – 2C•13
   removal – 2C•10
Cylinder block – 2C•10
Cylinder head – 2A•10, 2B•10, 2C•4, 2C•6
Cylinder head valve components – 2C•5

D

Dimensions and weights – REF•1
Disc brakes – 9•8
Door lock assembly
   front – 11•15
   rear – 11•16
Door removal, refitting and adjustment – 11•16
Door window glass and electric motor – 11•13
Driveplate – 2A•13, 2B•15
Driveshaft rubber – 1•12
Driveshafts – 8•1 *et seq*
   removal and refitting – 8•3
   rubber gaiters – 8•3

Note: *References throughout this index are in the form* **"Chapter number"** • **"Page number"**. *So, for example, 2C•15 refers to page 15 of Chapter 2C.*

E

Electrical system basic checks – 0•12
Electric windows components – 11•11
Emissions control and exhaust
   systems – 4B•1 *et seq*
   catalytic converter – 4B•3
   EGR cooler – 4B•2
   EGR valve – 4B•2
Engine in-car repair procedures
   2148 cc – 2A•1 *et seq*
   2143 cc – 2B•1 *et seq*
Engine removal and overhaul
   procedures – 2C•1 *et seq*
   removal – 2C•3
   overhaul – 2C•2, 2C•4
   start-up after overhaul – 2C•15
Engine oil – 1•6
   filter – 1•6
   level check – 0•11
Engine oil cooler – 2A•3
Engine/transmission mountings –
   2A•15, 2B•16
Exhaust manifold – 4A•17
Exhaust system – 1•12, 4A•20
Exterior mirror – 11•17

F

Facia panel assembly – 11•29
Fan (cooling) – 3•6
Fault finding – REF•16
   automatic transmission – REF•20
   braking system – REF•21
   clutch – REF•19
   cooling system – REF•18
   driveshafts/propeller shaft – REF•21
   electrical systems – REF•23
   engine – REF•17
   final drive – REF•21
   fuel and exhaust systems – REF•19
   manual transmission – REF•20
   steering and suspension – REF•22
Final drive – 8•1 *et seq*
   draining – 8•2
   removal – 8•3
   seal renewal – 8•2

Fluid capacities – 0•16
Fluid level checks – 0•11, 0•12
Flywheel – 2A•13, 2B•15
Front hub/bearings – 10•4, 10•5, 10•6
Front suspension – 10•1 *et seq*
Front suspension strut – 10•6
Fuel system – 4A•1 *et seq*
   common fuel rail – 4A•13
   components removal and refitting – 4A•13
   ECU – 4A•14
   fuel injectors – 4A•11
   fuel pump and sender unit – 4A•6
   switches and sensors – 4A•13 *et seq*
   testing – 4A•10
Fuel economy – REF•2
Fuel filter – 1•15
Fuel injectors – 4A•11
Fuel pump and sender unit – 4A•6
Fuel tank – 4A•5
Fuses – 0•12, 12•4, *et seq*

G

Gearbox oil (manual transmission) –
   1•16, 7A•1
Gearchange linkage removal – 7A•2
General repair procedures – REF•8

H

Handbrake adjustment – 9•10
Headlight beam alignment – 12•17
Heater/ventilation system – 3•8
   component removal and refitting –
   3•8 *et seq*
Horn – 12•18

I

Ignition lock control cable – 7B•3
Ignition switch – 12•6
Inlet manifold – 4A•17
Instrument panel – 12•17
Intercooler – 4A•20
Introduction – 0•4

J

Jacking and vehicle support – REF•9
Jump starting – 0•7

L

Leaks – 0•9, 1•10
Light units (exterior) – 12•14 *et seq*
Lubricants and fluids – 0•1, 0•16

M

Main bearings – 2C•12
Maintenance schedule – 1•3
Manual transmission – 7A•1 *et seq*
   gearchange linkage removal – 7A•2
   overhaul (general) – 7A•4
   removal and refitting – 7A•4
   reversing light switch – 7A•3
   transmission oil – 1•16, 7A•1
Master cylinder (braking system) – 9•9
MOT test checks – REF•12

O

Oil level check – 0•11
Oil pump – 2A•12 (2148 cc), 2B•15

P

Parktronic system – 12•26
Piston rings – 2C•13
Pistons and connecting rods – 2C•9,
   2C•11, 2C•15
Pollen filter – 1•13
Power steering system – 10•16
Propeller shaft – 8•1 *et seq*
   centre bearing – 8•5
   removal – 8•4
   universal joint – 8•6

Note: *References throughout this index are in the form* "**Chapter number**" • "**Page number**". *So, for example, 2C•15 refers to page 15 of Chapter 2C.*

R

Radiator – 3•3
  cooling fan – 3•6
  grille – 11•5
Radio/infotainment units – 12•21
Rain/light sensor – 12•18
Rear coil spring – 10•11
Rear hub bearings – 10•9, 10•10
Rear suspension – 10•1 et seq
Relays – 12•3
Reversing light switch – 7A•3
Roadside repairs – 0•6
Routine maintenance and servicing –
  1•1 et seq

S

Safety First! – 0•5
Seat belts – 11•20
Seats – 11•18 (front), 11•19 (rear)
Service indicator reset – 1•14
Shock absorber (rear) – 10•10
Speakers – 12•22
Starter motor – 5A•5
Starting and charging systems –
  5A•1 et seq
  battery – 5A•2
  charging system testing – 5A•4
  starting system testing – 5A•5

Steering column – 10•14
Steering rack assembly – 10•15, 10•16
Steering wheel – 10•14
Stop light switch – 9•13
Sump – 2A•11, 2B•13
Sunroof – 11•21
Suspension and steering – 10•1 et seq
  front anti-toll bar – 10•8
  front hub/bearings – 10•4, 10•5
  front strut – 10•6
  front suspension lower arm – 10•8
  power steering system – 10•16
  rear anti-roll bar – 10•13, 10•14
  rear coil spring – 10•11
  rear control arms – 10•12
  rear hub carrier – 10•9
  rear shock absorber – 10•10
  steering column – 10•14
  steering column lock – 10•15
  steering rack assembly – 10•15
  steering rack rubber gaiters – 10•16
  steering wheel – 10•14
  track rod end – 10•17
  wheel alignment – 10•17
Switches – 12•6 et seq

T

Tailgate – 11•6 et seq
  automatic opening/closing – 11•7
  lock and release handle – 11•6
Thermostat – 3•3

Timing chain – 2A•6, 2B•6
  cover – 2A•5, 2B•6
  tensioner and sprockets – 2A•7, 2B•7
Timing cover – 2A•5
Tools and working facilities – REF•10
Torque converter oil seal – 7B•5
Towing – 0•9
Track rod end – 10•17
Turbocharger – 4A•20 et seq
  turbocharger removal and refitting – 4A•18
Tyre checks – 0•15
Tyre pressures – 0•15

V

Valve components – 2C•5 et seq
Vehicle identification numbers – REF•7

W

Washer fluid check – 0•14
Water pump – 3•5
Wheel alignment – 10•17
Wheel changing – 0•8
Windscreen – 11•17
Windscreen/tailgate washer system –
  12•20 et seq
Windscreen wiper – 12•18 et seq
  motor and linkage – 12•19
  wiper arm – 12•18
Windscreen wiper blade check – 0•14
Wiring diagrams – 12•28 et seq

Preserving Our Motoring Heritage

> The Model J Duesenberg Derham Tourster. Only eight of these magnificent cars were ever built – this is the only example to be found outside the United States of America

Almost every car you've ever loved, loathed or desired is gathered under one roof at the Haynes Motor Museum. Over 300 immaculately presented cars and motorbikes represent every aspect of our motoring heritage, from elegant reminders of bygone days, such as the superb Model J Duesenberg to curiosities like the bug-eyed BMW Isetta. There are also many old friends and flames. Perhaps you remember the 1959 Ford Popular that you did your courting in? The magnificent 'Red Collection' is a spectacle of classic sports cars including AC, Alfa Romeo, Austin Healey, Ferrari, Lamborghini, Maserati, MG, Riley, Porsche and Triumph.

A Perfect Day Out

Each and every vehicle at the Haynes Motor Museum has played its part in the history and culture of Motoring. Today, they make a wonderful spectacle and a great day out for all the family. Bring the kids, bring Mum and Dad, but above all bring your camera to capture those golden memories for ever. You will also find an impressive array of motoring memorabilia, a comfortable 70 seat video cinema and one of the most extensive transport book shops in Britain. The Pit Stop Cafe serves everything from a cup of tea to wholesome, home-made meals or, if you prefer, you can enjoy the large picnic area nestled in the beautiful rural surroundings of Somerset.

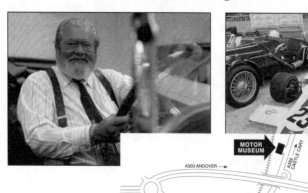

> John Haynes O.B.E., Founder and Chairman of the museum at the wheel of a Haynes Light 12.

> Graham Hill's Lola Cosworth Formula 1 car next to a 1934 Riley Sports.

The Museum is situated on the A359 Yeovil to Frome road at Sparkford, just off the A303 in Somerset. It is about 40 miles south of Bristol, and 25 minutes drive from the M5 intersection at Taunton.
Open 9.30am - 5.30pm (10.00am - 4.00pm Winter) 7 days a week, *except Christmas Day, Boxing Day and New Years Day*
Special rates available for schools, coach parties and outings Charitable Trust No. 292048